Lynda Weinman's | Hands-On Training

Adobe®
After Effects® 7
Includes Exercise Files and Demo Movies

lynda.com

By Chad Fahs with Lynda Weinman

Adobe® After Effects® 7
Hands-On Training

By Chad Fahs with Lynda Weinman

lynda.com/books | Peachpit Press
1249 Eighth Street • Berkeley, CA • 94710
800.283.9444 • 510.524.2178 • 510.524.2221(fax)
http://www.lynda.com/books
http://www.peachpit.com

lynda.com/books is published
in association with Peachpit Press,
a division of Pearson Education
Copyright ©2007 by lynda.com

ISBN: 0-321-39775-4

0 9 8 7 6 5 4 3 2 1

Printed and bound in the
United States of America

H•O•T Credits

Director of Product Development and Video Production: Tanya Staples

Operations Manager: Lauren Harmon

Project Editor: Karyn Johnson

Production Coordinator: Tracey Croom

Compositors: David Van Ness, Myrna Vladic

Developmental Editor: Jennifer Eberhardt

Copyeditor: Kim Wimpsett

Proofreader: Haig MacGregor

Interior Design: Hot Studio, San Francisco

Cover Design: Don Barnett

Cover Illustration: Bruce Heavin (bruce@stink.com)

Indexer: Jack Lewis, J & J Indexing

Video Editors and Testers: Scott Cuzzo, Steven Gotz, Eric Geoffroy

H•O•T Colophon

The text in *Adobe After Effects 7 H·O·T* was set in Avenir from Adobe Systems Incorporated. The cover illustation was painted in Adobe Photoshop and Adobe Illustrator.

This book was created using QuarkXPress and Microsoft Office on an Apple Macintosh using Mac OS X. It was printed on 60 lb. Influence Matte at Courier.

Table of Contents

Introduction

A Note from Lynda Weinman

Most people buy computer books to learn, yet it's amazing how few books are written by teachers. Chad and I take pride this book was written by experienced teachers, who are familiar with training students in this subject matter. In this book, you'll find carefully developed lessons and exercises to help you learn After Effects 7—one of the most capable Web development tools available today.

This book is targeted to beginning- to intermediate-level animators, filmmakers, and even Web designers who are looking for a way to learn about motion graphics and the basic features of After Effects 7 quickly and easily. The premise of the hands-on approach is to get you up to speed quickly with After Effects 7 while you actively work through the lessons in this book. It's one thing to read about a program and another experience entirely to try the product and achieve measurable results. Our motto is, "Read the book, follow the exercises, and you'll learn the program." I have received countless testimonials, and it is our goal to make sure this motto remains true for all our Hands-On Training books.

This book doesn't set out to cover every single aspect of After Effects 7, but it will build a strong foundation that will enable you to learn the more difficult techniques much more easily. What we saw missing from the bookshelves was a process-oriented tutorial teaching readers the core principles, techniques, and tips in a hands-on format.

I welcome your comments at **ae7hot@lynda.com**. If you run into any trouble while you're working through this book, check out the technical support link at **www.lynda.com/books/HOT/ae7**.

Chad and I hope this book will enhance your skills in After Effects 7 and motion graphics in general. If it does, we have accomplished the job we set out to do!

—Lynda Weinman

About lynda.com

lynda.com was founded in 1996 by Lynda Weinman and Bruce Heavin in conjunction with the first publication of Lynda's revolutionary book, *Designing Web Graphics*. Since then, lynda.com has become a leader in software training for graphics and Web professionals and is recognized worldwide as a trusted educational resource.

lynda.com offers a wide range of Hands-On Training books, which guide users through a progressive learning process using real-world projects.

lynda.com also offers a wide range of video-based tutorials, which are available on CD and DVD and through the lynda.com **Online Training Library**. lynda.com also owns the **Flashforward Conference and Film Festival**.

For more information about lynda.com, check out **www.lynda.com**. For more information about the Flashforward Conference and Film Festival, visit **www.flashforwardconference.com**.

Product Registration

Register your copy of *Adobe After Effects 7 HOT* today, and receive the following benefits:

- FREE 24-hour pass to the lynda.com Online Training Library with more than 13,000 professionally produced video clips from

over 200 titles by leading industry experts and teachers

- News, events, and special offers from lynda.com

- The lynda.com monthly newsletter

- To register, visit **www.lynda.com/register/ HOT/aftereffects7**

Additional Training Resources from lynda.com

To help you master and further develop your skills with After Effects 7, register to use the free, 24-hour pass to the lynda.com Online Training Library, and check out the following video-based training resources:

After Effects 7 Essential Training
with Jeff Foster and Lynda Weinman

After Effects 7 Animation Techniques
with Jeff Foster

After Effects 7 and Photoshop CS2 Integration
with Jeff Foster

Animation Principles
with Chris Casady and Lynda Weinman

About the Authors

Chad Fahs is an author, editor, and digital film-maker. What began as an obsession with film led him in 1998 to set up an Avid studio in Chicago, where he worked on commercials, music videos, electronic press kits, documentaries, and a variety of experimental film and video projects. In 2000, he began work as a Web producer for a company owned by United Airlines and continued to work on video projects at the same time. He also began writing about digital video with his first book about DVD-authoring software in 2001. Chad continued to write books and training materials, as well as train users in applying emerging video and multimedia technologies at colleges and private companies, including Future Media Concepts. While writing and teaching, Chad found time to edit and work on personal projects.

In 2004, Chad began work as an editor and animator at Concrete Pictures, located in the Philadelphia area, where over the next two years he created many hours of original, high-definition videos and animations for a channel on the VOOM and DISH satellite services.

To date, his books as author and coauthor include *HDV Filmmaking*, *iPod and iTunes Digital Field Guide*, *Final Cut Pro 4 for Dummies*, *Mac OS X Panther in Ten Simple Steps or Less*, *Apple Pro Training Series: DVD Studio Pro 2*, *Flash MX Design for TV and Video*, and *MacWorld DVD Studio Pro Bible*.

Recently, Chad has contributed to *Wired* magazine and is currently working on a documentary that takes place in the United States and Japan.

Lynda Weinman is an author, instructor, and conference speaker. She is the author of the best-selling book, *Designing Web Graphics*, and is the founder of lynda.com. Lynda has taught digital arts at numerous seminars and colleges, including Art Center College of Design in Pasadena. She is the founder and producer of the Flashforward Conference & Film Festival. Lynda Weinman is the originator of the Hands-On Training series. She develops each book with carefully selected instructors who are experts in their field.

Acknowledgments from Chad Fahs

I'd like to thank the editors I've worked with at lynda.com, especially Tanya Staples and Lauren Harmon, for their time and dedication to this book.

I'd also like to thank Meghann Matwichuk for her support throughout this project and all my writing endeavors.

How to Use This Book

The following sections outline important information to help you make the most of this book.

The formatting in this book

This book has several components, including
step-by-step exercises, commentary, notes, tips,
warnings, and video tutorials. Step-by-step exercises are numbered. Filenames, folder names,
commands, keyboard shortcuts, and URLs are in
bold so they pop out easily, such as **filename.htm**,
the **images** folder, **File > New**, **Ctrl+click**, and
www.lynda.com.

Commentary is in dark gray text: This is
commentary.

Interface screen shots

We took most of the screen shots in the book on
an Apple Power Mac G5 computer, as we do most
of our design, development, and writing on a Mac.
We note important differences between the
Windows and Mac platforms when they occur.

What's on the After Effects 7 HOT CD-ROM?

You'll find a number of useful resources on the
After Effects 7 HOT CD-ROM, including the
following: exercise files, video tutorials, and information about product registration. Before you
begin the hands-on exercises, read through the
following sections so you know how to set
up the exercise files and video tutorials.

Exercise files

The files required to complete the exercises are
on the **After Effects 7 HOT CD-ROM** in the
exercise_files folder. These files are divided into
chapter folders, so you should copy each chapter
folder onto your desktop before you begin the
exercise for that chapter. For example, if you're
about to start Chapter 5, copy the **chap_05** folder
from the **exercise_files** folder on the **After
Effects 7 HOT CD-ROM** onto your desktop.

On Windows, when files originate from a CD or
DVD, they automatically become write protected,
which means you cannot alter them. Fortunately,
you can easily change this attribute. For complete
instructions, read the "Making exercise files
editable on Windows computers" section below.

Video tutorials

Throughout the book, you'll find references to
video tutorials. In some cases, these video tutorials
reinforce concepts explained in the book. In other
cases, they show bonus material you'll find interesting and useful. To view the video tutorials, you
must have Apple QuickTime Player installed on
your computer. If you do not have QuickTime
Player, you can download it for free from Apple's
Web site at **www.apple.com/quicktime**.

To view the video tutorials, copy the videos from
the **After Effects 7 HOT CD-ROM** onto your hard
drive. Double-click the video you want to watch,
and it will automatically open in QuickTime Player.
Make sure the volume on your computer is turned
up so you can hear the audio content.

If you like the video tutorials, refer to the "Product
Registration" section earlier in this introduction,
and register to receive a free pass to the lynda.com
Online Training Library, which is filled with more
than 13,000 video clips from more than 200 different tutorials.

Making exercise files editable on Windows computers

By default, when you copy files from a CD to a Windows computer, they are set to read-only (write protected). This will cause a problem with the exercise files because you will need to edit and save many of them. You can remove the read-only property by following these steps:

1 Open the **exercise_files** folder on the **After Effects 7 HOT CD-ROM**, and copy one of the subfolders, such as **chap_02**, to your **Desktop**.

2 Open the **chap_02** folder you copied to your **Desktop**, and choose **Edit > Select All**.

3 Right-click one of the selected files, and choose **Properties** from the contextual menu.

4 In the **Properties** dialog box, click the **General** tab. Turn off the **Read-Only** check box to disable the read-only properties for the selected files in the **chap_02** folder.

Making file extensions visible on Windows computers

By default, you cannot see file extensions, such as **.htm**, **.fla**, **.swf**, **.jpg**, **.gif**, or **.psd**, on Windows computers. Fortunately, you can change this setting easily. Here's how:

1 On your **Desktop**, double-click the **My Computer** icon.

Note: If you (or someone else) changed the name, it will not say My Computer.

2 Choose **Tools > Folder Options** to open the **Folder Options** dialog box. Select the **View** tab.

3 Turn off the **Hide extensions for known file types** check box to make all the file extensions visible.

After Effects 7 System Requirements

Windows

- Intel Pentium 4 processor (multiprocessor recommended).

- Microsoft Windows XP Professional or Home Edition with Service Pack 2.

- 512 MB of RAM (1 GB recommended).

- 500 MB of available hard-drive space for installation (10 GB for disk caching and 1 GB for functional content recommended).

- 24-bit color display adapter.

- CD-ROM drive.

- QuickTime 6.5 software recommended.

- Internet or phone connection required for product activation.

- For the render engine (Professional edition only): System requirements are the same as application system requirements.

- For OpenGL support: Adobe After Effects–supported OpenGL 2.0 card (Nvidia recommended). For a current list, visit **www.adobe.com/products/aftereffects/opengl.html**.

Macintosh

- PowerPC processor (multiprocessor G5 recommended).

- Mac OS X version 10.3.9 (version 10.4 recommended for best OpenGL performance).

- 512 MB of RAM (1 GB recommended).

- 500 MB of available hard-drive space for installation (10 GB for disk caching and 1 GB for functional content recommended).

- 24-bit color display adapter.

- CD-ROM drive.

- Internet or phone connection required for product activation.

- For the render engine (Professional edition only): System requirements are the same as application system requirements.

- For OpenGL support: Adobe After Effects–supported OpenGL 2.0 card. For a current list, visit **www.adobe.com/products/aftereffects/opengl.html**.

Getting Demo Versions of the Software

If you'd like to try demo versions of the software used in this book, you can download them at the following Web sites:

Firefox: www.getfirefox.com

After Effects 7:
www.adobe.com/products/aftereffects/

Flash 8: www.adobe.com/products/flash/flashpro/

Illustrator CS2: http://www.adobe.com/products/illustrator/

Photoshop CS2: http://www.adobe.com/products/photoshop/

1

Getting Started

This chapter provides background information related to Adobe® After Effects® 7.0 Professional, as well as introduces motion graphics. If you are anxious to get into the hands-on exercises, feel free to skip ahead to Chapter 2, *"Understanding the Workspace."* This is not a required chapter; instead, it is here to help readers who are not familiar with the capabilities of After Effects or who want an overview of the application before getting started. Even if you're a seasoned After Effects veteran, you might want to read the "What's New in After Effects 7?" section to see what new, exciting, and creative features are in store!

What Is After Effects?

If you watch TV or movies, you've already seen footage developed in After Effects, though you might not have been aware of it at the time. For example, the title sequence with the raining text in the feature film *The Matrix* and the dancing silhouettes in Apple iPod commercials both use footage created in After Effects. After Effects is used professionally throughout the motion picture and video industries for title sequences, identity campaigns for TV stations, TV commercials, industrial videos, CDs and DVDs, Web animations, and much, much more. One of the coolest features of After Effects is that you can make a single project

yet publish it to a variety of formats for playback in video, film, CD, DVD, or Web content.

After Effects allows you to compose moving images in the same way an artist might compose a drawing or a painting. It gives you the ability to create relationships between images, sounds, and moving footage. You can compose an animation by positioning images in locations on the screen and moving them or changing their characteristics (such as opacity, scale, and rotation) over time. In addition, After Effects lets you synchronize audio to play back with your moving images.

What's New in After Effects 7?

For those of you who have worked with a previous version of After Effects, you are surely eager to know what new features have been added to this version. The following chart identifies the new features.

Note: For this release, Adobe released two versions of the software—After Effects 7 Standard

edition and After Effects 7 Professional edition. Some of the new features are unique to After Effects 7 Professional edition. Please refer to the notes in the following table and the Adobe Web site for more details:

After Effects 7 New Features	
Feature	**Description**
Unified user interface	After Effects 7 has a redesigned, unified user interface, which simplifies working in the application. For the first time, After Effects eliminates floating palettes and overlapping windows and features dockable panels, which are consistent with the other programs in the Adobe Production Studio. You can create custom workspaces by moving panels and resizing panel groups and by adjusting the brightness and colors. You'll take a tour of the redesigned interface in Chapter 2, *"Understanding the Workspace."*
Graph Editor	The new **Graph Editor** lets you set animation properties with a graph, which provides finer control over keyframe editing and the ability to visually align motions across multiple layers. You'll learn how to use the **Graph Editor** in Chapter 5, *"Creating Keyframes and Animation in the Timeline."*

continues on next page

After Effects 7 New Features *continued*

Feature	Description
Project templates and animation presets	Project templates and animation presets make setting up a project and creating complex motions a breeze. Animation presets include settings for text, effects, transitions, background movies, and expressions. As an added bonus, you can select from a variety of **behaviors**, which automate the animation process by eliminating the need to keyframe many types of motion. You'll learn how to use project templates and animation presets in Chapter 5, *"Creating Keyframes and Animation in the Timeline,"* and in Chapter 9, *"Working with Text Layers."*
New file format support	After Effects 7 supports a variety of new file formats, including HDV (**H**igh-**D**efinition **V**ideo), Camera Raw, OpenEXR, AAF, 10-bit YUV, and 32-bit TIFF and PSD. You'll learn more about how to work with these new file formats throughout the book. **Note:** File format support varies between After Effects 7 Standard and After Effects 7 Professional.
HDR color	After Effects 7 supports HDR (**H**igh **D**ynamic **R**ange) color, which more closely matches the properties of color and light in the real world. HDR is a bit of a step forward for high-end special effects and color correction work, allowing you to increase brightness without losing detail in an image. An example of an HDR file is an OpenEXR file, which was created by the special-effects company ILM (**I**ndustrial **L**ight & **M**agic) for feature-film work. **Note:** HDR color is available only in After Effects 7 Professional.
Timewarp	**Timewarp** lets you smoothly slow down or speed up footage, producing dramatic speed changes without the uneven results produced by ordinary methods of duplicating or eliminating frames. You'll learn about **Timewarp** in Chapter 8, *"Working with Layers."* **Note:** This feature is available only in After Effects 7 Professional.
Blur effects	After Effects 7 includes new blur effects. **Lens Blur** accurately simulates the properties of a defocused camera, and **Smart Blur** creates soft images and colors without destroying detail. Additional blur effects include **Fast Blur**, **Box Blur**, and **Compound Blur**. You'll learn about the blur effects in Chapter 10, *"Applying Effects."*
Enhanced OpenGL 2.0	After Effects 7 has enhanced support for OpenGL 2.0, which provides better previewing and rendering capabilities that support enhanced blending modes, motion blur on 2D layers, anti-aliasing, track mattes, shadows, and accelerated rendering of common effects. You'll learn about the enhanced OpenGL support in Chapter 7, *"Previewing Movies."*

continues on next page

After Effects 7 New Features *continued*	
Feature	**Description**
Integration with Adobe Bridge	After Effects 7 supports Adobe Bridge, Adobe's asset management application, which provides a better way to browse and search for assets (using metadata), manage files, and preview or apply presets and effects.
Enhanced integration with Adobe Photoshop CS2 and Adobe Premiere Pro 2	After Effects 7 provides enhanced integration with other applications in the Adobe Production Studio, including Adobe Photoshop CS2 and Adobe Premiere Pro 2. For example, you can create new Photoshop layers from within After Effects 7, export After Effects 7 projects as Premiere Pro 2 projects, or use Adobe Dynamic Link to update After Effects 7 compositions without rendering.

What Are Animation and Motion Graphics?

The word **animation** comes from the Latin word **anima**, which means life or soul. As an artist working with images, you bring them to life when you make them move. Still images can appear to move by arranging them in a specific order and changing from one image to the next in a fairly rapid sequence.

A flip book is a simple form of animation, but live-action filmmaking and video also bring still images to life. Although not all films and video are classified as being animated, they all share the same principle of animation.

The term **motion graphics** is used quite a bit in conjunction with After Effects 7. The term usually refers to taking a static image and making it move. In this context, the term **animation** contrasts with the term **motion graphics**, because animation involves creating new artwork for each frame within a sequence. Often, the terms are used interchangeably.

NOTE:

Why Does Animation Appear to Make Still Images Move?

Our eyes have sensors that retain an image for a moment. Stare at a high-contrast image for a while and then close your eyes. You'll see a ghost image even though your eyes are closed. This is called **persistence of vision** or an **after effect** of vision. The name of the computer program After Effects comes from this sensory phenomenon.

The trick of animation is to move a series of related images quickly enough so our eyes do not perceive the difference between the separate images. It takes about 24 individual images per second to overcome the tendency for the images to appear separate and to gain an illusion of fluid motion.

What Formats Does After Effects 7 Produce?

You can use After Effects 7 for film, video, digital video, CD, Web, and print output. It produces a wide variety of file formats that are specifically tailored to each medium. After Effects 7 provides ample options to meet the demands of artists and media professionals.

The most common video formats to output from After Effects 7 are QuickTime (MOV), Windows Media Video (WMV), and Video for Windows (AVI), which can be published at a variety of resolutions, supporting everything from Web content to feature-film quality. In addition to QuickTime for Mac and WMV or AVI for Windows, After Effects 7 supports all of the following formats and more (refer to the After Effects 7 documentation or visit the Adobe Web site for information about additional formats):

QuickTime Movie (MOV)

Video for Windows (AVI)

Windows Media Video (WMV)

DV Stream

MPEG-2

MPEG-4

Image Sequences

Macromedia Flash (SWF)

Macromedia Flash Video (FLV)

FLIC (FLC, FLI)

Animated GIF (GIF)

Audio Interchange File Format (AIFF)

WAV

MP3

AU audio file (AU)

How Is After Effects Different from Adobe Photoshop?

Photoshop is designed to work with still images. If your project demands high-quality still images, Photoshop is probably the best tool for the job. You can use Photoshop images in After Effects projects with great results, so many people use Photoshop and After Effects together. To differentiate the two tools, think of them this way: Photoshop is great for still images, and After Effects is great for moving images.

How Is After Effects Different from Avid Xpress DV, Apple Final Cut Pro, and Adobe Premiere Pro?

Software such as Avid Xpress DV, Apple Final Cut Pro, and Premiere Pro are for nonlinear editing. They are geared toward putting finished video shots together as a single short-form or long-form movie. They don't focus on creating frame-by-frame animation, creating sophisticated video title effects, or manipulating special effects. You can do some similar work in these programs, but After Effects has far more features for creating professional animation and motion graphics. You wouldn't want to cut a movie in After Effects, and you probably wouldn't choose to do a complex title sequence in a nonlinear editing program.

How Is After Effects Different from Apple Motion?

Recently, Apple introduced their own animation and motion graphics software called Apple Motion. If you are working on a Mac, you may wonder about the differences between these two applications. Motion relies heavily on using a real-time workflow, manipulating images, and instantly viewing the results of the preset patterns, particles, and animation behaviors you have applied. It requires the fastest video cards on the market to produce a satisfactory working experience. Motion was created to integrate closely with other Apple software in the Apple Final Cut Studio suite. Generally speaking, it is for creating title sequences and DVD menu designs (although it can be used for general compositing and effects work as well), with an emphasis on ease of use, which is appealing to the casual user.

Although After Effects has many of the same features (particularly in the latest release), it is suited to the most intricate and professional projects and situations you might encounter. For example, arranging layers in 3D space is possible only with After Effects (although available in other applications, such as Autodesk Combustion). It also provides high-end features, such as motion tracking, image stabilization, and flexible keying options, with numerous available plug-ins and support from third-party software developers. In addition, After Effects provides a more traditional workspace, familiar to users of Photoshop and Premiere Pro. It also runs on a wider variety of machines, both Macs and PCs, and has less-intensive hardware requirements (although it does benefit from newer video cards and faster processors). In addition, After Effects integrates seamlessly with other Adobe applications while providing files that can be used just as easily in Final Cut Pro, Avid Xpress DV, or other professional video software.

How Is After Effects Different from Macromedia Flash?

Macromedia Flash lets you combine still images, video, and sound, just like After Effects. Flash also offers, through its native scripting language called ActionScript, the capability to create interactive presentations, making it ideal for creating graphical Web sites. After Effects does not offer ActionScript and can be used only for animation and sound. However, you can use After Effects to create and export animations into SWF, which is the same format used to export movies from Flash.

Apart from the lack of ActionScript capabilities and interactivity, After Effects is different from Flash in more subtle ways. For example, Flash writes files with vectors and bitmaps; After Effects writes movie files that are converted entirely to bitmaps, even if the movie contains vector artwork to start. **Vector artwork** is composed of mathematically generated lines and shapes; **bitmap artwork** is generated by turning pixels on or off. The key advantage to vector artwork is its crisp, pristine appearance (as well as smaller file sizes), whereas bitmap artwork can look more realistic with shadows, gradients, glows, and blurs.

In general, After Effects is used for TV and film, which require larger frame sizes and faster frame rates. This is particularly the case with new digital formats, such as HD (**H**igh **D**efinition) and film projects, all the way up to IMAX. However, because of the nature of vector artwork, you can easily increase the scale of Flash animations to any size you want, although they are generally less sophisticated in appearance (bold colors and outlines are the norm) and therefore most often used solely for the Web. Examples where Flash technology has overlapped with video and film are the movies *Waking Life* and *Through a Scanner Darkly*, which began as videos that were later traced with similar vector-based software.

After Effects also has much more sophisticated effects and keyframe manipulation than Flash. You can bring an After Effects sequence into Flash, however, After Effects does not offer any interactive features like Flash does. Also, After Effects is time based, whereas Flash is frame based. This makes it possible to change the timing of an After Effects piece easily and stretch it from two seconds to two minutes without losing any of the animation relationships. This is not true in Flash.

What Is Compositing?

Compositing is the process of combining multiple sources of images, film footage, animation, text, or sound. Just like in Photoshop, After Effects uses **layers** (stacks of content laying on top of each other) to create composites. Compositing can be as simple as using two layers or as complex as using hundreds of layers. After Effects has wonderful features that support sophisticated masking with alpha channels, as well as tools for extracting subjects from a background for placement on top of new layers. (You'll learn more about alpha channels in Chapter 13, *"Creating Masks,"* and about separating objects from a solid color background in Chapter 15, *"Working with Color Keys."*)

How Do I Get Video Content into After Effects?

You can get video content into After Effects in a number of ways. The first method involves a digital video format, such as DV (**D**igital **V**ideo) or HDV (a new, high-definition video format), and an Apple FireWire connection. For this method, you need the following: a DV or HDV camera or playback deck with a FireWire port, a computer with a FireWire port, a FireWire cable to connect the camera to your computer, and software that controls the transfer of digital video into your computer, such as Premiere Pro 2 or Final Cut Pro.

Most computers with FireWire ports also include the software required to transfer digital video. Examples of software products supporting this process include Premiere Pro and Adobe Premiere Elements, Microsoft Windows Movie Maker, Final Cut Pro, Apple Final Cut Express, and Apple iMovie. Transferring the footage from a camera or video deck to the computer is usually a simple process using this method.

In the second method, using analog video, you must convert an analog video signal into a digital format as part of the process. You can do this using numerous tools, including the following: an analog video camera or playback deck, a computer with video-digitizing hardware, an appropriate cable to connect the camera with the digitizing hardware, and software to control the digitizing process.

Digitizing analog video is generally not a simple process and can require a fair amount of time and technical knowledge to ensure success. In general, we recommend using digital video (such as DV) and FireWire connections rather than analog video as source footage for your video projects. The image quality is usually higher with formats such as DV and much more so with HDV, and today's technologies make it easy to bring digital video directly into your computer.

In the third method, video already transferred to a computer may be available to you on CD, portable hard drives, or other computer storage media. You can copy this video directly to your computer system, and then After Effects can use it.

Ultimately, all of the footage content After Effects requires must be in a digital format.

What Tools Do I Need in Addition to After Effects?

If you are using After Effects to produce animations for the Web, you may need only an image scanner. For a video project, you'll need access to appropriate hardware for your chosen video system. A motion-picture film project might require you to utilize an outside service to scan your film images into digital form and provide recordings of your finished output on film.

The extra software tools, if you need any, depend mostly on the type of media you plan to create.

After Effects can import a wide variety of file formats, allowing you to work with many types of computer art, such as bitmap images (from programs such as Photoshop), vector graphics (from programs such as Adobe Illustrator), and 3D content (from programs such as Autodesk Maya or MAXON Computer CINEMA 4D). You don't need extra programs, but it's great to know that if you create artwork in them, you can use these images easily in After Effects.

How Do I Learn More About Animation, Video, and Compositing?

This book introduces all of these subjects, and you'll get a strong foundation to make the process clear. In Appendix B, *"After Effects 7 Resources,"* you'll find a reference section of books, videos, and CDs you can use to further your knowledge.

In summary, this chapter has offered an overview of some of the concepts and features of After Effects and related applications. We're sure you're anxious to move from passively reading to actively completing hands-on exercises. In that case, see you in Chapter 2, *"Understanding the Workspace."*

2

Understanding the Workspace

Adobe provides a consistent interface throughout most of their products, which makes learning and using Adobe products easier. For example, if you've used Adobe Premiere Pro and Adobe Photoshop, many of the tools in After Effects 7 will already be familiar to you, and the way you work in the application is fundamentally the same even though its interface is unique. With After Effects 7, the traditional interface of separate floating windows and palettes has changed, but the current interface is nearly identical in function to its predecessors.

Because After Effects 7 requires assets (called **footage**), such as movie files, sounds, and still images, it has a **Project** panel to store all these items. After Effects 7 also has a **Timeline** panel for setting up the motion for your moving images and a **Composition** panel for building, editing, and previewing your projects. When working in After Effects 7, you'll primarily use these three panels. This chapter gives you a quick overview of these panels and walks you through a simple project so you can see how the interface changes in relation to your content. As you'll see throughout this book, the After Effects 7 interface gives you a lot of functionality when you start to build projects and work with moving pictures.

Viewing After Effects 7 for the First Time

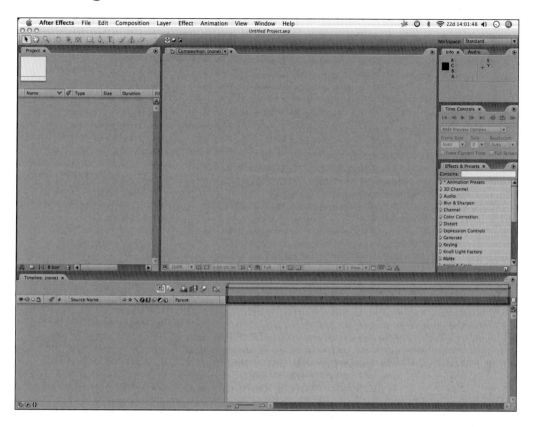

Shown in the illustration here is what you see the first time you open After Effects 7 and create a new project, as described in the next section. The main area of the program is referred to as the **application window**, and the various panels comprise the **workspace**, or panel layout, you see on your screen.

You can dock panels together or separately in the dockable areas (**frames**) of the workspace. The panels opened by default include **Project**, **Composition**, **Timeline**, **Tools**, **Info** and **Audio** (docked together in the same frame as a panel group), **Time Controls**, and **Effects & Presets**. These panels don't do anything until you import content such as movie footage, Adobe Photoshop files, Adobe Illustrator files, or other supported document types. (You'll learn how to import footage in Chapter 3, "Beginning a New Project.")

Tips for working with After Effects 7 appear by default each time you open the program. These tips can be incredibly useful. You can cycle through more than one tip by clicking the **Next Tip** button. If you don't want to see tips on startup, turn off the **Show Tips at Startup** check box. You can always get them back by choosing **Help > Tip of the Day**.

In the next sections, you'll look at each of these panels in detail, starting with the three panels you'll use most often: **Project**, **Composition**, and **Timeline**.

Introducing the Project Panel

After Effects 7 is different from many other programs you might be familiar with because it uses something called a **project** to organize content and store the settings you create to produce animation and output audio. When you bring artwork into Photoshop, for example, the artwork is saved with the Photoshop document. The project file in After Effects 7 is quite different because (when it comes to imported artwork) the project file merely references the footage residing on your hard drive. For this reason, the file sizes of After Effects 7 projects are quite small. This method of working is similar to working with project files from most NLE (**N**on**L**inear **E**diting) software, such as Premiere Pro and Apple Final Cut Pro.

The **Project** panel is one of the three primary panels you use in After Effects 7. Think of the **Project** panel as the place where you will store all the media you'll be working with—from still images to video footage to sounds. The word **footage** is an umbrella term for most media, including even still images and audio. Importing or adding footage to your project creates references in the **Project** panel.

Whenever you open a new After Effects 7 project, a new workspace with an empty **Project** panel appears. When you import footage, it appears in the **Project** panel. When you save your work, you save a project file—hence, it has the file extension **.aep** (**A**fter **E**ffects **P**roject). The project file memorizes all kinds of features including, but not limited to, the footage references of content you've imported. Think of After Effects 7 as "linking" to the footage, whereas programs such as Photoshop or Illustrator "embed" content. This process will become much clearer as you work through the book.

In the **Project** panel, you can view details about your footage or composition using columns of information showing the name, label, type, size, duration, file path, date, and comment of each item. A **composition** in After Effects is a type of file in which you combine all your layers of content and set them to animate over a **Timeline**. (You'll learn all about compositions in Chapter 4, *"Creating a Composition."*)

The **Project** panel shown in the illustration here is full of footage; footage and compositions appear as a list in the **Project** panel. To see all this content, you need to expand the **Project** panel by dragging its lower-right corner (the point where the **Project** panel intersects with all other frames). Alternatively, you can drag the horizontal intersection of the **Project** panel and the **Timeline** panel directly below, or (if you don't want to resize panels) you can use the scrollbars.

To see all the columns in the **Project** panel, you can stretch this panel wider by dragging the vertical intersection of the **Project** panel and the **Composition** panel to the right. You'll learn more about the features of the **Project** panel in Chapter 3, *"Beginning a New Project."*

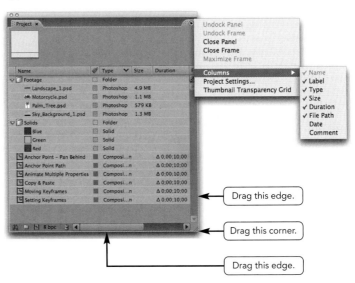

Introducing the Composition Panel

Whereas the **Project** panel lists the footage in your project, the **Composition** panel is where the visual preview, or **playback**, of your project appears. Think of the **Composition** panel as the equivalent of the screen at the front a movie theater, except you can have multiple compositions within a single project. The project is like a movie theater complex showing lots of movies, and each movie represents a composition. That's a silly analogy perhaps, but the point is you are not limited to one composition per project. In fact, you can have hundreds of compositions per project. You can even create compositions within compositions, known as **nesting**.

The **Composition** panel is available when you start After Effects 7, but no content appears until you create a new composition. You can create a composition from the **Project** panel or the **Composition** menu, which you will learn to do in Chapter 4, *"Creating a Composition."*

As shown in the illustration here, the **Composition** panel offers several controls for previewing your compositions. You'll learn more about the features of this panel in Chapter 4, *"Creating a Composition."*

Introducing the Timeline Panel

Like the **Composition** panel, the **Timeline** panel is available when you start After Effects 7, although no content appears until you open a composition.

The main function of the **Timeline** panel is to give you the ability to control time relationships between the various footage in your composition, such as multiple layers of video or graphics synchronized to create an animation.

As shown in the illustration here, footage appears in layers in the **Timeline** panel. The length of each layer represents its duration in time. You can set each layer to start or stop (be visible or invisible) at any point in the composition by adjusting it in the **Timeline**. You will learn more about the **Timeline** panel in Chapter 5, "*Creating Keyframes and Animation in the Timeline.*"

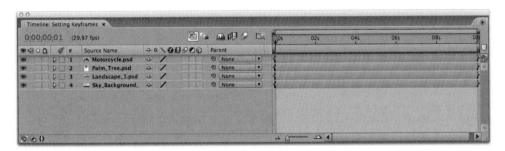

Organizing Panels

You can pull apart, reorganize, and restore the various panels in After Effects 7 easily. By rearranging panels, you can modify the workspace to match your working style and computer setup; for example, larger monitors can display more panels simultaneously. At times, you may choose to reorganize panels to create a workspace better suited for specific tasks, such as painting.

Each panel includes a **tab**, which you can use to view or move a panel to a dockable area of the program, known as a **frame**, where you can arrange multiple panels into panel groups. **Panel groups** are areas where multiple panels appear in one frame grouped "on top of" each other. In other words, in a panel group, you can see the topmost panel in its entirety, but you can't see the other panels—only their tabs—because the panels themselves are hidden underneath the topmost panel. You can also separate panels and move them just like floating panels (similar to windows in previous versions of After Effects).

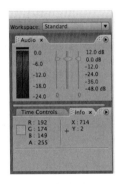

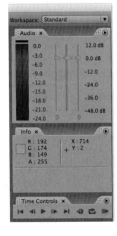

The illustration on the left shows where to drag when moving a panel into a panel group (top two images) and when creating a new frame (bottom two images).

To move a panel, simply select its tab (located in the upper part of the panel) and drag it into another frame. To create a panel group, select the tab of the panel you want to group and then drag it onto the tab of the panel with which you want to group it. Alternatively, you can also create panel groups by dragging and dropping one panel into the middle of another panel. For example, you can drag and drop the **Audio** panel tab onto the middle of the **Time Controls** panel tab. This action groups the two panels in a single frame, creating a panel group. However, if you drag and drop a panel onto the area directly beneath another panel's name, it will create a new frame with each panel appearing in its entirety.

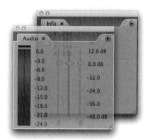

If you separate a panel, such as the **Audio** panel shown in the illustration above, from its current position by holding down the **Cmd** key (Mac) or **Ctrl** key (Windows) as you click and drag, you will be able to access it independently as a **floating panel**.

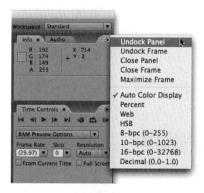

When panels are separated from a panel group and floating freely, they are **undocked**. When panels are reattached to a panel group, they are **docked**.

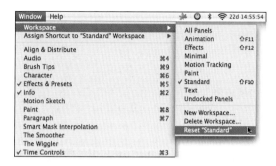

Note: To reset all your panels to their default positions (which comes in handy if you change your screen layout accidentally), choose the **Window > Workspace > Reset "Standard"** menu item.

When you click a panel, its selected status is indicated by an orange outline around the panel. Additionally, panels react to functions such as the scroll wheel on your mouse—no clicking is necessary. This is useful because you can navigate in any panel without having to click it first or without leaving another panel you may already be using.

If you want to close a panel, simply click the **Close** button (the X in the panel tab). To reopen a panel you have closed or to open panels not appearing as part of the default workspace, choose **Window**, and then choose the name of the panel you want to open.

By default, the **Tools** panel opens as a bar in the upper-left corner of the screen (the only panel positioned in the upper part of your screen by default). This is a unique setup, which is new to After Effects 7. You can separate the **Tools** panel from the upper part of the screen by selecting its tab and dragging it into another area of the screen, just like any other panel. You can also access it independently as a floating panel.

Now that you have some experience organizing After Effects 7 panels, you'll learn about the other panels you'll be using.

Introducing the Time Controls Panel

The **Time Controls** panel allows you to preview your compositions as moving images. Using these controls, you can play back the entire composition or select a specific frame.

Chapter 5, *"Creating Keyframes and Animation in the Timeline,"* defines these buttons in more detail.

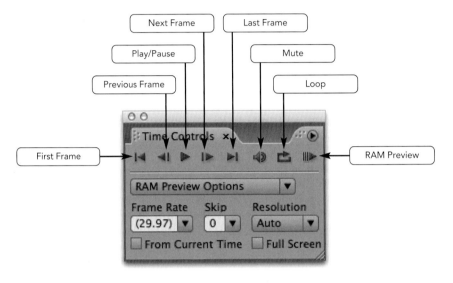

Introducing the Audio Panel

By default, the **Audio** panel appears in the same panel group as the **Info** panel. You can use the **Audio** panel for viewing and adjusting volume levels in your source audio.

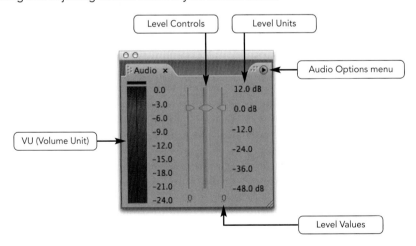

The level controls allow you to set the volume for each audio layer. The VU meter displays the audio levels during playback. You will learn about these terms in Chapter 19, *"Working with Audio."*

Introducing the Info Panel

The **Info** panel gives you information about images in the **Composition** panel, such as the position of your cursor within the **Composition** panel, the name and duration of the currently selected layer, and the specific color values within your graphics.

You'll learn more about the **Info** panel throughout the book.

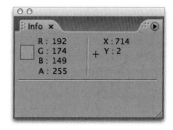

Introducing the Tools Panel

The **Tools** panel provides functionality for drawing in the **Composition** panel or for selecting elements and objects.

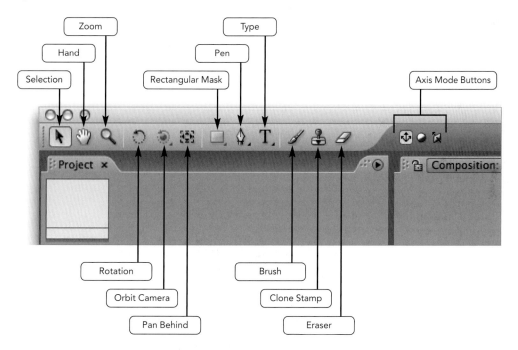

Using Shortcut Keys

After Effects 7 provides many shortcut keys, and all of them are listed in your program manual. We'll refer to specific shortcut keys throughout this book as you encounter reasons to use them, so don't spend too much time memorizing them here. The following chart lists some of the most useful shortcuts:

Shortcuts in After Effects 7		
Command	Mac	Windows
Import file	Cmd+I	Ctrl+I
Project settings	Cmd+Option+Shift+K	Ctrl+Alt+Shift+K
Suspend window updates	Caps Lock	Caps Lock
Display/hide panels	Tab	Tab
Step forward one frame	Cmd+right arrow	Ctrl+right arrow
Step backward one frame	Cmd+left arrow	Ctrl+left arrow
Start/pause playback	Spacebar	Spacebar
RAM preview	0 on numeric keypad	0 on numeric keypad
Nudge layer one pixel in specific direction	Arrow key	Arrow key
Select next layer back	Cmd+down arrow	Ctrl+down arrow
Select next layer forward	Cmd+up arrow	Ctrl+up arrow
Zoom in	. (period)	.(period)
Zoom out	, (comma)	, (comma)
Zoom in and resize window	Option+. (period)	Alt+. (period)
Zoom out and resize window	Option+, (comma)	Alt+, (comma)
Hand tool	H (or hold down spacebar)	H (or hold down spacebar)

Tip: Consider copying the previous chart and taping it to your monitor. Shortcuts will prove invaluable as you learn more about After Effects 7.

1 | Exploring the After Effects 7 Workspace

This exercise introduces you to the three primary panels in After Effects 7—**Project**, **Composition**, and **Timeline**—and lets you explore the basic functionality of each. In this exercise, you will open an After Effects 7 project file already prepared for you and use it to move within each of the primary panels to see how they relate to each other.

1 Copy the **chap_02** folder from the **After Effects 7 HOT CD-ROM** onto your **Desktop**. Launch **After Effects**, and choose **File > Open Project**. In the **Open** dialog box, navigate to the **chap_02** folder you copied to your **Desktop**, click **Interface.aep** to select it, and click **Open**.

2 If necessary, reset your panels to their default locations by choosing **Window > Workspace > Reset "Standard."** In the **Reset Workspace** dialog box, click **Discard Changes**.

If you moved your panels in Chapter 1, *"Getting Started,"* this step returns them to their defaults. If your panels are already in their default locations, you won't notice any change in the workspace.

As shown in the illustration here, notice the Composition panel and the Timeline panel contain content. In the Composition panel, you'll see a preview of some artwork. In the Timeline panel, you'll see a number of layers. You will learn more about layers and settings for layers in later chapters.

3 In the **Time Controls** panel, click the **Play/Pause** button, or press the spacebar. In the **Composition** panel, watch the preview of the animation. After a few seconds, click the **Play/Pause** button in the **Time Controls** panel, or press the **spacebar** to pause the animation.

The Play/Pause button and spacebar controls represent simple methods for previewing your animations. However, you can move more quickly back and forth in the Timeline using the CTI (Current Time Indicator), which you will do next.

Current Time Indicator

4 In the **Timeline** panel, locate the **CTI**. Drag the **CTI** left and right, and observe how its position affects the preview in the **Composition** panel.

This process is also known as **scrubbing** in the video-editing industry.

The CTI is also referred to as the **playhead**, which points to the exact playback location in your animation or movie.

Notice the green line in the Timeline panel? This appears as After Effects 7 **renders** (prepares the content for preview and playback). This green line will become a familiar cue as you work through this book's exercises. As you add elements such as effects and 3D layers, playback can take longer because it takes longer to render the footage. It's helpful to position the CTI at a specific frame, because sometimes you want to check a certain part of the Timeline but don't want to watch the playback of the entire composition.

5 Choose **File > Close Project**. You do not need to save your changes.

In this exercise, you worked with panels in the standard After Effects 7 workspace. In the next section, you will look at ways to customize the After Effects 7 workspace to suit the requirements of different projects and computer setups.

Customizing Your Workspace

Because your working style and computer setup may be unique, After Effects 7 allows you to easily rearrange and save custom workspaces. You can also choose from preset workspaces.

You can rearrange the location of panels to suit your aesthetic taste or the requirements of your project. For example, you might make your **Timeline** panel taller to accommodate several layers, make your **Project** window wider to view more information for files you have imported, or add the **Character** panel to the workspace to help you format text. After Effects 7 provides many ways to set up your workspace, and as you progress through the book, you will find advice on using different panels.

After Effects 7 also comes with several preset workspaces, including **Animation**, **Effects**,

Motion Tracking, and **Paint**. However, for general work, especially as you begin using the application, the **Standard** workspace should be sufficient. You can open the **Standard** workspace by choosing **Window > Workspace > Standard**.

If you have a second monitor connected to your computer, you may even detach individual panels and place them on another screen. This is particularly useful for large projects (large either in screen dimension or in the number of files), because you may want to see a bigger image preview in the **Composition** panel, you may want to see more layers in the **Timeline** panel, or you may want to view long lists of file names you have imported into the **Project** panel.

EXERCISE
2 | Creating and Saving an After Effects 7 Workspace

In this exercise, you will rearrange panels and then save a custom workspace so you can use the workspace later.

1 If you followed the previous exercise, After Effects should still be open. If it's not, launch the program.

2 In the upper part of the **Info** panel, click the tab with the panel's name and drag it onto the **Time Controls** panel tab, as shown in the illustration here.

This creates a panel group with the Info panel and Time Controls panel.

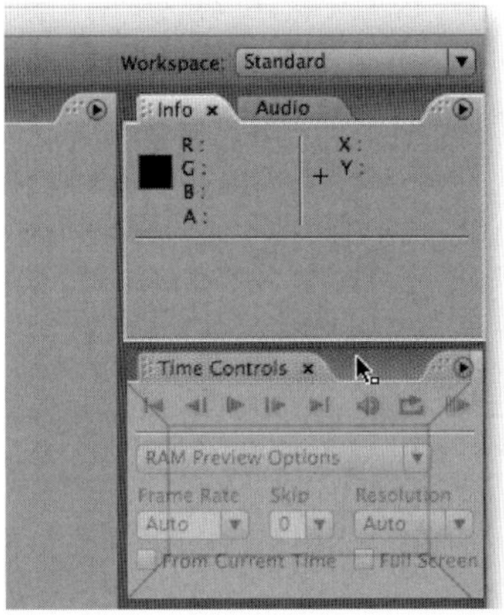

3 In the upper part of the **Audio** panel, click the **Close** button to close the **Audio** panel.

Closing panels you don't use helps you keep your interface uncluttered.

4 Choose **Window > Character** to open the **Character** panel.

You can use the Character panel to apply style changes, such as changing the font and font size, to any text you add to your project. You'll learn more about text in Chapter 9, *"Working with Text Layers."*

You can open new panels not appearing as part of the standard workspace or reopen closed panels by choosing Window > Panel Name. This technique works for any panel you want to view.

After you open a panel, you can resize it, which you'll do next.

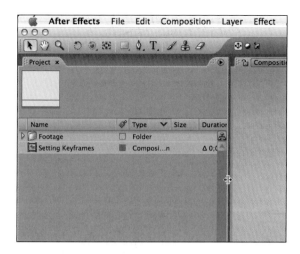

5 In the **Project** panel, click between the intersection of the **Project** panel and the **Composition** panel, and then drag to the right.

This makes the Project panel wider so it is easier to view information for files imported into your project.

Notice how the Composition panel dynamically resizes with the Project panel. All the panels in After Effects 7 dynamically resize in this way, eliminating the need to manually adjust every panel separately.

Now that you've customized the layout of panels in the workspace, it's time to save the custom workspace so you can use it again.

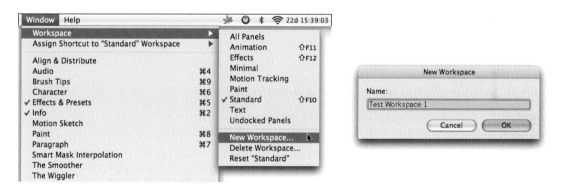

6 Choose **Window > Workspace > New Workspace**. In the **New Workspace** dialog box, type **Test Workspace 1** in the Name text box, and click **OK**.

This saves the new workspace you just created, and it will now appear in the Workspace menu.

7 Choose **Window > Workspace** to view the name of the new workspace you just created. Click anywhere outside the menu to close the menu.

Next you'll reset your workspace to the default settings and then reset the workspace to the custom workspace you just created.

---

8 Choose **Window > Workspace > Standard** to revert to the default workspace.

---

9 Choose **Window > Workspace > Test Workspace 1**.

Notice the workspace automatically reconfigures to the workspace you created in this exercise. As you can see, custom workspaces are a great way to remember specific panel configurations.

Next, you'll learn how to delete custom workspaces.

---

10 Choose **Window > Workspace > Standard** to return to the default workspace layout, and then choose **Window > Workspace > Delete Workspace** to open the **Delete Workspace** dialog box. Choose **Test Workspace 1** from the **Name** pop-up menu, and click **Delete**.

You can easily add or delete workspace presets whenever you want. However, make sure you leave all the default presets intact and delete only the test workspace you created for this exercise. Also, you cannot delete the workspace you are currently using, so you must first switch to a different workspace, as you did in this step by first returning to the Standard workspace before deleting Test Workspace 1.

11 Choose **File > Close**. You do not need to save your changes.

Congratulations! You've completed your first two exercises, and you've gotten a good look at the After Effects 7 interface. Best of all, you've been able to interact with After Effects 7 and see some results first-hand. In the next chapter, you'll learn more of the details involved in creating After Effects 7 projects, including how to import assets and organize footage into folders. Soon you'll be creating your own compositions, making them move, and saving movies. Keep reading!

3

Beginning a New Project

Animations, motion graphics, and visual effects often require a large number of individual images to make up the finished piece. For example, a typical title sequence for a film or video includes multiple layers of text, video, and moving textures. When creating these kinds of pieces with programs such as Adobe Photoshop and Adobe Illustrator, you'd store all the artwork for a picture either on multiple layers or flattened inside a single layer. Adobe After Effects 7 is different in that it keeps art, video, and audio elements separate, allowing you to combine different kinds of elements in unrestricted ways. This is why an After Effects document is called a *project*, since it is more than a simple file.

As you learned in Chapter 2, *"Understanding the Workspace,"* the **Project** panel is where After Effects 7 stores references to all the footage and image elements for your project. This panel helps you organize the images, movies, audio tracks, and compositions used by your project.

In this chapter, you'll learn exactly what a project is, and you'll see how to set up a project, import images, and organize items using the tools provided in After Effects 7. Setting up and organizing a project is the first step toward creating animations in After Effects 7 and is necessary for properly managing and using the media you import.

Introducing Projects

An After Effects 7 **project** is a single file containing references to all the images, video, and audio files you'll need for your work. A **reference** is a pointer to the location of a file on your hard drive. After Effects 7 uses references instead of copying the images, video, and audio files into the project file. Your project knows where to find the files it needs because After Effects automatically creates the reference to the files when you import them into After Effects 7.

In After Effects 7, all images, video, and audio elements—any media that After Effects 7 uses inside a project—are your **footage**. These elements are also often called **assets**.

In addition to holding references to footage, the project holds one or more compositions you create in After Effects 7. You'll learn about compositions in detail in Chapter 4, *"Creating a Composition."* For now, think of compositions as the editing environment in which all the action happens. You can't edit inside the **Project** panel. The project merely holds all the footage and compositions making up the product you're creating.

The project can contain more footage and compositions than appear in the final product, though. For example, as you probably know, in live-action filmmaking, a **shot** is the viewpoint from a single camera that is edited into a film. In After Effects 7, you can think of a shot in the same way. You can create many versions, or **takes**, of the same shot and keep all the takes in one project file. This is

valuable when working with clients; for instance, you can automatically maintain a record of exactly what you do in each take during the course of a project or easily show multiple versions of the same assignment.

When you save a project in After Effects 7, you are saving the project and its compositions, not the individual footage. In other words, each time you save in After Effects 7, you're saving the *reference* to where all your footage resides on your hard drive, and you're saving the updated composition files. For this reason, projects have small file sizes, whereas the footage items they reference might be huge.

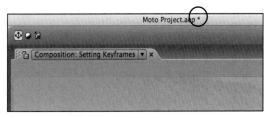

If you see an asterisk, save your project!

Because saving is so important, After Effects 7 puts an asterisk by the file name whenever the project has not been saved since a new change was made, as shown in the illustration here.

Finally, you can have only one project open at a time. Closing a project will close all the project's assets that are open in various panels and leave only the empty panels on the screen.

NOTE: **Working on the Motorcycle-Themed Project**

Throughout this book, you will be working with a series of motorcycle-themed files, which you will use to create a project for a fictional motorcycle company. Additional exercises and media will also illustrate a variety of topics. By following the exercises in this book, you will be able to assemble your own commercial and export the finished piece to DVD or the Web.

1 | Creating and Naming a Project

Setting up a project in After Effects 7 is quite simple. In this exercise, you'll create your first project and learn how to save the project. Creating a new project is the first step toward constructing any animations, motion graphics, and visual effects you create in After Effects 7.

1 Copy the **chap_03** folder from the **After Effects 7 HOT CD-ROM** onto your desktop.

2 Launch **After Effects 7**. If necessary, create a new project by choosing **File > New > New Project**.

When you open After Effects 7, in most cases an Untitled Project.aep project appears, with the project name displayed at the top of the application window. The project is untitled because you haven't saved it yet.

The Project panel holding your footage and compositions displays in the upper-left corner of the screen. Right now it is empty because you haven't imported any footage or created any compositions.

3 Choose **File > Save As**. In the **Save As** dialog box, navigate to your desktop. Click the **New Folder** button (Mac) or the **Create New Folder** icon (Windows). Name the folder **AE7_HOT_Projects**, and click **Create**.

The AE7_HOT_Projects folder is where you will be instructed to store all the exercises you work on in this book. Saving your exercises in this folder is important so you don't write over the originals.

4 With the **Save As** dialog box still open, navigate to the **AE7_HOT_Projects** folder you just created. Name the file **Moto_Project.aep**, and click **Save**.

5 Leave **Moto_Project.aep** open for the next exercise.

You've now successfully created your first project and saved it. It's time to import footage into your project. You'll learn how to do this next.

Importing Assets

As stated earlier, the images, video, and audio tracks you use in a project are the footage, or assets, of your project. Think of assets as valuable items necessary to create new compositions. Given how long it can take to create images, video, or sounds, assets truly live up to their name.

Remember, when you import assets into After Effects 7, you don't actually copy and paste the files into your project. With the import process, After Effects 7 creates references inside your project to files residing on your hard drive. In the following exercises, you will learn to import several types of footage into your new After Effects 7 project. Each type of footage has its own characteristics, and After Effects 7 offers many options to take advantage of various file formats.

After Effects 7 is a forgiving program. It will import almost any format—PSD, TIF, EPS, AIF, WAV, MOV, AVI, and so on.

2 | Importing Photoshop Documents

Photoshop files are one type of document that is commonly used in After Effects 7 projects. The main advantage of Photoshop files is their ability to utilize transparency, as well as multiple layers of images, organized in a single file. In this exercise, you will learn how to import a series of Photoshop files (which have been provided for you). Although this exercise provides an introductory look at bringing Photoshop files into an After Effects 7 project, you will learn additional ways to work with Photoshop files as you progress through the book.

---

1 If you followed the previous exercise, **Moto_Project.aep** should still be open in After Effects 7. If it's not, choose **File > Open Project**. Navigate to the **chap_03** folder you copied to your desktop, click **Moto_Project_2.aep** to select it, and click **Open**.

---

2 Choose **File > Import > File**. Navigate to the **chap_03** folder you copied to your desktop. Click the **Moto_Scene** folder to open it, and click **Landscape_1.psd**. Hold down the **Cmd** key (Mac) or **Ctrl** key (Windows), and click the **Palm_Tree.psd**, **Motorcycle.psd**, and **Sky_Background_1.psd** files. When you have selected all the files, release the **Cmd** key (Mac) or **Ctrl** key (Windows). Be sure the **Import As** pop-up menu is set to **Footage**, and click **Open**.

Note: In addition to using the Cmd key (Mac) or Ctrl key (Windows) to select files that are not adjacent to each other, you can hold down the Shift key to select multiple files that are next to each other in the same folder. This is referred to as a **contiguous selection**.

---

3 For each item containing multiple layers, you'll see an import prompt box, as shown in the illustration here. Click **OK** for each item to choose the default settings.

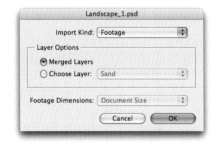

Because some of the Photoshop files you are importing contain multiple layers, you will see this import prompt box asking you whether you want to use merged layers with this file. Clicking OK tells After Effects 7 to flatten all the layers.

Congratulations! You just imported your first assets!

Note: You will learn how to work with more complex layered Photoshop files in future chapters.

---

4 Click inside a blank area of the **Project** panel to deselect the PSD files, and then widen the **Project** panel by clicking between the intersection of the **Project** panel and the **Composition** panel and dragging.

This allows you to observe the additional information available.

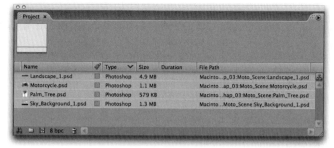

Also, you can click any of the column headings in the Project panel (Name, Label, Type, Size, Duration, or File Path) to sort the project's files by those criteria. You'll try this next.

---

5 Click the **Size** column name, and notice how the items in the **Project** panel rearrange themselves according to size, biggest to smallest. Narrow the **Project** panel to return it to a smaller view by clicking between the intersection of the **Project** panel and the **Composition** panel and dragging.

---

6 Click the **Name** column to select it; notice that the files now appear alphabetically.

---

7 Choose **File > Save**, or press **Cmd+S** (Mac) or **Ctrl+S** (Windows). Leave **Moto_Project.aep** open for the next exercise.

The asterisk at the top of the application window goes away as soon as you save the file. Again, the asterisk is a handy message from After Effects 7 to remind you to save your work—take advantage of it!

Note: You can import Photoshop files in many ways, including with the capability to use all the layers of a file. Before you learn to import this way, you'll need to understand what a composition is. You'll learn about this in Chapter 4, *"Creating a Composition."*

NOTE:

Locating Your Footage

After Effects 7 is pretty powerful when it comes to locating footage on your hard drive. Even if you move or rename footage after you've quit the program, After Effects 7 can often locate it without much effort on your part. If you ever want to give your After Effects 7 project to a client or coworker, a handy feature lets you collect all the footage into one neat folder. You'll learn how to do this in Chapter 20, *"Rendering Final Movies."*

Meanwhile, what do you do if After Effects 7 can't find your footage? For example, say you move some files on your hard drive without realizing that they are being used in an After Effects 7 project. In this case, the files will appear in your **Project** panel as empty reference links (the thumbnail previews disappear), and a placeholder item containing color bars will appear, along with the names in italics.

To fix the broken links, just double-click the name of an unlinked footage item to open the Import File dialog box. Navigate to the lost footage on your hard drive, click **Open**, and After Effects 7 will reconnect the link. If other unlinked footage items appear in the **Project** panel and they are in the same location on your hard drive as the first item you reconnected, After Effects 7 will automatically reconnect them as well.

3 | Importing Illustrator Documents

Illustrator files are great to work with in After Effects 7. That's because they are vector based and resolution independent, unlike Photoshop files. In other words, if you zoom into an Illustrator file during an animation, it will stay crisp and in focus. A Photoshop file would get progressively pixilated, depending on how much you zoomed into the artwork. For this reason, After Effects 7 and Illustrator work really well together. Importing Illustrator files is quite simple, as you'll learn in this exercise. Although you could import Illustrator documents using the same method of importing you used in the previous exercise, you'll practice a different method of importing here.

Note: Unfortunately, the support for Macromedia FreeHand, CorelDRAW, or other vector-based applications is not as good as for Adobe tools. If you're not an Illustrator user, save the file as an EPS and import it that way. Sadly, you lose the advantage of working with layers this way.

---

1 If you followed the previous exercise, **Moto_Project.aep** should still be open in After Effects 7. If it's not, choose **File > Open Project**. Navigate to the **chap_03** folder you copied to your desktop, click **Moto_Project_3.aep** to select it, and click **Open**.

---

2 In a blank area of the **Project** panel, **Ctrl+click** (Mac) or **right-click** (Windows). From the contextual menu, choose **Import > File** to open the **Import File** dialog box.

This is another method of accessing the Import command. Some users find this method faster and easier than choosing File > Import > Import File. Another method is to simply double-click in an empty area of the Project panel to launch the Import File dialog box.

---

3 In the **Import File** dialog box, navigate to the **chap_03** folder you copied to your desktop. Click the **Illustrator_File** folder to open it. Click **Palm_Tree_Vector.ai**, and click **Open**.

---

4 In the import prompt box, click **OK** to accept the **Merged Layers** option and the **Footage Dimensions** setting of **Layer Size**.

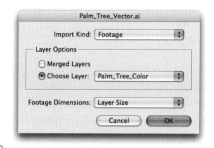

After Effects 7 includes the capability to choose the footage dimension of Layer Size or Document Size for a layer. For now, this decision is unimportant, and its significance is lost until you learn to work with compositions (Chapter 4, *"Creating a Composition"*) and to set keyframe properties (Chapter 5, *"Creating Keyframes and Animation in the Timeline"*).

Notice this adds the Illustrator file to the Project panel, and the asterisk in the application window's title bar indicates you have changed your project and have not yet saved it.

---

5 Choose **File > Save**, or press **Cmd+S** (Mac) or **Ctrl+S** (Windows). Leave **Moto_Project.aep** open for the next exercise.

In this exercise, you imported an Illustrator file. The process is similar to importing Photoshop files and other still images with multiple layers. In the next exercise, you will import an Apple QuickTime file that consists of video (a series of moving images). Although video files do not contain layers in the same way Photoshop or Illustrator files do, they can contain transparent areas (these transparent areas, or **alpha channels**, will be discussed throughout the book), and therefore After Effects 7 treats them a little differently.

---

4 | Importing QuickTime Movies

QuickTime movies (the standard video format on a Mac) and AVIs (the standard video format in Windows) are easy to import into an After Effects 7 project. The efficiency and portability of these file types are truly time-savers when working with moving images because these movie files contain a sequence of images in one neat package. In this exercise, you'll learn how to import QuickTime movies.

1 If you followed the previous exercise, **Moto_Project.aep** should still be open in After Effects 7. If it's not, choose **File > Open Project**. Navigate to the **chap_03** folder you copied to your desktop, click **Moto_Project_4.aep** to select it, and click **Open**.

2 In a blank area of the **Project** panel, **Ctrl+click** (Mac) or **right-click** (Windows). From the contextual menu, choose **Import > File** to open the **Import File** dialog box.

3 Navigate to the **chap_03** file you copied to your desktop. Click the **Moto_Scene** folder to open it. Click the **Motorcycle.mov** file. Hold down the **Cmd** key (Mac) or **Ctrl** key (Windows), and click **Smoke.mov** to multiple-select the QuickTime files, and click **Open**.

This adds the QuickTime footage to your Project panel.

Note: Using the Cmd key (Mac) or Ctrl key (Windows) allows you to select multiple files that are not next to each other in the same folder. This is referred to as a **discontiguous selection**. In this case, making a discontiguous selection is useful because you want to select only the QuickTime files from the list of available files.

You have now added the QuickTime footage to your Project panel.

4 In the **Project** panel, click a blank area to deselect the files you just imported. In the **Project** panel, double-click **Motorcycle.mov**, and press the **spacebar**.

Double-clicking opens the Motorcycle.mov file, and pressing the spacebar plays the movie. If you double-click any of the footage you've imported so far, you can view it in its own preview panel.

5 Close the **Motorcycle.mov** file by clicking the **Close** button in the upper-left corner (Mac) or the upper-right corner (Windows) of the preview panel.

Notice once more the asterisk in the application window's title bar, which indicates you have changed your project and have not yet saved it.

---

6 Choose **File > Save**, or press **Cmd+S** (Mac) or **Ctrl+S** (Windows). Leave **Moto_Project.aep** open for the next exercise.

In the previous few exercises, you imported individual files one at a time. Next, you will learn how to import multiple files in a folder at one time, which is a real time-saver.

NOTE:

What Are QuickTime Movies and AVIs?

Think of a QuickTime movie or an AVI file as an extremely handy container. Rather than having many different image files and a separate audio file, a QuickTime movie or AVI file allows you to place all the frames (individual images that are a part of a sequence, which makes up the completed movie) and synchronized audio into one neat package. With the QuickTime Player or Windows Media Player installed on your computer, a single QuickTime or AVI file will play hundreds or thousands of images with synchronous sound.

Numerous settings are available for these file types, and we'll cover many options throughout this book. If you are working on a Mac, you will use QuickTime files. If you are working in Windows, the standard video format is AVI, although Windows users can also use QuickTime files (make certain to download the free QuickTime Player application if you haven't already done so). The files created for each format are similar to each other and function in the same way.

5 | Importing a Folder Containing Various File Types

In the previous few exercises, you imported Photoshop, Illustrator, and QuickTime files separately. But you don't have to work this way. Instead, you can choose to import many different file types at once, and After Effects 7 will figure out what type of files are being imported automatically. In this exercise, you'll learn how to delete the files you've imported thus far from the **Project** panel and import all the files in one fell swoop.

1 If you followed the previous exercise, **Moto_Project.aep** should still be open in After Effects 7. If it's not, choose **File > Open Project**. Navigate to the **chap_03** folder you copied to your desktop, click **Moto_Project_5.aep** to select it, and click **Open**.

2 In the **Project** panel, press **Cmd+A** (Mac) or **Ctrl+A** (Windows) to select all the files. Press the **Delete** key to delete the selected files. When prompted, click **Delete** to confirm you really want to delete the references to these files.

Note: Remember, you are deleting only the references to these files from the After Effects 7 project. The original files are still on your hard drive.

3 In a blank area of the **Project** panel, **Ctrl+click** (Mac) or **right-click** (Windows). From the contextual menu, choose **Import > File** to open the **Import File** dialog box.

Note: Again, you can also double-click an empty area of the Project panel to automatically open the Import File dialog box.

4 Navigate to the **chap_03** folder you copied to your desktop, click the **Moto_Scene** folder to select it, and click the **Import Folder** button. Click **OK** as needed to accept the merged layer versions of the files.

When you import a folder into the Project panel, all the files will appear within the same folder you selected on your hard drive.

Tip: Click the arrow to the left of the folder name to reveal the folder contents.

Another neat feature of importing the folder is being able to organize your content so you can find it more easily. As you progress with your project, you may need hundreds of files in the Project panel. Using folders is a great way to stay organized.

5 Choose **File > Save**, or press **Cmd+S** (Mac) or **Ctrl+S** (Windows). Leave **Moto_Project.aep** open for the next exercise.

Opening the different types of files in separate exercises gave you the opportunity to focus on each file type; however, in reality, importing all the footage at once, as you did in this exercise, is much faster. Next, you'll learn how to create a folder, which helps you organize the files in your Project panel.

6 | Creating Folders

By creating folders and organizing project assets in the **Project** panel, you can access footage in a way that makes the most sense to you. For example, you could create separate folders for your Illustrator files, your QuickTime movies and AVIs, and your compositions. You might also choose to create a "final" folder for your finished compositions or an "old" folder for footage you no longer need. This is a great way to organize footage; in fact, it can be really helpful when you have a deadline and you're desperately looking for files you need immediately. In this exercise, you'll learn two different methods of creating folders.

1 If you followed the previous exercise, **Moto_Project.aep** should still be open in After Effects 7. If it's not, choose **File > Open Project**. Navigate to the **chap_03** folder you copied to your desktop, click **Moto_Project_6.aep** to select it, and click **Open**.

2 Choose **File > New > New Folder**.

This creates a new folder inside the Project panel. The folder name will be highlighted and ready to accept a new name.

3 In the **Project** panel, type **Stills**, and press **Return** (Mac) or **Enter** (Windows) to name the folder.

Note: If you need to rename the folder for any reason, select the folder, and press the Return key (Mac) or Enter key (Windows). This allows you to type a new name.

4 In the **Project** panel, click **Landscape_1.psd**. Hold down the **Cmd** key (Mac) or **Ctrl** key (Windows), and click each of the other PSD files in the list to multiple-select the remaining Photoshop files. When you have selected all the files, drag the files to the **Stills** folder.

Tip: You can click the arrow to the left of the Stills folder to hide or show the contents of the folder.

5 Click the **arrow** next to **Stills** to view its contents and verify you dragged the Photoshop files to the right place. Click the **arrow** next to **Stills** again to hide its contents.

6 At the bottom of the **Project** panel, click the **Create a new Folder** icon.

Clicking the Create a new Folder icon is another way to create a new folder.

7 In the **Project** panel, type **Movies**, and press **Return** (Mac) or **Enter** (Windows) to name the folder.

8 In the **Project** panel, click the **Motorcycle.mov** file. Hold down the **Cmd** key (Mac) or **Ctrl** key (Windows), and click **Smoke.mov** to multiple-select the QuickTime files. Drag the files to the **Movies** folder.

The project is now much more nicely organized. You have a Stills folder containing all your Photoshop files and a Movies folder containing all your movies.

9 In the **Project** panel, select the **Moto_Scene** folder, and press the **Delete** key to remove it.

You no longer need this folder, so getting rid of it further tidies up your workspace.

10 Choose **File > Save**, or press **Cmd+S** (Mac) or **Ctrl+S** (Windows). Choose **File > Close**.

In this chapter, you practiced naming and saving a new project, importing footage, and organizing your footage.

You've now successfully completed everything you need to do to set up, organize, and import footage assets into your first project! You'll learn some of the deeper nuances of using the Project panel as you work through the later exercises in this book.

If you feel ready, continue to the next chapter to learn all about compositions—or feel free to pick the book up again after taking a break.

4

Creating a Composition

In Chapter 3, *"Beginning a New Project,"* you learned how to create a project. The project holds references to all your footage, but the composition is where you use this footage. Without a composition, you cannot create animation, video, graphics, or audio. Think of the composition as the instructions telling Adobe After Effects 7 what to do with your footage, and as the preview showing you how those instructions affect your creation.

In this chapter, you'll learn exactly what a composition is and how to create one. You'll also learn how to work with the **Composition** panel—your main visual panel where you can preview and edit the animations you compose.

Understanding Compositions

A **composition** is where you make your footage come to life through creating animation, using filters, combining footage, and performing all the other tasks you will learn about throughout this book.

Compositions appear within the **Project** panel along with your footage and have their own special icons, as shown in the illustration here. To open a composition, double-click its name from the **Project** panel. This simultaneously opens the composition in the **Composition** panel and opens the composition's layers in the **Timeline** panel.

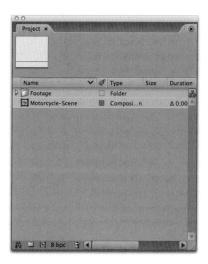

*You can preview your composition's design in the **Composition** panel.*

In the **Composition** panel, you can graphically interact with the images in your composition by clicking, dragging, and resizing items (for example). In fact, you can think of the **Composition** panel as being similar to a painter's canvas because you can see your design in it. You can also preview animation in the **Composition** panel.

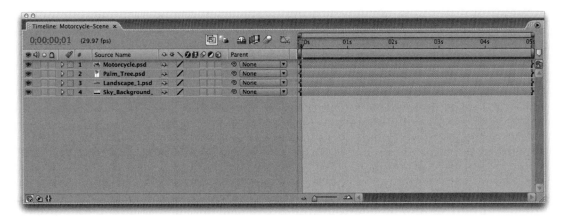

*You can preview your layers and their settings in the **Timeline** panel.*

In the **Timeline** panel, you can view the elements of your composition and their settings (such as **In** and **Out** points, **Position**, **Scale**, and a host of others). Think of the **Timeline** panel as the equivalent of a musical score interpreted to create your finished piece. The settings you make here are like musical notations, and the finished piece is your final symphony.

Although the **Composition** and **Timeline** panels are separate panels, one will not function properly without the other. If you are working and lose your **Composition** and **Timeline** panels, you may need to reopen them from your **Project** panel.

Now that you know a little about the **Composition** and **Timeline** panels, let's talk more about compositions. Essentially, compositions are your frame-by-frame instructions to After Effects 7. After Effects 7 will read your instructions, interpret them for each frame, and output your final product based on the settings you specify in your composition.

Your project can have as many compositions as you want. For example, you might want to try multiple versions of an idea by creating multiple compositions and keeping all of them in the project file. When you are finished, you can also choose to delete the compositions you no longer need.

When creating a composition, you must make some basic decisions about the dimensions of the document, its frame rate, its duration, and other attributes necessary for a film or video project. The **Composition Settings** dialog box is where you adjust these settings, and you will become intimately familiar with this dialog box as you work through this book. In the following exercise, you will create a composition and learn about some of the settings in the **Composition Settings** dialog box necessary for working with compositions in After Effects 7.

1 | Defining Composition Settings

Creating a composition requires defining a few settings, such as its **Width** and **Height**, **Pixel Aspect Ratio**, **Frame Rate**, **Start Timecode**, and **Duration**. In this exercise, you will learn to define these settings by using the **Composition Settings** dialog box, which opens automatically when you create a new composition. It's best to set all the options in the **Composition Settings** dialog box when creating your composition because these settings will also affect the way After Effects 7 handles the footage you add into your compositions (which is especially important with footage dimensions and aspect ratios). Most of the options are obvious, particularly if you've worked with video applications before, but we'll explain any new terms along the way.

1 Copy the **chap_04** folder from the **After Effects 7 HOT CD-ROM** onto your desktop.

2 Launch **After Effects 7**. If necessary, create a new project by choosing **File > New > New Project**.

3 Choose **File > Save As**. In the **Save As** dialog box, navigate to the **AE7_HOT_Projects** folder on your desktop. Name the file **Composition_Chapter.aep**, and click **Save**.

Soon you'll be filling this project with footage and a composition.

4 In the **Project** panel, click the **Create a new Composition** button.

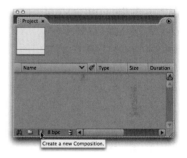

5 In the **Composition Settings** dialog box, type **First Comp 1** in the highlighted **Composition Name** text field.

Naming your composition appropriately is important. Because most projects go through several iterations, it's a good idea to give each version a number. If you have to output to two different media types (such as video and film), you'll want different names for each set of compositions to distinguish the two output types. In addition, your client may make changes as the project continues, so giving each composition its own name or version number will allow you to keep track of version changes.

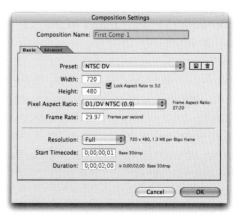

6 In the **Start Timecode** text field, type **0;00;00;01**. In the **Duration** text field, type **0;00;02;00**.

These timecode settings determine the number of frames, seconds, minutes, and hours necessary to create your completed animation. Although you may already be familiar with timecodes from using a VCR, DVD player, or camcorder, many of those devices do not provide the same frame-level accuracy you see here.

Reading from left to right, you will see the number of hours, minutes, seconds, and frames in your composition, with each set of numbers separated by a colon or semicolon. As you work through projects in this book, you will become more fluent with timecode nomenclature.

---

7 In the **Composition Settings** dialog box, match the remaining settings to the illustration shown in Step 5. Click **OK**.

Note: For now, trust that these settings are appropriate. The following section contains a chart you can use to learn more about the different options.

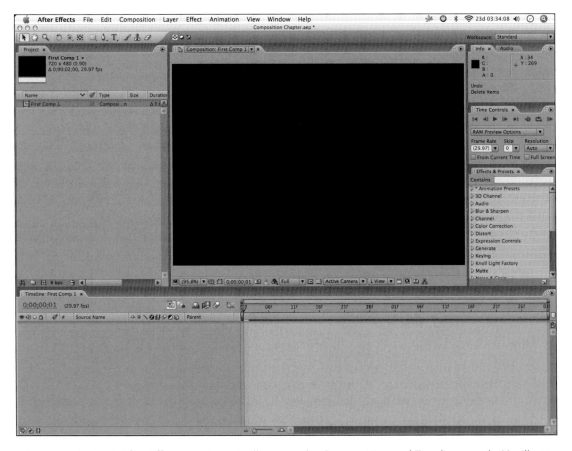

When you click OK, After Effects 7 automatically opens the Composition and Timeline panels. You'll get to work directly with these two panels in the next exercise.

---

8 In the **Project** panel, make sure **First Comp 1** is selected, and choose **Composition > Composition Settings**. Alternatively, you can press **Cmd+K** (Mac) or **Ctrl+K** (Windows).

The Composition Settings dialog box reopens. If you ever need to change your composition settings, you can do so at any time. However, as mentioned, setting them when you create your composition is most beneficial. Leave them alone for now, and be sure to review the upcoming chart so you understand what these settings mean.

---

9 Choose **File > Save**, or press **Cmd+S** (Mac) or **Ctrl+S** (Windows). Leave **Composition_Chapter.aep** open for the next exercise.

Now that you've created your composition and specified the composition settings, you'll be taking a short break. You need to do some reading before you get going again, so you can better understand the significance of what you just did.

Exploring the Composition Settings

In general, although it is ideal to decide up front what composition settings you will need for your composition before you start adding footage and creating animations, sometimes you may need to make adjustments along the way. For example, you can work with certain settings as you're brainstorming and creating a product and then output it with different settings when you're finished. Or you might decide your program needs to be longer, in which case a simple change to your composition's duration is in order. You might also choose to adjust your composition's width and height to accommodate widescreen video or high-definition projects.

Few programs offer the level of flexibility that After Effects 7 does, and one of the best features of the composition settings is they can be changed later. In fact, since the composition settings are at the hub of many critical choices, it may be hard to

determine some settings until you're further along in the creative process. No problem—once you've created a composition and fixed its settings, just reopen the **Composition Settings** dialog box by choosing **Composition > Composition Settings**, and then adjust the settings.

Note: As mentioned earlier, just be certain the changes you make to the composition settings do not adversely affect any settings you have made to existing footage in your project (particularly in regard to screen dimensions).

As you work through this book and learn more about the elements making up a project, you will come to learn how footage relates to your compositions. Here's a handy chart to help you better understand what all those settings in the **Composition Settings** dialog box mean (next page):

Composition Settings

Setting	Description
Preset	The **Preset** pop-up menu contains many choices for common sizes and resolutions. It contains settings for video, film, Web, HDTV (**H**igh-**D**efinition **Tele**Vision), and others. The exercises in this book will primarily use the NTSC settings because they represent the majority of projects that users are currently creating. (NTSC is the TV standard for the United States, Japan, and a few other countries, and PAL is used throughout most of Europe.) As you take on professional projects, you may need to use a different preset to match your output goals. The **Custom** option allows you to specify your settings manually.
Width, Height, Aspect Ratio	As you change your presets, the **Width** and **Height** fields will change depending on your needs. You can use the **Preset** pop-up menu to change these settings, or you can type custom values in the fields. If you leave the **Lock Aspect Ratio to 3:2** check box turned on, you can type a width, and After Effects 7 will automatically calculate the height. A 3:2 aspect ratio (the numerical relationship between width and height) is correct for DV (**D**igital **V**ideo), although 4:3 is popular for many multimedia formats and some film format sizes. The numbers appearing in the **Lock Aspect Ratio to 3:2** check box may change if you choose another preset. With widescreen televisions and the new HDTV devices, for example, 16:9 is another popular choice.
Pixel Aspect Ratio	Computer screens and digital televisions are composed of perfectly square pixels; however, standard-definition video screens are composed of rectangular pixels (taller then they are wide), known as **nonsquare pixels**. Because the goal of this book is to teach After Effects 7, you will be working on your computer screen instead of a video screen, so working with square pixels is fine. As you proceed through the book, you will encounter instances of both square and nonsquare pixels, although it is not necessary for you to know too much about them at this time.

If you take on any projects that need to be output to standard-definition video, you may want to change this setting to one of the many video options that this pop-up menu offers, such as **D1/DV NTSC (0.9)**, **D1/DV NTSC Widescreen (1.2)**, **D1/DV PAL (1.07)**, or even the new **HDV 1080/DVCPRO HD 720 (1.33)** and **DVCPRO HD 1080 (1.5)** settings.

Note that when you change the format from square pixels to a nonsquare format, your footage may look slightly squished. It will "unsquish" once you output the final material to video. In the latest versions of Photoshop (Photoshop CS and CS2), you can actually create images in nonsquare pixel format for preview purposes so they don't appear squished as you work on them. Pixel aspect ratios can be a difficult topic to grasp, and you will learn more about them as you work through the book. |

continues on next page

Composition Settings *continued*	
Setting	**Description**
Frame Rate	Different kinds of output require different frame rates. Video usually runs at 30 frames per second, and this number is fine for the purposes of this chapter. As you'll soon learn firsthand, these settings are not set in stone and can be changed easily at a later time. (The upcoming "Determining Duration" sidebar and the "Project Settings" chart cover the frame rate choices and describe in more detail what they mean and when to use them.)
Resolution	You can choose to work at **Full**, **Half**, **Third**, **Quarter**, or **Custom** resolution. This means you will preview the footage at 1:1, 1:2, 1:3, 1:4, or a custom setting. When working on large formats for film or when using intense effects, filters, or 3D (which take extra time to render), many After Effects artists scale down the resolution so they can get a quick preview. You can always change this setting when you render the final movie. The great thing about this setting is that it is not permanent. You can choose to work at half resolution, but this won't alter your full-resolution footage. This means you can always output at full resolution later, and you won't lose any of the quality. (You'll learn more about rendering in Chapter 20, *"Rendering Final Movies."*)
Start Timecode	Timecode, which measures time in units of frames, seconds, minutes, and hours (the smallest building block is an individual frame), is utilized extensively by film and video hardware and software, including After Effects. **Frame 0:00:00:00** or **Frame 0:00:00:01** is the first frame of the duration of a composition. Sometimes, when dealing with footage being combined later with a film or video project, After Effects artists want to have their numbers match an edited sequence with a specific timecode. If you were to change this setting to not start on **Frame 1**, you could set it to match the timecode of the external video footage. Many animators, especially beginners, start on **Frame 1**, although other video professionals will choose to start on **Frame 0**. By the way, **Frame 0:00:00:01** is the same as **Frame 1**. The zeros stand for hours, minutes, seconds, and frames.
Duration	Duration specifies the length of the composition. As an example, 0:00:30:00 specifies the duration of the composition is set to 30 seconds. You can always change the duration of a composition, which you will also learn to do in Chapter 5, *"Creating Keyframes and Animation in the Timeline."*

Determining Duration

The abbreviation **fps** (frames **per** second) refers to the number of frames changed sequentially before your eyes each second to create the illusion of moving pictures. To compute the number of frames for your composition, divide the duration by the number of frames per second.

For example, you might be using a standard video frame rate of 30 fps. If you have 300 frames in your composition, the calculation is 300 / 30 = 10. Thus, your composition is 10 seconds long.

Or you might be using a standard motion-picture frame rate of 24 fps. If you have 240 frames in your composition, the calculation is 240 / 24 = 10. Here, too, the length of time for your composition is 10 seconds.

Determining Pixel Aspect Ratio

Most display devices in computer graphics use square pixels. This means the height and width of the pixels are the same. However, many video systems and anamorphic film projects (shot with a special lens) use nonsquare display systems. The height of a nonsquare display system is not the same as its width, so these pixels are rectangular in shape.

How do you determine when you need to use square pixels or choose another option? The basic rule is this: If you are working on a project that will not be output to video or film, use square pixels.

If you are working on a video project, determine which video format you are using and select it from the menu. In the United States, the most common video format is D1/DV NTSC. In Europe, the most standard video format is D1/DV PAL. However, the new high-definition formats, such as HDV or DVCPRO HD, have their own unique, nonsquare pixel dimensions, which you can select from the **Pixel Aspect Ratio** pop-up menu.

If you are working on a film project or certain high-definition projects, talk with your supervisor or client before deciding to use square pixels or Anamorphic 2:1. Although standard operating procedures exist, many film productions have special requirements. Motion-picture production is expensive, and making assumptions can lead to formidable difficulties. Make sure you communicate with the producer of the project about the settings needed.

Learning More About Timecode

The **Start Timecode** setting can be critical when working on a video project. Video editors, for example, use timecode as a system to log all editing decisions. You may be asked to start a sequence or animation at a certain point in time, based on timecode numbering. Timecode specifies the exact hour, minute, second, and frame within a video piece.

0;00;00;01

Notice the semicolons separating the numbers in the illustration here. The first number is the hour (0), followed by a semicolon; the second number is the minute (00), followed by a semicolon; the third number is the seconds (00), followed by a semicolon; and the last number is the frame (01). You may have noticed that some timecode numbers are separated by semicolons and others by colons. Semicolons denote the use of **Drop Frame** timecodes, and colons denote **Non-Drop Frame** timecodes (see the NTSC setting in the "Project Settings" chart that follows for more information). Basically, it is more accurate to count the frame rate of NTSC video as 29.97 fps, rather than an exact 30 fps. To denote the difference using timecode notations, a semicolon is used for the odd, **Drop Frame** timecode of NTSC video.

Exploring the Project Settings

In Chapter 3, *"Beginning a New Project,"* you learned about a project and its significance to the After Effects 7 workflow. That chapter didn't cover the project settings because they actually relate more to compositions (even though they also relate to projects). Basically, the project settings affect all the compositions you create by creating global settings for the entire project. The composition settings, by contrast, create settings specific to an individual composition.

To see the project settings for a project, choose **File > Project Settings**.

It's important to understand these settings, so the following handy chart describes what the most important settings mean (next page):

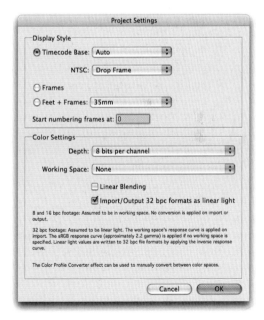

Project Settings

Setting	Description
Timecode Base	This is the radio button to click when you are authoring for video, Web, DVD, or multimedia. Most video is set to 30 fps, but the **Timecode Base** pop-up menu offers other choices in the event you want something different.
NTSC	Unfortunately, NTSC video counts frames in an unusual way, dropping frames every so often, as compared with a normal clock. No actual frames are lost—they are just counted differently. This makes it difficult to count frames in a linear fashion. Most people set this to **Non-Drop Frame** so the frame numbers will advance sequentially in the After Effects 7 **Timeline**. The reality is that when you output to video, you will be working with 29.97 fps. For this book's purposes, you'll keep the **Non-Drop Frame** setting. In fact, most After Effects artists leave this setting to **Non-Drop Frame** in order to count frames more easily. This setting doesn't affect the final output to video and is really there for preview and editing purposes.
Frames	If you click this radio button, After Effects 7 counts frames instead of hours, minutes, seconds, and frames. Most animators doing cel or character animation are accustomed to working this way because animators typically number their drawings sequentially and refer to their artwork by its frame numbers. You will not use this setting in this book, but it exists if you want it.
Feet + Frames	This is the radio button to click when you are authoring for film. Film is measured by feet and frames, and most film, including 35 mm film, runs at 24 fps. Therefore, with 35 mm film, a foot is 24 frames. If you were looking at **Frame 120** in this context, you would divide the number into 24, and it would result in a measurement of 4 feet and 6 frames. It's a confusing way to measure time to anyone who isn't a filmmaker, so using this setting is not advised unless you are working on an actual film project. You have the choice here of **35mm** or **16mm**.
Start numbering frames at	The **Start numbering frames at** field refers to the numbering for the first frame. Typically, filmmakers call the first **Frame 1**, but this setting allows you to enter any value you want.
Depth	For most projects, 8 bits per channel is the correct setting. However, if you need the highest-quality output, particularly for film projects, you may also choose 16 bits per channel or 32 bits per channel. In general, 16 or 32 bits per channel are necessary only for high-end projects because the majority of video projects are delivered and viewed in 8-bit formats anyway. However, you can use even some of the high-end settings for general color correction or special-effects purposes.

2 | Importing Footage into the Composition

Now that you've created and opened a composition, you're probably wondering how to get it to do something. The first step is to bring in some footage, and the next step is to animate that footage. In this exercise, you will learn to import footage into a composition. (In Chapter 5, *"Creating Keyframes and Animation in the Timeline,"* you'll learn how to animate footage in the **Composition** panel.) You cannot animate footage without the **Timeline**, and you cannot gain access to the **Timeline** without a composition. Understanding the relationship between the project, composition, and **Timeline** is key to understanding After Effects 7. This exercise should be a great help in unfolding the mystery of why you need all these elements.

---

1 If you followed the previous exercise, **Composition_Chapter.aep** should still be open in After Effects 7. If it's not, choose **File > Open Project**. Navigate to the **chap_04** folder you copied to your desktop, click **Composition_Chapter_2.aep** to select it, and click **Open**.

---

2 In the **Project** panel, double-click the blank area to open the **Import File** dialog box. Navigate to the **chap_04** folder and then to the **chap_04** folder (an additional folder named **chap_04** exists inside the main folder), and click **Import Folder**. Click **OK** as many times as needed to merge the PSD layers and accept the layer dimensions.

This imports the entire folder of footage in one action. You learned in Chapter 3, *"Beginning a New Project,"* that you don't need to import footage items separately; you can import individual footage items or an entire folder of footage at once, depending on your needs.

When you get ready to display the footage you just imported, you'll need to use a twirly. If you remember, a **twirly** is the official and affectionate After Effects 7 term describing the arrow to the left of a folder name.

---

3 In the **Project** panel, click the **twirly** next to **chap_04** to reveal the footage you just imported. Drag the file **Palm_Tree.psd** into the **Composition** panel.

You should observe several noteworthy events once you complete this task. Notice the file appears in the Timeline at the same time? The Timeline and Composition panels are tied together—nothing can happen in one panel without affecting the other.

Notice also the duration in the Timeline is the full 2 seconds, represented by the bar stretching across the Timeline panel. By default, a still picture will stretch as long as the duration of the composition if the CTI (Current Time Indicator) is set to the first frame.

4 With **Palm_Tree.psd** selected, either in the **Composition** panel or in the **Timeline** panel, press **Delete**.

Notice the footage has been deleted only from the Composition and Timeline panels, not from the project. This is significant. Your footage exists in the project whether it is in a composition or not.

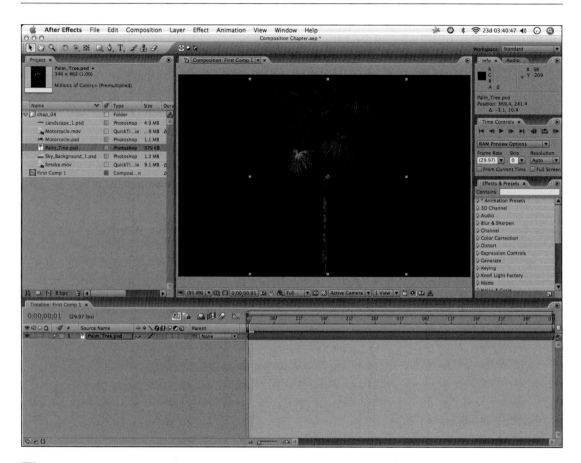

5 From the **Project** panel, drag **Palm_Tree.psd** directly into the **Timeline** panel.

The Palm_Tree.psd footage appears in both the Composition and Timeline panels.

The benefit of using this technique (dragging directly into the Timeline) is that the footage is automatically centered in the middle of the Composition panel. Get into the habit of dropping footage into the Timeline whenever you need it centered. Other than that, either method works fine.

6 From the **Project** panel, drag **Motorcycle.mov** into the **Composition** panel.

Notice that the Motorcycle.mov footage appears above Palm_Tree.psd in both the Composition and Project panels.

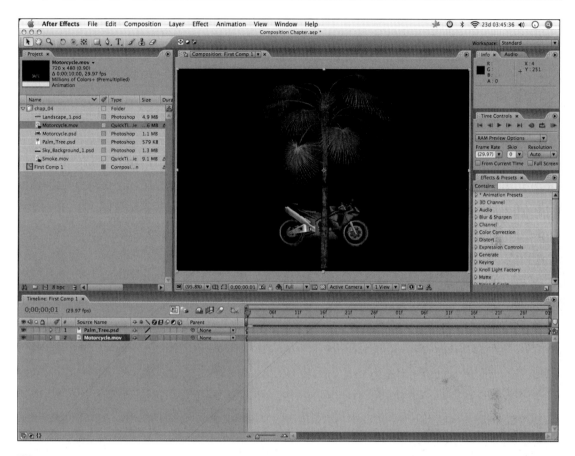

7 In the **Timeline** panel, drag **Motorcycle.mov** below **Palm_Tree.psd** to change the stacking order.

You can easily move layers around within the Timeline panel by dragging them into different positions. The topmost files are visible in the foreground of the Composition panel and have smaller numbers in the Timeline.

8 From the **Project** panel, drag **Sky_Background.psd** to the bottom of the footage stack in the **Timeline** panel.

The sky will appear behind the motorcycle.

9 Press the **spacebar** to play a preview of the contents of your composition. Press the **spacebar** again to stop the preview.

Using the spacebar is a fast way to observe your work. You'll learn a lot more about previewing work in future chapters.

10 Choose **File > Save**, or press **Cmd+S** (Mac) or **Ctrl+S** (Windows). Leave **Composition_Chapter.aep** open for the next exercise.

When you save the project, After Effects 7 saves all the footage references and the composition, so you don't need to save them separately.

In this exercise, you learned how to add individual footage items to a new composition. In the next exercise, you will utilize a convenient feature of After Effects 7 that allows you to import a Photoshop file as its own composition. This will allow you to access all the layers inside the original Photoshop document.

3 | Importing a Photoshop File as a Composition

So far, you have learned how to ⟨...⟩tion from scratch and how to import footage into a composition. In this exercise, yo⟨...⟩Photoshop files. The After Effects 7 **Timeline** has layers, and Photo⟨...⟩mpose the layers in Photoshop and have them a⟨...⟩

Setting up a complex compos⟨...⟩s can be extremely useful, especially when you ar⟨...⟩mple), graphics, photographs that have been ⟨...⟩te image), or characters with elements (such as⟨...⟩r Effects 7. This exercise shows you how to i⟨...⟩

---

1 If you followed the pre⟨...⟩open in After Effects 7. If it's not, choose **File > O**⟨...⟩to your desktop, click **Composition_Chapter_3**⟨...⟩

---

2 In the **Project** panel⟨...⟩ area to open the **Import**⟨...⟩ Navigate to the **chap_0**⟨...⟩ **chap_04** folder, and cli⟨...⟩ select it. From the **Imp**⟨...⟩ choose **Composition,**⟨...⟩

Notice two files appe⟨...⟩ panel: a folder called⟨...⟩ a new composition n⟨...⟩ Whenever you impo⟨...⟩ as a composition, A⟨...⟩ files in the Project p⟨...⟩ and a composition⟨...⟩ name the Photosh⟨...⟩ confusing because⟨...⟩ but one displays a⟨...⟩ displays a compo⟨...⟩

In previous exerc⟨...⟩ from the Import As pop-up menu.⟨...⟩d, After Effects 7 preserves the layers of the Photoshop file. You also can choose Comp⟨...⟩d Layers. With this option, After Effects 7 will look at the Photoshop transparency in the different layers and will crop each layer's content tightly. This is helpful once you start to animate because the center of each layer is dictated by the size of the layer, not the overall Photoshop document size.

---

3 In the **Project** panel, double-click the **Landscape 1** composition to open it.

It's OK that your other composition is still open.

In the Composition panel, notice you can have two (or more!) compositions open at once. A tab appears in the Timeline panel with the name of the composition, and the tab in the Composition panel allows you to select an open composition from a convenient pop-up menu (open compositions appear in the second group of options). This illustrates that you can also have multiple compositions inside a project. Often, when you're working on a big project, you might choose to separate elements into individual compositions or keep different versions active within a single project.

4 In the **Project** panel, click the **twirly** next to **Landscape_1 Layers** to view its contents.

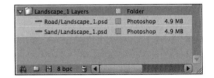

The Landscape_1 Layers folder contains the two layers of the composition as two separate footage items. If you import Photoshop footage as merged layers, as you've done in previous exercises, you won't be able to access individual layers as you can now. Also, notice the same Photoshop layer names appear inside the Timeline panel.

5 Choose **File > Save**, or press **Cmd+S** (Mac) or **Ctrl+S** (Windows). Leave **Composition_Chapter.aep** open for the next exercise.

As you have seen, creating compositions from Photoshop files has its advantages, namely, the ability to access multiple layers from the original Photoshop document (as opposed to importing Photoshop documents as merged, or flattened, files). In the next exercise, you will learn how to further speed up creating a composition by using the settings of an already imported file to automatically determine the settings for the new composition.

Creating a Composition from Footage Settings

You can also create a composition in After Effects 7, and save a lot of time, by basing a composition on a footage file. Creating a composition based on a piece of footage is especially useful when working with video clips, whose settings often dictate the settings for the entire composition you're creating. For example, if you have some footage you want to use as a background for your composition, you might use the footage to determine the width, height, duration, and other settings of the composition, rather than setting them all manually. In this exercise, you'll see firsthand how and why this will be a valuable skill in your After Effects 7 arsenal.

1 If you followed the previous exercise, **Composition_Chapter.aep** should still be open in After Effects 7. If it's not, choose **File > Open Project**. Navigate to the **chap_04** folder you copied to your desktop, click **Composition_Chapter_4.aep** to select it, and click **Open**.

2 In the **Project** panel, click **Motorcycle.mov** to select it, and observe the information about this footage that appears at the top of the panel.

Notice the file is 720x480 pixels, is 0;00;10;00 long, and was recorded at 29.97 fps. You could create a composition with the same size, duration, and fps and then drag Motorcycle.mov into the composition. Or, you can follow the next series of steps instead.

3 Drag the **Motorcycle.mov** file onto the **Create a new composition** icon at the bottom of the **Project** panel.

Notice this drag-and-drop action instantly creates a new composition and Timeline, which are named after the footage.

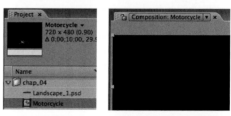

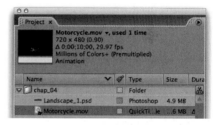

4 If necessary, select the **Motorcycle** composition by clicking its name in the **Project** panel. Choose **Composition > Composition Settings**.

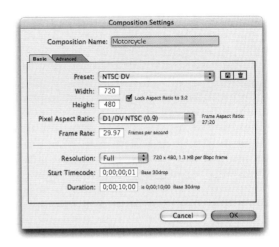

5 In the **Composition Settings** dialog box, notice how the settings match the footage properties. Click **OK**.

In this step, you're not really changing anything; you're just looking. Because Motorcycle.mov was 720x480 pixels, so is this composition. This is a great technique when you want one footage item to dictate the settings for a composition. It's especially useful with movie footage, which can vary in fps, timecode, and duration.

6 Choose **File > Save**, or press **Cmd+S** (Mac) or **Ctrl+S** (Windows). Choose **File > Close**.

You just learned a quick and easy way to create a composition, a technique you will use frequently throughout your After Effects 7 career, particularly when working with video footage, whose frame size and duration are often fixed.

Throughout this chapter you also learned other ways to create compositions, including manually adjusting all settings. As you work through the book and as you create your own projects in the future, feel free to refer to the tables and notes in this chapter as references when you are uncertain about the meaning of a particular setting. In future chapters, you will learn more about composition settings for particular projects and review the topics already covered here.

In the next chapter, you will finally put your project and compositions settings to use when you learn about the numerous animation techniques available to you in After Effects 7. So, if you're ready to continue, let's get animating!

5

Creating Keyframes and Animation in the Timeline

Because Adobe After Effects 7 is a motion graphics tool, creating motion is at the heart of its power. Professional animators and motion graphics artists need to know how to create deliberate and oftentimes complex movement. Some motion projects require subtle movement (such as a slowly drifting title); others require wild, erratic movement (the flight path of a firefly, for example). You can achieve any of these motion styles by mastering the use of keyframes.

You set up keyframe action using the After Effects 7 **Timeline**. As you work through the exercises in this chapter, you'll see that some kinds of keyframes can create movement that speeds up or slows down, other kinds of keyframes can create curved paths, and still other kinds can create smooth or jerky movement. Once you complete this chapter, you will have a good foundation of motion skills that will last your entire professional life.

Viewing the Timeline

This chapter focuses on using the **Timeline** for setting keyframes and on animating properties of layers. The **Timeline** has a few navigation and viewing features you haven't seen yet that are important to understand when working on a project in After Effects 7.

Specifically, you can reduce the **Timeline** to fit a smaller panel, in case you have a long animation or you're already zoomed in on a specific portion of your sequence, by using the **Time Navigator** slider. Simply drag to stretch it to the location you want the **Timeline** content to fill, as shown in the illustration here.

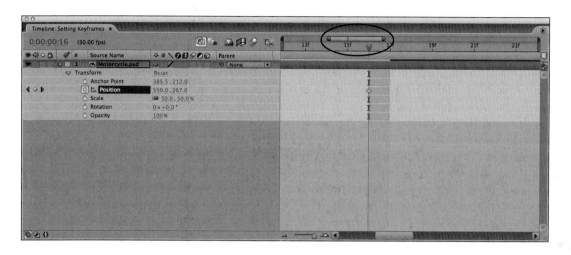

You can also use the **Time Navigator** slider to zoom into the specific part of the **Timeline** where the **CTI** (**C**urrent **T**ime **I**ndicator) resides. This is useful for checking a frame you are working on or for closing the surrounding frames. To do this, drag the **Zoom into frame level** slider.

For example, dragging the **Zoom into frame level slider** to the right zooms in. Moving the slider to the left widens the **Time Navigator** and reveals the entire **Timeline** again, as shown in the illustration below.

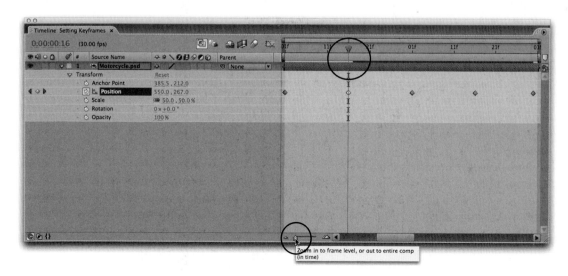

Understanding Keyframes

Keyframe is an animation term used to describe a point at which something changes. The best way to plan and design animation is to determine the start point and end point for particular actions. These start and end points are the "keys" to your animation. If the action is complex, you might need to indicate numerous other points of change as well.

Animators use keyframes to describe main points of action, such as when an image moves from the left side of the screen to the right side of the screen. In this example of a simple lateral movement, you would need two keyframes: one for the left side of the screen and another for the right.

Once you have created keyframes, you can create the frames between the keyframes. For example,

in traditional hand-drawn animation, an animator can draw two keyframes. An assistant can then draw the frames between those keyframes (the in-between frames). If artwork moves from the left side of the screen to the right in 30 frames with 2 keyframes, then the assistant would need to draw 28 connecting frames. The keyframes act as a guide for all the frames that fall between them.

In computer animation, you can define the keyframes and have an application like After Effects 7 draw, or **interpolate**, the in-between frames for you. Again, the keyframes act as guides for the frames that After Effects 7 creates automatically.

VIDEO: | **keyframes.mov**

To help you learn more about the fundamentals of keyframes, check out **keyframes.mov** in the **videos** folder on the **After Effects 7 HOT CD-ROM.**

---

1 | Setting Keyframes

You've learned to import footage into your project, create a composition, and add artwork from the project into the composition. Now, it's finally time to start animating! In this exercise, you will learn how to set keyframes. Specifically, you will learn how to create start and end points as keyframes, and you'll preview the results of your animation.

---

1 Copy the **chap_05** folder from the **After Effects 7 HOT CD-ROM** onto your desktop.

---

2 Launch After Effects 7, and choose **File > Open Project**. In the **Open** dialog box, navigate to the **chap_05** folder you copied to your desktop, click **Keyframe_Animation.aep** to select it, and click **Open**.

This is a project file, just like the project files you learned to make in Chapter 3, *"Beginning a New Project."*

---

3 Choose **File > Save As**. Navigate to the **AE7_HOT_Projects** folder on your desktop, name the file **Keyframe_Animation.aep**, and click **Save** to save a copy of the project.

---

4 In the **Project** panel, double-click the **Setting Keyframes** composition to open it. Click the **twirly** next to **Footage** to expand the folder.

Tip: Remember, the arrow used to display properties is affectionately called the **twirly**.

The Project panel contains numerous compositions, as well as a Footage folder. Notice the Footage folder contains a file called Motorcycle.psd. Notice also the Timeline panel contains a single footage item called Motorcycle.psd, which was imported from the project into the Setting Keyframes composition as a merged Adobe Photoshop file.

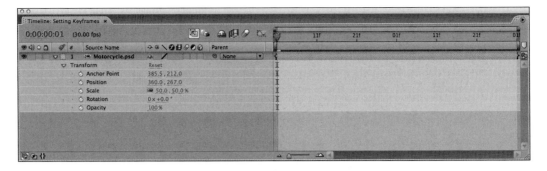

5 In the **Timeline** panel, click the **twirly** to the left of the **Motorcycle.psd** layer, and then click the **twirly** to the left of **Transform** underneath.

Clicking the twirly next to a layer expands its properties. Notice the Transform setting for the layer and each of its properties: Anchor Point, Position, Scale, Rotation, and Opacity.

Every layer in a Timeline has at least one twirly, with the same five Transform properties you see for the Motorcycle.psd layer. These properties are part of the After Effects 7 interface and are the most important properties you will work with when animating a layer.

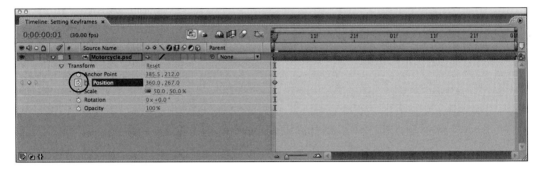

6 In the **Timeline** panel, click the **stopwatch** icon next to the **Position** property.

Clicking the stopwatch icon causes After Effects 7 to place a keyframe icon in the Timeline at the current CTI position (Frame 0:00:00:01).

Clicking the stopwatch icon not only inserts a keyframe at the current CTI but also turns on the capability to set keyframes for the property at other locations in the Timeline, as you'll do shortly.

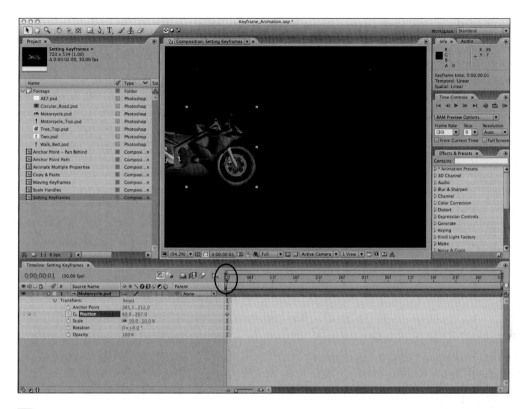

7   In the **Timeline** panel, make sure the **CTI** is on the first frame. In the **Composition** panel, click and drag the **Motorcycle.psd** image to the position in the illustration shown here.

Having already clicked the stopwatch icon and set the Position property of the image, you have created your first keyframe. This keyframe will be the starting point for animating the Position property.

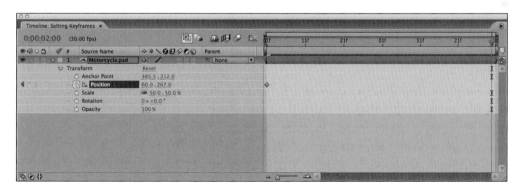

8   In the **Timeline** panel, drag the **CTI** to the last frame (**0:00:02:00**).

Notice the Current Time display in the upper-left corner changes based on the CTI position. You will frequently need to refer to the Current Time display as you work in After Effects 7, since it is a frame-accurate reference for your location within the Timeline.

Avoiding the Dreaded Gray Frame

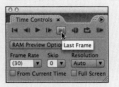

If you manually move the **CTI** to the last frame in the **Timeline** panel (or click the **Next Frame** button when you are already at the end), you may see a blank, gray frame. This means you've dragged the **CTI** too far.

You can use a few methods to get the **CTI** back to the true end. You can click the **Current Time** display and type the correct value; you can use the **Time Controls** panel and click the **Last Frame** button, as shown in the illustration here; or you can press the **End** key. If you have a laptop that doesn't have an **End** key, you can press the shortcut **Cmd+Option+right arrow** (Mac) or **Ctrl+Alt+right arrow** (Windows). Or, you can readjust the playhead manually.

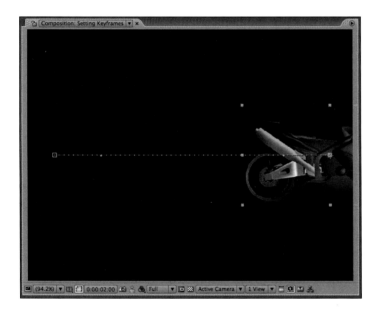

9 In the **Composition** panel, drag the **Motorcycle.psd** image to the position shown in the illustration here to create a new keyframe.

Notice this creates a motion path between the two keyframe points. A motion path will appear only if the change is to the Position property. If the change is to some other property, such as Opacity or Scale, you will not see a motion path.

When you click the stopwatch icon for the Position property, moving the artwork in the Composition panel sets a keyframe automatically at the location of the CTI in the Timeline.

10 In the **Timeline** panel, drag the **CTI** back and forth to preview your animation.

Dragging the CTI back and forth is also known as **scrubbing** the Timeline.

To review, the steps to create keyframe animation are as follows: First, click the stopwatch icon to establish that the property will accept keyframes and to set the first keyframe. Second, move the CTI, and make a change to the position of the layer at a new point in time. This causes a new keyframe to appear automatically.

---

11 Choose **File > Save**, or press **Cmd+S** (Mac) or **Ctrl+S** (Windows). Leave **Keyframe_Animation.aep** open for the next exercise.

Now that you understand a bit about setting keyframes, you will look at some of the basic properties you are able to set keyframes for in After Effects 7. In the next exercise, you will learn how to quickly preview the motion you have created via your keyframes. But first you'll learn a little more about properties.

Understanding Properties

In the previous exercise, you set keyframes for the **Position** property. But what exactly is a property?

Transform properties are inherent to all footage layers. When you bring a footage item into the **Timeline**, that footage becomes a **layer**. Think of layers as the individual components making up your composition.

Each layer has properties you can access and change on a frame-by-frame basis to create an animation. Think of properties as options for a layer. **Properties** provide the means to change the color, size, position, and other attributes associated with a layer. The variety of properties in After Effects 7 is impressive. They are organized into groups to make them easy to find.

In addition to the **Transform** properties, After Effects 7 has a few primary groups of properties: **Masks**, **Effects**, **Text**, **3D**, and **Expressions**. The **Transform** properties are automatically assigned to all footage layers. To access some of the other types of properties, you need to take other steps or create other types of layers. You'll learn about other types of properties throughout this book.

The good news is that you can animate all the properties by setting keyframes. And once you learn how to set keyframes for a **Transform** property in this chapter, you can use the same process on other types of layer properties.

2 | Using RAM Preview

A significant part of creating animation is being able to preview the results. In the previous exercise, you watched the motion you created using a technique called **scrubbing**. In this exercise, you will learn to preview your motion using the **Time Controls** panel and the **RAM Preview** button, which allows you to render a preview of your composition into your system's memory. Consequently, the more RAM (**R**andom **A**ccess **M**emory) you have in your computer, the better.

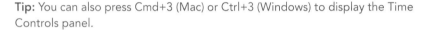

1 If you followed the previous exercise, **Keyframe_Animation.aep** should still be open in After Effects 7. If it's not, choose **File > Open Project**. Navigate to the **chap_05** folder you copied to your desktop, click **Keyframe_Animation_2.aep** to select it, and click **Open**.

---

2 If necessary, double-click the **Setting_Keyframes** composition to open it. If the **Time Controls** panel is not visible, choose **Window > Time Controls** to display it.

Tip: You can also press Cmd+3 (Mac) or Ctrl+3 (Windows) to display the Time Controls panel.

---

3 In the **Timeline**, set the **CTI** to **Frame 0:00:00:01** to manually rewind your animation, or press the **Home** key. If you have a laptop without a **Home** key, press **Cmd+Option+left arrow** (Mac) or **Ctrl+Alt+left arrow** (Windows).

---

4 In the **Time Controls** panel, click the **Play/Pause** button to preview your animation.

Your animation may play roughly the first time.

---

5 Press the **spacebar** to stop playing the looping animation.

Tip: Because the spacebar shortcut is so much faster, it's rarely necessary to use the Play/Pause button. Press the spacebar once to play the animation, and press it again to stop.

---

6 In the **Time Controls** panel, click the **First Frame** button to rewind your animation.

Another way to get to the first frame of an animation is to press the Home key.

---

7 In the **Time Controls** panel, click the **RAM Preview** button to preview your animation. Click anywhere, or press any key to stop the preview.

The RAM Preview feature causes your computer to store the movie in its memory (RAM) to give you a real-time preview. The term **real time** refers to the timing that would occur in a video or film playing at ordinary speed. When you click the Play button instead of using RAM Preview, After Effects 7 has to render each frame, which can cause the preview to slow down. RAM Preview is useful for getting a sense of what the final timing of your movie will look like. If RAM Preview doesn't work well, it might be because your computer doesn't have enough RAM.

---

8 Press the **End** key to go the last frame.

---

9 Choose **File > Save**, or press **Cmd+S** (Mac) or **Ctrl+S** (Windows). Leave **Keyframe_Animation.aep** open for the next exercise.

Now that you have practiced previewing your composition using the Time Controls panel, spacebar, and RAM Preview functions, it is time to learn how to modify the motion in your animation by altering keyframes.

---

3 | Editing the Motion

Remember (if you're old enough) how typewriters didn't have undo keys? If you made a typing mistake, you sometimes had to retype everything. Fortunately, computers are great for editing, and the old days of worrying about changing your mind are gone forever. What good would setting keyframes be if you couldn't change them? In this exercise, you will learn the basics of editing keyframe animation. Specifically, you'll learn how to select individual keyframes and add more keyframes. You'll also learn how to change keyframe properties. Nothing is ever cast in stone in After Effects 7—you can always change your mind (and so can your clients!).

---

1 If you followed the previous exercise, **Keyframe_Animation.aep** should still be open in After Effects 7. If it's not, choose **File > Open Project**. Navigate to the **chap_05** folder you copied to your desktop, click **Keyframe_Animation_3.aep** to select it, and click **Open**.

---

2 If necessary, double-click the **Setting_Keyframes** composition to open it. Press the **End** key to move the **CTI** to the last keyframe.

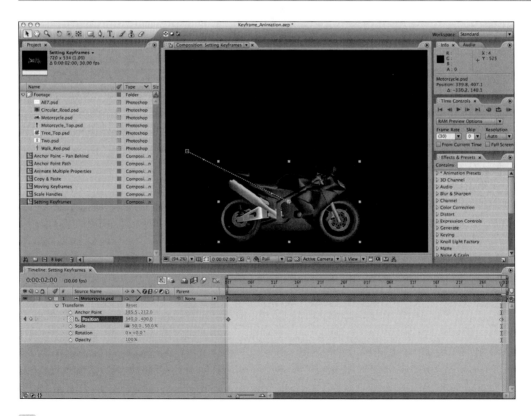

3 In the **Composition** panel, drag the **Motorcycle.psd** image to the position shown in the illustration here.

Notice the motion path has changed because you altered the last keyframe. In the Timeline panel, notice the Position property values of the Motorcycle.psd layer have changed. Any changes you make in the Composition panel take effect in the Timeline panel as well.

4 In the **Timeline** panel, locate the **Keyframe Navigator**, and click the **Go to previous keyframe** icon (left arrow), as shown in the illustration here. Once you do this, notice that the **CTI** moves to the previous keyframe (**Frame 0:00:00:01**).

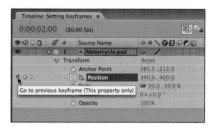

The Keyframe Navigator appears whenever you have more than one keyframe set in the Timeline. Clicking the right arrow will take you forward to the next keyframe; clicking the left arrow will take you to the previous keyframe. These arrows will appear only if keyframes are present to the right or left of the CTI's position. Using the Keyframe Navigator arrows is a great way to locate existing keyframes. The only way to change a keyframe is to go to it first, so you'll find the Keyframe Navigator to be invaluable.

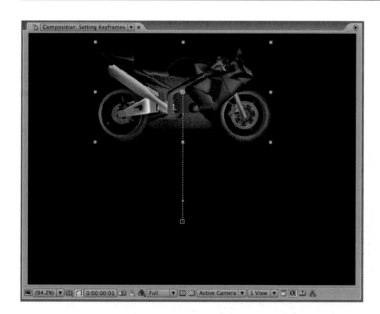

5 In the **Composition** panel, drag the **Motorcycle.psd** image to the top of the panel, as shown in the illustration here.

You've changed the motion path again by editing the keyframe for the beginning position.

6 Set the **CTI** to **Frame 20**.

Currently no keyframe appears at Frame 20, but you'll learn how to set one in the next step.

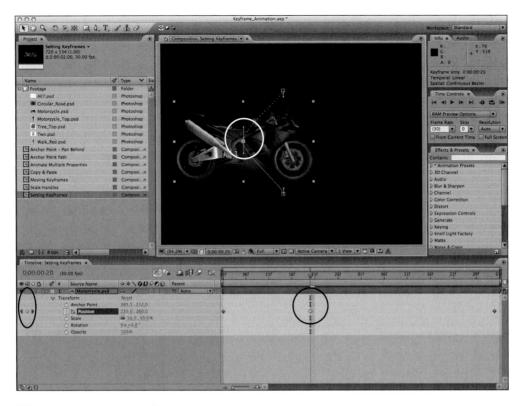

7 Drag the **Motorcycle.psd** image to the left. Notice this action adds a new keyframe to your animation at **Frame 0:00:00:20**.

When you want to create a new Position keyframe, go to a frame that does not already have a keyframe and then move the object to that frame, as you did in this step. This requires you to first click the stop-watch icon, as in Exercise 1. From that point on, when you want to change an existing keyframe, go to that keyframe, and then move the object. Going to an existing keyframe is easy with the Keyframe Navigator arrows (circled in the illustration here).

---

8 Set the **CTI** to **Frame 0:00:01:10**.

You might notice tiny green marks next to the frame numbers in the Timeline; these represent rendered frames. It's not important in this exercise to understand the green marks. Chapter 7, *"Previewing Movies,"* explains them fully.

---

9 In the **Timeline** panel, locate the **Position** values. Position your cursor over the *x* value until the cursor changes into a hand with a double arrow. Click and drag to the right to increase the value to approximately **400** pixels.

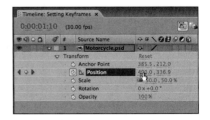

The Position property's *x* value is the first field on the left. This represents the horizontal position of the object.

10 In the **Timeline** panel, locate the **Position** values. Hold your cursor over the **y** value until the cursor changes into a hand with a double arrow. Click and drag to the left to decrease the value to approximately **260** pixels.

The Position property's y value is the second field on the right. This represents the vertical position of the object.

Tip: Moving the Position sliders in the Timeline panel moves the object in the Composition panel and is another way to set a position keyframe. Observe the resulting motion path in the Composition panel. The path is curved by default. You'll learn ways to alter the shape of this path soon.

---

11 Press the **spacebar** or click the **RAM Preview** button in the **Time Controls** panel to view the animation.

---

12 Choose **File > Save**, or press **Cmd+S** (Mac) or **Ctrl+S** (Windows) to save the **Keyframe_Animation.aep** project.

This automatically saves the Setting Keyframes composition along with the project.

---

13 Choose **Close Setting Keyframes** from the pop-up menu in the upper-left corner of the **Composition** panel to close the **Setting Keyframes** composition. Alternatively, you can click **Close** in the **Timeline** panel to close the composition.

Notice the Keyframe_Animation.aep project does not close with the composition. If you clicked Close in the Timeline panel, also notice the workspace layout changes because the Timeline panel has disappeared. Do not be alarmed—the Timeline panel will return when you open another composition.

You still may be confused at this point about the relationship between the project and the composition. Remember, the composition you've been working with in this exercise is inside the project file. The composition name is Setting Keyframes, and the project name is Keyframe_Animation.aep. The only way to save the composition is to save the project.

This is one of the distinctive features of After Effects 7—the project, not the individual compositions, is what you open and save. In fact, you cannot open a composition without being in an open project. You'll get used to this, but in the beginning it is confusing to most users.

---

14 Choose **File > Save**, or press **Cmd+S** (Mac) or **Ctrl+S** (Windows). Leave **Keyframe_Animation.aep** open for the next exercise.

You have just learned how to modify keyframe values for a composition. In the next exercise, you will learn how to save time on repetitive motions by copying and pasting keyframes.

VIDEO: | **HoldKeyframes.mov**

We've prepared a short video that demonstrates how to set hold keyframes using the **Keyframe Navigator** in the **Timeline**. You'll find **HoldKeyframes.mov** in the **videos** folder on the **After Effects 7 HOT CD-ROM**.

Typing Property Values

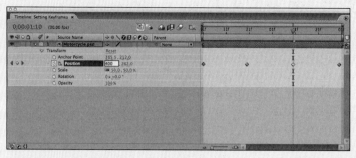

In addition to dragging or using the sliders, you can type **Property** values directly into the **Timeline**. Click the value, type a number in the resulting value box, and press **Return** (Mac) or **Enter** (Windows).

Double-Clicking a Keyframe Icon to Adjust Values

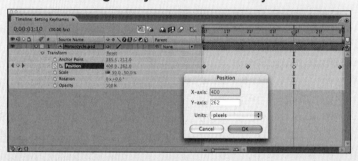

You can also adjust keyframe values by double-clicking a **keyframe** icon. This opens a **Position** dialog box in which you can type values.

Adding a Keyframe Via a Check Box

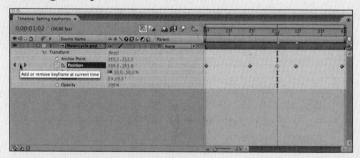

You can add a keyframe by clicking the **Add or remove keyframe at current time** icon (the diamond-shaped icon between the left and right arrows). This adds a keyframe wherever the **CTI** is without changing the value of the frame. In effect, it copies the information from the previous keyframe and makes a new keyframe with the same information. This icon can come in handy when you want to retain a value for a specific frame, which is necessary when you want to apply a change from this point forward without affecting the previous values.

4 | Copying and Pasting Keyframes

Just as you copy and paste text in a word processor, you can copy and paste keyframes in After Effects 7. This technique is useful if you've set up a repetitive motion, such as a blinking light, and want to continue using it in your composition. In this exercise, you'll use this process to make a light (in this case, a "don't walk" light) flash on and off.

---

1 If you followed the previous exercise, **Keyframe_Animation.aep** should still be open in After Effects 7. If it's not, choose **File > Open**. Navigate to the **chap_05** folder you copied to your desktop, click **Keyframe_Animation_4.aep** to select it, and click **Open**.

---

2 In the **Project** panel, double-click the **Copy & Paste** composition to open it.

This is an empty composition you will set up yourself.

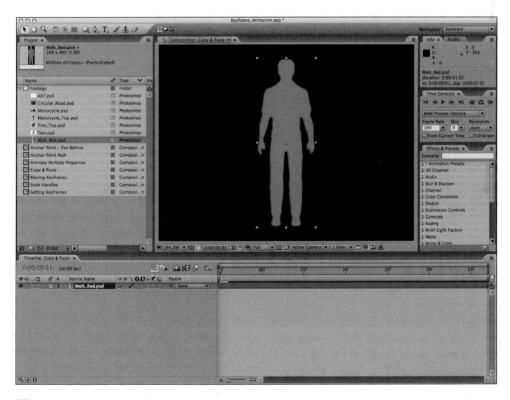

---

3 In the **Timeline**, make sure the **CTI** is on the first frame. In the **Project** panel, click the **twirly** next to **Footage** to expand its contents. Drag **Walk_Red.psd** into the **Timeline**.

The image of a red figure (the "don't walk" light) appears in the Copy & Paste Composition panel.

---

4 In the **Timeline** panel, click the **twirly** next to the **Walk_Red.psd** layer. Click the **twirly** next to **Transform** to reveal the **Transform** properties for this layer. Click the **stopwatch** icon for the **Opacity** property.

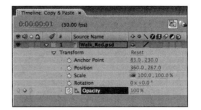

This sets a keyframe for the opacity of the Walk_Red.psd image at the current CTI, which should be on Frame 1. The Walk_Red.psd image currently has an Opacity value of 100%, which makes it fully visible.

---

5 In the **Timeline** panel, click the **Current Time** display. In the **Go to Time** dialog box, type **0:00:00:05**, and click **OK**.

This moves the CTI to Frame 5. You can either move the CTI to the desired frame in the Timeline panel or use this more precise method of specifying the frame in the Go to Time dialog box; both techniques achieve the same result.

It's important to move the CTI before you make a change to the property. This might take some time to understand, but you will eventually get the hang of it. In the next step, you'll change the property value and set a new keyframe.

Tip: Another way to access the Go to Time dialog box is by pressing the shortcut Cmd+G (Mac) or Ctrl+G (Windows).

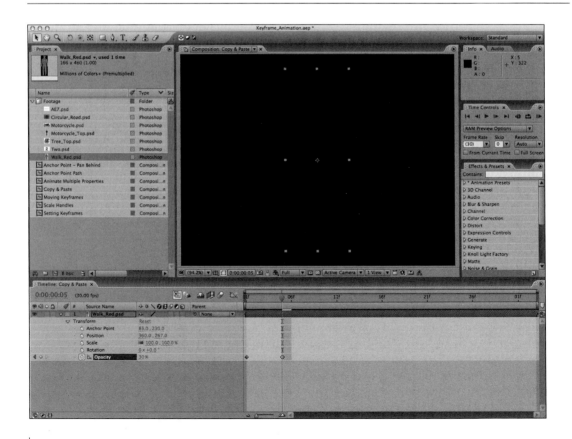

6 In the **Timeline** panel, change the value of the **Opacity** property to **30%**.

The red figure will appear less opaque in the Composition panel. Also notice this sets a new keyframe at Frame 5. Once you set a property to contain one keyframe, which you do by clicking the stopwatch icon for that property, you automatically set a keyframe anytime you move the CTI and change that property's setting.

---

7 Scrub the **CTI** over the first few frames, and observe the existing keyframe animation.

The red figure fades out quickly. You created this effect automatically by changing the Opacity property from 100% to 30% over two keyframes.

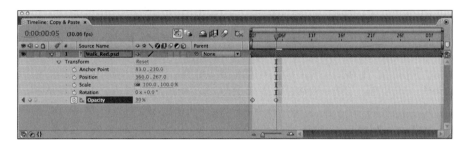

8 With the first keyframe already selected, hold down the **Shift** key, and click the second **Opacity** keyframe to select them both.

You will copy these two keyframes so the fading effect will repeat itself.

---

9 Choose **Edit > Copy**, or press **Cmd+C** (Mac) or **Ctrl+C** (Windows).

---

10 Move the **CTI** to **Frame 10**.

It's important to move the CTI before you paste the keyframes into the new location. Keyframes are always pasted wherever the CTI resides.

11 Choose **Edit > Paste**, or press **Cmd+V** (Mac) or **Ctrl+V** (Windows).

Notice the keyframes are pasted at the current CTI position on Frame 10.

12 Move the **CTI** to **Frame 20**. Press **Cmd+V** (Mac) or **Ctrl+V** (Windows) to paste the keyframes again.

Once you have the keyframes in the computer's memory, you can paste them indefinitely (until you select and copy something else).

---

13 Press the **spacebar** to preview the animation. Notice the action occurs three times.

---

14 Choose **File > Save**, or press **Cmd+S** (Mac) or **Ctrl+S** (Windows) to save the **Keyframe_Animation.aep** project.

---

15 In the top-left corner of the **Composition** panel, choose **Close Copy & Paste** from the pop-up menu to close this composition.

---

16 Choose **File > Save**, or press **Cmd+S** (Mac) or **Ctrl+S** (Windows). Leave **Keyframe_Animation.aep** open for the next exercise.

Using these copy-and-paste techniques instead of re-creating keyframes manually will save you a lot of time. In the next exercise, you will learn how to easily move keyframes within the Timeline, which can be another great time-saver.

EXERCISE

5 | Moving Keyframes

So far you've set keyframes at the position of the **CTI**. This is the only way to create a keyframe because the keyframe appears wherever the **CTI** is positioned in the **Timeline**. Sometimes, after you've created keyframes, you might change your mind about where you want them to occur. The good news is that once you've made a keyframe, you can always move it to a different frame position. Moving keyframes farther apart makes the movement or property changes slower; moving them closer together makes the movement or property changes faster. In this exercise, you'll learn how to move keyframes and see the effect moving a keyframe has on animation.

---

1 If you followed the previous exercise, **Keyframe_Animation.aep** should still be open. If it's not, choose **File > Open Project**. Navigate to the **chap_05** folder, click **Keyframe_Animation_5.aep** to select it, and click **Open**.

---

2 In the **Project** panel, double-click the **Moving Keyframes** composition to open it.

We have already set up keyframes in this composition for both the Position and Scale properties.

---

3 Press the **spacebar** to preview the movement, and observe the animation of the motorcycle moving through the **Composition** panel and getting smaller.

---

4 In the **Timeline** panel, click **Motorcycle.psd** to select it. Press the **P** key.

Pressing the P key reveals only the Position property. (You can find some charts of other shortcut keys later in the "Using Shortcut Keys for Properties" section of this chapter.)

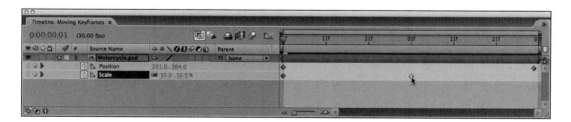

---

5 Hold down the **Shift** key, and press the **S** key. Click the last **Scale** keyframe (at **0:00:02:00**) to select it, and drag it onto the **Timeline** at **0:00:01:00**.

Holding the Shift key when pressing shortcut keys allows you to reveal multiple properties without using the twirlies.

Chapter 5 : **Creating Keyframes and Animation in the Timeline**   79

6 Press the **spacebar**, and observe the results of moving the **Scale** keyframe.

The motorcycle now gets smaller more quickly and continues to traverse the Composition panel.

You can move the first or last Scale keyframe wherever you want in the Timeline to change the timing of the scaling in your composition. The closer together the keyframes are, the faster the scaling; the farther apart they are, the slower the scaling.

---

7 Choose **File > Save**, or press **Cmd+S** (Mac) or **Ctrl+S** (Windows) to save the **Keyframe_Animation.aep** project.

---

8 In the top-left corner of the **Composition** panel, choose **Close Moving_Keyframes** from the pop-up menu to close this composition.

---

9 Choose **File > Save**, or press **Cmd+S** (Mac) or **Ctrl+S** (Windows). Leave **Keyframe_Animation.aep** open for the next exercise.

You just learned how to modify the position of keyframes within the Timeline, saving you the step of re-creating them at another point in your composition. After learning about some shortcut keys, you will learn how to modify the Scale property of a layer from within the Composition panel.

TIP:

Moving Multiple Keyframes

You can also move multiple keyframes at once. Using the cursor, click and drag a selection box around the keyframes you want to move, or hold down the **Shift** key to multiple-select keyframes. Once you have the keyframes selected, simply drag them to the new location and release.

Using Shortcut Keys for Properties

As you know, you can press keyboard shortcuts to display individual layer properties. Individual properties are hidden unless you use these shortcut keys or click a twirly to reveal all the properties at once.

But how do you view more than one property at a time using shortcut keys? Let's say you want to change the scale and rotation of a layer, and you want to know the shortcut to show these two properties. You can add only the properties you want to see. To display more than one layer property in the **Timeline** at a time, you must first show a single property. Then, hold down the **Shift** key, and press the shortcut key for the other property you want to view.

The following charts list all the shortcut keys for displaying **Transform** properties and for adding **Transform** properties to the **Timeline** display:

Shortcut Keys for Individual Transform Properties	
Shortcut Key	Property
A	Anchor Point
P	Position
R	Rotation
S	Scale
T	Opacity

Shortcut Keys for Adding Transform Properties	
Shortcut Key	Property
Shift+A	Anchor Point
Shift+P	Position
Shift+R	Rotation
Shift+S	Scale
Shift+T	Opacity

Automatic keyframe shortcuts

If you want to set a keyframe automatically while you display a property, press **Option** (Mac) or **Alt+Shift** (Windows) and the shortcut key for the property. This reveals the property you want and sets a keyframe in one operation.

Shortcut Keys for Setting a Keyframe with the Transform Property		
Mac Shortcut Key	Windows Shortcut Key	Property
Option+A	Alt+Shift+A	Anchor Point
Option+P	Alt+Shift+P	Position
Option+R	Alt+Shift+R	Rotation
Option+S	Alt+Shift+S	Scale
Option+T	Alt+Shift+T	Opacity

VIDEO: **Display_Properties.mov**

A short video that demonstrates using shortcut keys to display properties is called **Display_Properties.mov** and is located in the **videos** folder on the **After Effects 7 HOT CD-ROM**.

6 | Animating Scale Using Control Handles

When working with the **Scale** property, you have two ways to access its settings: by altering values in the **Timeline** for the **Scale** field or by working with its control handles. Sometimes you may want to change the proportions of an object by making it taller, wider, shorter, or narrower than the original artwork. This exercise will show you both ways, so you can choose which one you want to use.

---

1 If you followed the previous exercise, **Keyframe_Animation.aep** should still be open. If it's not, choose **File > Open Project**. Navigate to the **chap_05** folder, click **Keyframe_Animation_6.aep** to select it, and click **Open**.

2 Double-click the **Scale Handles** composition to open it.

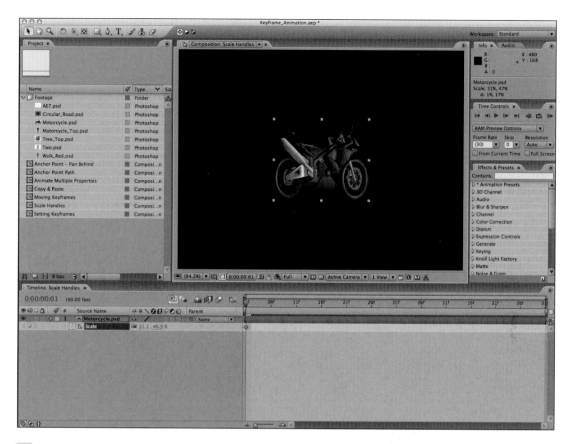

3 In the **Timeline** panel, make sure the **CTI** is at the first frame, and select the **Motorcycle.psd** layer. Press **Option+S** (Mac) or **Alt+Shift+S** (Windows) to display the **Scale** property and automatically add a keyframe at the **CTI** position (**Frame 0:00:00:01**).

Pressing Option+S (Mac) or Alt+Shift+S (Windows) not only reveals and isolates the Scale property from the others but also automatically activates the stopwatch to set keyframes.

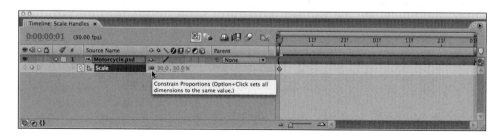

4 In the **Timeline** panel, change the value of the **Scale** property to **30%**.

Note that if you change one value, the other changes because the Constrain Proportions icon (to the left of the values) is set to constrain the *x* and *y* values proportionally.

5 In the **Timeline** panel, move the **CTI** to **Frame 0:00:01:00**. In the **Composition** panel, drag the upper-right **control handle** of the **Motorcycle.psd** image up and to the right.

Did you notice you are able to scale the object differently in the x and y values using this technique? This is a great way to override the link icon, which is set to constrain the scale.

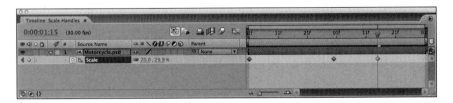

6 In the **Timeline** panel, move the **CTI** to **Frame 0:00:01:15**. Type **20** into the first field of the **Scale** property.

Even though the link icon is still activated, the second field does not update with this new value. Once you use the scale handles, you disrupt the relationship between the x and y values. It's fine if you want them to be disproportional, but what if you want to resynchronize them?

7 Click the **link** icon to deselect it. Type **20** into the second field, and press **Return** (Mac) or **Enter** (Windows). Once these two values match again, click the **link** icon to activate it.

Now, anytime you type a new value here, the x and y values will match.

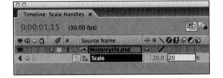

Note: You can use the scale handles to scale proportionally as well. Holding down the Shift key causes both the x and y values to scale identically. You have to first select the object in the Composition panel and then press Shift for this to work. This is different from most programs, such as Photoshop, for example, where you have to hold down the Shift key to scale proportionally before you select the handle.

8 Choose **File > Save**, or press **Cmd+S** (Mac) or **Ctrl+S** (Windows) to save the **Keyframe_Animation.aep** project.

9 In the **Timeline** panel, click **Close** to close the **Scale Handles** composition.

10 Choose **File > Save**, or press **Cmd+S** (Mac) or **Ctrl+S** (Windows). Leave **Keyframe_Animation.aep** open for the next exercise.

Adjusting a property such as Scale in the Composition panel can be an intuitive way to work. Until now, you've adjusted only one property at a time. In the next exercise, you'll learn how to adjust more than one property at once.

7 | Animating Multiple Properties

Most professional animation is obviously more complex than what you've created so far. To achieve more complex motion, you'll want to animate several properties for an individual layer. In this exercise, you'll learn to animate the **Position**, **Scale**, **Rotation**, and **Opacity** properties for a simple title graphic, a process you can use to create a more dynamic animation to engage your viewers.

---

1 If you followed the previous exercise, **Keyframe_Animation.aep** should still be open. If it's not, choose **File > Open Project**. Navigate to the **chap_05** folder, click **Keyframe_Animation_7.aep** to select it, and click **Open**.

---

2 Double-click the **Animate Multiple Properties** composition to open it.

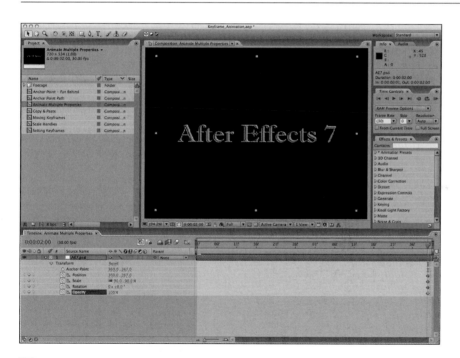

3 In the **Timeline** panel, select the **AE7.psd** layer, and click the **twirlies** (one twirly for the layer and another for **Transform**) to reveal the **Transform** properties.

Note: The Scale property in After Effects 7 shows both x and y scale percentage values, and they are currently each set to 90%. When you type a value other than the default (in the case of Scale, the default value is 100%) without a keyframe, you simply change that value throughout the composition as a constant value. This is great when you want a value to stay the same throughout the animation but also want it to be different from the default.

---

4 Press the **End** key to go to the end of the **Timeline**, or press **Cmd+Option+right arrow** (Mac) or **Ctrl+Alt+right arrow** (Windows) if your laptop doesn't have an **End** key. Click the **stopwatch** icons for **Position**, **Scale**, **Rotation**, and **Opacity**.

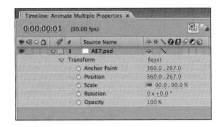

Pressing End positions the CTI at 0:00:02:00. Checking the stopwatch icons will set a keyframe at the last frame for all those properties. Nothing will have changed in the Composition panel because all you've done is set keyframes; you haven't changed their values.

This is a common technique for setting keyframes. It allows you to set the final frame first and then animate the beginning keyframes so the animation will resolve where you set the final frame. It's animating in reverse, which is often easier than animating forward.

---

5 In the **Timeline** panel, move the **CTI** to the first frame. Press either the **Home** key or **Cmd+Option+left arrow** (Mac) or **Ctrl+Alt+left arrow** (Windows), or drag the **CTI** into place. Set the **Scale** value to **25%**.

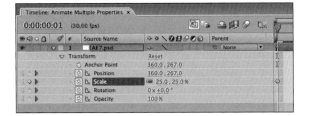

Typing a value in either the x field or the y field will set both fields if the link icon is present. This will set a new keyframe for Scale at 0:00:00:01.

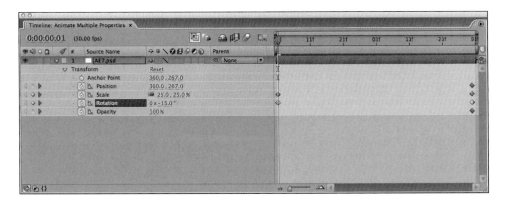

6 Set the **Rotation** value to **-15** degrees.

Note the keyframe was automatically set for Frame 0:00:00:01. Anytime you click the stopwatch icon for a property, move the CTI (which you did a few steps ago), and then change the property value, and you will create a new keyframe automatically.

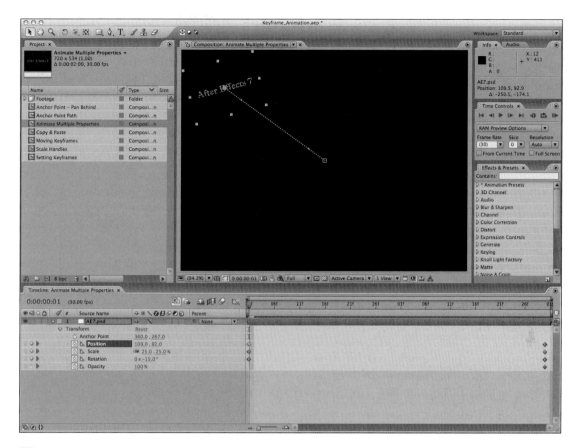

7 Click and drag the artwork in the composition to the location shown in this illustration. Notice this automatically sets a **Position** keyframe at the same location where the **CTI** resides in the **Timeline**.

8 Press the **spacebar** to preview what you've done so far. To get rid of the motion path in the **Composition** panel, click an empty area in the **Timeline**, and preview the animation again.

If the animation preview is sluggish, click the RAM Preview button in the Time Controls panel.

9 In the **Timeline** panel, move the **CTI** to **0:00:01:14**. To the left of the **Opacity** property, click the **Add or remove keyframe at current time** icon (between the arrows for the **Keyframe Navigator**).

This automatically inserts an Opacity keyframe at this frame. Why do you want to do this? This maintains the Opacity value of 100% between this keyframe and the last keyframe. This might make more sense after you complete the next step.

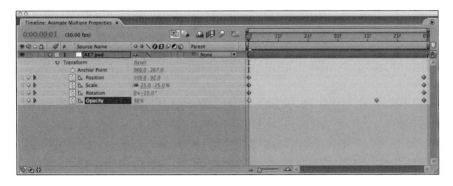

10 In the **Timeline** panel, move the **CTI** to **Frame 0:00:00:01**. Change the **Opacity** value to **30%**. Press the **spacebar** to preview the animation so far.

This sets a new keyframe. You'll see that the logo fades all the way up to 100% once it hits the second keyframe and then maintains its value of 100% from the second to the third keyframe.

Tip: We taught you an interesting workflow here, though it might not be too obvious. You could have set the keyframes for the Opacity property in order, starting at 30%, then setting another at 100%, and finally setting another at 100%. Instead, by clicking the stopwatch icon when the CTI was on the last frame, you set the Opacity to 100% automatically. By clicking the "Add or remove keyframe at current time" icon, you set another keyframe at 100% without typing any value in the Opacity property. This allowed you to type only one value, with the CTI at the first frame. It sounds lazy, but when you're working on a real-world project with a real-world deadline, these subtle shortcuts add up.

Next, you'll learn another interesting workflow trick.

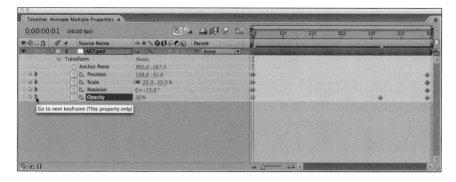

11 Click the **Go to next keyframe** icon to precisely position the **CTI** on the second keyframe.

Note: This icon is sometimes referred to as the Keyframe Navigator arrow.

12 Click the last keyframe of the **Rotation** property, and press **Cmd+C** (Mac) or **Ctrl+C** (Windows) to copy it. Place your cursor at the location of the **CTI** on the **Rotation** property, and press **Cmd+V** (Mac) or **Ctrl+V** (Windows) to paste the keyframe.

In this step, initially you're causing the Rotation property to become selected in the Timeline. Then you're pasting the value of the last keyframe in the Rotation property into the same location in time as the second keyframe for the Opacity keyframe.

Two different ideas are at play here. First, you can use keyframe locations from one property to set a keyframe for another property in the same location. Second, you can paste the value of a keyframe into another keyframe location based on where the CTI is. This kind of copy-and-paste action will become second nature to you eventually, and it saves a lot of time. In addition, using the Go to next keyframe and Go to previous keyframe icons is a great time-saver over trying to manually position the CTI at the exact keyframe location.

13 Press the **spacebar** to preview the motion.

If it's sluggish, you can use a couple of different techniques to try to speed up the preview.

First, as mentioned, you can click the RAM Preview button in the Time Control panel instead of the spacebar. This might take a moment to render, but once it does, the preview will be much faster.

Second, if it isn't there already, change the quality to Draft by clicking the Quality button in the Timeline panel. Basically, Best (high quality) looks the best but takes the longest to render. By changing the quality setting to Draft, the spacebar technique of previewing the footage will work much faster. You'll learn more about the quality settings in Chapter 7, *"Previewing Movies."*

---

14 Choose **File > Save** to save the **Keyframe_Animation.aep** project.

---

15 Choose **Close Animate_Multiple_Properties** from the pop-up menu in the top-left corner of the **Composition** panel to close the composition.

---

16 Choose **File > Save**, or press **Cmd+S** (Mac) or **Ctrl+S** (Windows). Leave **Keyframe_Animation.aep** open for the next exercise.

You just learned how to create keyframes and animate several properties for a layer in your composition. Most projects involve at least a couple, if not more, properties requiring animation, so it is important to become comfortable working with several properties at once. Next, you will learn about working with another property: Anchor Point.

Understanding the Anchor Point

The **anchor point** of an image is a designated point used for positioning, scale, and rotation. It looks like a circle with an *X* through it. Each layer has its own anchor point. By default, After Effects 7 places the anchor point at the center of each layer. If the object rotates or scales, it will do so around the anchor point.

It is often necessary to move the anchor point to make an object rotate or scale around a point other than the center of the image. Another reason to move the anchor point is to rotate an object around another object. You'll get to move the anchor point in the next exercise.

Animating the Anchor Point Using the Pan Behind Tool

This exercise will give you a real-world example of why you would want to change an animation's anchor point, which determines the fixed point on a layer that affects its rotation, scale, and position when it is animated. Altering the anchor point is particularly important when animating the rotation of a layer. For example, creating an animation of a satellite orbiting a planet or a car circling a racetrack requires the anchor point to be set to the correct center of an object on a layer. In this exercise, you'll modify the anchor point using a special **Pan Behind** tool in After Effects 7 to create an animation of a motorcycle circling a tree.

1 If you followed the previous exercise, **Keyframe_Animation.aep** should still be open. If it's not, choose **File > Open Project**. Navigate to the **chap_05** folder, click **Keyframe_Animation_8.aep** to select it, and click **Open**.

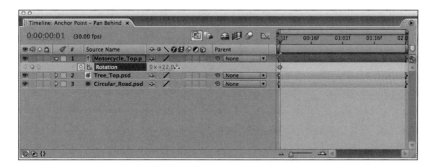

2 Double-click the **Anchor Point – Pan Behind** composition to open it. Notice the motorcycle and tree images in the **Composition** panel. Select the **Motorcycle_Top.psd** layer. Press **Option+R** (Mac) or **Alt+Shift+R** (Windows).

This simultaneously reveals the Rotation property for this layer and activates the stopwatch icon for keyframes.

The Rotation property has two values. The first is how many full 360-degree rotations are being set, and the second is the degrees of rotation other than 360.

3 Scrub the value of the Rotation property's degrees field, and notice the motorcycle rotating on its own axis.

This is great for spinning knobs and gears, but a motorcycle generally does not spin on its own axis. In fact, you're going to make a motorcycle rotate around the tree in this composition. This sounds like a simple idea, but it will require changing the anchor point. You'll want to change the axis to the center of the tree to give the motorcycle the motion needed in this animation.

4 If your **Tools** panel isn't open, choose **Window > Tools**. From the **Tools** panel, select the **Pan Behind** tool.

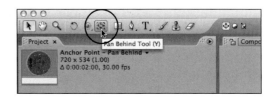

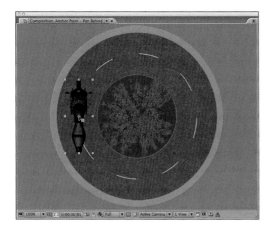 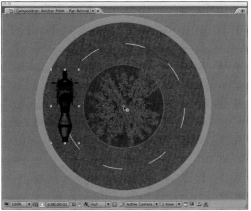

5 In the **Composition** panel, click the **motorcycle** (if it isn't already selected) to display its anchor point, and then drag the motorcycle's **anchor point** to the center of the tree. Notice the cursor changes its shape when you use the **Pan Behind** tool.

To rotate around the tree, you need to change the default rotation axis of the motorcycle, which is in the middle of the motorcycle. Changing the anchor point to the middle of the tree allows the rotation to occur around the tree instead of around the motorcycle itself.

Note: The Pan Behind tool moves the anchor point of the motorcycle but doesn't alter the position of the motorcycle. If you hadn't used this tool and simply changed the anchor point position in the Transform properties, the motorcycle would move along with the anchor point. The Pan Behind tool is popular because it moves the anchor point without moving the object to which the anchor point is attached.

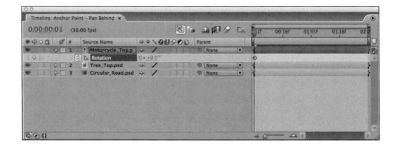

6 If necessary, reset the Rotation property to **0** rotations and **0** degrees. Make sure the **stopwatch** icon is activated.

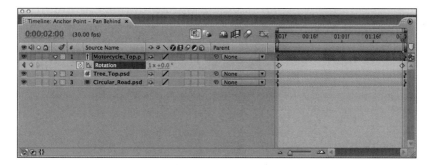

7 In the **Timeline** panel, move the **CTI** to the last frame, and then set the **Rotation** value to **1**. Press the **spacebar** to watch the motorcycle rotate around the tree instead of its own axis.

---

8 Choose **File > Save**, or press **Cmd+S** (Mac) or **Ctrl+S** (Windows) to save the **Keyframe_Animation.aep** project.

---

9 Choose **Close Anchor Point – Pan Behind** from the pop-up menu in the upper-left corner of the **Composition** panel to close this composition.

---

10 Choose **File > Save**, or press **Cmd+S** (Mac) or **Ctrl+S** (Windows). Leave **Keyframe_Animation.aep** open for the next exercise.

As you have seen, altering the anchor point allows you to rotate layers in the way your animation requires.

WARNING: **Pan Behind Alters the Motion Path**

If you attempt to use the **Pan Behind** tool to move the anchor point on a layer with an existing motion path, you will alter your motion path. These alterations can be significant. Therefore, while you are learning After Effects 7, use the **Pan Behind** tool to move an anchor point only when the selected layer does not have a motion path.

NOTE:

What About Animating the Anchor Point Property?

In the previous exercise, you moved the anchor point, but you didn't set values in the **Anchor Point** property to do so. Using the **Pan Behind** tool, you moved the anchor point to a new location. By doing so, you changed the axis of the motorcycle artwork from its middle point to an outside location. When animating the **Anchor Point** property, you change the center location of your object. The center of an object is what many other properties are based on, including **Scale**, **Position**, and **Rotation**. You can animate the **Anchor Point** property by setting keyframes and changing its value if that's the effect you want.

Let's say you want something to rotate from the center for part of the animation, but then you want it to pivot from a corner point later. You can do this by animating the **Anchor Point** property. Often, After Effects 7 artists use the **Pan Behind** tool or **Parenting** techniques (see Chapter 11, *"Parenting Layers"*) instead of animating the **Anchor Point** property because of the impact it has on so many other properties.

Understanding Bézier Curves and Handles

The title of this section might sound scarier than it is. Bézier curves and handles are something that digital artists love because they give artists artistic control. Those of you who are familiar with Adobe Illustrator will likely be familiar with Bézier curve editing. In After Effects 7, you'll use Bézier curves to influence the shape of motion paths. You can also use them for other purposes, such as for mask shapes and speed graphs, which you'll learn about in future chapters. If you are not familiar with Bézier curves and points, don't worry—this section will explain them.

A **Bézier curve** contains points with control handles. To see the Bézier handles in the **Composition** panel, you must click a keyframe in the **Timeline** (or on a point in the motion path) to select that keyframe. The control **handles** influence the curves around the **Bézier point**.

VIDEO:

bezier_points.mov

To learn more about how to use Bézier points, check out **bezier_points.mov** in the **videos** folder on the **After Effects 7 HOT CD-ROM**.

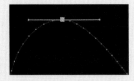

As shown in the illustration here, the series of tick marks represents the animation path. By dragging the Bézier handles, you affect the Bézier curve and influence the motion path.

Bézier points have two handles: one for the portion of the curve preceding the Bézier point and another for the portion of the curve following the Bézier point.

The term **Bézier** comes from the name of a French mathematician, Pierre Bézier. He developed a mathematical formula for describing curves. After Effects 7 and many other computer graphics programs use this formula. Luckily, you don't have to worry about formulas. All you have to do is click and drag to get the curve you want.

EXERCISE

9 | Using Bézier Handles with Motion Paths

In this exercise, you will learn to select Bézier points and adjust Bézier handles to influence the motion path. This gives you added control over the way your objects move and, for that reason, is an invaluable skill.

---

1 If you followed the previous exercise, **Keyframe_Animation.aep** should still be open. If it's not, choose **File > Open Project**. Navigate to the **c:\ chap_05** folder, click **Keyframe_Animation_9.aep** to select it, and click **Open**.

---

2 In the **Project** panel, double-click the **Setting Keyframes** composition to reopen it.

---

3 In the **Composition** panel, click the **Motorcycle.psd** image to select it. Press the **spacebar** to preview the motion and see how the artwork indeed travels along this exact path.

With the layer selected, the motion path will appear as an outline with little dots, as shown in the illustration here. The dots represent frames and speed, which you'll learn more about in Chapter 6, *"Playing with Time."*

---

4 Press the **Home** key, or move the **CTI** to **Frame 0:00:00:01**. In the **Composition** panel, click the second **Bézier point** in the motion path to select it.

Notice Bézier handles appear. These handles influence the curve of the motion path.

---

5 Drag the upper **Bézier handle** upward, and observe the influence on the motion path.

The curve becomes rounder and less angular.

6 Drag the bottom **Bézier handle** outward and to the left.

This bends the curve and alters its appearance even more.

7 Click the third **Bézier point** in the motion path to select it. Drag its handles to be longer.

This widens the curve and angles it to the left.

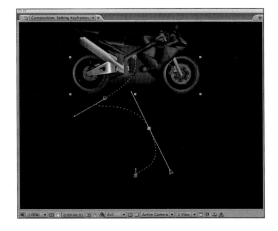

8 Press the **spacebar** to see the new animation.

Getting used to pulling on handles to influence the motion path takes practice, but once you get the hang of it, you'll gain a lot more control over the way your artwork moves.

---

9 Choose **File > Save**, or press **Cmd+S** (Mac) or **Ctrl+S** (Windows) to save the **Keyframe_Animation.aep** project.

---

10 Choose **Close Setting Keyframes** from the pop-up menu in the top-left corner of the **Composition** panel to close this composition.

---

11 Choose **File > Save**, or press **Cmd+S** (Mac) or **Ctrl+S** (Windows). Leave **Keyframe_Animation.aep** open for the next exercise.

In this exercise, you learned how to alter a motion path using Bézier curves, which produce curved motion and more interesting animations. Next, you will learn different ways to work with these curves and modify the way points are created in a motion path to follow a specific shape.

TIP:

Orienting Objects Automatically

To make the motorcycle, or any object for that matter, orient to the path as it moves, choose **Layer > Transform > Auto Orient**.

The Auto-Orientation dialog box appears. If you click **Orient Along Path**, the object's orientation in space will follow the shape of the motion path.

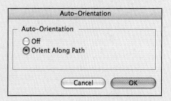

Using Spatial Interpolation Types

This section will teach you how to control a motion path by showing you how to give the path straight lines and curves. You will accomplish this with a feature in After Effects 7 called **spatial interpolation**. Spatial interpolation types are visible in the **Composition** panel because they influence the appearance of the motion path.

You can identify **Linear** interpolation by a sharp curve and even distribution of tick marks. No Bézier controls appear in a **Linear** type. Placing the **Pen** tool over any point in the curve in the **Composition** panel and clicking toggles the shape between a straight path and a curved one.

You can identify **Auto Bézier** interpolation by the smooth curve. You'll see control handles but no handle bars. If you attempt to move a control point on an **Auto Bézier** type, you will convert it to a **Continuous Bézier** type. You'll get to try this in the next exercise.

You can identify **Continuous Bézier** interpolation by the straight handle bars. The handle bars may be of different lengths, but they are always straight.

Angled handle bars identify the Bézier interpolation type, and you can adjust the angle and length of the handle bars independently. Using the **Selection** tool, if you hold down the **Cmd** key (Mac) or **Ctrl** key (Windows) and click any Bézier handle, you can create this type of path by pulling the handles in different directions. To change a control point from a smooth to a corner point (or vice versa), press **Cmd** (Mac) or **Ctrl** (Windows) as you click the point with the **Selection** tool.

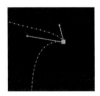

Mixing spatial interpolation types

After Effects 7 sometimes uses esoteric terms to explain common tasks. Take the term **spatial interpolation**, for example. The word **spatial** refers to the way an object moves in physical space, as with the **Position** property.

Interpolation is what After Effects 7 does to create fluid movement between keyframes. If you set a keyframe to move its position from screen left to screen right, you are affecting its spatial appearance. Interpolation is what makes it move from point A to point B. You may be familiar with the terms **tweening** and **in-betweening**; interpolation is the same.

In previous exercises, the motorcycle moved from the top of the frame to the bottom of the frame using spatial interpolation. The default type of movement is **Auto Bézier**, which you learned to control manually in Exercise 9. Other types of spatial interpolation methods are possible. Often you will need to create straight lines and complex curves within the same motion path. To accomplish this, you must use both **Linear** and **Bézier** spatial interpolation types on the motion path, as you will learn in the next exercise.

10 | Following a Complex Motion Path

When you create a keyframe, the default interpolation type is **Auto Bézier**. However, in some instances, you will need to change the spatial interpolation to another type, such as **Linear** or **Continuous Bézier** to create a motion path that can better match the path of a particular shape. In this exercise, you will change the interpolation type for each point to make the motion path follow a desired shape.

---

1 If you followed the previous exercise, **Keyframe_Animation.aep** should still be open. If it's not, choose **File > Open Project**. Navigate to the **chap_05** folder, click **Keyframe_Animation_10.aep** to select it, and click **Open**.

---

2 In the **Project** panel, double-click an empty area to launch the **Import File** dialog box. In the **Import File** dialog box, navigate to the **chap_05 > Footage** folder, and select **Two.psd**. Before you click the **Open** button, be sure to choose **Composition > Cropped Layers** (Mac) or **Composition > Layer Size** (Windows) from the **Import As** pop-up menu. Click **Open**.

This is a multilayered Photoshop file. You are choosing to import it as its own composition with cropped layers. What does this mean? Well, once the file comes into After Effects 7, a composition will automatically appear with this layered file inside. All the Photoshop layers will automatically become layers in the After Effects 7 Timeline. A bounding box area will be defined to crop the artwork, instead of matching the size of the Photoshop document. You'll learn more in upcoming steps about why this is important.

Once the import is accepted, two new files appear inside the Project panel, as shown in the illustration here: a footage folder called Two Layers and a composition called Two. The names are automatically generated because the PSD file was named Two.psd.

---

3 Click the **twirly** next to the **Footage** folder to reveal three footage files. Double-click the **Two** composition to open it.

Once the composition is open, notice it contains three layers. The layer names match the layer names in the Photoshop document. (If you have Photoshop, open the file there, and you'll see them.)

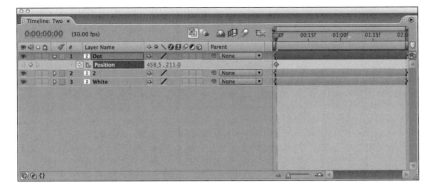

4 Click the layer visibility **eye** icons to toggle the visibility on and off for each layer to see what they look like, but make sure you turn them all back on. (This will familiarize you with the content of the composition.) Make sure the **CTI** is on the first frame, and select the **Dot** layer.

5 Press the **P** key to reveal the **Position** property. Click the **stopwatch** icon for the **Position** property, and you'll be ready to start animating.

This is the only property you'll animate in this exercise. Once you start working with compositions containing lots of layers and properties, using the shortcut keys to isolate a single property makes your screen a lot less cluttered and easier to use.

Note: For this exercise, if your composition isn't already 2 seconds in duration, open the Composition Settings panel by choosing Composition > Composition Settings, and then type 0:00:02:00 in the Duration field. Click OK to accept the new duration. The default Start Timecode for compositions created using Photoshop files is 0:00:00:00. You'll keep it that way for this exercise, although you can change it if you want.

6 In the **Composition** panel, move the **Dot** layer to the position shown in the illustration here, on top of the **2**.

This sets the first keyframe's position. Notice the Dot layer is smaller than the composition. That's the result of the cropped layer setting you chose upon import. It's extremely helpful because the center of the Dot layer is the center of the actual artwork.

7 In the **Timeline** panel, move the **CTI** to **Frame 0:00:00:20**. In the **Composition** panel, move the **Dot** layer to the position shown in the illustration here.

You'll adjust the path later; for now, you're just blocking out the rough keyframe positions.

8 In the **Timeline** panel, move the **CTI** to **0:00:01:10**. In the **Composition** panel, move the **Dot** layer to the position shown in the illustration here.

This sets the third keyframe.

9 In the **Timeline** panel, move the **CTI** to the last frame, and in the **Composition** panel move the **Dot** artwork to the position shown in the illustration here.

This sets the last keyframe. Now it is time to tweak the motion path.

---

10 Locate the handle of the **start** keyframe, and drag it upward to the position shown in the illustration here.

This new position affects the motion path curve of the second keyframe. You'll see the result in a minute.

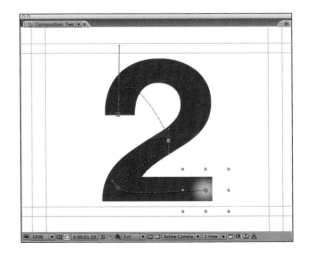

---

11 In the **Composition** panel, drag the **Bézier handle** of the second keyframe to the position shown in the illustration here. Notice how the path is more closely resembling the shape of the **2**.

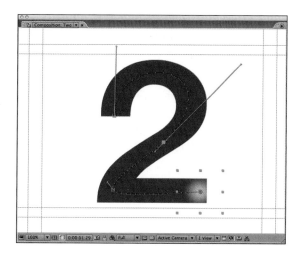

12 In the **Tools** panel, click and hold down the **Pen** tool button, and choose **Convert Vertex Tool** from the pop-up menu.

13 Click the third keyframe point, and notice that, at this point, it shifts from a curve to an angle. Using the techniques discussed (particularly the **Convert Vertex** tool), adjust all the points and curves to best fit into the shape of the **2**.

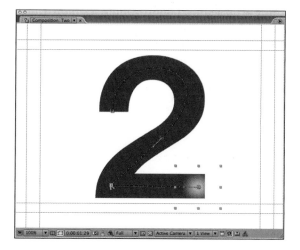

14 Press the **spacebar** to preview the animation.

You might notice that the speed of the movement is faster at the beginning than it is at the end. The difference in speed is because the dots are farther apart between Keyframe 1 and Keyframe 2 than they are between the other keyframes. Although the keyframes are evenly spaced over time in the Timeline, the actual time it takes to move evenly around the 2 shape is not equal between these keyframes. In the Timeline panel, drag the second keyframe to the right, and notice that this more evenly spaces the dots. Press the spacebar again, and the acceleration between the four keyframes will seem more consistent, even though the keyframes are no longer evenly spaced in time.

When you are roughing out motion, you rarely know how it will look until you preview it. In other words, it's hard to calculate how long it will take to move around the shape of the 2 until you try it. It's great that After Effects 7 offers the feedback of these dots to help you visualize the speed of the movement. It's also great that the speed is so easy to change. Chapter 6, *"Playing with Time,"* offers other techniques to achieve the same result. The best part about After Effects 7 is that it lets you change your mind about everything you'd ever need to change—it's just a matter of learning how to access the appropriate controls.

15 Choose **File > Save**, or press **Cmd+S** (Mac) or **Ctrl+S** (Windows). Choose **File > Close Project**.

The precise adjustment of motion paths using Bézier curves is an important ability to have if you need to match a specific shape, as you saw in this exercise. Users of Illustrator and similar applications already know the importance of using Bézier curves to create images, and in After Effects 7 they are also important to create the motion paths for masks (as you will learn in Chapter 13, *"Creating Masks"*).

NOTE:

Previewing Without the Dots

As mentioned before, the dots in the **Composition** panel represent time, with each dot representing a single frame. The dots are incredibly useful because they're offering visual feedback about the timing of the movement. Still, when you preview the artwork, seeing the dots and the motion path can be distracting. You can turn them off by deselecting the layer the **Position** keyframes are on. Just click anywhere in the **Timeline** panel that is not directly on a layer.

In this chapter, you learned the fundamental principles necessary to create animation in After Effects 7. Using keyframes, which determine the changes of a property over time, you create animation by filling the in-between frames. You experienced what is involved with placing keyframes, copying and pasting them, and modifying them in a variety of ways.

In the next chapter, you will learn more about manipulating keyframes, particularly in regard to the effects of time, including slowing down or speeding up your animations.

6

Playing with Time

This chapter deals specifically with time and the features controlling time in Adobe After Effects 7. As you become more experienced with creating animation, you'll start to recognize the nuances of motion and see how timing plays a critical role. The term **timing** refers to whether objects move quickly, move slowly, or change speed in the middle of an animation. During an animation, an object taking 10 seconds has the potential to move at the same speed over the entire 10 seconds; or, it can start slow, maintain a constant speed, and then go faster at the end, still occupying only 10 seconds of time.

The tools described in this chapter will help you learn how to finesse the timing of your animation. After Effects 7 is one of the most powerful desktop motion graphics tools because of its capability to give you, the animator and motion designer, the utmost control.

Understanding Spatial Versus Temporal Interpolation

After Effects 7 distinguishes between keyframes in your animations using spatial and temporal interpolation. In animation terms, **spatial** means space (such as the shape of a curve), **temporal** means time (such as the speeding up or slowing down of an object), and **keyframe interpolation** describes the types of changes that occur between keyframes having both spatial and temporal attributes. Although those terms might sound a little technical or intimidating, their meanings are really simple. For example, an object, such as a motorcycle, moves from point A to point B in a given amount of time. The path it travels is the spatial aspect, and the time it takes to travel that path is the temporal part of the equation. When put together using different forms of interpolation (smooth motions versus sudden motions, for example), these two components create animations.

So, in After Effects 7, you can set footage to change in both space and time. You use distinct tools to adjust the spatial and temporal aspects of your compositions. In Chapter 5, *"Creating Keyframes and Animation in the Timeline,"* you worked primarily with spatial issues in the **Composition** panel. By learning to change the curves of your motion paths, for example, you adjusted the spatial qualities of your animation. In this chapter, you will work with temporal issues in the **Timeline** panel.

In fact, the **Timeline** panel is the primary tool for playing with time. Just as you adjust spatial interpolation in the **Composition** panel, you can adjust temporal interpolation in the **Timeline** panel.

All properties have temporal interpolation. In other words, you can adjust the timing of any property. After Effects 7 contains sophisticated tools you can use to affect time in both subtle and dramatic ways. How you use these tools is up to your imagination and artistic sensibility.

It has been said that timing is everything. Indeed, timing is perhaps the most important aspect of animation. Although books such as this one can provide vital information, as an artist you'll develop your sense of timing through experience. Just like a musician must practice to develop a full sense of rhythm, the same is true for an animator. You'll master the subtlety of timing and rhythm through a commitment to the art form.

EXERCISE

1 | Using the Graph Editor and Keyframe Assistant

In this exercise, you will learn to work within the **Graph Editor** and use the **Keyframe Assistant** to ease the timing of objects. **Easing** the timing means creating a smooth transition in timing. Rather than having something start moving and continue moving at the same speed, it slowly builds acceleration or deceleration. Imagine an animation of a motorcycle slowing down at a stop sign. The motorcycle doesn't move at 40 miles per hour continuously between its starting and stopping points. First it accelerates, reaches a constant maximum speed, and then gradually slows down.

The **Keyframe Assistant** offers ease tools to automate the acceleration and deceleration of objects to create the appearance of natural movement. Specifically, you'll learn to use the **Easy Ease In** and **Easy Ease Out** tools to smooth timing changes.

You can see timing changes in the **Timeline** panel by observing the graph associated with time (the **Speed** graph). Using a graph helps you to visualize the changes in speed, or other properties, created by the addition of keyframes. At a glance, you can see the changes you've created over the entire length of your animation. In addition, by using the **Keyframe Assistant**, you will be introduced to the new **Graph Editor** and will learn to interpret speed changes in the graph.

---

1 Copy the **chap_06** folder from the **After Effects 7 HOT CD-ROM** onto your desktop.

---

2 Choose **File > Open Project**. Navigate to the **chap_06** folder you copied to your desktop, click **Time.aep** to select it, and click **Open**.

---

3 Choose **File > Save As**. In the **Save As** dialog box, navigate to the **AE7_HOT_Projects** folder on your desktop. Name the file **Time.aep**, and click **Save**.

---

4 In the **Project** panel, double-click the **Ease In and Out** composition.

We have already prepared this composition to teach you the principles of this exercise.

---

5 In the **Time Controls** panel, click the **RAM Preview** button to view the animation.

The motorcycle moves at a steady, constant speed. This is called **linear timing**. Linear timing has no acceleration or deceleration in speed.

6 In the **Timeline** panel, select the **Motorcycle_ Top.psd** layer, and open its **Position** property by pressing the **P** key. Click the **Include this property in the graph editor set** icon.

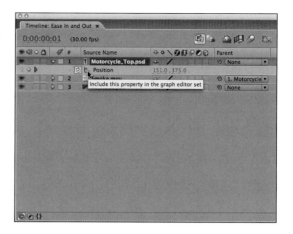

Every property has one of these special buttons, a new feature in After Effects 7, which allows you to determine the properties to display in the Graph Editor. You'll find out more about the Graph Editor in a moment.

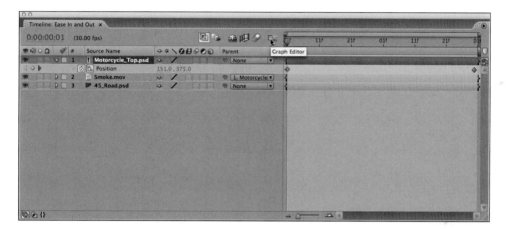

7 In the **Timeline** panel, click the **Graph Editor** button to display the **Graph Editor** for the **Position** property. Observe the straight line in the **Speed** graph, as shown in the illustration here.

This straight line reflects the linear timing of the motorcycle. The graph is part of the built-in After Effects 7 interface called the Graph Editor, which allows you to view and edit keyframe values and other properties using a two-dimensional graph in the Timeline, thus replacing the traditional layer bar view. You can view a simple graph for any layer that has keyframed motion for the Position, Rotation, Scale, or Opacity properties. As you work through the exercises in this chapter, you'll begin to understand how the Graph Editor helps you adjust values fluidly.

Note: When you click the Graph Editor button, you will see graphs for any properties that have the "Include this property in the graph editor set" icon activated.

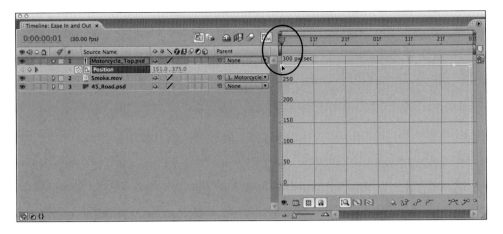

8 In the **Motorcycle.psd** layer, click **Frame 0:00:00:01** to select it.

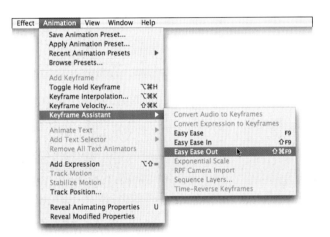

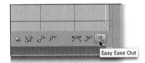

9 Choose **Animation > Keyframe Assistant > Easy Ease Out**, or click the **Easy Ease Out** button in the **Graph Editor**.

Note: You can also Ctrl+click (Mac) or right-click (Windows) on the keyframe, and choose **Keyframe Assistant > Easy Ease Out**.

Observe that the Speed graph is now curved. This indicates the movement is no longer linear. At the lower part of the curve, the timing of the object (in this example, the motorcycle artwork layer) slows down. At the higher part of the curve, the timing of the object is faster.

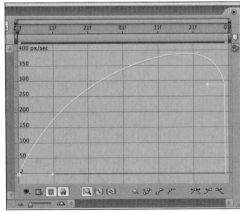

10 Click **RAM Preview** to see the results. Notice the motorcycle starts slowly and gains speed.

11 In the **Graph Editor**, click the last keyframe to select it.

12 Choose **Animation > Keyframe Assistant > Easy Ease In**, or click the **Easy Ease In** button in the **Graph Editor**.

The Speed graph now curves upward until it gets to the middle and then curves downward at the end. This means the object starts out slowly, moves faster as it approaches the center of the curve, and then slows down as it reaches the end.

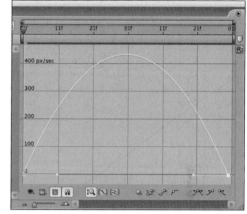

Notice in the Composition panel the dots get closer together as they reach the last keyframe.

13 Click **RAM Preview** to preview the animation.

Notice the motorcycle slows down at the end of the movie.

So, when do you use Easy Ease In, and when do you use Easy Ease Out? Use the Easy Ease In function when you want movement to start fast and end slow. If you think of a car pulling *in* to a driveway, it might be an easy way to remember Easy Ease In means to slow down. Use the Easy Ease Out function when you want movement to start slow and end fast. Think about a car pulling *out* of a driveway to remember Easy Ease Out means to speed up. If you want something other than slow and fast or fast and slow, you'll have to learn how to adjust the timing curves on your own. (You'll learn how to do that in the next exercise!)

---

14 Choose **File > Save**, or press **Cmd+S** (Mac) or **Ctrl+S** (Windows). Leave **Time.aep** open for the next exercise.

NOTE:

Learning More About Speed Dots

After Effects 7 provides a graphical way to see the timing of your animations, even when you're not looking at the **Graph Editor**. When you select an object in the **Timeline** or **Composition** panel with the **Position** keyframe properties set, dots will appear in the **Composition** panel. Each dot indicates a frame in time. The spacing between the dots indicates how fast, slow, or evenly paced the keyframed movement is. Dots closer together mean slower movement, and ones farther apart mean faster movement.

Shown in the illustration here, the top red *X* has evenly spaced dots associated with its motion. This indicates linear movement. The middle *X* uses an **Easy Ease In**, shown by dots that are spaced farther apart at the beginning and closer together at the end. In this instance, the movement will start fast and then slow down. The bottom *X* uses an **Easy Ease Out**. The dots are spaced closer together at the first keyframe and get farther apart at the end.

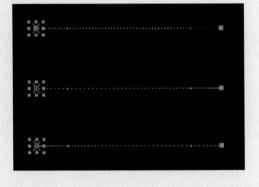

The only way to see these dots is to select artwork in which **Position** keyframe properties are set, either in the **Timeline** panel or in the **Composition** panel. One way to change the spacing between the dots is with the **Speed** graph in the **Graph Editor**, which you just learned how to do.

Editing the Speed Graph in the Graph Editor

In this exercise, you will learn to work with the **Speed** graph. You've seen that the **Easy Ease In** and **Easy Ease Out** tools will automatically ease timing for you. However, it's often preferable to set the timing exactly as you want it, especially when you want to create a more fluid, less mechanical feel for an animation. In this exercise, you'll learn to ease animation timing manually.

1 If you followed the previous exercise, **Time.aep** should still be open in After Effects 7. If it's not, choose **File > Open Project**. Navigate to the **chap_06** folder you copied to your desktop, click **Time_2.aep** to select it, and click **Open**.

2 Double-click the **Time Graph** composition to open it.

3 Click **RAM Preview**, and observe the linear timing of the motorcycle driving off.

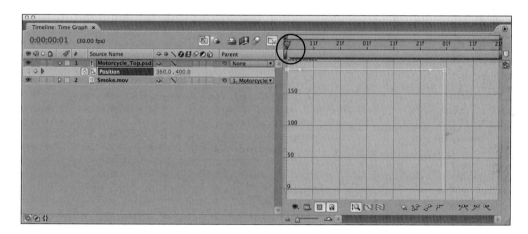

4 In the **Timeline** panel, select the **Motorcycle_Top.psd** layer, and press the **P** key to reveal the **Position** property by itself. Click the **Include this property in the graph editor set** button, and then click the **Graph Editor** button to reveal the **Speed** graph. Click the first keyframe for the **Motorcycle_Top.psd** layer.

When the keyframe is selected, control handles will appear on the Speed graph.

5 Click the center of the keyframe, and drag it down to slow the speed of the motorcycle. Notice the information about the speed change appears next to the keyframe in the **Graph Editor** as you drag.

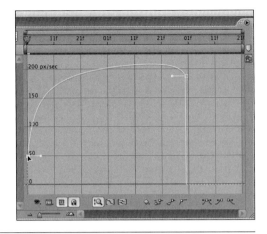

You can also grab the handle and drag it downward to slow the speed. Be aware, however, by dragging the handle you may inadvertently influence your curve (a function you'll get to in the next step).

Dragging the keyframe down on the graph slows the timing. Dragging the keyframe up speeds up the timing.

6 Drag the **control handle** to the right to influence more outgoing frames. Notice that the graph adjusts as you drag the handle. Release the handle when you're finished dragging.

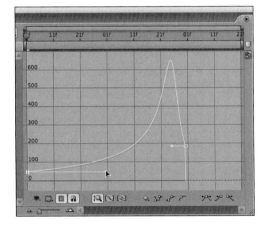

Dragging the control handle away from the point influences more frames. Dragging it toward the point affects fewer frames.

7 Click **RAM Preview**, and notice the motorcycle now drives off slowly and then speeds up.

8 Choose **File > Save**, or press **Cmd+S** (Mac) or **Ctrl+S** (Windows) to save. Leave **Time.aep** open for the next exercise.

In this exercise, you learned how to create natural-looking motion by adjusting the rate of speed manually. In the next exercise, you will look at **Hold interpolation**, which keeps the value of a keyframe steady, without a gradual transition.

Using the Hold Temporal Interpolation Method

In this exercise, you'll learn to use the Hold interpolation method, which is useful when you want movement in an animation to stop and hold, such as when producing a freeze-frame or strobe-light effect or when you simply want to pause before continuing with a particular gesture. In the process of learning how to use the Hold interpolation method, you'll get more experience building compositions and setting keyframes.

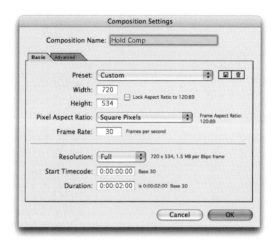

1 If you followed the previous exercise, **Time.aep** should still be open in After Effects 7. If it's not, choose **File > Open Project**. Navigate to the **chap_06** folder you copied to your desktop, click **Time_3.aep** to select it, and click **Open**.

2 In the **Project** panel, click the **Create a new Composition** button, which opens the **Composition Settings** dialog box. Name your composition **Hold Comp**, match the settings to those shown in the illustration here, and click **OK**.

You haven't made a new composition for a few chapters, so you'll now get a refresher on how to do it.

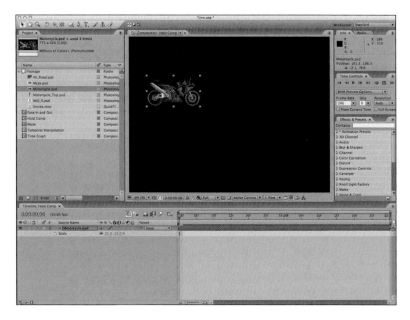

3 In the **Project** panel, drag **Motorcycle.psd** from the **Footage** folder into your **Timeline**. Set **Scale** to **25%**. Move the motorcycle to the position shown in the illustration here by dragging it into place in the **Composition** panel.

Tip: Pressing the S key will show the Scale properties, or you can click the Transform twirly in the Timeline to display the Scale property.

In the next step, you will duplicate the layer so you have two identical motorcycles in the Composition panel. This is a little easier said than done, so perform the steps carefully.

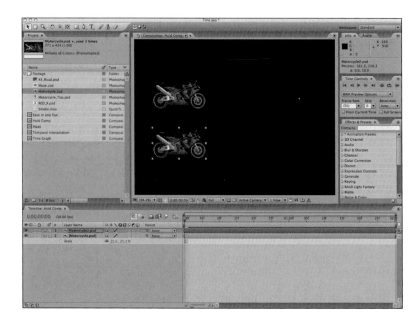

4 In the **Timeline** panel, select the **Motorcycle.psd** layer, and press **Cmd+D** (Mac) or **Ctrl+D** (Windows) to duplicate the layer. In the **Timeline**, change the name of the new **Motorcycle.psd** layer by selecting it, pressing **Return** (Mac) or **Enter** (Windows), typing a new name such as **Motorcycle2.psd**, and then pressing **Return** (Mac) or **Enter** (Windows) again to accept the change. With the copy selected, use the **arrow keys** on your keyboard to nudge the copy of the motorcycle image down in the **Composition** panel until it matches what's shown in the illustration here.

Tip: Hold down the Shift key while you use the arrow keys to move it more quickly.

You may not realize what you've just accomplished. By changing the scale in Step 3 and not setting a keyframe by not clicking the stopwatch icon, you created a global change for the object. This means it will have 25% scale throughout any animation unless you change your mind, set keyframes, and make changes to the scale between keyframes. By duplicating the object with the global scale change, you now have two identical motorcycle images. After Effects professionals often use this duplicate-and-rename technique to save time.

Next, you'll set position keyframes to make the motorcycle layers move across the screen. You can do this to both layers at once.

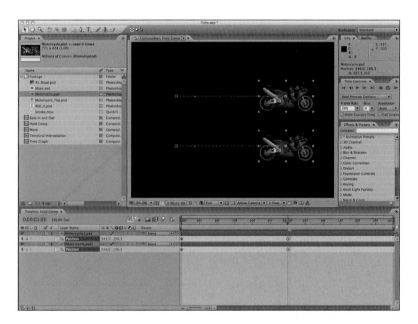

5 Hold down the **Shift** key, and select the **Motorcycle2.psd** and **Motorcycle1.psd** layers. Once you have both layers selected, press the **P** key. This causes the **Position** property to appear on both layers. Click the **stopwatch** icon to set starting keyframes for both layers. Move the **CTI** (Current Time Indicator) to **Frame 0:00:01:00**. In the **Composition** panel, grab one of the motorcycle objects, and move it to the right.

Since you selected both motorcycle objects, they should move together. This sets two identical keyframes.

You could have created this keyframe animation in one motorcycle layer and then duplicated the layer. After Effects 7 always offers multiple ways to perform tasks.

6 In the **Timeline**, click a blank area to deselect all the layers. Select the keyframe on the first frame (0:00:00:00) for the **Motorcycle2.psd** layer. Choose **Animation > Keyframe Interpolation**.

You can also press Cmd+Option+K (Mac) or Ctrl+Alt+K (Windows).

---

7 In the **Keyframe Interpolation** dialog box, choose **Hold** from the **Temporal Interpolation** pop-up menu. Click **OK**.

This sets the first keyframe as a Hold interpolation keyframe. You'll see the result when you preview the motion in the next step. As you can see, the Keyframe Interpolation dialog box is rather complex. Be sure to read the "Interpolation Icons and Functions" chart on the following page to understand its settings.

---

8 Click **RAM Preview** or press the **spacebar**, and observe the change in timing between the two motorcycles. In particular, notice that the **Motorcycle2.psd** layer holds in time (remains in the same place) before appearing at the next keyframe.

The Hold interpolation keyframe type makes objects stop or jump from frame to frame. If you wanted to make Motorcycle2.psd move on the first frame, you could change the keyframe interpolation type to Linear or another type of interpolation. You can also mix and match interpolation types within an animation if you set numerous keyframes.

---

9 Choose **File > Save**, or press **Cmd+S** (Mac) or **Ctrl+S** (Windows). Click the drop-down menu in the upper-left corner of the **Composition** panel and choose **Close Hold Comp** to close this composition. Leave **Time.aep** open for the next exercise.

Understanding the Temporal Interpolation Icons

The shape of the **keyframe** icon in the **Time** graph represents the temporal interpolation type. If you ever want to change a temporal keyframe interpolation type, select the keyframe you want to change, and choose **Animation > Keyframe Interpolation**. This causes the Keyframe Interpolation dialog box to appear, in which you can choose another temporal interpolation type, depending on the effect you are trying to achieve. For example, you can easily change a **Linear** keyframe to **Hold** when you want to freeze an animation property at that point in time.

◇	Linear Icon
⊠	Bezier or Continuous Bezier Icon
○	Auto Bezier Icon
◁	Hold Icon

It's not important to memorize what these icons look like. You'll probably be more interested in making your artwork move the way you want it to visually than in worrying about what icon appears in your **Timeline**. Still, you might notice the icons for keyframes change. The following is a handy chart to refer to if your curiosity gets aroused:

Interpolation Icons and Functions

Icon	When to Use
Auto Bézier	This type of interpolation maintains a smooth transition between keyframes. The **Speed** graph will show handles, and After Effects 7 applies curves automatically.
Bézier or Continuous Bézier	Anytime you change the curves on the **Speed** graph, manually or through the **Easy Ease In** or **Easy Ease Out** function, the icon changes to reflect a **Bézier** or **Continuous Bézier** interpolation type. The difference between the two is that the **Continuous Bézier** handles adjust both sides of the curve, and **Bézier** handles adjust each side of the curve separately.
Linear	This is the default temporal interpolation type. Use this interpolation method when you don't want the speed of movement to change.
Hold	Use this interpolation method when you want movement to stop or pause.

4 | Using Roving Keyframes

When you set multiple keyframes, it can be hard to get the speed of the movement to be even, which is sometimes necessary when the distance between keyframes is different, as this exercise will demonstrate. Some of the moves are short, and others are longer. It's hard to know where to set the keyframes on the **Timeline** because you probably aren't going to spend the time to measure the distance, divide it into frames, and figure out where to set your keyframes. Fortunately, After Effects 7 provides a way to determine even timing for you. The **Roving Keyframe** command ensures the speed from keyframe to keyframe is consistent, even if you didn't set it up that way to start.

In this exercise, you will learn to use roving keyframes by applying the **Roving Keyframe** command to a prepared composition. This exercise will provide a good example of when you'd want to use roving keyframes.

---

1 If you followed the previous exercise, **Time.aep** should still be open in After Effects 7. If it's not, choose **File > Open Project**. Navigate to the **chap_06** folder you copied to your desktop, click **Time_4.aep** to select it, and click **Open**.

---

2 Double-click the **Maze** composition to open it.

---

3 Click **RAM Preview**, and observe the *X* moving through the maze. Notice the timing of the movement is uneven—the *X* speeds up and slows down.

To make the *X* shape go around the maze in this example, you would have to set numerous keyframes. Unfortunately, the physical distance the *X* has to travel from keyframe to keyframe varies, which results in the uneven speed.

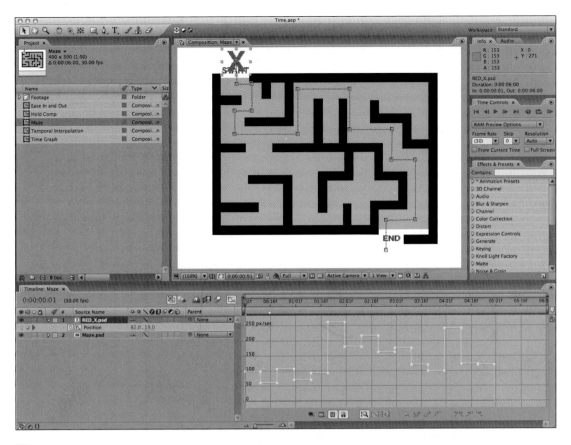

4 In the **Timeline** panel, select the **Red_X.psd** layer, and press **P** to reveal the **Position** property. (We have already set the keyframes.) Click the **Include this property in the graph editor set** button, and then click the **Graph Editor** button at the top of the **Timeline** panel.

You should now be able to see the Speed graph in the Graph Editor. The high portions of the graph are where the Red_X.psd layer is moving faster. The low portions of the graph are where the Red_X.psd layer is moving slower.

5 With your cursor, drag a selection box around all the keyframes in the **Graph Editor** to select all the keyframes at once.

You can also hold down the Shift key to select each keyframe, but the dragging method is much faster.

6 At the bottom of the **Graph Editor**, click the **Edit selected keyframes** button, and choose **Keyframe Interpolation** from the contextual menu. In the **Keyframe Interpolation** dialog box, choose **Rove Across Time** from the **Roving** pop-up menu. Click **OK**.

You can also choose Animation > Keyframe Interpolation or press Cmd+Option+K (Mac) or Ctrl+Alt+K (Windows).

As you can see, the options in the Keyframe Interpolation dialog box are rather complex. Be sure to read the "Keyframe Interpolation Dialog Box Settings" chart later in this chapter for an explanation of the various options.

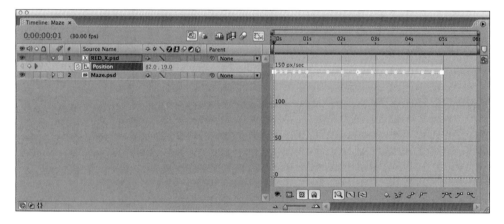

7 In the **Graph Editor**, observe that the selected keyframes have moved. Also observe that the **Speed** graph is flat and even.

Allowing keyframes to "rove across time" means After Effects 7 will mathematically adjust the keyframes you set manually to even increments of time. The position of the keyframes on the Timeline will not look even, but After Effects 7 will even out the time it takes to get from point to point in the composition. This smoothes the timing of the movement when the distance of travel between points varies. This kind of timing would be difficult to figure out manually!

8 Click **RAM Preview** to see the result of the roving keyframes.

---

9 Choose **File > Save**, or press **Cmd+S** (Mac) or **Ctrl+S** (Windows) to save your project. Choose **File > Close Project**.

Using roving keyframes, you've easily smoothed out the timing of your animation across multiple keyframes, which is a real time-saver. Before completing this chapter, refer to the following discussion of various keyframe interpolation methods.

Understanding Keyframe Interpolation

The term **interpolating** refers to the process of creating changes between keyframes. It's often referred to as **tweening** in animation terminology.

The **Keyframe Interpolation** dialog box is where you can set temporal and spatial attributes for keyframes. One way to access this dialog box is to choose **Animation > Keyframe Interpolation**. You must select single or multiple keyframes before you can access this dialog box. Any changes you make in the dialog box will apply to the selected keyframes.

In addition, you can mix keyframe interpolation types on different keyframes on a **Timeline**. For example, a set of position keyframes might have **Auto Bézier** for its temporal interpolation and **Linear** for its spatial interpolation, and the next set of position keyframes might be set to **Continuous Bézier** for its temporal interpolation and **Bézier** for its spatial interpolation. You can create all sorts of combinations for an individual keyframe or for sets of keyframes.

In the **Keyframe Interpretation** dialog box, you can choose whether you want to use temporal interpolation or spatial interpolation. All properties have temporal interpolation. Of the **Transform** properties, **Opacity** is the only one without spatial attributes because its changes are marked by time only, not by space. Here's a chart that explains all the complex settings in this dialog box:

Keyframe Interpolation Dialog Box Settings

Category	Option
Temporal Interpolation	Affects how a property changes over time in the **Timeline** panel. Here are the **Temporal Interpolation** settings: **Linear:** This creates a uniform rate of change between keyframes. You can use **Linear** keyframes to form a corner or sharp turn in the graph line. This method is useful for giving a mechanical or rhythmic feel to animation timing. **Bézier:** This is a completely manual interpolation method. The two control handles operate independently of one another in both the motion path and the **Value** graph. Use this type of temporal interpolation when you want to manually control the timing in and out of the keyframe. **Continuous Bézier:** This creates a smooth rate of change through a keyframe. You set the positions of the control handles manually. Use this method where you want a smooth change in time and need specific control. **Auto Bézier:** This creates a smooth rate of change through a keyframe. You cannot manually adjust the handles of an **Auto Bézier** point. The handles adjust automatically based on the nearest keyframes and create smooth transitions through the **Auto Bézier** point. Use this method when you want a smooth change in time and do not need manual control. **Note:** If you do adjust the **Auto Bézier** handle manually, you'll automatically convert it to a **Continuous Bézier** keyframe. **Hold:** This creates an abrupt change. Use this method when you want an image to appear or disappear suddenly. It's also useful when you want a strobe effect. It can hold any point in time steady until the next keyframe.
Spatial Interpolation	Affects the shape of the path in the **Composition** panel. Here are the **Spatial Interpolation** settings: **Linear:** This creates a straight motion path. **Bézier:** You can identify this type by the angled handle bars. You can adjust the handle bars independently in both angles and length. **Continuous Bézier:** You can identify this type by the straight handle bars. The handle bars may be different lengths, but they are always straight. **Auto Bézier:** You can identify this type by the smooth curve. This type has control handles but no handle bars. (If you attempt to move a control point on an **Auto Bézier** type, you'll automatically convert it to a **Continuous Bézier** type.)
Roving	Drifts across time to smooth the **Speed** graph. The first and last keyframes cannot rove. Here are the **Roving** settings: **Lock to Time:** This allows you to set the keyframe position on the **Timeline**. This is the default setting for **Roving**. **Rove Across Time:** This changes the position of the keyframe on the **Timeline** to mathematically smooth the speed of the motion. Use this when you want After Effects 7 to create a consistent speed between multiple keyframes.

That's it for this chapter! Remember, learning the tools of timing is a skill, but applying that skill to the art of animation is a real talent. Developing your talent takes time and experience, but you have now taken your first steps toward that goal.

In the next chapter, you will investigate the options you have when previewing the animations you create.

7

Previewing Movies

To preview animation in the "olden days" of filmmaking, you had to photograph your hand-drawn cel, send the film to a lab, and wait until the next day to see what you had created. Adobe After Effects 7 has made life much easier, but some science is still involved with previewing.

When you create animation in After Effects 7, the program has to render what each frame should look like. The rendering process can take a long time if you have lots of layers, effects, or property settings. Although this is barely noticeable when you're looking at a single frame, it is possible After Effects 7 will have trouble keeping up with rendering complicated compositions containing many frames. For this reason, the speed of your previews can be problematic.

You've already previewed your animations using the **spacebar** and the **Play/Pause** and **RAM Preview** buttons in the **Time Controls** panel; you've also learned to scrub the **CTI** in the **Timeline** panel. It's hard to believe previewing encompasses much more than what you've already learned, but it does. Between the two extremes of fast previews and accurate previews are numerous mix-and-match settings you can tune to maximize the type of detail you're looking for and to minimize the time it takes to see the results. In this chapter, you'll see a number of scenarios to help you understand when and how to use each preview setting.

Using the Time Controls Panel

You've already worked with the **Time Controls** panel in previous chapters, but like most features of After Effects 7, the **Time Controls** panel is a lot more complex than you might think at first glance. This chapter gives you the opportunity to really learn its features. The chart below describes the various controls in this panel.

The **Time Controls** panel is the main tool for controlling previews, but as you'll see in this chapter, settings in the **Composition** and **Timeline** panels also affect the preview of movies.

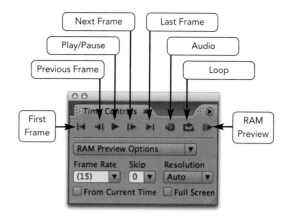

Time Controls Panel	
Option	**Description**
First Frame	Like a rewind button on a VCR (**V**ideo **C**assette **R**ecorder), this button will always quickly jump the **CTI** to the first frame.
Previous Frame	This button allows you to view the composition in single-frame increments in reverse.
Play/Pause	This button plays the composition not in real time but as fast as it can—which is sometimes slow.
Next Frame	This button allows you to view the composition in single-frame increments going forward.
Last Frame	This button moves the **CTI** to the last frame in the composition.
Audio	This button needs to be clicked to hear sound. (Sound is audible only by clicking the **RAM Preview** button, not the **Play/Pause** button.)
Loop	This button allows you to watch the same composition over and over. Clicking this button repeatedly makes After Effects 7 access the **Play Once** and **Ping Pong** (play forward and then play in reverse over and over) play modes.
RAM Preview	This button causes After Effects 7 to do its best to show you the composition at its true speed. It might take a moment for the program to render the preview, but once it does, it will play back faster than when clicking the **Play/Pause** button. The green bar in the **Timeline** indicates what your computer can play in RAM (**R**andom **A**ccess **M**emory).

Understanding Preview Types

Four types of previews exist: manual, standard, RAM, and wireframe. The following chart gives an in-depth description of each type and explains how to access these features:

Preview Types and Uses	
Preview Type	**Use**
Manual	You should use this primarily when you want to step through your animation one frame at a time to analyze motion or when you want to set the current time to a specific frame. The **CTI** playhead in the **Timeline** panel, the **Shuttle** playhead, and the **Preview Frame/Next Frame** and **Play/Pause** buttons in the **Time Controls** panel are all manual preview types.
Standard	You can access this by either clicking the **Play/Pause** button in the **Time Controls** panel or pressing the **spacebar**. This mode is useful if you want to see every frame. You can use it to analyze motion at slower than real-time playback. You can also choose to use standard preview when you are running low on available RAM and you need to see the entire animation play from beginning to end.
RAM	This is most useful when you need to see real-time playback. The **RAM Preview** button is located in the **Time Controls** panel. You can set up two different RAM preview modes and switch between them to optimize your workflow. The best use of the two modes is to set one for high image detail and the other for low image detail. Using higher image detail will reduce the number of frames that can be played back from RAM. Based on your available system RAM, you may also choose to skip frames to optimize the playback.
Wireframe	You should use this when you need real-time preview and image outlines to provide enough detail to allow for broad compositional choices. Wireframe previews use relatively little RAM and can be valuable when you have numerous frames and little available RAM. This method allows you to view a long animation piece in its entirety. You access wireframe settings by choosing **Composition > Wireframe Preview** (Mac) or **Composition > Preview > Wireframe Preview** (Windows).

NOTE:

You Need RAM for RAM Preview

It's common to have problems with RAM preview stopping before it has finished displaying your entire composition. This can be for a few reasons, one of which is not having enough RAM in your computer to run the entire composition. You can solve this problem by buying more RAM (a total of 512 MB is required, Adobe recommends 1 GB, and more is even better!) or by using some of the workarounds you'll learn about in this chapter, such as skipping frames or lowering the preview resolution. Another solution is to render a final movie, which you'll learn how to do in Chapter 20, "Rendering Final Movies."

NOTE:

Knowing When to Use RAM Preview

RAM preview is preferable to pressing the **spacebar** or clicking the **Play/Pause** button on the **Time Controls** panel because it gives you a better sense of how fast your animation plays in real time. You won't always need to know how fast your animation plays, however. Sometimes you'll just want to check movement, not timing. It's fine to use any preview method you want—RAM preview simply offers the fastest preview.

Working with Play Modes in the Time Controls Panel

Three play modes are available in the **Time Controls** panel. These three modes determine whether you will see your animation play once, play in a continuous loop, or play forward and backward continuously. Although you probably won't need to change play modes often, each is necessary at times. In this exercise, you'll learn how to access each play mode, and you'll understand the reasons to choose each one.

1 Copy the **chap_07** folder from the **After Effects 7 HOT CD-ROM** onto your desktop.

2 Choose **File > Open Project**. Navigate to the **chap_07** folder you copied to your desktop, click **Preview.aep** to select it, and click **Open**.

3 Choose **File > Save As**. In the **Save As** dialog box, navigate to the **AE7_HOT_Projects** folder on your desktop. Name the file **Preview.aep**, and click **Save**.

4 In the **Project** panel, double-click **Face_Comp** to open it.

We have created this composition for you. It contains a different layer for each feature of the face. We animated the layers using the Scale, Position, and Rotation properties. It also contains a video layer called Sparks.mov.

5 In the **Time Controls** panel, click the **Loop** button until it displays the **Loop** icon, as shown in the illustration here. Click the **RAM Preview** button to play your animation.

As you continue to click the Loop button, it cycles through different icons. You will learn about them all in the course of this exercise. For now, make sure you click until you see the Loop icon.

Clicking until you see the Loop icon causes your animation to continue to loop until you click in After Effects 7 or press a key on the keyboard. This play mode is generally the most useful for analyzing motion.

6 Click the **Loop** button until it shows the **Play Once** icon, and click **RAM Preview**.

In Play Once mode, your animation plays once and stops on the last frame. This mode is good if you are the type of person who likes to see something once and quickly move on to making changes. It can also be useful for presenting work to a client for a first impression.

7 Click the **Loop** button again to display the **Ping Pong** icon, and press the **spacebar**.

Pressing the spacebar is a shortcut for clicking the Play/Pause button to preview an animation.

The Ping Pong mode (sometimes referred to as Palindrome) plays forward and backward continuously. This mode can be good for analyzing complex motion. It can sometimes help to see an action in reverse, perhaps running slowly, to understand the subtleties of the motion.

---

8 When you're finished watching the animation, press any key to stop the preview. Return to the **Loop** icon by clicking the **Loop** button two more times.

Loop is the default setting for the Time Controls preview.

---

9 From the pop-up menu in the upper-left corner of the **Composition** panel, choose **Close Face_Comp**. Choose **File > Save**, or press **Cmd+S** (Mac) or **Ctrl+S** (Windows). Leave **Preview.aep** open for the next exercise.

EXERCISE

2 | Skipping Frames for Faster RAM Previews

You may find yourself creating a large, ambitious project that takes a long time to preview. This usually happens when your composition has several layers, animated properties, and effects applied to it. This exercise presents a great method for speeding up preview and playback: skipping frames.

---

1 If you followed the previous exercise, **Preview.aep** should still be open in After Effects 7. If it's not, choose **File > Open Project**. Navigate to the **chap_07** folder you copied to your desktop, click **Preview_2.aep** to select it, and click **Open**.

---

2 In the **Project** panel, double-click **Motorcycle_Text_Comp** to open it.

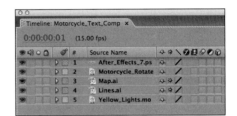

We have already created this composition for this exercise. It contains Adobe Illustrator and Apple QuickTime footage items. We have set all the footage to Best quality so it looks as good as it possibly can. You can find the Best quality setting in the Switches panel; Chapter 8, *"Working with Layers,"* discusses the Best setting in more detail. Although this setting makes the artwork look great, it makes the composition take longer to render in RAM preview.

We have set the Illustrator items in the Timeline to Continuous Rasterization, which means they will look crisp even if you enlarge the artwork. This also makes the composition more difficult to render. This composition was designed to demonstrate what happens when you have artwork that is difficult to preview using RAM preview.

---

3 Move the **CTI** to any frame in the **Timeline**, and notice the arrow cursor flashes black and white for a moment.

This is a visual indicator that After Effects 7 is rendering and cannot show that frame. Moving the CTI to any other unrendered frame in the Timeline will cause the same result.

---

4 Move the **CTI** to the first frame of the composition (or press the **Home** key). Click the **Play/Pause** button in the **Time Controls** panel to play the animation.

You'll see that After Effects 7 struggles to play this animation. This is what happens as you start to work on larger and more complicated compositions; this is a common issue for After Effects 7 artists.

5 In the **Time Controls** panel, click the **RAM Preview** button.

It will take After Effects 7 a little while to build the preview. Once the preview is ready to play, it's possible it will not play all the way to the end. You must have a sufficient amount of RAM.

The green line at the top of your Timeline panel is the After Effects 7 visual display of how many frames it can play in RAM. The green line will appear, disappear, and redraw itself every time you preview a change in your Timeline. It indicates which frames have been rendered.

---

6 To reset the render bar in the **Timeline**, click the **Video** button (the **eye** icon) for the **After_Effects_7.psd** layer, which turns the layer off, and then click the **eye** icon again to turn it on. In the **Time Controls** panel, choose **1** from the **Skip** pop-up menu. (Alternatively, type **1** in the **Skip** field of the **Time Controls** panel, and press **Enter**.) Click the **RAM Preview** button again.

This time, it should take only half as long to prepare this preview, and the preview should also play to the end. If it doesn't, type 2 in the Skip field, and press Enter.

Skipping frames helps you see an entire composition even if you don't have enough RAM to play every frame. This preview technique is useful when you want to see a real-time preview but you don't care about seeing each frame. It gives you an accurate sense of timing but not a completely accurate sense of appearance.

---

7 Choose **0** from the **Skip** pop-up menu in the **Time Controls** panel.

---

8 Choose **File > Save**, or press **Cmd+S** (Mac) or **Ctrl+S** (Windows). Leave **Preview.aep** open for the next exercise.

In this exercise, you learned how skipping frames can help when you need to quickly preview your animations. In the next exercise, you will learn how lowering the preview resolution can also help you to achieve faster playback results.

Skipping Frames to Preserve RAM

Choosing **1** from the **Skip** pop-up menu causes the preview to alternately display one frame and then skip one frame. This process continues for the length of the preview.

Skipping frames can help preserve RAM. Every frame skipped preserves memory. However, the more frames you skip, the rougher the preview. If you need to preserve RAM, it is best to start by skipping one frame and seeing whether this saves the amount of RAM necessary for your playback.

Another reason you may choose to skip frames is to speed the time it takes to render your preview. Just setting the option to skip one frame will cut the preview rendering time in half.

Answering More RAM Questions

You might be curious about other RAM limitations. If RAM is such a big problem, how does it affect your ability to create After Effects 7 projects or the ability of your audience to see your final movies?

Insufficient RAM can affect your RAM preview, but you can get around this problem in several ways. RAM preview is simply a handy way to help you see your animations quickly as you're working. If you don't have enough RAM in your computer, you have other options. Clicking the **Play/Pause** button, moving the **CTI** control, and scrubbing the **CTI** in the **Timeline** panel will allow you to preview your work; these methods just won't play as fast as the RAM preview will.

The amount of available RAM won't have much of an impact on your ability to create and render After Effects 7 compositions. You can create complicated movies in After Effects 7 using the minimum RAM requirement of the program. You can also render final movies in After Effects 7 without much RAM. The real issue with RAM is related to using the RAM preview (and to some of the 3D features, which you'll learn about in Chapter 16, "Working with 3D Layers").

EXERCISE

3 | Lowering Preview Resolution

In this exercise, you will learn about the RAM preview **Resolution** setting, which allows you to preview your animation at a lower resolution than the resolution assigned to the composition. This is an excellent way to speed up the playback of a composition you are creating when you need to preview the motion of animation properties. In this case, it's more important to preview the paths and movement of objects—therefore, you can temporarily sacrifice resolution. You can combine skipped frames with lowered resolution settings, but you'll learn about these features one at a time in this exercise so you'll understand them better.

1   If you followed the previous exercise, **Preview.aep** should still be open in After Effects 7. If it's not, choose **File > Open**. Navigate to the **chap_07** folder you copied to your desktop, click **Preview_3.aep** to select it, and click **Open**.

2   Make sure **Motorcycle_Text_Comp** is still open. If it isn't, in the **Project** panel, double-click **Motorcycle_Text_Comp** to open it.

3   In the **Time Controls** panel, choose **0** from the **Skip** pop-up menu if necessary. Choose **Quarter** from the **Resolution** pop-up menu.

These settings take whatever resolution After Effects 7 is set at (in this case, 720 x 534 pixels) and reduce it by 75 percent.

4   Click the **RAM Preview** button. When you are done previewing, click the **RAM Preview** button again to stop playback.

All frames render at quarter resolution and preview in real time. This setting is good for previewing all the frames in your composition while preserving RAM. It also speeds up preview rendering time because lower-resolution images render more quickly. Unfortunately, the moving footage doesn't look nearly as good at quarter resolution. Although it does give you a good indication of motion, it gives a bad indication of appearance.

5   Choose **File > Save**, or press **Cmd+S** (Mac) or **Ctrl+S** (Windows). Choose **Close Motorcycle_Text_Comp** from the drop-down menu in the upper-left corner of the **Composition** panel to close this composition. Leave **Preview.aep** open for the next exercise.

In this exercise, you learned how to vary the resolution of your previews to save render time and effort on the part of your computer's processor. In the next exercise, you will revisit resolution issues by working with your composition settings as a more permanent alternative. But first you'll learn more about frame rate settings.

Speeding Up Rendering via Frame Rate Settings

Occasionally, you will want to preview your movie faster or slower than the composition settings permit. To do this, choose an option from the **Frame Rate** pop-up menu in the **Time Controls** panel. This technique changes the speed your composition plays at and can provide another way to analyze motion.

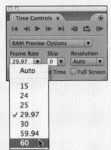

In the **Time Controls** panel, you can choose **60** fps (frames per second) from the **Frame Rate** pop-up menu. With an original composition setting of **30** fps (or 29.97 fps), the animation will play at twice the speed of the composition setting if you click the **RAM Preview** button. In the same instance, with **Frame Rate** set to **15** fps, the animation will play at half speed.

Choosing **Auto** from the **Frame Rate** pop-up menu automatically adjusts the frame rate to match the composition settings.

Using the Shift+RAM Preview Option

Now that you've learned how to set up the RAM preview with all its different settings, you might want to take advantage of **Shift+RAM preview**, which allows you to work with two kinds of RAM previews. You can set the first RAM preview to be full resolution, to not skip frames, and to use a high frame rate. Do this by choosing **RAM Preview Options** in the **Time Controls** panel.

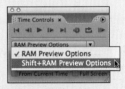

If you want, you can then set up a second type of RAM preview, the Shift+RAM preview. You access this setting by choosing **Shift+RAM Preview Options** from the **RAM Preview Options** pop-up menu in the **Time Controls** panel, as shown in the illustration here.

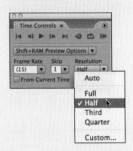

Next, make your changes to the **Frame Rate**, **Skip**, and **Resolution** options, such as choosing **Half** from the **Resolution** pop-up menu (as shown in the illustration here). Once you're finished, choose **RAM Preview Options** from the **Shift+RAM Preview Options** pop-up menu in the **Time Controls** panel again.

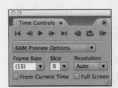

You can access the standard settings simply by clicking the **RAM Preview** button. If you want to access the Shift+RAM preview settings, hold down the **Shift** key, and then click the **RAM Preview** button. Now you have two groups of settings with which to preview, as shown in the illustrations here.

Changing the Resolution in the Composition Panel

You can change the **Resolution** setting in the **Composition** panel as an alternative to changing the RAM preview resolution in the **Time Controls** panel. When you make this change in the **Composition** panel, it affects the way the **Composition** panel appears all the time, until you change it back to **Full**. When you change the setting in the **Time Controls** panel, the **Composition** panel will look normal, but the RAM preview will display with the lower resolution.

Why, then, would you want to change the resolution in the **Composition** panel? Well, if your composition has a lot of render-intensive filter effects, such as **Blur** or **Motion Blur**, and the **Composition** panel is set to full resolution, After Effects 7 will take a long time to render a still frame. This extended render time gets cumbersome when you're trying to position objects and set keyframes. For this reason, knowing how to use the **Composition** panel's **Resolution** setting is an important skill.

---

1 If you followed the previous exercise, **Preview.aep** should still be open in After Effects 7. If it's not, choose **File > Open Project**. Navigate to the **chap_07** folder you copied to your desktop, click **Preview_4.aep** to select it, and click **Open**.

---

2 In the **Project** panel, double-click **Large_Motorcycle_Comp** to open it.

We have also added some Motion Blur and Best quality settings to this composition, which can make it challenging to render. You will learn about Motion Blur in Chapter 10, *"Applying Effects."*

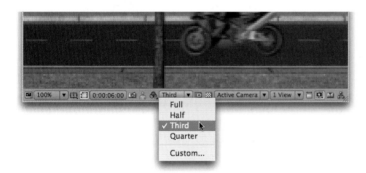

---

3 Press the **spacebar** to play the composition (it may play slowly). When you are done previewing, press the **spacebar** again to stop playback. In the **Composition** panel, choose **Third** from the **Resolution** pop-up menu. Press the **spacebar** to play the composition.

As it plays, you'll notice the image resolution is degraded but the animation plays more quickly.

---

4 In the **Time Controls** panel, choose **Full** from the **Resolution** pop-up menu. Click the **RAM Preview** button.

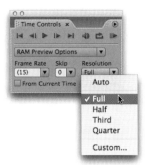

Notice that your animation plays back at Full resolution, even though it is still set in the Composition panel to the Third resolution setting. This is because the RAM preview resolution option is independent of the Composition panel's Resolution setting. You can make a resolution change in either spot—in the RAM preview options of the Time Controls panel or in the Composition panel. When you press the spacebar, the Composition panel setting will play the composition at the resolution selected (currently Third). However, if you click the RAM Preview button, the composition will play at its current setting as defined in the Time Controls panel, which is Full. Just remember that RAM preview may not be able to play the entire composition because you may not have enough RAM in your computer.

---

5 In the **Time Controls** panel, choose **Auto** from the **Resolution** menu. Click the **RAM Preview** button.

The animation plays with the Third resolution setting. The Auto setting allows the RAM preview to use the same resolution as the current Resolution setting in the Composition panel.

---

6 In the **Composition** panel, choose **Full** from the **Resolution** pop-up menu. Click the **RAM Preview** button.

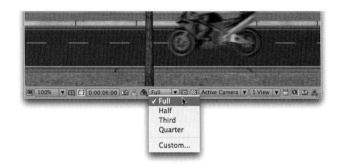

With the RAM preview resolution set to Auto, the preview adjusts to full resolution. Now the playback will be slower, and it might not be able to play all the frames again.

---

7 Choose **File > Save**, or press **Cmd+S** (Mac) or **Ctrl+S** (Windows). Leave **Large_Motorcycle_Comp** open for the next exercise.

Now that you've learned about the different ways you can set playback resolution for a composition, you will learn how to define a region of interest to speed up your previews even more.

VIDEO: **resolution.mov**

If you still have questions about changing the resolution in the **Time Controls** palette versus the **Composition** window, please watch **resolution.mov**, located in the **videos** folder on the **After Effects 7 HOT CD-ROM**.

5 | Previewing a Region of Interest

Defining a **region of interest** allows you to preview a specific area of the image. By specifying a smaller area for preview, you decrease the rendering time and speed up your workflow. This method also allows you to visually concentrate on the details of a limited area.

A region of interest is easy to use. Once you've set it up, it is always available, and you can turn it on or off with the click of a button. In this brief exercise, you'll learn everything you need to know about this feature.

---

1   If you followed the previous exercise, **Preview.aep** should still be open in After Effects 7. If it's not, choose **File > Open Project**. Navigate to the **chap_07** folder you copied to your desktop, click **Preview_5.aep** to select it, and click **Open**.

---

2   Double-click **Large_Motorcycle_Comp** in the **Project** panel to open the composition, if it is not already open.

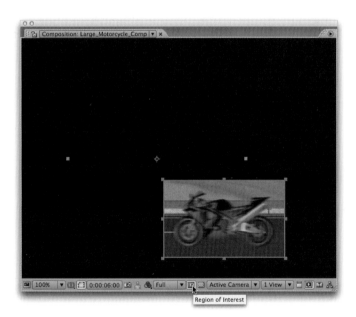

3   In the **Timeline**, move the **CTI** to approximately **0:00:05:00**. In the **Composition** panel, click the **Region of Interest** button, which changes the cursor to a **Marquee** tool. Drag this tool inside the **Composition** panel to define a region of interest. Use the control handles on the resulting bounding box to adjust the size of the region.

Once you complete the shape, everything else will disappear except the area you have selected. This helps you focus previews on challenging or important areas of the composition.

Magnification ratio popup

4 In the **Composition** panel, set **Magnification** to **200%**. Hold down the **spacebar**, and position your cursor in the **Composition** panel to display the **Hand** tool. Click the **Hand** tool, and drag the image to position the region of interest in the center of the panel.

Note: You can also use the Zoom tool from the Tools panel to zoom into a document and look at a specific area. Holding the Opt key (Mac) or the Alt key (Windows) will cause the Zoom tool to zoom out and decrease magnification. Press the spacebar to view your animation.

---

5 Set **Magnification** to **100%**. Click the **Region of Interest** button to turn the region of interest off. Hold down the **spacebar**, and use the **Hand** tool once again to reposition your frame so it is centered in the **Composition** panel.

Once you have set a region of interest, you can click the Region of Interest button to turn it on and off as you work on your composition.

---

6 With the region of interest turned off, hold down the **Opt** key (Mac) or the **Alt** key (Windows), and click the **Region of Interest** button at the bottom of the **Composition** panel.

This clears the region of interest. The Marquee tool appears again so you can draw a new region of interest.

---

7 Choose **File > Save**, or press **Cmd+S** (Mac) or **Ctrl+S** (Windows) to save your project. Leave **Large_Motorcycle_Comp** open for the next exercise.

Specifying a region of interest is a great way to narrow the focus of your previews in the Composition panel, especially for previewing details in a complex composition. In the next exercise, you will learn how to limit the amount of your composition that plays back by working in the Timeline.

Limiting Previews with Work Area Settings

Sometimes, if your animation is long, you might want to preview only the small section you are in the process of refining. You can limit your preview by defining the work area settings in the composition time ruler area of the **Timeline** panel. In this exercise, you will learn to use the work area. First, you'll learn the keyboard shortcuts to set it; then, you'll learn to set the work area by simply dragging the handles at the top of the **Timeline** panel.

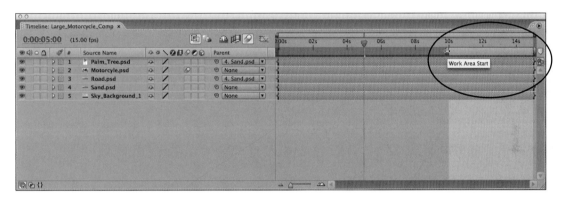

1 If you followed the previous exercise, **Preview.aep** and **Large_Motorcycle_Comp** should still be open. If they're not, choose **File > Open Project**. Navigate to the **chap_07** folder you copied to your desktop, click **Preview_6.aep** to select it, and click **Open**. In the **Project** panel, double-click **Large_Motorcycle_Comp** to open it.

2 In the **Timeline** panel, drag the left side of the **Work Area Start** marker to begin the work area at **10 seconds**.

3 In the **Time Controls** panel, click the **RAM Preview** button.

The preview includes only the frames within the work area. The animation should start playing at 0:00:10:00, where the work area begins, instead of at 0:00:00:00. This is useful if you want to preview a small section of your Timeline. If the animation won't play in full, try reducing the resolution in the RAM preview options to Half.

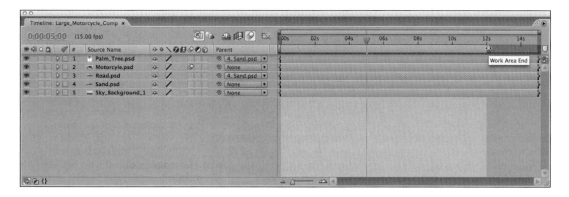

4 Drag the left **Work Area Start** marker to **0:00:00:00** and the right **Work Area End** marker to **0:00:12:00**.

This defines the work area as beginning on the first frame and ending on 0:00:12:00.

Tip: In addition to dragging the work area marker, you can use keyboard shortcuts in the following chart to set these points:

Work Area Keyboard Shortcuts		
Action	Mac	Windows
Set beginning of work area to current time	B	B
Set end of work area to current time	N	N

5 In the **Time Controls** panel, click **RAM Preview**.

You'll see a preview of the new work area. If the animation won't play in full, try reducing the resolution in the RAM preview options to Half or lower. Sometimes you have to combine techniques. If you make this change, be sure to set it to Auto once you've finished this exercise.

6 Choose **File > Save**, or press **Cmd+S** (Mac) **or Ctrl+S** (Windows) to save your project. Close all open compositions by selecting **Close All** from the pop-up menu in the upper-left corner of the **Composition** panel. Leave **Preview.aep** open for the next exercise.

7 | Using Wireframe Previews

Sometimes in a preview, you want to focus on the motion of your objects, not on the appearance. In such cases, you can use a specialized type of preview that allows you to see a wireframe of your artwork instead of the full-pixel version. A **wireframe** outline shows the shape of the layers of artwork in your composition. In this mode, a white outline gives you a quick impression of the shape of your artwork but without the color, fill, effects, or texture.

Using the **Wireframe** setting is useful for previewing motion quickly because the computer doesn't have to render as much information as it does in other modes. You can use two types of wireframe previews: basic wireframe and wireframe with motion trails. You'll learn to use both types of previews in this exercise.

---

1 If you followed the previous exercise, **Preview.aep** should still be open. If it's not, choose **File > Open Project**. Navigate to the **chap_07** folder you copied to your desktop, click **Preview_7.aep** to select it, and click **Open**.

---

2 In the **Project** panel, double-click **Face_Comp** to open it.

---

3 In the **Time Controls** panel, click the **Play/Pause** button to view the animation. Click it again to stop the animation.

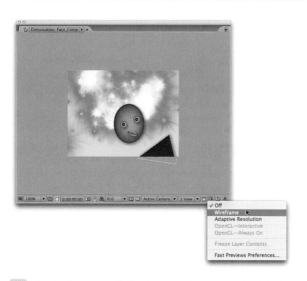
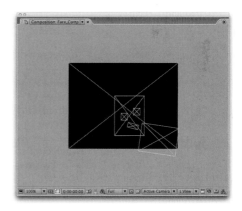

4 At the bottom of the **Composition** panel, click the **Fast Previews** button, and choose **Wireframe** from the pop-up menu. Press the **spacebar** to play the composition, and press it again when you are finished previewing.

The Wireframe option allows your composition to play in real time because After Effects 7 doesn't have to render much content to the screen. In this preview, it's easy to see the compositional relationship between all the objects while viewing the animation in its entirety. You can use this setting when you have a complicated animation and want to see parts hidden by other objects. The wireframe preview is also faster for the computer to generate than a full-frame view, so it's used sometimes as a quick-and-dirty preview method.

---

5 Choose **Composition > Preview > Motion with Trails**. When you are finished previewing, click in the **Timeline** or **Composition** panel to stop playback.

In this type of preview, the wireframe view repeats itself in every frame, leaving a trace of its motion. Motion with Trails is useful for observing the motion paths of your objects as they are moving.

---

6 Choose **File > Save** or press **Cmd+S** (Mac) or **Ctrl+S** (Windows) to save the project, and then choose **File > Close Project** to close **Preview.aep**.

That's all there is to previewing with wireframes. You won't use this feature all the time. You'll want to use this feature only when you have a complicated composition that takes a long time to render. If you want to return to using the standard preview options, simply click the Play/Pause or RAM Preview button, and the preview will return to normal.

Viewing with Adaptive Resolution

Choosing **Adaptive Resolution** from the **Fast Previews** pop-up menu at the bottom of the **Composition** panel, as shown in the illustration here, decreases the preview resolution of layers as necessary in order to maintain the selected playback speed. You can choose this option if you are most concerned with smooth playback and not as interested in maintaining the best image resolution. With **Adaptive Resolution**, After Effects 7 makes all the necessary resolution changes for you whenever necessary, eliminating the hassle of experimenting with different frame rates manually until you are able to see your animation play back smoothly.

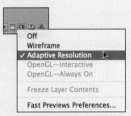

You might want to use this option if you work with a lot of complex animations and effects (and don't want to think a lot about your preview settings), especially when you need a consistent playback speed. Of course, even **Adaptive Resolution** cannot maintain playback speed on all your animations—those with especially intensive rendering and memory requirements may require additional preview methods.

In addition, you can set the maximum amount of resolution reduction for adaptive resolution. Click the **Fast Previews** button at the bottom of the **Composition** panel, and choose **Fast Previews Preferences**. In the **Preferences** dialog box, you can choose **1/2**, **1/4**, or **1/8** from the **Adaptive Resolution Limit** pop-up menu (**1/4** is the default and is usually appropriate). Click **OK** when you are done with the **Preferences** dialog box.

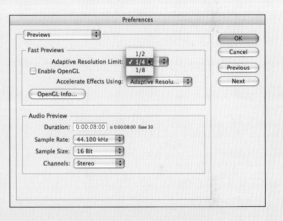

Note: Choosing **Off** from the **Fast Previews** pop-up menu will disable adaptive resolution and wireframes as appropriate, limiting you to the standard previewing methods discussed earlier in this chapter.

NOTE:

Learning More About OpenGL

If your computer has the appropriate video card installed, you may be able to take advantage of the high-quality previews offered by the OpenGL standard in After Effects 7 (specifically, OpenGL 2.0). **OpenGL** is a standard built into some video cards. It renders common motion and special effects in real time, allowing you to play your composition without a loss of resolution. This can significantly speed up the creation of projects, saving additional time over other playback modes, even RAM preview.

The particular video card and version of OpenGL your system supports will determine what types of features you can use for OpenGL previews. If your card does not support certain features (shadows, for example), they will not appear in your previews. As a result, you may want to use the other previewing methods discussed in this chapter.

For high-end graphics work, consider one of the cards known to support advanced Open GL features. To determine whether the video card in your system supports OpenGL, click the **Fast Previews** button at the bottom of the **Composition** panel, and choose **Fast Previews Preferences** from the pop-up menu. In the **Preferences** dialog box, click the **OpenGL Info** button. You'll get information similar to the information in the illustration shown here.

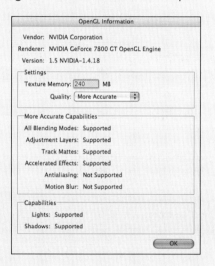

Choosing the Proper Setting

At this point, you've learned about several preview settings, so you might be confused as to which setting to use at which time. The following chart recaps the preview setting options and can help you determine the best solution for a particular project:

	Summary of Preview Settings	
Location	**Feature**	**Reason to Use**
Timeline panel	Set the work area in the **Timeline**, and use RAM preview in the **Time Controls** panel.	This is useful for reducing the number of frames shown during a preview when you have a long animation that takes too long to render.
Composition panel	Select the **Resolution** option: **Full**, **Half**, **Third**, **Quarter**, or **Custom**.	This is useful when the static preview takes a long time to render when you are trying to move an object.
Composition panel	Set the region of interest.	This is useful if you want to focus only on one small part of your screen.
Time Controls panel	Select a play mode: **Play Once**, **Loop**, or **Ping Pong**.	This is useful for choosing whether to watch something once, over and over, or forward and backward.
Time Controls panel	Select the RAM or Shift+RAM preview options.	This is useful for previewing in real time. The ability to access a secondary group of settings with the **Shift** key is useful for easily toggling between an accurate or a fast preview.

Getting used to previewing movies and using the options takes time and experience. You won't necessarily need everything you've learned right away, but this information will come in handy as you work on larger projects. Give yourself some time to absorb everything here, and feel free to return to this chapter when you want to remember exactly how a certain preview option functions.

8

Working with Layers

You might be used to the concept of layers from programs such as Adobe Photoshop and Adobe Illustrator. In After Effects 7, many of the same principles apply, yet its use of layers is much more complicated than in programs dealing only with still images.

Layers reside in the **Timeline** of After Effects 7, and they relate not only to what appears visually in your composition but also to the timing of your graphics and animations. This chapter will expose you to the possibilities provided by layers, which are the building blocks of any project. Some of the tasks you'll learn to perform include moving layers, renaming layers, replacing layers, trimming layers, sliding layers, and organizing layers. You'll even learn how to manipulate the speed and timing of your layers. It's a long chapter but an invaluable part of your After Effects 7 education.

1 | Understanding Layers

You've used layers throughout the previous chapters. In this exercise, you'll start with a couple of tasks you've performed before, and then you'll quickly move into new territory. You'll learn how to rename a layer, how to change the stacking order of layers, and how to use the keyboard to lock and unlock layers. In the process, you'll get practice making a composition and importing a layered Photoshop file. These are tasks you will perform often while using After Effects 7.

---

1 Copy the **chap_08** folder from the **After Effects 7 HOT CD-ROM** to your desktop.

---

2 Choose **File > New > New Project**.

---

3 Choose **File > Save As**. In the **Save As** dialog box, navigate to the **AE7_HOT_Projects** folder on your desktop. Name the file **Layers.aep**, and click **Save**.

---

4 Double-click the empty **Project** panel to open the **Import File** dialog box. Navigate to the **chap_08** folder on your desktop, and select **Outdoor_Stage.psd**. From the **Import As** pop-up menu, choose **Composition – Cropped Layers** (Mac) or **Footage Dimensions: Layer Size** (Windows), and then click **Open**.

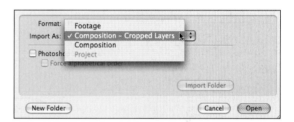

---

5 In the **Project** panel, click the **twirly** icon next to the **Outdoor_Stage Layers** folder. Notice you have imported each layer in the Photoshop file as a separate piece of footage.

Both a Layers folder and a corresponding composition will appear in the Project panel. The composition is Outdoor_Stage, and the footage folder is Outdoor_Stage Layers. This is how you will most often import a layered Photoshop file into After Effects 7—as a composition.

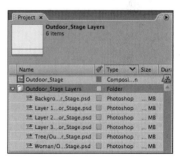

---

6 In the **Project** panel, click the **Outdoor_Stage** icon, and choose **Composition > Composition Settings**. In the **Composition Settings** dialog box, verify the settings match those shown in the illustration here, and click **OK**.

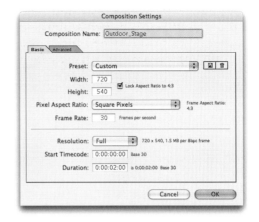

How did these settings get in the Composition Settings dialog box?, you might wonder. We created the Photoshop document at 720 x 540 pixels, which is how the composition got its dimensions. All the other settings carry over from the last time you made a composition.

---

7 Double-click the **Outdoor_Stage** composition to open the **Composition** and **Timeline** panels. In the **Timeline** panel, select **Layer 3**, and press **Return** (Mac) or **Enter** (Windows). Rename the layer **Bird 1**. Rename **Layer 2** to **Bird 2** and **Layer 1** to **Bird 3**.

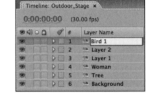

Sometimes you'll want to rename layers imported from Photoshop, or you'll simply change your mind about a layer's name you imported from another source.

---

8 In the **Composition** panel, choose **50%** from the **Magnification ratio popup** pop-up menu to change the size of the composition preview.

---

9 One at a time, click and drag each of the three bird layers to the work area of the **Composition** panel (the gray area outside the main view).

This is how you set artwork to a position out of view from the composition. The bird will animate eventually onscreen from the left and exit off-screen to the right. This is the first step in accomplishing such an animation.

10 In the **Timeline** panel, select **Bird 1**. Hold down the **Shift** key, and select **Bird 2** and **Bird 3** to multiple-select the layers. Press the **P** key to reveal the **Position** property of each layer. Click the **stopwatch** icon for any of the layers. Do not deselect.

Because you selected all three layers, you can turn on the stopwatch icon for all the selected layers with a single click.

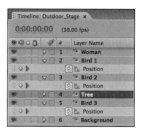

11 In the **Timeline** panel, drag the **CTI** (**C**urrent **T**ime **I**ndicator) to the last frame, or press the **End** key. Drag the selected objects to the other side of the **Composition** panel, as shown in the illustration here.

All three layers should still be selected in the Timeline along with the three associated objects in the Composition panel. Once you have moved the three items, After Effects 7 automatically sets a second keyframe on all three layers.

Tip: You can also move the selected objects by using the arrow keys on your keyboard.

12 In the **Composition** panel, choose **100%** from the **Magnification ratio popup** pop-up menu. Press the **spacebar** to preview the animation.

You can also choose Fit from the Magnification ratio popup pop-up menu to size the image preview to fit your current panel dimensions. If you don't want to see the motion paths as you preview the movement, deselect the layers by clicking an empty area of the Timeline panel.

13 In the **Timeline** panel, click and drag the **Woman** layer to the top of the stack of layers, above **Bird 1**. Click and drag the **Tree** layer above **Bird 3**. Press the **spacebar** to watch the animation.

You should notice how the stacking order of the layers changes the preview in the Composition panel. After Effects 7 stacks its layers from bottom to top, with the topmost layer being in front of all other layers.

Note: For a list of keyboard shortcuts you can use to change the stacking order of layers, see the handy chart after this exercise.

14 In the **Timeline** panel, click the **Lock** switch next to the **Background** layer to lock it.

Because you wouldn't want the background layer to be animated, locking a layer is a great way to ensure you don't accidentally move or bump a layer you want to stay still. With the lock turned on, you will be unable to move or otherwise edit this layer.

15 Choose **File > Save**, or press **Cmd+S** (Mac) or **Ctrl+S** (Windows). Leave the **Outdoor_Stage** composition and the **Layers.aep** project open for the next exercise.

In this exercise, you learned some important layer basics, such as how to reorder and rename layers in the Timeline. The next exercise will demonstrate how to add labels, which are useful for organizing and sorting layers.

TIP:

Using the Keyboard to Change the Stacking Order

The following chart shows keyboard shortcuts you can use to change the stacking order of the layers in a composition:

Stacking Order Keyboard Commands		
Stacking change	**Mac**	**Windows**
Move down one level	Cmd+[	Ctrl+[
Move up one level	Cmd+]	Ctrl+]
Move to bottom of stack	Cmd+Shift+[	Ctrl+Shift+[
Move to top of stack	Cmd+Shift+]	Ctrl+Shift+[

Now that you briefly looked at the way stacking order affects layers, you can proceed to the next exercise, where you will learn to label layers more effectively. Labeling helps keep layers organized and makes them easier to identify, which is particularly important when working with a lot of layers stacked in the **Timeline** panel.

2 | Labeling Layers

All layers have color-coded labels. You probably haven't paid too much attention to these labels yet; they appear in the **Timeline** panel in the second column from the left and are just little colored squares. You can assign and control the color coding of each layer using these labels. Labels can help you identify layers when you are working with large projects. For example, you could assign one label color to layers containing text and another color to layers containing photographs. Once layers have color codes, you can select them using the label color. Label colors can help you quickly organize a lot of content. In this exercise, you'll learn how to assign label colors and then select layers based on the label assignment.

---

1 If you followed the previous exercise, **Layers.aep** should still be open in After Effects 7. If it's not, choose **File > Open Project**. Navigate to the **chap_08** folder you copied to your desktop, click **Layers_2.aep** to select it, and click **Open**.

---

2 In the **Timeline** panel, click the **Bird 1** layer to select it. Hold down **Cmd** (Mac) or **Ctrl** (Windows), click the **Bird 2** layer, and then click the **Bird 3** layer to multiple-select all three layers.

Clicking while holding down Cmd (Mac) or Ctrl (Windows) allows you to select noncontiguous layers. Notice the column of color squares to the left of the # column. At the moment, they are all lavender, which is the default color code for layers. You'll learn to change the color of selected layers in the next step.

---

3 Choose **Edit > Label > Sunset**, and notice the color codes on all the selected bird layers turn a reddish color.

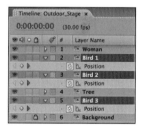

---

4 In the **Timeline** panel, click the **Woman** layer to select it. Choose **Edit > Label > Select Label Group**.

Notice this selects all layers with the same lavender color in the Timeline panel as the Woman layer (in this case, the Tree layer). Also notice a locked layer is not selected unless you unlock it, which is why the Background layer is not selected.

---

5 Choose **File > Save**, or press **Cmd+S** (Mac) or **Ctrl+S** (Windows). Choose **File > Close Project**.

In this exercise, you learned how to use labels to better identify and select certain layers. In the next exercise, you'll learn to use a special Shy switch for layers in the Timeline panel, which helps you view and sort layers in a different way.

NOTE:

Setting the Label Color Preferences

You can change the available label colors and names by choosing **After Effects > Preferences > Label Colors** (Mac) or **Edit > Preferences > Label Colors** (Windows). (Label Preferences don't appear in the **Edit** menu in OS X; they appear in the **After Effects** menu.) To rename a label in the **Preferences** dialog box,

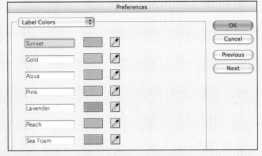

type a new color name in one of the text fields next to a particular label. You can also use the eyedropper or click a color field to access the **color picker** to change a label color. When you are finished changing the label colors in the **Preferences** dialog box, click **OK**.

Introducing Switches

Switches let you display layers in After Effects 7 in different ways. Depending on your work process, you may want to use switches to hide layers from display in the **Timeline**, turn off the sound from an audio layer, or show only an individual layer in the **Composition** panel. Switches also affect the preview and final rendering of your movie.

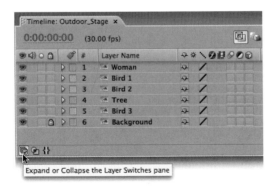

Each layer has its own set of switches affecting only that layer. Switches appear in the **Timeline** panel, and if they're not currently visible, you can make them appear by clicking the **Expand or Collapse the Layer Switches pane** button in the lower-left corner of the **Timeline** panel. In After Effects 7, the **Video**, **Audio**, **Solo**, and **Lock** switches are always present for a layer and are not turned on or off (unless you specifically choose to hide the column). These switches appear at the far-left side of the **Timeline** panel, separate from the other switches such as the **Shy** and **Quality** switches.

We introduced you to the **Lock** switch in Exercise 1. In the following exercises, you'll learn about more switch options, and we'll introduce you to others throughout the rest of this book.

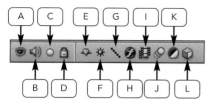

Switches form columns of options for your layers.

The following is a practical chart describing each switch. The letters correspond to the labels in the illustration:

Switch Functions	
Switch name	**Definition**
A. Video	Turns video on and off. This is available only if your layer contains footage.
B. Audio	Turns audio on and off. This is available only if your layer contains audio.
C. Solo	Allows you to easily isolate one or more layers and turn off all the other layers. This saves you the effort of turning off the layers you don't want to see. This switch turns off the visibility of layers only in the **Composition** panel; the **Shy Layers** switch turns off the visibility of layers only in the **Timeline** panel.
D. Lock	Allows you to lock a layer so you cannot move or edit it. This is useful when you want to ensure a layer doesn't change.
E. Shy Layers	Allows you to turn off a layer in the **Timeline** panel, even though it will still be visible in the **Composition** panel. This allows you to limit the number of visible layers to make it easier to work with a complicated **Timeline**. You can turn on and off the shy layers with the click of a button. You'll work with shy layers in the next exercise.
F. Continuous Rasterization	Allows vector artwork to rasterize when different transformations are applied, causing the artwork to have a crisp appearance. You'll work with this switch a little later in this chapter.
G. Quality	Allows you to specify either **Draft** quality or **Best** quality. The default is **Draft** quality. You can click this switch to see the effect the two settings produce. The **Quality** setting is especially noticeable when artwork is transformed using scaling or rotation.
H. Effect	Allows you to turn off effects temporarily so they don't have to be rendered. You don't lose your effects settings when you turn them off. You'll work with this switch in Chapter 10, *"Applying Effects."*
I. Frame Blend	When you use the time-remapping or time-stretching features (which you'll do later in this chapter), After Effects 7 **holds**, or duplicates, frames, which often results in jerky movement. Frame blending smoothes the jerkiness by creating dissolves between frames.

continues on next page

Switch Functions *continued*	
Switch name	**Definition**
J. Motion Blur	Uses the built-in motion blur feature in After Effects 7, which emulates a motion-picture camera using a long exposure (or shutter duration). You'll learn to use this feature later in this chapter.
K. Adjustment Layers	Allows you to apply effects to more than one layer at a time. You'll learn to work with adjustment layers in Chapter 10, *"Applying Effects."*
L. 3D Layer	Allows you to specify a 3D layer, which can move in three-dimensional space. You'll learn to work with 3D layers in Chapter 16, *"Working with 3D Layers."*

Tip: If you forget the name of a switch, you can position the cursor over any of the switch icons to see its tool tip.

3 | Using Shy Layers

When you have a composition with a lot of layers, it's sometimes helpful to hide one or more layers in the **Timeline** but leave the artwork visible. This eliminates visual clutter in the **Timeline** when you're trying to focus on setting keyframes. When you mark a layer as shy, you can hide it in the **Timeline** panel until you're ready to display it again. Shy layers are still active in your composition and display normally in the **Composition** panel. They are just hidden from view in the **Timeline** panel so you can concentrate on the task at hand without scrolling up and down in search of the layers needing attention. In this exercise, you'll learn to mark shy layers and to hide or display all shy layers by clicking the **Hide Shy Layers** button.

---

1 Choose **File > Open Project**. Navigate to the **chap_08** folder you copied to your desktop, click **Switches.aep** to select it, and click **Open**. Choose **File > Save As**. In the **Save As** dialog box, navigate to the **AE7_HOT_Projects** folder on your desktop. Name the file **Switches.aep**, and click **Save**.

---

2 In the **Project** panel, double-click the **Switches** composition to open it and its associated **Timeline** panel.

---

3 Press the **spacebar** to preview the animation.

---

4 In the **Timeline** panel, press **Cmd+A** (Mac) or **Ctrl+A** (Windows) to select all the layers. Press the **U** key to reveal all the properties containing keyframes.

In After Effects 7, the letter U is known as the **überkey**. It's a great shortcut key to know about when you want to quickly see what properties have been animated in an unfamiliar (or even a complicated but familiar) composition. However, this causes quite a few layers and properties to open in the Timeline, and once your Timeline gets to this level of complexity, it becomes difficult to focus on an individual layer. Using the shy layers feature, which you'll do in the next steps, will help simplify your Timeline.

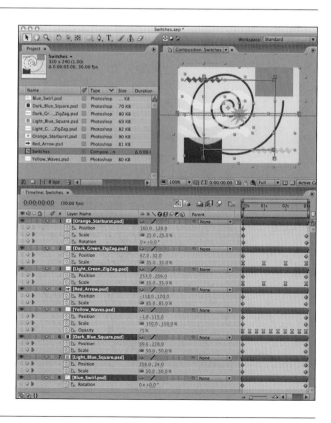

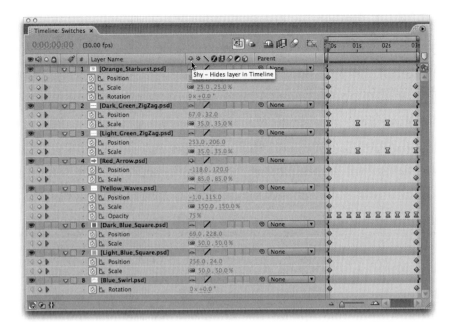

5 Click an empty area of the **Timeline** panel to deselect the layers. Click the **Shy Layers** switch for all the layers except **Layer 4**, **Red_Arrow.psd**.

Nothing noticeable happens in the Timeline or composition yet, except the icons for the Shy Layers change to identify each layer as shy. When a layer is shy, the icon looks flat (as though the guy is hiding), and when a layer isn't shy, it shows a picture of him with his nose peeking out.

---

6 In the **Timeline** panel, click the **Hide Shy Layers** button. Notice the shy layers you created in Step 5 are now hidden in the **Timeline** panel. Click the **Enable Shy Layer** button again so all your layers appear.

Why would you do this? In this example, you might want to set keyframes for the opacity of the Red_Arrow.psd layer and modify or add Position keyframes. To add animation keyframes to it, you might want to isolate it so you aren't distracted by all the other layers in the Timeline panel. Once you've worked on it and set keyframes, you'd want to see all the other layers again, which you could do easily by clicking the Hide Shy Layers button at the top of the Timeline panel. Basically, shy layers offer a way to organize your Timeline when it gets too cluttered with layers and property settings.

---

7 Choose **File > Save**, or press **Cmd+S** (Mac) or **Ctrl+S** (Windows). Leave the **Switches.aep** project and composition open for the next exercise.

You just learned how to use shy layers to organize and manage layers in your composition's Timeline. In the next exercise, you will learn another way to manage layers—using the Solo switch.

4 | Using the Solo Switch

The **Solo** switch provides a quick way to hide certain layers temporarily and to leave selected layers displayed. Unlike shy layers, which remain visible in the **Composition** panel when they're hidden in the **Timeline**, solo layers hide the artwork in the **Composition** panel but leave it visible in the **Timeline** panel. They're opposites: Whereas shy layers can help clear some real estate in the **Timeline** panel, the **Solo** switch can help you quickly focus attention on the contents of a layer (or layers) in the **Composition** panel.

Sometimes it's useful to see a few layers together. Fortunately, despite its name, the **Solo** switch is not limited to displaying just one layer at a time. In this exercise, you will learn to "solo" individual and multiple layers. You'll also learn how to stop soloing layers and return to normal display.

---

1 If you followed the previous exercise, **Switches.aep** should still be open in After Effects 7. If it's not, choose **File > Open Project**. Navigate to the **chap_08** folder on your desktop, click **Solo_Switches.aep** to select it, and click **Open**.

---

2 Click the **Timeline** panel to make it active. Press **Cmd+A** (Mac) or **Ctrl+A** (Windows) to select all the layers. Press the **U** key to hide all the layer properties.

Selecting all layers and pressing the U key is a great technique to quickly collapse your Timeline.

---

3 Click an empty area of the **Timeline** panel to deselect all the layers.

---

4 In the **Timeline** panel, locate the **Solo** column and click the **Solo** switch next to the **Blue_Swirl.psd** layer to solo the layer in the **Composition** panel. Notice the other layers no longer appear.

Why would you want to turn off all the other layers in the Composition panel? You may want to work on this individual layer without the distraction of all the other artwork onscreen.

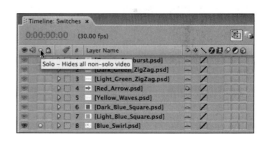

---

5 Click the **Solo** switch next to the **Dark_Green_ZigZag.psd** and **Light_Green_ZigZag.psd** layers.

These layers (Dark_Green_ZigZag.psd and Light_Green_ZigZag.psd) turn on, and the previous solo layer stays on as well.

---

6 Click the **Solo** switch next to **Dark_Green_ZigZag.psd**, and keep pressing your mouse. With the mouse held down, drag straight down the **Solo** switch column to clear all the active **Solo** switches.

Once you've cleared them, the artwork for all the layers will reappear in the Composition panel.

You can turn the Solo switch on or off, meaning you can also click each Solo switch to clear soloing for the corresponding layer.

---

7 Choose **File > Save**, or press **Cmd+S** (Mac) or **Ctrl+S** (Windows). Choose **File > Close Project**.

As you learned, the Solo switch can be useful when you need to focus attention on a small number of layers. In the next exercise, you'll discover the Quality switch. Although this switch won't help you organize your layers, it will help you adjust the quality of your animations as you view them in the Composition panel.

---

5 | Using the Quality Switch

In this exercise, you will learn to use the **Quality** switch, which toggles the quality for artwork on a layer between the **Best** and **Draft** settings for previewing purposes. As a rule, **Best** quality looks better but takes longer to render. **Draft** is the default and is good for speeding up your previews on complex or render-intensive projects.

The **Quality** switch affects pixel-based images such as those originating in Photoshop, also known as **raster** images. If you scale or rotate a pixel-based image, the **Best** setting will improve the quality. This exercise demonstrates when to use the **Best** setting and how to do so.

---

1 Choose **File > New > New Project**. Choose **File > Save As**. In the **Save As** dialog box, navigate to the **AE7_HOT_Projects** folder on your desktop. Name the file **Quality.aep**, and click **Save**.

---

2 Double-click the empty **Project** panel to launch the **Import File** dialog box. Navigate to the **chap_08** folder, and select **Mo.psd**. Make sure **Footage** is selected in the **Import As** pop-up menu, click **Open**, and then click **OK** to accept the merged layers.

The file will appear as footage in the Project panel. This is a Photoshop document, also known as a raster image.

Note this import method brings in a flattened PSD file whereas the method you learned in Exercise 1 brought in a Photoshop file as a composition. It's up to you to know the different importing methods and to choose accordingly, depending on whether you want a flattened footage element or layers imported as separate footage items. In this exercise, a flattened PSD layer is all you need.

---

3 In the **Project** panel, drag **Mo.psd** onto the **Create a new Composition** button.

After Effects 7 automatically names the composition Mo and opens it immediately. This is our favorite way to make a new composition because it always scales to the size of the content and automatically names itself.

In the next step, you will learn how to change the default background color appearing in the Composition panel. Although it's not related to the Quality switch, it can be useful when you want to create a background other than black or when you need a color to make it easier to see what's on the layers above it.

---

4 Choose **Composition > Background Color**. In the **Background Color** dialog box, click the **color swatch** to launch the **color picker**. Change the color from black to yellow, and click **OK**.

You can change the background color of any composition at any time by using the Background Color dialog box. You can also use the eyedropper, rather than the color picker, to select a color already onscreen. The eyedropper technique is helpful when you want to match the background to a color in your animation, keeping the color palette consistent.

---

5 Click the **Quality** switch for the **Mo.psd** layer to change it to **Best** quality if it is not already there (the line will slant up to the right). Continue clicking the switch to toggle between **Best** and **Draft** quality, and then return it to **Draft** quality (slanted up to the left).

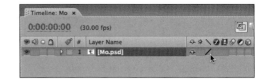

At this point, you shouldn't see a difference between the quality settings. The next steps will show you when and why you would want to change this switch.

---

6 In the **Timeline** panel, select the **Mo.psd** layer, if it's not already selected. Press the **R** key to display the **Rotation** property. Set the **Rotation** value to **15** degrees.

Adding rotation makes the edges of your layer look jagged.

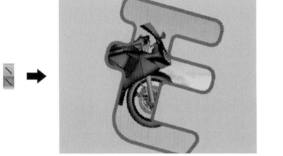 

7 Click the **Quality** switch to set the layer to **Best** quality.

Switching the layer quality to Best removes all the jagged edges.

---

8 Hold down the **Shift** key, and press the **S** key to open the **Scale** property while leaving the **Rotation** property visible. Change **Scale** to **50%**, and click the **Quality** switch repeatedly to compare the settings.

You'll see what a big difference Best quality makes when the Scale or Rotation property changes.

---

162 Adobe After Effects 7 : H·O·T

9 Change the **Scale** property to **200%**, and click the **Quality** switch to set the layer to **Best**.

The Best quality setting makes the image look much better. Note, however, that whenever you scale a raster image larger than its original size, the image will look a little out of focus. It's always best to prepare your Photoshop artwork bigger than what you will need if you plan to animate the Scale property. The Best quality setting helps improve the appearance, but it can't totally compensate for a raster image scaled larger than 100 percent.

In summary, the Quality switch will make a difference to your source footage only if the footage is scaled or rotated. Many After Effects 7 artists leave the Quality switch set to Draft mode to speed up rendering. When you make a final movie (which you'll learn to do in Chapter 20, *"Rendering Final Movies"*), you can set the overall Quality setting in the Render Queue to Best and override the switch setting so your movie will look the best it can. Otherwise, you can set the Quality switch to Best occasionally to check the quality but leave it set to Draft otherwise to allow you to work faster.

---

10 Choose **File > Save**, or press **Cmd+S** (Mac) or **Ctrl+S** (Windows). Leave **Quality.aep** open for the next exercise.

In this exercise, you learned how the Quality switch in the Timeline panel affects what you see in the Composition panel. You will continue to explore the Quality switch in the next exercise, along with the Continuous Rasterization switch. Whereas the Quality switch is best for raster images (such as Photoshop documents), the Continuous Rasterization switch is best for Illustrator files, or vector-image formats, as you'll see in the next exercise.

Understanding the Quality Switch Versus Continuous Rasterization

Vector images, such as the type created by Illustrator, are mathematical descriptions of curves, lines, and colors; they do not consist of pixels. When After Effects 7 displays vector images in the **Composition** panel, it converts the display of the vector information to pixels. The **Quality** switch determines whether the vector image appears in **Draft** or **Best** quality. The difference between the two settings is quite noticeable when working with vector images.

As you learned in the previous exercise, if you scale an image larger than 100 percent, the **Best** quality setting will improve its appearance, but the image will still look out of focus. If you are working with raster images, you can't get around this problem except to remake your artwork larger than the composition size so you won't have to scale it larger than 100 percent in After Effects 7.

With vector images, however, this problem has a solution: It's called **Continuous Rasterization**. The **Continuous Rasterization** switch appears next to the **Quality** switch, and it allows vector artwork to scale to any size and always look perfectly crisp. You'll gain working knowledge of this important feature in this exercise.

---

1 If you followed the previous exercise, **Quality.aep** should still be open in After Effects 7. If it's not, choose **File > Open Project**. Navigate to the **chap_08** folder you copied to your desktop, click **Quality_Switch_2.aep** to select it, and click **Open**. Choose **File > Save As**. In the **Save As** dialog box, navigate to the **AE7_HOT_Projects** folder on your desktop. Name the file **Quality_Switch_2.aep**, and click **Save**.

---

2 Choose **File > Import > File**. Navigate to the **chap_08** folder, click **Palm_Tree_Vector.ai** to select it, and click **Open**. Click **OK** to accept the merged layers for the Illustrator layers as you did with the PSD artwork.

---

3 In the **Project** panel, drag **Palm_Tree_Vector.ai** onto the **Create a new Composition** button.

This automatically makes the comp size match the artwork and names the composition Palm_Tree_Vector. At this point, you should know how to do this without a lot of instruction. If you don't, please revisit the previous exercise. If your Composition panel isn't large enough, you may have to resize it to see the entire graphic.

4 In the **Timeline** panel, click the **Quality** switch next to the **Palm_Tree_Vector.ai** layer to change it from **Draft** to **Best**, causing the tree to look crisp.

5 Press the **S** key to open the Scale property and change the scale of the tree to **300%**, causing the tree to look blurry.

6 Click the **Continuous Rasterization** switch to improve the quality of the vector image.

The Continuous Rasterization switch is available only for vector-based footage items. If you reopen the Mo composition you made previously, you'll see this switch is missing for raster images. The Continuous Rasterization

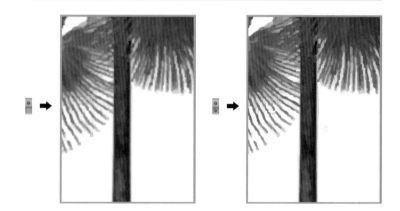

switch will cause a vector image to look pristine at any Scale or Rotation setting. It does slow down previews and your work, however. You can test this by creating an animation in this composition using different Scale settings on different keyframes and clicking the Continuous Rasterization switch. If you preview your animation, you'll see it takes a bit longer to render with Continuous Rasterization in effect. For this reason, most After Effects 7 artists use the Continuous Rasterization switch sparingly or until they render the composition to a final movie.

7 Choose **File > Save**, or press **Cmd+S** (Mac) or **Ctrl+S** (Windows). Choose **File > Close Project**.

Now that you are familiar with both the Quality and Continuous Rasterization switches in After Effects 7, you will learn about motion blur and how to activate it for layers in a composition.

Introducing Motion Blur

Cameras have shutters that expose film to light. When the shutter is open, the image is recorded onto film. When you use your snapshot camera, the clicking sound you hear while taking a picture is the sound of the shutter opening and closing. The shorter the time the shutter is open, the less motion is recorded on the film image. The longer the shutter is open, the more motion is recorded on the film image.

If an object is in motion when it is photographed, any recorded motion will display as a blur. This is called **motion blur**. For example, if you take a picture of someone on a bicycle speeding past you on the street, the photograph may be blurred if the camera shutter is open long enough to record the motion. In the images shown in the illustration here, the motorcycle on the left shows no motion blur, and the motorcycle on the right has some motion blur.

In motion-picture photography, motion blur is useful and often desirable. In everyday life, we don't see the world as individual snapshots; we see continuous motion. Fast-moving objects are naturally blurred to our eyes. When a series of images is projected in a movie theater, fast-moving action appears natural to our eyes because motion blur caught by the camera helps blend images and produce the perception of smooth action. Including motion blur can produce a natural feel to animation created in After Effects 7.

After Effects 7 offers a useful tool, motion blur, for smoothing motion, as you'll see in the next exercise.

7 | Applying Motion Blur

You can use the **Motion Blur** switch to make quick movements in your animations look more realistic. For example, if your animation has a motorcycle driving through the scene, motion blur will add a natural blurred look to the vehicle as it passes through the composition, simulating the properties of a film camera. After Effects 7 makes it easy to apply motion blur. In this exercise, you will learn to use the **Motion Blur** switch and the **Enable Motion Blur** button.

---

1 Open **Motion_Blur.aep** from the **chap_08** folder you copied to your desktop. Choose **File > Save As**. In the **Save As** dialog box, navigate to the **AE7_HOT_Projects** folder on your desktop. Name the file **Motion_Blur.aep**, and click **Save**.

---

2 In the **Project** panel, double-click the **Motorcycle** composition. Drag the **CTI** to scrub the **Timeline** so you can see how the motion looks before you apply motion blur. Drag the **CTI** back to the beginning frame of the **Timeline** by dragging it or pressing the **Home** key.

---

3 In the **Timeline** panel, locate the **Motorcycle.psd** layer, and then locate the column for the **Motion Blur** switches. Click the **Motion Blur** switch to turn on motion blur for the **Motorcycle.psd** layer.

You won't notice any change in the composition yet.

---

4 At the top of the **Timeline** panel, locate the group of buttons to the left of the **CTI**. Click **Enable Motion Blur** for all the layers with the **Motion Blur** switch turned on.

In the Composition panel, this applies motion blur to the motorcycle image, which you will see if you move to a later frame in the Timeline.

Why are there two settings, the Enable Motion Blur button and the Motion Blur switch? Motion blur is render intensive. Lots of people set it up and then turn it off while they're working to get speedier previews. It's nice to have a local switch on the layer and a master switch for the entire composition.

---

5 Drag the current **CTI** to **Frame 0:00:00:25**. Repeatedly click the **Motion Blur** switch for the **Motorcycle.psd** layer to turn the motion blur off and on.

Note: In After Effects 7, the Motion Blur switch is intelligent. It applies more motion blur to objects moving faster.

6 With the **Motion Blur** switch still on, click **RAM Preview** in the **Time Controls** panel to view your animation.

You'll probably notice your animation takes longer to render than it did before you added motion blur. As stated, motion blur is render intensive, but it looks great on many projects.

---

7 Choose **File > Save**, or press **Cmd+S** (Mac) or **Ctrl+S** (Windows). Choose **File > Close Project**.

In the previous few exercises, you worked with the different layer switches to change the quality, rasterization, and motion blur for layers. In the following sections, you will learn how to influence the position and duration of specific layers in your Timeline, which you can set independently from the overall settings for your compositions.

TIP:

Adding Motion Blur and Rendering

Motion blur slows down rendering to the screen. When you are designing a composition, it's generally best to apply motion blur only when you want to check the effect it has on the image. To speed your workflow, turn on all the layers that will need motion blur and then turn on or off motion blur with the **Enable Motion Blur** button.

Moving and Trimming Time in Layers

You can control two basic items when working with layer time. First, you can define where a layer starts in your composition, and second, you can control how many frames on a layer are actually displayed. This provides you with a great deal of control over the timing of your animation, particularly when working with multiple layers in a composition.

When you import footage and add it to your composition, by default the new layer starts on the first frame of the **Timeline**. Of course, you'll often need to change where the layer starts, which you can accomplish by sliding the layer duration bar to the right or left in the **Timeline**. This is called **moving** a layer.

The layer added to your composition has a default frame length, as well. Sometimes you'll need to shorten the length of a layer. This is known as **trimming** a layer.

In the illustration shown here, the top layer has been moved, and the second layer has been trimmed. Observe that the moved layer (the top one) has an **In** point handle, but the

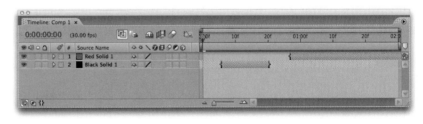

Out point handle is offscreen in the **Timeline** panel. You can move a layer in time to the right or the left. Notice the trimmed layer (the bottom one) has a lighter bar to its left and right. That is a visual cue a layer has been trimmed. It indicates you can pull the handles out to their original durations.

After Effects 7 provides several means to accomplish these two essential tasks. You'll learn some new tricks and shortcuts as you work through the next exercises.

8 | Working with In and Out Points for Layers

In this exercise, you will first learn to move the point at which a layer starts and stops in the **Timeline**, creating the appearance of a **cut**, which is familiar to anyone who has edited film or video. The starting point is called the **In** point, and the stopping point is called the **Out** point. You'll learn to drag a layer in the **Timeline** to change the **In** and **Out** points.

---

1 Choose **File > New > New Project**. Choose **File > Save As**. In the **Save As** dialog box, navigate to the **AE7_HOT_Projects** folder on your desktop. Name the file **In_Out_Points.aep**, and click **Save**.

---

2 Double-click an empty area of the **Project** panel to open the **Import File** dialog box. Navigate to the **chap_08** folder you copied to your desktop. Click **Sky.mov** to select it. Hold down **Cmd** (Mac) or **Ctrl** (Windows), and click **Sky_Text_1.psd** and **Sky_Text_2.psd** to multiple-select the Photoshop files. Click **Open**, and then click **OK** to accept the merged layers for the Photoshop layers as you import the PSD items.

---

3 In the **Project** panel, drag **Sky.mov** onto the **Create a new Composition** button.

This creates a new composition with the same settings (and name) as the movie. Notice the Composition and Timeline panels both open in the process and the layer Sky.mov exists in the Timeline, without having to drag it there separately.

This is a great technique for making a new composition if you have movie footage and you want the composition to be the same length in both frames and the same frame rate as the movie file. If you want to check out the composition settings, choose Composition > Composition Settings. You'll see the settings may be different from other compositions you've made. The composition got all these settings automatically from the movie footage.

---

4 In the **Project** panel, drag **Sky_Text_1.psd** to the **Timeline** panel. Make sure to place it above the **Sky.mov** layer. Press the **spacebar** to watch the composition. Notice the **Sky_Text_1.psd** artwork is visible over the movie footage in the **Composition** panel.

We created this artwork in Photoshop and saved it in a transparent layer. The areas transparent in Photoshop are also transparent in After Effects 7. Also notice the movie footage has an abrupt cut midway through, and a different moving cloud image appears. This abrupt change is built into the movie footage. In the following steps, you'll add a different title to begin when this new footage appears.

5 In the **Timeline** panel, scrub the **CTI** to where the abrupt sky change occurs in the movie (**0:00:02:03**). Pull the right handle of the **Sky_Text_1.psd** layer to the left to match the **CTI** position, as shown in the illustration here. Press the **spacebar** to watch the composition.

You have just adjusted this layer's Out point, trimming the number of frames of footage in this layer. Notice the lettering disappears at the same point as the abrupt change in the movie footage. Observe the lighter bar to the right of the Out point in the Sky_Text_1.psd layer. This means you could drag the handle back to the right, and the footage would reappear all the way to the end of that bar.

---

6 Make sure the **CTI** is still at **Frame 0:00:02:03**.

An alternative to moving the CTI to a specific frame is to press Cmd+G (Mac) or Ctrl+G (Windows). In the Go To Time dialog box, type a number.

Hint: You can easily see what frame the CTI is on by looking at the readout in the upper-left corner of the Timeline panel.

7 Drag **Sky_Text_2.psd** to the **Timeline** panel, and make sure it is the top layer. Notice it appears in the **Timeline** panel at the same position as the **CTI**.

After Effects 7 sets the In point of any footage item in the Timeline to the same position as the CTI when you import the footage using the Project panel. If you accidentally import footage at the wrong In point, you can always slide the layer's duration bar to the right or left to make a change.

Creating Layers at the Composition Start Time

If your layer's **In** points appear at the beginning of your **Timeline** and not at the **CTI** position, you must make a small change to your **Preferences** in After Effects 7. Choose **After Effects > Preferences > General** (Mac) or **Edit > Preferences > General** (Windows), and turn off the **Create Layers at Composition Start Time** check box (if it is currently on).

In previous versions, After Effects always set the **In** point of any footage item in the **Timeline** to the same position as the **CTI** when you imported the footage using the **Project** panel. In After Effects 7, you have the option of setting the **In** point for all layers to automatically begin at the beginning of the **Timeline**, which is the same as the composition start time. With this check box turned on, any layers you drag from the **Project** panel automatically start on the first frame of the **Timeline** panel instead. For the exercises in this book, make sure this check box is turned off so that (when dragging from the **Project** panel) all your layers begin at the **CTI** location.

8 Press the **spacebar** to preview the movie. Notice where each layer begins and ends.

---

9 Choose **File > Save**, or press **Cmd+S** (Mac) or **Ctrl+S** (Windows). Choose **File > Close Project**.

In this exercise, you successfully trimmed a layer and set the In point of another. These are useful features to understand. You'll be adding to your knowledge of layers in the following exercises, including using keyboard commands to help you trim layers more efficiently.

EXERCISE

9 | Using Keyboard Methods for Trimming Layers

Trimming is a useful method for shortening a layer within the composition. For example, you can trim a graphic layer (such as a title) if you want it to appear only for a short time in a longer composition. You can trim an **Out** point or an **In** point in After Effects 7. With trimming, you can always change your mind and modify the **In** or **Out** point for a layer at any time.

The difference between moving and trimming footage is that when you move footage, you don't change its physical length in the **Timeline**; you just move it to a different location. With trimming, you can shave off time from the beginning or end of a layer. You trimmed footage in the previous exercise by using the layer handles. In this exercise, you'll learn to trim footage using the **CTI** and bracket keys, which is often a quicker and more precise way to trim layers in the **Timeline**.

---

1 Choose **File > Open Project**. Navigate to the **chap_08** folder you copied to your desktop, click **Trimming.aep** to select it, and click **Open**. Choose **File > Save As**. In the **Save As** dialog box, navigate to the **AE7_HOT_Projects** folder on your desktop. Name the file **Trimming.aep**, and click **Save**.

2 In the **Project** panel, double-click the **Traffic_Light** composition to open the composition and its associated **Timeline** panel.

---

3 In the **Timeline** panel, click the **Expand or Collapse the In/Out/Duration Stretch panes** button.

Alternatively, you can click the Options menu in the upper-right corner of the Timeline panel (the small arrow icon), choose Columns > In, and then repeat the process but choose Columns > Out.

This causes the In and Out panels to appear in your Timeline panel. These panels are not necessary for performing trimming functions, but they give you numeric feedback about where your footage starts and ends. To hide these panels, repeat the process. Leave them displayed for now.

In the Composition panel, notice the images. They don't move at all, even though they are in the Timeline for 4 full seconds. You'll make the lights turn off and on over time by using trimming methods.

---

4 Drag the right layer handle for the **Red_Light.psd** layer, and set the **Out** point to **Frame 0:00:01:00**. Use the **Out** panel (the column labeled **Out** on the left side of the **Timeline** panel) as a frame reference as you drag the layer handle to trim this layer.

5 Drag the right layer handle for the **Yellow_Light.psd** layer, and set the **Out** point to **Frame 0:00:01:12**.

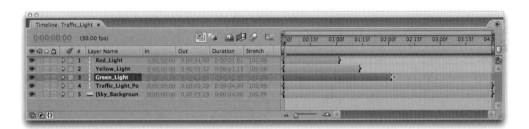

6 Drag the right layer handle for the **Green_Light.psd** layer, and set the **Out** point to **Frame 0:00:02:00**.

7 Select the **Traffic_Light_Post.psd** layer. Drag the **CTI** to **Frame 0:00:02:15**. Alternatively, press **Cmd+G** (Mac) or **Ctrl+G** (Windows), and type the timecode.

8 Press **Opt+]** (Mac) or **Alt+]** (Windows). Notice the **Out** point is trimmed to the current **CTI** position.

This is the keyboard shortcut to trim the Out point of any layer, based on the location of the CTI. You'll use this shortcut frequently to make changes to a layer's Out point.

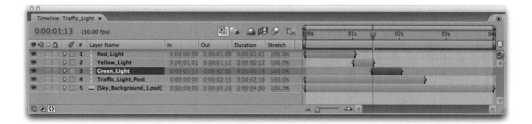

9 In the **Timeline** panel, click an empty area to deselect the **Traffic_Light_Post.psd** layer. Select the **Yellow_Light** layer. Set the **CTI** to **Frame 0:00:01:01**. Press **Opt+[** (Mac) or **Alt+[** (Windows).

This keyboard shortcut trims the In point of any selected layer, based on the location of the CTI. You'll use this shortcut frequently to make changes to a layer's In point.

The In points of the selected layers are trimmed to the current CTI position. These keyboard shortcuts are also the quickest way to trim multiple layers to the same In or Out point.

---

10 Select the **Green_Light** layer to select it. Set the **CTI** to **Frame 0:00:01:13**. Press **Opt+[** (Mac) or **Alt+[** (Windows).

---

11 Press the **spacebar** to watch your animation play, and notice how the lights appear to change as a result of setting **In** and **Out** points for each layer.

---

12 Choose **File > Save**, or press **Cmd+S** (Mac) or **Ctrl+S** (Windows). Choose **File > Close Project**.

In this exercise, you learned how to manually set In and Out points for a series of layers, Next, you'll learn about an interesting technique called **splitting layers**, which assists you in setting In and Out points while also separating a layer into two parts for specialized animation purposes.

NOTE: | **Using In and Out Panels**

You can type values in the **In** and **Out** panels, and your footage will move to the frame position you type. You cannot use the **In** or **Out** panels in the **Timeline** panel to trim footage. Although they will display the current trimmed points, the **In** and **Out** panels are useful only for moving layers or for displaying the numeric **In** and **Out** point frame values of footage.

Using the Bracket Keys

The left and right bracket keys are important in After Effects 7. You can use them to move layers, change the stacking order, and trim layers. The following chart summarizes the different types of bracket key commands:

Bracket Key Commands			
Command type	Command	Mac	Windows
Move	Move In point to Current Time Indicator	[	[
Move	Move Out point to Current Time Indicator	]	]
Stacking order	Bring forward	Cmd+]	Ctrl+]
Stacking order	Send backward	Cmd+[	Ctrl+[
Stacking order	Bring to front	Cmd+Shift+]	Ctrl+Shift+]
Stacking order	Send to back	Cmd+Shift+[	Ctrl+Shift+[
Trim	Trim In point to Current Time Indicator	Opt+[	Alt+[
Trim	Trim Out point to Current Time Indicator	Opt+]	Alt+]

10 | Splitting Layers

Most of the time when you drag a footage item into your composition, you want that footage to be used as a single layer in your composition. Sometimes, however, that isn't the case. For example, let's say you want an item to travel in front of a layer and then behind the same layer. You might, for instance, want a car to drive in front of a tree in one part of your animation and then behind the tree in another. The long way to do this would be to duplicate the car layer, put it above and below the tree layer, and trim its **In** and **Out** points correctly.

After Effects 7 offers a much simpler way of dealing with such a situation: You can **split** a layer. When you split a layer, you cut the layer into two pieces. The two pieces contain all the properties originally included on the single layer. Each piece is actually an entire layer placed in your **Timeline** panel and trimmed automatically according to the **CTI** position. This is a real time-saver. In this exercise, you'll learn how to split a layer and learn when you'll want to do so.

---

1 Choose **File > Open Project**. Navigate to the **chap_08** folder you copied to your desktop, click **Split_Layer.aep** to select it, and click **Open**. Choose **File > Save As**. In the **Save As** dialog box, navigate to the **AE7_HOT_Projects** folder on your desktop. Name the file **Split_Layer.aep**, and click **Save**.

---

2 In the **Project** panel, double-click the **Split_Layer** composition to open it and its associated **Timeline** panel. Press the **spacebar** to preview the animation.

Notice the text goes behind the tree twice. This is appropriate for the first half of the movie. However, the text should go in front of the tree during the second half of the movie. You'll learn how to split the layer to achieve this effect.

---

3 In the **Timeline** panel, set the **CTI** to **Frame 0:00:01:20**, and select the **Test_Drive.psd** layer.

You chose this frame because it is the first frame in which you want the text to appear in front of the tree, instead of behind the tree.

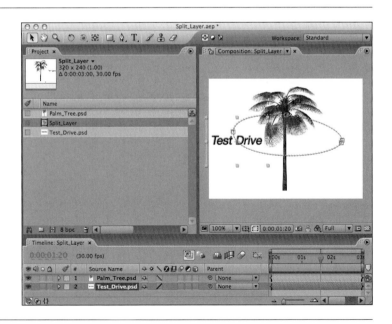

4 Choose **Edit > Split Layer**.

After the split, your Timeline panel looks like the one shown in the illustration here. Notice After Effects 7 automatically duplicated the layer and set its In and Out points to line up exactly in the frame at which you specified the layer to be split.

5 Drag the second half of the split **Test_Drive.psd** layer above the **Palm_Tree.psd** layer.

Remember, the stacking order of your layers determines which layers are visible as they pass in front of or behind other layers. Because you want the top Test_Drive.psd layer to appear in front of the tree, you need to place it above Palm_Tree.psd in the Timeline.

6 Press the **spacebar** to preview the results of your split layer animation.

Using split layers is much easier and less painful than duplicating and trimming manually.

7 Choose **File > Save**, or press **Cmd+S** (Mac) or **Ctrl+S** (Windows). Choose **File > Close Project**.

Splitting layers is a great way to automatically duplicate and trim layers so you can use them in the correct order in your Timeline. In the next exercise, you will use a new technique allowing you to stretch layers in time, rather than trimming them to make them shorter.

EXERCISE

11 | Stretching Time and Blending Frames

You've learned how to trim (shorten) layers, but what about stretching layers? After Effects 7 is capable of not only adjusting the **In** and **Out** points of layers but also is able to slow down or speed up time within a layer to adjust its duration, which is known as **stretching**. The ability to adjust the timing, or speed, of a clip allows you to make a fast clip slower or a slow clip faster—whatever your project requires. This exercise shows you how to define, set, and adjust the duration of layers.

---

1 Open **Time_Stretch.aep** from the **chap_08** folder you copied to your desktop. Choose **File > Save As**. In the **Save As** dialog box, navigate to the **AE7_HOT_Projects** folder on your desktop. Name the file **Time_Stretch.aep**, and click **Save**.

This project contains two footage items: an Apple QuickTime movie and a Photoshop document.

---

2 Choose **Composition > New Composition**, or press **Cmd+N** (Mac) or **Ctrl+N** (Windows) to start a new composition. Set its duration to **1** second long. Change your composition settings to match those shown in the illustration here. Name the composition **Short**.

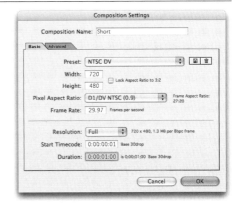

3 Drag the two footage items to this **Timeline** panel. Make sure **Speed_Title.psd** is above **Road.mov** in the **Timeline** panel. Play the composition by pressing the **spacebar**.

Notice the Photoshop layer stops at Frame 0:00:01:00, and the movie footage item that extends beyond the Timeline seems to get cut off by the short length of the composition. That's because a still footage item, such as a Photoshop or Illustrator document, scales automatically to

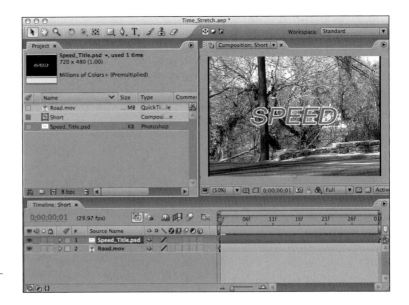

178 | Adobe After Effects 7 : H•O•T

the duration of the composition into which it is inserted. The movie footage has a fixed time associated with it. You can change the length of the composition to fit the movie, or you can change the duration of the movie to fit the length of the composition. You'll learn to do both in this exercise.

4 Select the layer **Road.mov**. Choose **Layer > Time > Time Stretch**.

This opens the Time Stretch dialog box, which makes it possible to alter the duration of the movie.

5 In the **Time Stretch** dialog box, type **0:00:01:00** for **New Duration**, and click **OK**. Press the **spacebar** to preview your video.

You will see the Road.mov footage is now only 1 second long in the Timeline. If you play the composition by pressing the space-bar, you'll see the panning action in the video is quite a bit faster now. That's because After Effects 7 has compressed the footage to span a much shorter duration.

How did After Effects 7 do it? It divided the original length by the requested length and temporarily discarded the unnecessary frames. In this case, you used Time Stretch to shorten the dura-tion of the layer. It might not seem like the terms *stretch* and *time stretch* should be appropriate, but you can use the time-stretching feature to reduce as well as stretch. You'll try both operations in the next few exercises.

You can stretch or reduce the duration of footage based on the frame values or percentage values you type. Hold In Place means After Effects 7 will stretch or reduce the duration of the footage to make sure the In point is preserved, the Out point is preserved, or the current CTI position (Current Frame) is pre-served, depending on the option you choose.

6 Choose **Composition > Composition Settings** to change the length of the composition. In the **Composition Settings** dialog box, type **0:00:10:00** for **Duration**, and click **OK**.

This lengthens the composition to 10 seconds.

7 At the top of the **Timeline** panel, drag the **Time Navigator** handle to the right to reveal all 10 seconds in the **Timeline**.

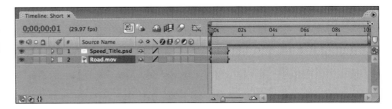

You can always zoom in and out on your Timeline by using this handle (try stretching it back and forth to try it). Notice the two layers are much shorter than the length of the Timeline. That's because the layers were automatically set to the original duration of the length of the original composition. Now that you've changed the composition's duration, these layers no longer fit to size.

---

8 Drag the right layer handle for **Speed_Title.psd** to the end of the Timeline (the entire length of the composition) to change its **Out** point.

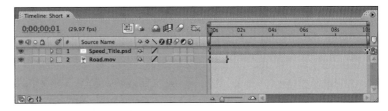

If you pressed the spacebar to preview the composition, you'd see the title now extends much longer than the movie. The PSD layer has a movable handle, but the Road.mov layer does not. That's because movie footage has to be time-stretched to change its duration. Still footage is always a lot more flexible than movie footage.

---

9 Select the **Road.mov** layer, and choose **Layer > Time > Time Stretch**. Type **0:00:10:00** for **Duration**, and click **OK**. Press the **spacebar** to view the animation.

Now the panning motion is very, very slow because of the time stretching. How is After Effects 7 achieving this? It's repeating frames. Most of the frames are being repeated at least two times. After Effects 7 has a solution for smoothing the motion between frames, called **frame blending**, and you'll get to try it in the next step.

---

10 In the **Timeline** panel, click the **Frame Blend** switch for the **Road.mov** layer in the **Timeline** once to set it to **Frame Mix** (simply speaking, **Draft** quality), and then click

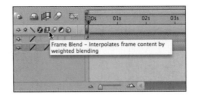 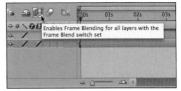

the **Enable Frame Blending** button at the top of the **Timeline** panel. If necessary, set the general **Quality** switch to **Best** by clicking it a second time. Click the **RAM Preview** button in the **Time Controls** panel to preview your animation with smooth, frame-blended motion.

You'll see After Effects 7 has created soft opacity transitions between the held frames using the Frame Blend switch. If you click the Frame Blend switch twice, you will set frame blending to Pixel Motion, or

Best quality, which takes longer to render, although it's preferable when outputting a finished movie. The Quality switch also affects frame blending and should be set to Best (rather than Draft) when you want to see the best results. You'll have to wait longer for your movie to render, but it is worth the extra time.

NOTE:

Using Frame Mix and Pixel Motion Frame Blending

Anytime you apply frame blending to a footage layer, you have a choice of blending types: **Frame Mix** or **Pixel Motion**. You can set the frame-blending type by selecting them from the **Layer** menu (**Layer > Frame Blending**). Alternatively, you can click the **Frame Blend** switch in the **Timeline** panel to toggle among **Off**, **Frame Mix**, and **Pixel Motion**.

Frame Mix is the simplest and least render-intensive frame-blending option. It is essentially a lower, draft-quality setting good for previewing and reducing render times. **Pixel Motion**, on the other hand, provides better results (especially for sloweddown footage), but it takes longer to render. Basically, **Pixel Motion** analyzes the movement of pixels from frame to frame, using this information to create new, highly accurate, in-between frames resulting in smooth motion. Both options are acceptable for finished movies, although **Pixel Motion** is the best choice for maximum quality.

11 Press the **spacebar** to watch the final results. Click the **Frame Blend** switch, and click the **Enable Frame Blending** button. Watch the movie again.

The frame-blending feature makes time-stretched footage look significantly better.

You can set up frame blending with the switch, but click the Enable Frame Blending button to speed up rendering while you're working on your project.

Note: Frame blending works only on moving footage. It has no effect on still frames.

12 Choose **File > Save**, or press **Cmd+S** (Mac) or **Ctrl+S** (Windows). Choose **File > Close Project**.

In this exercise, you learned to use the time-stretching and frame-blending techniques, which affect the temporal (time-based) motion properties of your video. The next exercise covers a related technique called **time remapping**, which is great when you need to create variable speed effects.

NOTE:

Using Timewarp Instead of Time Stretch

If you are working with the Professional edition of After Effects 7, you may have noticed a new effect called **Timewarp**, which is a special-effects filter allowing you to apply extremely smooth speed changes to your footage with the maximum amount of control over the speed-up or slow-down process. (We discuss effects in Chapter 10, "*Applying Effects.*") To apply **Timewarp**, you simply select your footage layer, choose **Effect > Time > Timewarp**, and in the **Effect Controls** panel, adjust settings for **Speed**. You'll practice adding a **Timewarp** effect in Exercise 13.

12 | Using the Time Remapping Feature

Time remapping lets you change the way After Effects 7 interprets time for a live-action movie. For example, you can use time remapping to create a variable speed effect, starting with footage at normal speed that gradually slows down and then speeds up again. You might also use time remapping to reverse the speed of footage to play it backward. In this exercise, you'll use the same panning road footage you worked with in the previous exercise to see how time remapping lets you speed up and reverse the footage layer over time.

1 Choose **File > New > New Project**. Choose **File > Save As**. In the **Save As** dialog box, navigate to the **AE7_HOT_Projects** folder on your desktop. Name the file **Time_Remapping.aep**, and click **Save**.

2 Double-click an empty area of the **Project** panel to open the **Import File** dialog box. Navigate to the **chap_08** folder you copied to your desktop, click **Road.mov** to select it, and click **Open**. After you've imported the **Road.mov** file, in the **Project** panel, drag this footage onto the **Create a new Composition** button.

This creates a composition with the right length and frame rate. After Effects 7 automatically names the composition Road and opens the Timeline and Composition panels. Whenever we work with live action in a project, we usually like to create the composition using this technique because of all the behind-the-scenes work After Effects 7 does automatically.

3 In the **Timeline** panel, select the **Road.mov** layer. Choose **Layer > Time > Enable Time Remapping**.

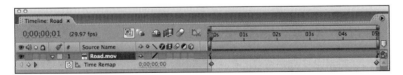

A Time Remap property, which allows you to shift between constant and variable speeds for a layer (expanding, contracting, or holding the layer duration), appears for the Road.mov layer. Your screen should look like the one shown in the illustration here. Notice start and end keyframes have been set and the stopwatch icon is active. This happens automatically when you choose the Enable Time Remapping option.

4 Next to the **Time Remap** property, click the **Include this property in the graph editor set** button. At the top of the **Timeline** panel, click the **Graph Editor** button.

The Time Remap property shows a graph, called the Time Remap graph, represented in the Graph Editor. The line represents the length of the layer. The value graph shows a gradual incline, which means the movie footage plays at the expected speed. You will add keyframes to this graph to change the playback speed.

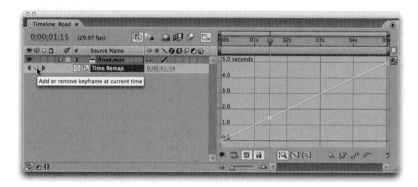

5 Drag the **CTI** to **0:00:01:15**, and turn on the **Add or remove keyframe at current time** check box.

Turning on this check box inserts a keyframe at this frame. Nothing else happens yet.

Once you've placed a keyframe at 0:00:01:15, you'll see a keyframe handle (represented by a yellow dot) appear on the graph in the Graph Editor at that frame.

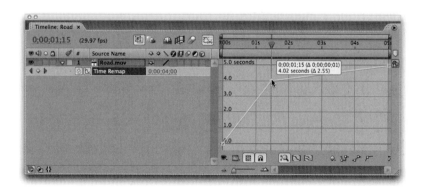

6 Drag the keyframe handle to the point shown in the illustration here (approximately **4** seconds).

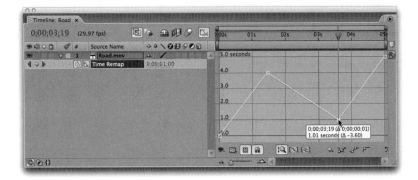

7 Drag the **CTI** to **0:00:03:19**, and turn on the **Add or remove keyframe at current time** check box to add another keyframe. On the new keyframe, move the graph to the point in the illustration shown here (approximately **1** second).

By reversing the direction of the graph and making it point downward, the playback of your footage will reverse at this point in time.

---

8 Press the **Home** key, or drag the **CTI** to the beginning of the **Timeline** manually. Press the **spacebar** to preview the animation.

The time of this movie speeds up, then reverses, then slows down, and finally reverses again. That's what time mapping does—allows you to play with, or remap, time! Feel free to add more keyframes and move the graph to new places.

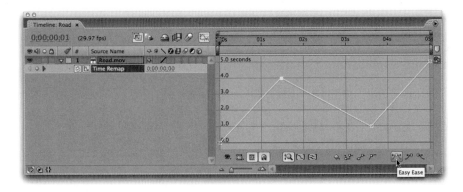

9 In the **Graph Editor**, click the keyframe handle at **0:00:01:15** to select it. With the keyframe selected, click the **Easy Ease** button.

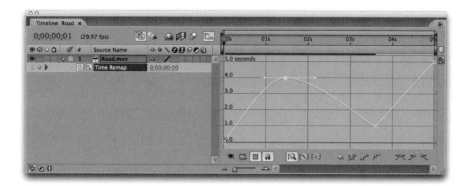

Easy Ease applies both an Ease Out and an Ease In to your keyframe animation, which smoothes the motion into and out of the selected keyframes. Notice the curved shape of your graph in the Graph Editor now.

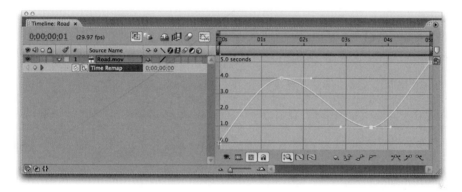

10 In the **Graph Editor**, click the keyframe handle at **0:00:03:19** to select it. With the keyframe selected, click the **Easy Ease** button.

With Easy Ease applied to both your keyframe points in the graph, you should see two smooth curves, indicating a gradual change in speed at those positions in time.

11 Press the **Home** key, or drag the **CTI** to the beginning of the **Timeline**. Press the **spacebar** to preview the animation.

When you play the animation this time, you should notice a more gradual change in speed when the footage reverses and speeds up again. This is the result of those smoothed keyframes created using Easy Ease. The difference between using Easy Ease and not using it is often quite dramatic.

Understanding the Time Remap Graph

You might be wondering what kinds of results you can get by making changes to the **Time Remap** graph. Here are some visual examples to help you.

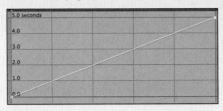

This Time Remap graph will play at a constant speed.

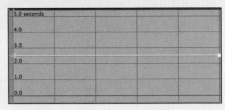

This Time Remap graph will freeze the motion in a frame.

This Time Remap graph, with a steep incline, will play faster than normal speed at the beginning.

This Time Remap graph will play in reverse.

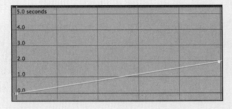

This Time Remap graph will play slower than normal speed.

The illustration shown here puts these graphs into practice. The steep incline at the beginning of this graph will speed up the footage. The decline in the graph will cause the footage to play in reverse. The flat portion in the middle of the graph will cause the movie to freeze. The gradual incline at the end will cause it to play at a constant speed again.

12 Choose **File > Save**, or press **Cmd+S** (Mac) or **Ctrl+S** (Windows). Choose **File > Close Project**.

Time remapping can be a lot of fun and worth some experimentation. Try following the steps in this exercise using your own footage to see what kinds of speed changes you can come up with on your own.

13 | Applying a Timewarp Effect

Although it does not have anything specifically to do with layers, the **Timewarp** effect (which is designed to produce professional results when speeding up or slowing down a layer) is another way to achieve changes in speed for your footage. Although you'll learn more about using effects in Chapter 10, *"Applying Effects,"* this exercise will show you how you can use them within the context of speed changes. For most of your speed change needs, you will probably use the basic time-remapping features outlined in the previous exercise. For those projects with more demanding time alteration requirements, you might also opt for using the **Timewarp** effect, where you can adjust parameters other than simply slowing down or speeding up footage at different rates.

To use the **Timewarp** effect, you will need the Professional edition of After Effects 7. This exercise is optional; we have included it to let you know about a new way to achieve speed changes in After Effects 7. It will also demonstrate some of the differences between using **Timewarp** rather than using the time-stretching and time-remapping features discussed previously in this chapter.

---

1 Choose **File > New > New Project**. Choose **File > Save As**. In the **Save As** dialog box, navigate to the **AE7_HOT_Projects** folder on your desktop. Name the file **Timewarp.aep**, and click **Save**.

---

2 Double-click an empty area of the **Project** panel to open the **Import File** dialog box. Navigate to the **chap_08** folder you copied to your desktop, click **Road.mov** to select it, and click **Open**.

---

3 In the **Project** panel, drag the **Road.mov** footage onto the **Create a new Composition** button. Press the **spacebar** to preview the animation.

---

4 In the **Timeline** panel, select the **Road.mov** layer, and choose **Effect > Time > Timewarp**.

The Effect Controls panel appears automatically, docked in the same frame as the Project panel (its default position in the Standard workspace layout), with the Timewarp parameters visible. Whenever you apply an effect in After Effects 7, you will use either the Effect Controls panel shown in the illustration here or the effect properties in the Timeline panel to adjust any effects you have applied. You'll learn more about using and modifying effects in Chapter 10, *"Applying Effects."*

---

5 In the **Effect Controls** panel, change the **Speed** value to **50** if it's not already set. Press the **spacebar** to preview the effect.

A Speed value of 100 indicates normal (full) playback speed; a value of 50 indicates half speed, or twice the original duration.

In addition to Speed, you can change many other properties to change the quality of your finished movie. (Most are in the Tuning section of the Effect Controls panel for the Timewarp effect.) These properties include Vector Detail, Smoothing, and Error Threshold, to name a few. You can also easily apply keyframes to the speed change, making your footage speed up or slow down at different rates, which is similar in some ways to using the Time Map graph.

You'll notice Timewarp does not operate in the same way as applying Time Stretch to a layer. Applying Time Stretch to a layer (as you did previously) actually affects the length of your layer in the Timeline. When you apply the Timewarp effect, speed changes apply to the selected footage in the Timeline, although the layer's duration does not appear to change. In fact, you cannot change the actual duration (the length between In and Out points) on a layer using this effect, even if you changed your composition settings. The Timewarp effect also works independently of the Frame Blend switch in the Timeline panel.

---

6 Choose **File > Save**, or press **Cmd+S** (Mac) or **Ctrl+S** (Windows). Choose **File > Close Project**.

Although knowing how to use the Timewarp effect is not necessary for achieving speed changes in your footage (the time-stretching and time-remapping techniques discussed in the previous exercises should suffice for most users), it is helpful to know how to use this effect in case the need arises or in case you want to explore some of the more advanced options After Effects 7 has to offer.

Now that you have learned a bit about speed changes using layer settings and effects, in the next exercise you will learn how to replace existing layers with new footage—a real time-saver.

---

14 | Replacing Layers

As you know by now, After Effects 7 allows you to import a layer into the **Timeline**, set keyframes, and change properties. What you may not realize is how easy it is to then swap out different footage for the layer. This new footage will retain all the animation and property settings of the layer it replaces.

Why would you need to replace layers? Imagine you are creating a motion-graphic design for different language versions of a main title sequence. Replacing titles could get rather complicated if you had to start from scratch and replace each English title with a French title, for example. You would have to rework **Position** keyframes for each title, add mask properties, add effect properties, add various layer options, and so on. Luckily, After Effects 7 makes replacing a layer easy. All the properties and options of the original layer apply automatically to the new layer. In this exercise, you will see how easy it is to replace a layer with new footage.

---

1 Choose **File > Open Project**. Navigate to the **chap_08** folder you copied to your desktop, click **Replace_Layer.aep** to select it, and click **Open**. Choose **File > Save As**. In the **Save As** dialog box, navigate to the **AE7_HOT_Projects** folder on your desktop. Name the file **Replace_Layer.aep**, and click **Save**.

---

2 In the **Project** panel, double-click the **Title_Comp** composition to open it and its associated **Timeline** panel.

---

3 Press the **spacebar** to preview the animation.

In the next steps, you will learn to use the Replace Layer command. When you replace a layer, all the animation and keyframes applied to the original layer continue to work with the new layer.

---

4 In the **Timeline** panel, select the **English_Title.psd** layer. In the **Project** panel, select the **French_Title.psd** footage. Hold down **Opt** (Mac) or **Alt** (Windows), and drag the French title footage from the **Project** panel to the **Timeline** panel. Release the footage in the **Timeline** panel.

Notice the French_Title.psd layer replaces the English_Title.psd layer in the Timeline panel.

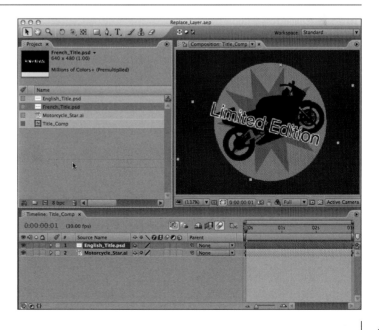

It doesn't matter where you drop the French_Title.psd footage in the Timeline, because After Effects 7 knows it should replace the English_Title.psd layer. Why? It's because you selected that layer before you dragged the replacement layer to the Timeline.

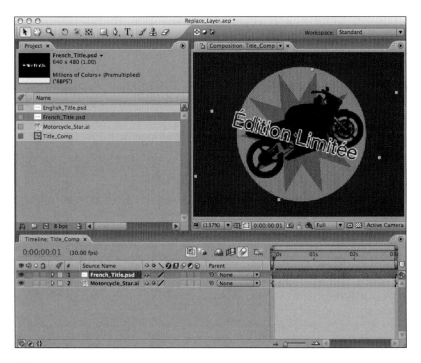

5 Press the **spacebar** to preview your work, and notice the French title uses the original animation.

You can use this technique for a lot of purposes besides language translations. You might design a template for a title sequence and swap out the appropriate titles. For example, if you have a commercial, you might make the same animation for different products and just swap out the animations.

Practice this on your own so you really understand how it works. You'll use this timesaving technique often in your real work.

6 Choose **File > Save**, or press **Cmd+S** (Mac) or **Ctrl+S** (Windows). Choose **File > Close Project**.

Knowing how to replace layers, as you learned in this exercise, will save you a lot of time and headaches during your After Effects 7 career and beyond. In the next exercise, you will learn about a lesser-known technique that also can save you a lot of time in certain instances. Using **sequencing layers**, you can automatically create a sequence of several layers in the Timeline without manually moving layers and setting In and Out points.

15 | Sequencing Layers

Quite often in motion graphics, you'll want to create a sequence of frames in which the first piece of artwork shows on the screen, followed by each successive piece of artwork playing in order. You might do this, for example, if you have a number of still photographs or scanned images you need to put into a sequence to create an animation, a time-lapse effect, or a slideshow. When you learned how to move and trim layers, you saw you could accomplish something like this by having layers start and end on different frames. The manual method of sequencing layers would be to move each layer in the **Timeline** to sequentially follow another. However, After Effects 7 provides a way to select multiple layers and sequence them automatically in the **Timeline**.

After Effects 7 also provides options for overlapping the layers rather than simply having one end and the next begin. When you overlap layers, you can transition a certain number of frames with **cross dissolves**, which means fading in on one picture while fading out on another. Cross dissolves are a transitional device filmmakers use all the time. In this exercise, you'll learn to sequence layers, overlap them, and use cross dissolves on the overlapping layers.

---

1 Choose **File > New > New Project**. Choose **File > Save As**. In the **Save As** dialog box, navigate to the **AE7_HOT_Projects** folder on your desktop. Name the file **Layer_Sequence.aep**, and click **Save**.

---

2 Double-click the empty **Project** panel to open the **Import File** dialog box. Navigate to the **chap_08** folder you copied to your desktop, click the **Sky_Slides** folder to select it, and click the **Import Folder** button.

This step imports an entire folder of images into your project at once, keeping all the images organized in a single folder.

---

3 At the bottom of the **Project** panel, click the **Create a new Composition** button to create a new composition. Name it **Sky_Sequence**, and change the composition settings to match those shown in the illustration here. Click **OK**.

This opens empty Timeline and Composition panels.

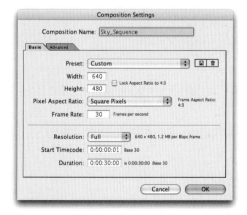

4 Click the **twirly** icon next to the **Sky_Slides** folder to reveal its contents in the **Project** panel.

This reveals the list of images in the folder. If you click an image, you will see a thumbnail with some information about the document at the top of the Project panel. This folder contains 15 different sky images generated at 640 x 480 square pixels. You will soon learn how to create a slideshow from these still images using the sequencing layers feature.

5 In the **Project** panel, select **Sky001.tif**. Press the **Shift** key, and click **Sky015.tif** to multiple-select all 15 images in the **Sky_Slides** folder. (You may have to use the scroll bar in the **Project** panel to see all the files.) Drag the selected files to the **Timeline**.

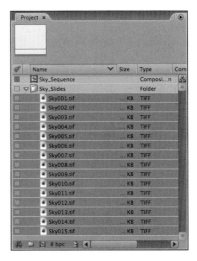

Warning: Make sure you don't select the Sky_Sequence composition you just made when you select these images. If you do, you won't be able to drag the images into the composition.

Notice all 15 layers in the Timeline are 30 seconds long. After Effects 7 automatically creates a duration for still footage that is the length of the composition. As you have learned already, you can trim this footage to be a different length, and you can also stretch footage to be longer than a composition. For this exercise, you want each layer to be 2 seconds long so you can create a slideshow. You'll do this next.

6 Position the **CTI** at **0:00:02:00**. If all the layers are not still selected, press **Cmd+A** (Mac) or **Ctrl+A** (Windows) to select them. Press **Opt+]** (Mac) or **Alt+]** (Windows) to trim each layer to the **CTI**.

In this case, you made the layers 2 seconds long.

You can see why keyboard shortcuts for trimming are useful. You could have dragged 15 handles to trim each layer, but After Effects 7 can automate the whole process instead. With the layers trimmed, you'll learn to automatically position each layer in a sequence in the Timeline.

7 With all the layers still selected in the **Timeline**, choose **Animation > Keyframe Assistant > Sequence Layers**. The **Sequence Layers** dialog box appears. *Do not* click the **Overlap** button. Click **OK**.

At this point, you want the layers sequenced end to end in the Timeline. Clicking the Overlap button would allow you to apply a cross dissolve between the layers, which you will do later in this exercise.

We will explain the settings in the Sequence Layers dialog box in a chart after this exercise.

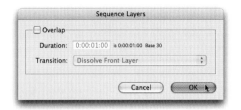

Notice the layers are now perfectly positioned in the Timeline to create a 2-second sequence 15 times. Press the spacebar to preview the animation. It might be cooler if there were little cross dissolves between each pair of layers, don't you think? You've learned how to set Opacity property keyframes—can you imagine the labor involved in manually setting keyframes for this kind of animation? Of course, there's a better solution, which you'll learn in the next step.

Note: The order in which you select the images is important. If you want to specify which image comes first in the sequence order, you can press Cmd (Mac) or Ctrl (Windows) to select images in a noncontiguous order. When you use the Shift key to select the images (as you did in the Project panel when you imported these images), the order in which you select the images will affect which image appears first in the layer sequence (top to bottom or bottom to top).

8 With all the layers still selected, choose **Animation > Keyframe Assistant > Sequence Layers**. In the **Sequence Layers** dialog box, turn on the **Overlap** check box. Set **Duration** to **0:00:00:10**, and choose **Cross Dissolve Front and Back Layers** from the **Transition** pop-up menu. Click **OK**.

This adds a cross dissolve between each layer. Check out the chart after this exercise to understand all the possible settings in the Sequence Layers dialog box.

---

9 Press the **spacebar** to play the composition, and notice the cross dissolve between the layers. Press the **T** key to reveal the **Opacity** settings, and notice each layer has keyframes automatically set for opacity changes. Drag the **Zoom** slider to see a larger view of the **Timeline** content.

After Effects 7 has placed four keyframes per layer to fade the image in and out. After Effects 7 has just saved you a lot of work!

Notice the composition is now too long for the animation. That's because, with the overlapping of each layer by 10 frames, the footage no longer takes up the entire 30 seconds. The last frame containing an image is at 0:00:25:10. Fortunately, you can also trim a composition. The next step will show you how.

---

10 Choose **Composition > Composition Settings**, and change **Duration** to **0:00:25:10**. Click **OK**.

When you change the value for Duration, you'll see you have shortened your composition. Now when you play the slideshow, the composition will end at the same time the images do.

---

11 Choose **File > Save**, or press **Cmd+S** (Mac) or **Ctrl+S** (Windows). Choose **File > Close Project**.

Sequencing layers is great time-saver, particularly when you have a lot of still images or graphics you want to arrange one after the other in the Timeline. Using the techniques you learned in this exercise, you can create slideshows or even animations from an imported sequence of images in no time.

In the next exercise, you'll learn about working with solid layers in After Effects 7, but first, you'll learn more about the Sequence Layers dialog box.

Using the Sequence Layers Dialog Box

In the previous exercise, you worked with the sequencing layers feature of After Effects 7. The **Sequence Layers** dialog box has many options. Here's a useful chart outlining those options:

Sequence Layers Dialog Box	
Option	**Description**
Overlap	Allows you to overlap two adjacent layers with a cross dissolve. This causes each layer to look as though it is fading in or out or fading both in and out. You control the cross dissolve using the **Cross Dissolve** option.
Duration	Indicates the number of frames over which the overlap of layers occurs. You can type any value in this field that does not exceed the duration of the layer.
Transition: Dissolve Front Layer	Fades out at the end of the layer's duration. **Opacity** keyframes lasting the duration of the overlap are automatically set. For a layer that is 15 frames long with a five-frame overlap, the fade-out will occur from **Frame 10** to **Frame 15**.
Transition: Cross Dissolve Front and Back Layers	Fades in the layer at the beginning and fades it out at the end of the layer's duration. **Opacity** keyframes lasting the duration of the overlap are automatically set. For a layer that is 15 frames long with a five-frame overlap, the fade-in will occur from **Frame 1** to **Frame 5**, and the fade-out will occur from **Frame 10** to **Frame 15**.

Introducing Solid Layers

A **solid** layer is exactly what it sounds like: a layer containing a solid-colored shape. You can make a solid layer of any size, from a layer with 1 x 1 pixels to a layer with 32,000 x 32,000 pixels. The color can be any color you want. Solid layers are useful when you want a quick graphic in the shape of a rectangle, such as for a button in a DVD interface. Later in the book, you'll also learn to mask solid layers to create shapes other than rectangles.

At first it might seem like having a layer of a solid color is of minimal use—say, only for a background color. However, because solid layers have all the properties of a normal layer, you'll find

yourself using them all the time. You can add effects, masks, and transformations to solid layers and make them useful in many ways.

In the following exercise, you'll learn how to create solid layers and change their color, dimensions, and settings. You can make solid layers smaller than the shape of your composition so they don't cover other layers of artwork, or you can make them partially transparent so you can see through them. You can animate all the properties of a solid layer as well.

EXERCISE

16 | Creating Solid Layers

In this exercise, you will create and make settings for solid layers in After Effects 7. Solid layers are the simplest type of layer generated by After Effects 7. You can use them for a variety of purposes, such as backgrounds, rectangular "card" graphics, and placeholders for other footage. Alternatively, you can cut them into different shapes using masks (as discussed in Chapter 13, "Creating Masks"). This exercise introduces you to the most common ways you can create and manipulate solid layers in After Effects 7.

1 Choose **File > New > New Project**. Choose **File > Save As**. In the **Save As** dialog box, navigate to the **AE7_HOT_Projects** folder on your desktop. Name the file **Solid_Layers.aep**, and click **Save**.

2 Choose **Composition > New Composition** to create a new composition. In the **Composition Settings** dialog box, name the composition **Solid Layers 1**. Set **Duration** to **0:00:01:00**. Click **OK**.

3 Choose **Layer > New > Solid**. Alternatively, press **Cmd+Y** (Mac) or **Ctrl+Y** (Windows).

4 In the **Solid Settings** dialog box, leave **Dark Gray Solid 1** as the name for the solid layer. If the color doesn't appear automatically, click the **color swatch**. In the **color picker**, select dark gray, and click **OK**. In the **Solid Settings** dialog box, make sure **Width** is **720** and **Height** is **480**. Click **OK**.

Notice the default name for the solid is the same as the color in the color swatch. This will be the color of your solid layer.

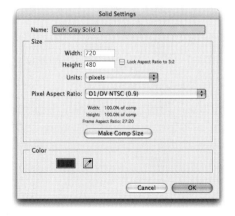

Your Composition panel should look like the one shown in the illustration here. Notice when you create a solid layer, the layer appears in the Timeline and in a folder in the Project panel called Solids. You cannot create a solid without a composition; it's a special kind of artwork After Effects 7 allows you to create for the purpose of working in a composition's Timeline.

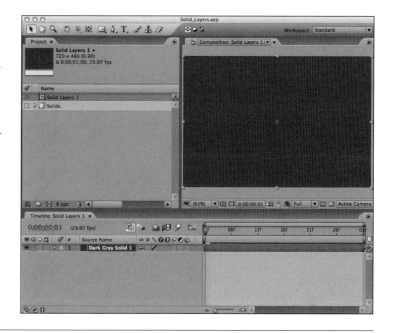

5 With the solid selected in the **Timeline**, choose **Layer > Solid Settings**. In the **Solid Settings** dialog box, click the **color swatch**. In the **color picker**, select dark red, and click **OK**. In the **Solid Settings** dialog box, click **OK**.

This step reopens the Solid Settings dialog box, which allows you to make color changes.

Tip: You can also press Cmd+Shift+Y (Mac) or Ctrl+Shift+Y (Windows) to open the Solid Settings dialog box.

Notice the solid layer has changed color and has also assumed the name Deep Red Solid 1 automatically. You can always change the name of a layer by selecting it first and then pressing Return (Mac) or Enter (Windows). Leave the name at its default for now; it's a nice convenience to let After Effects 7 do the naming for you.

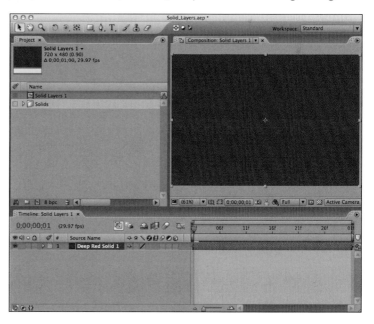

6 Make sure the **CTI** is on **Frame 1**. In the **Timeline** panel, select the **Deep Red Solid 1** layer, and press the **T** key to display the **Opacity** property. Click the **stopwatch** icon, and set **Opacity** to **0%**. Press the **K** key to move the **CTI** to the last frame of the composition. Set **Opacity** to **100%**.

The Opacity property (or amount of transparency) for this solid layer now changes from fully transparent to completely opaque over the course of the composition.

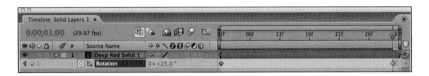

7 With the **Deep Red Solid 1** layer selected, press the **R** key to display the **Rotation** property. Press the **J** key to move the **CTI** to the first frame. Click the **stopwatch** icon. Press the **K** key to move the **CTI** to the last frame. Set **Rotation** to **25.0** degrees.

The amount of rotation applied to the solid layer now changes from 0 to 25 degrees over the course of the composition.

8 With the **Deep Red Solid 1** layer selected, press the **S** key to display the **Scale** property. Press the **J** key to move the **CTI** to the first frame. Click the **stopwatch** icon, and set **Scale** to **20%**. Press the **K** key to move to the last frame. Set **Scale** to **100%**. Click the **Quality** switch, and make sure it is set to **Best** quality (forward slanting line).

The Scale property (or relative size) of this solid layer now changes from 20 percent to 100 percent of its original size over the course of the composition. Solid layers preview much better at Best quality.

---

9 Press the **Home** key, or drag the **CTI** manually to the beginning of your **Timeline**. Press the **spacebar** to preview the animation.

Notice the solid layer responds to all property settings just as imported footage does.

In the following step, you will learn to change the dimensions of a solid layer.

---

10 Choose **Layer > Solid Settings**, or press **Cmd+Shift +Y** (Mac) or **Ctrl+Shift+Y** (Windows). If it isn't already unchecked, turn off the **Lock Aspect Ratio** check box. For both **Width** and **Height**, type **400**. Click **OK**.

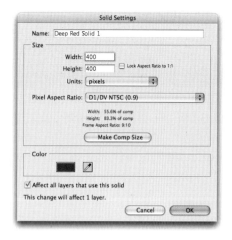

---

11 Press the **spacebar** to watch the animation, and observe the square dimensions of the solid layer.

Even though you changed the size, the layer retains all the animation properties you set in the previous steps.

---

12 Choose **Layer > New > Solid**, or press **Cmd+Y** (Mac) or **Ctrl+Y** (Windows).

---

13 In the **Solid Settings** dialog box, click the **color swatch**, and in the **color picker**, select dark purple. Click **OK**. In the **Solid Settings** dialog box, click the **Make Comp Size** button, and observe that the **Width** and **Height** values change to match the composition size. Click **OK**.

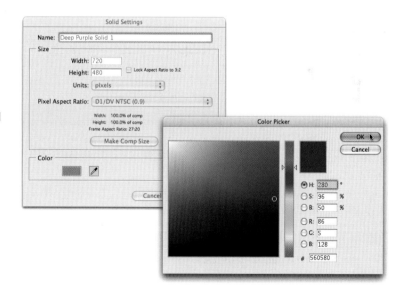

14 In the **Timeline** panel, drag the **Deep Purple Solid 1** layer below the **Deep Red Solid 1** layer. In the **Composition** panel, notice the new solid layer displays at the composition dimensions.

---

15 Choose **File > Save**, or press **Cmd+S** (Mac) or **Ctrl+S** (Windows). Choose **File > Close Project**.

This exercise introduced you to the settings for a solid layer. You'll work with these layers in other chapters as well, to get ideas for their usefulness. For now, you could make an abstract moving composition with lots of animating rectangles set to different scales, opacities, and rotations. In future chapters, you'll learn to combine solid layers with other footage, text, and effects.

As you work on your own After Effects 7 projects, you will find solid layers are infinitely useful in helping you quickly generate colored layers you can manipulate without having to create and import Photoshop graphics or other simple, still images.

In the next section, you'll learn about ways to align and distribute the layers you have created (whether solid layers or other footage) to create pleasing and accurate compositions.

Aligning and Distributing Layers

Sometimes you need to align multiple layers mathematically—for example, if you are creating a motion menu interface (with a moving background video or animation) for a DVD, you may want your buttons to line up perfectly. You could use a ruler to calculate what constitutes perfect distribution and alignment, but it's much easier to let the computer do these sorts of tasks for you.

In After Effects 7, you can move layers using the **Align** panel. You access this panel by choosing **Window > Align & Distribute**.

The top row contains the alignment icons, which set how the artwork on layers aligns. These icons represent horizontal left, horizontal center, horizontal right, vertical top, vertical center, and vertical bottom alignment.

The bottom row contains the distribution icons. To **distribute** something means to space it evenly. You can space multiple pieces of artwork by clicking the icons in this row, choosing from vertical top, vertical center, vertical bottom, horizontal left, horizontal center, or horizontal right distribution.

17 | Using the Align Panel

In this exercise, you will use After Effects 7's alignment and distribution tools for the first time. The alignment and distribution tools are particularly useful when creating a design for a DVD interface or for a title sequence. In these scenarios, you often need to space layers uniformly. For example, if you have several buttons on a page, the alignment and distribution tools can help you make sure the buttons are lined up and spaced evenly, ensuring a pleasing aesthetic.

1 Choose **File > Open Project**. Navigate to the **chap_08** folder you copied to your desktop, click **Align_Distribute.aep** to select it, and click **Open**. Choose **File > Save As**. In the **Save As** dialog box, navigate to the **AE7_HOT_Projects** folder on your desktop. Name the file **Align_Distribute.aep**, and click **Save**.

2 If necessary, in the **Project** panel, double-click **Menu** to open the composition.

3 If necessary, choose **Window > Align & Distribute**.

This opens the Align panel. The top row contains the alignment icons. The bottom row contains the distribution icons.

4 In the **Timeline** panel, **Shift+click** to select all the layers. Notice this also selects them in the **Composition** panel.

Tip: Alternatively, you can Shift+click the images in the Composition panel. This selects the layers in both places.

5 Click the **horizontal left alignment** icon, and notice the menu items move to align with the left edge of the button shape.

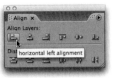
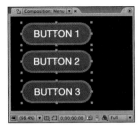

When you specify left alignment, the selected layers align with the selected object farthest to the left. The far-left edge does not move; it identifies the alignment edge.

6 Click the **vertical center distribution** icon, and notice the menu items are distributed evenly from top to bottom.

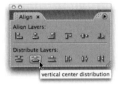

Clicking this icon spaces the centers of the items evenly, starting from the most extreme vertical positions.

This technique is useful for static or animated graphics. In the next few steps, you'll see how you can incorporate this alignment technique to create an animation of the menu items flying around the screen.

7 With all three layers still selected, press **Opt+P** (Mac) or **Shift+Alt+P** (Windows) to reveal the **Position** property for each layer, and set a keyframe. Drag the **CTI** to **0:00:00:29**, and turn on the **Keyframe Navigator** check boxes for each layer.

Notice the stopwatch is active, and a check mark already appears in the Keyframe Navigator check box. This happens automatically when you use the Opt (Mac) or Alt (Windows) keyboard shortcut. Moving the CTI and turning on the Keyframe Navigator check box inserts a keyframe at the current position of each layer at this point in the Timeline.

8 Press the **J** key to move the **CTI** to the first frame of your composition.

9 If necessary, reselect all three objects. Press the **Shift** key, and press the **right arrow** key to move the artwork to the right. Repeat this process until the artwork moves offscreen.

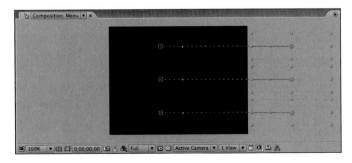

Holding down the Shift key when pressing the right arrow key moves the artwork in larger increments than using the right arrow key alone. Because two keyframes have been set and the layers are selected, you should see the motion path of the animation you just created.

TIP: | **Using the Keyboard to Move an Object**

You can move an object in the **Composition** panel by selecting its layer in the **Timeline** panel and pressing the arrow keys. Pressing an arrow key moves the selected layer or layers 1 pixel in the direction of the arrow. Holding down the **Shift** key while pressing an arrow key moves the selected layers 10 pixels at a time.

10 In the **Timeline** panel, click an empty area to deselect all the layers. Press the **spacebar** to view your animation.

11 Choose **File > Save**, or press **Cmd+S** (Mac) or **Ctrl+S** (Windows). Choose **File > Close Project**.

You just learned how to neatly arrange and organize layers by using the tools in the Align & Distribute panel. In the next exercise, you will look at **layer modes**, which affect the way layers interact with each other.

NOTE: | **Reversing Keyframes**

If you want to reverse the direction of the **Position** keyframes, select the keyframes you want to reverse by holding down the **Shift** key and clicking each keyframe. Choose **Animation > Keyframe Assistant > Time Reverse Keyframes** to reverse the animation.

Introducing Layer Modes

You may have worked with layer modes in Photoshop, and if you have, you'll find they are quite similar in After Effects 7. **Layer modes** affect the way multiple layers in the **Timeline** appear when **composited** (or combined) in the **Composition** panel. A normal layer, if put on top of another normal layer in the **Timeline**, will cover the lower layer completely. If set to a layer mode, however, the top layer will interact with the layer beneath it to change its appearance.

 **+**  **=**

If the top layer is set to **Normal** mode, it obscures the layer(s) beneath it. If the top layer is set to **Multiply** mode (for example), you can still see the layer beneath it. Layer modes offer alternative compositing effects in multilayered After Effects 7 documents.

After Effects 7 creates layer modes using mathematical formulas that add, subtract, multiply, and divide pixels. Depending on the formula used, a different result occurs. Most After Effects 7 artists use layer modes in an experimental way. It's hard to remember what each layer mode does, and it's much easier to use trial and error to search for a desired effect.

18 | Exploring Layer Modes

Layer modes (also called **blending modes** or **composite modes**) can add, subtract, divide, and multiply pixel values of different layers. Because After Effects 7 is programmed to do this in many ways, you have a wide variety of blending modes from which to choose. You can use these modes to create special effects in the way images look when they are composited.

Layer modes don't have too many practical uses; in general, they are more of a visual effect you might choose to use when you want your movie footage to look different from normal or when you want to blend foreground and background images without simply lowering the opacity. For example, you might use a layer mode when you need an interesting way to blend text with a background image. This exercise lets you experiment with layer modes.

1 Choose **File > Open Project**. Navigate to the **chap_08** folder you copied to your desktop, click **Layer_Modes.aep** to select it, and click **Open**. Choose **File > Save As**. In the **Save As** dialog box, navigate to the **AE7_HOT_Projects** folder on your desktop. Name the file **Layer_Modes.aep**, and click **Save**.

2 In the **Project** panel, double-click the **Spring_Flowers** composition to open it and its associated **Timeline** panel.

3 In the **Timeline** panel, click the **Expand or Collapse the Transfer Controls pane** button to display the **Mode** pane.

This button appears at the bottom of the Timeline panel. Try clicking it several times. You'll see it makes the Mode pane appear and disappear. Make sure you leave it set to the Mode pane when you're finished clicking.

4 Click the **Mode** pop-up menu next to the **Spring_Flowers.psd** layer, and choose **Multiply**.

This changes the layer mode on Spring_Flowers.psd from Normal to Multiply. Make sure the Mode menu selection is on the top layer. You always apply the layer mode to the layer above the one you want to affect.

Tip: Alternatively, select the layer, and then choose Layer > Blending Mode > Multiply. This transfer mode menu is the same as the Mode pop-up menu. (Remember, layer modes are also known as transfer modes and blending modes.)

---

5 Experiment with other modes to see what they do by choosing them from the **Mode** pop-up menu. When you are finished, choose **Multiply** once again from the **Mode** pop-up menu.

There is no better way to learn which ones you like than to experiment. Typically, you'll use modes such as Multiply, Add, Screen, Overlay, Hard Light, and Soft Light the most, although it really depends on your footage and the look you want. You can also reduce the opacity on the Spring_Flowers.psd layer, which will have varying effects with different layer modes. Also, moving the Blue_Sky.psd layer to the top of the Timeline and applying the same blending modes to it will change the results. Although the blending modes work by applying them to the top layer, it is up to you to decide on the layer order.

---

6 Choose **File > Save,** or press **Cmd+S** (Mac) or **Ctrl+S** (Windows). Choose **File > Close Project.**

TIP:

Changing Layer Modes

Unlike with layer properties, you cannot animate layer modes over time using keyframes. If you want to use another layer mode on the same layer at any point in a **Timeline**, you should split the layer and apply a new layer mode. You learned how to split a layer previously in this chapter.

This chapter was a big one. As you can see, layers are quite a bit more complex in After Effects 7 than in many other programs. Take a nice break before moving on to the next chapter, *"Working with Text Layers."*

9

Working with Text Layers

The text layer is a useful feature in After Effects 7. Instead of importing text from another application, such as Adobe Photoshop or Adobe Illustrator, you can create and edit text directly in After Effects 7, which allows you to easily modify and animate your type in all sorts of ways.

With text layers, you can create and edit text with the same precision and ease you find in Photoshop or Illustrator. The advanced formatting options let you adjust the layout of every character in a single word or create a single-line or paragraph-length text block. If you prefer to develop your text layouts in other applications, you can also retain the editability of unrasterized text imported from other applications.

With the animator properties, you can create text transformations in exciting ways. With the selector properties, you can increase or decrease the range of transformations across your text. By combining multiple selectors and animators and by applying Wiggly selectors and shape modifiers, you have an unlimited arsenal of text effects at your disposal. This chapter describes these terms through hands-on exercises.

Specifically, the exercises in this chapter will familiarize you with creating text directly, importing text from other applications, and putting text on a path. You'll also learn all about animators and selectors.

Using Text Layers and the Animate Text Menus

With text layers, you can set up text blocks of any length and then apply changes to any character or set of characters over time. Using the **Animation > Animate Text** menu, you can add **animators**, special attributes that control changes in text over time. Using the **Animation > Add Text Selector** menu, you add text **selectors**, which control which parts of the text blocks each animator affects. You can apply multiple animators, each with its own combination of animated text properties, to a single text layer, and you can apply multiple selectors to a single animator. If this sounds confusing, don't worry. You'll get to try all this in the first exercise.

1 | Adding and Animating Text

Adding text to a composition is as easy as adding any other type of layer. In this exercise, you will add text to a composition and apply some basic animations, causing it to stretch and glow over time.

---

1 Copy the **chap_09** folder from the **After Effects 7 HOT CD-ROM** onto your desktop.

---

2 Open **Text.aep** from the **chap_09** folder you copied to your desktop. Choose **File > Save As**. In the **Save As** dialog box, navigate to the **AE7_HOT_Projects** folder you created on your desktop, name the file **Text.aep**, and click **Save**.

---

3 In the **Project** panel, open the **Finished** composition to preview what you'll be doing in this exercise. Press the **spacebar** to view the contents of the composition. Close the **Finished** composition once you've explored it. Double-click the **Start** composition to open the **Timeline** and **Composition** panels.

We created the Finished composition entirely in After Effects 7—we didn't import any artwork. You'll be making this same composition on your own. The Start composition should be empty, but you'll change that soon.

---

4 In the **Tools** panel, select the **Type** tool. In the **Composition** panel, click near the center of the composition, and type the word **Motion**.

Once you finish typing, a text layer named Motion will appear in the Timeline.

Clicking an empty part of the Composition panel with the Type tool automatically creates a text layer in the Timeline. You can also create an empty text layer by choosing **Layer > New > Text**. This automatically selects the Type tool, and the cursor appears in the center of the screen for you.

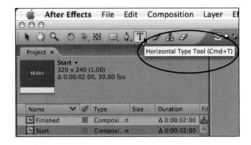

The default Type tool is the Horizontal Type tool. To select the Vertical Type tool, hold down the Type tool button in the Tools panel and then select Vertical Type Tool from the flyout menu that appears.

---

5 Choose **Window > Character** to open the **Character** panel if it is not already open. Select all the text in your composition by clicking and dragging across the word **Motion**. In the **Character** panel, set the font to **Arial Regular** and the size to **36 px**.

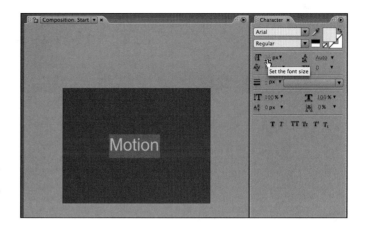

Because After Effects 7 projects are intended for screen-based output, fonts are measured in pixels instead of points. However, at 100 percent magnification, the pixels and points will appear roughly equivalent, so don't let the alternative measurement throw you.

NOTE:

Using Fonts and Collecting Files

For the exercises in this book, we've chosen standard fonts that almost everyone has on their systems, but feel free to jazz up these projects with more exciting fonts. The only caveat when working on your own projects is you must make sure the fonts are available on any system on which you'll edit or render your work.

If you're passing on a project to someone else, you might want to check your font usage by choosing **File > Collect Files**. This feature will generate a report of the fonts, files, and effects necessary for rendering your project. It can also copy and save those items, even if they reside in different locations on your computer, into a single folder that can be easily transferred to another user. However, the **Collect Files** feature does not do all the work for you. Although it gathers your media source files in one place, it leaves the complexities of installing any extra necessary fonts and effects to you.

---

6 With the **Type** tool still selected, move the cursor away from the text until it changes from the **I-beam** cursor to the **Move Layer** cursor. Drag the layer until your text is centered on the stage.

The Type tool remains selected so you can immediately return to editing text.

7 With the text still selected, click the **Fill Color** box in the **Character** panel. Select light gray from the **color picker**, and click **OK**.

The appearance of the color picker may vary by system.

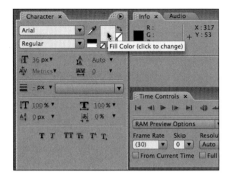

8 Click once to bring the **Stroke Color** box to the top; then click the **Stroke Color** box, select light yellow, and click **OK**.

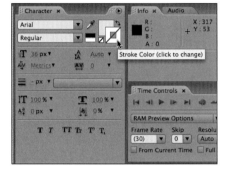

9 In the **Character** panel, type **0** in the **Stroke Width** field. If it isn't already selected, choose **Stroke Over Fill** from the pop-up menu next to the **Stroke Width** field. Click the type to deselect it.

It's hard to see the color changes until you deselect the type.

10 Choose **Animation > Animate Text > Stroke Width**.

This adds Animator 1 and Range Selector 1, along with the Stroke Width property, to your Timeline. Note the initial value of 0 for the Stroke Width property comes from the setting you chose in the Character panel.

In the Animate Text submenu, you might notice the other options, including one for animating the stroke color. You'll learn about this option soon. We'll also explain the Range selector in Exercise 2.

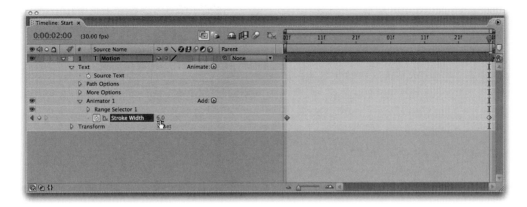

11 In the **Timeline**, click the **stopwatch** icon next to the **Stroke Width** property. Move the **CTI** (**C**urrent **T**ime **I**ndicator) to **0:00:02:00**, and set the value of the **Stroke Width** property to **6**. Press the **spacebar** to preview your animation and watch the text glow.

You should now have two keyframes set.

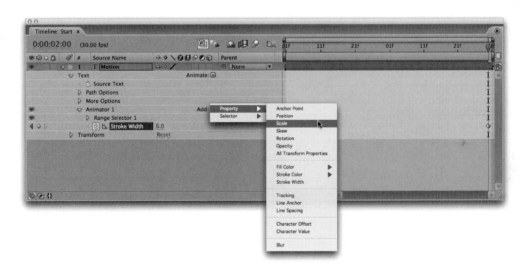

12 In the **Layer Switches** area of the **Timeline**, click the **Add** arrow next to **Animator 1**. Select **Property > Scale** from the pop-up menu to add a new **Scale** property beneath **Animator 1**.

If your hierarchy of animators and selectors gets too complicated, you might want to rename them by selecting each one, pressing Return (Mac) or Enter (Windows), and typing a new name—just like renaming any layer. You can't rename animated properties, but if you pay attention to the indentation, you'll be able to tell which properties belong to which animators. Note the layerwide versions of the properties (which you're not touching in this exercise) are still in a separate Transform category for each layer and aren't part of the animator hierarchy.

13 Click the **Link** icon next to the **Scale** values to remove the proportion constraints on scaling. Move the **CTI** to **0:00:00:00** in the **Timeline**, and click the **stopwatch** icon next to the **Scale** property beneath **Animator 1** to set the first keyframe with both **Horizontal Scale** and **Vertical Scale** set to **100%**. Move the **CTI** to **0:00:02:00** in the **Timeline**, and set **Vertical Scale** to **200%**.

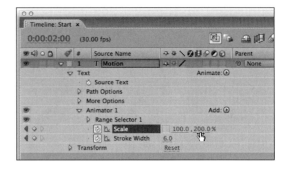

The scaled-up and glowing text looks a bit cramped now.

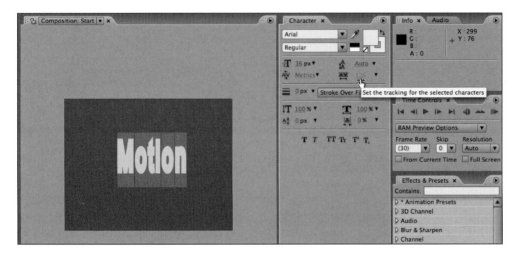

14 Using the **Type** tool, select the word **Motion** by dragging across it in the **Composition** panel. In the **Character** panel, type **125** in the **Tracking** field.

15 Click in the **Timeline** panel, and press the **spacebar** to play your animation.

The text appears to stretch and glow.

16 Choose **File > Save**, or press **Cmd+S** (Mac) or **Ctrl+S** (Windows). Leave **Text.aep** open for the next exercise.

You just learned how to use the text animator properties in After Effects 7. If you're wondering what some of the other animators do, apart from Stroke Width, refer to the following chart. After you've looked at these definitions, continue to the next exercise, where you'll learn about the Range selector, which determines what characters are affected by the animator properties.

Animator Properties

Animator	Description
Anchor Point	Allows you to set and animate the alignment of text characters.
Position	Relates to the position of characters. You can set values for this property in the **Timeline** panel, or you can set values in the **Composition** panel using the **Selection** tool, which changes to a **Move** tool when positioned over text characters.
Scale	Allows you to set and animate the scale of the text characters.
Skew	Allows you to set and animate the slant of the text characters. The skew axis specifies the axis along which the character is skewed.
Rotation	Allows you to set and animate the rotation of the text characters.
Opacity	Allows you to set and animate the opacity of the text characters.
All Transform	Allows you to add all the **Transform** properties at once to the animator group. You will work with this property in Exercise 5.
Fill Color (RGB, Hue, Saturation, Brightness, Opacity)	Allows you to set and animate the color values of the text characters, based on the type of color animator property you choose.
Stroke Color (RGB, Hue, Saturation, Brightness, Opacity)	Allows you to set and animate the color of the text character's stroke or outline. You worked with this property in Exercise 1.
Stroke Width	Allows you to set and animate the width of the text character's stroke. You worked with this property in Exercise 1.
Tracking	Allows you to set and animate the space between each text character in a word.
Line Anchor	Allows you to set the alignment of the tracking for each line of text. A value of **0%** specifies left alignment, **50%** specifies center alignment, and **100%** specifies right alignment.
Line Spacing	Allows you to set and animate the space between lines of text in a multiline text layer.
Character Offset	Allows you to offset a number or letter by whatever value you type. For example, if you used a value of **5** for the letter **a**, it would become an **e**. You'll work with this property in Exercise 6.
Character Value	Allows you to substitute the value for selected characters, replacing each character with one character represented by the new value.
Character Range	Limits the range of the character. You'll work with this property in Exercise 6.
Blur	Allows you to set and animate blur for text characters. This is new in After Effects 7.

2 | Using the Range Selector Property

In the previous exercise, you practiced animating an entire text layer using animator properties. In this exercise, you will apply the animator properties, such as **Scale** and **Stroke Width**, to different portions of the text by animating the **Range selector property**. Frankly, the **Range selector property** is better shown than explained. Basically, the **Range selector property** determines which characters in a text layer the text animator properties affect. If this explanation seems fuzzy to you, try this exercise, and then read it again. It will make more sense.

1 If you followed the previous exercise, **Text.aep** should still be open in After Effects 7. If it's not, choose **File > Open Project**. Navigate to the **chap_09** folder you copied to your desktop, click **Text_2.aep** to select it, and click **Open**.

2 Choose **File > Save As**. In the **Save As** dialog box, navigate to the **AE7_HOT_Projects** folder you created on your desktop. Name the file **Text.aep**, and click **Save**.

3 In the **Project** panel, open the **Finished** composition to preview what you'll be doing in this exercise. Press the **spacebar** to view the contents of the composition. Close the **Finished** composition once you've looked at it.

4 Double-click the **Start** composition to open the **Timeline** and **Composition** panels. Move the **CTI** to the first frame of the **Timeline** before you begin.

In this exercise, you'll be making the same effects shown in the Finished composition on your own. The Start composition should be familiar to you; it's where you left off in the previous exercise.

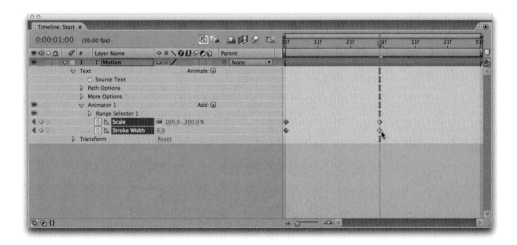

5 In the **Timeline**, open the **Animator 1** property for the **Motion** text layer, if it is not already open. Hold down the **Shift** key, and click to multiple-select the two end keyframes for the **Scale** and **Stoke Width** properties. Drag the keyframes to the **1-second mark** (**0:00:01:00**) in the **Timeline**.

The first goal in this exercise is to modify the animation, which is identical to the one you created in Exercise 1. The objective is to have the scale and glow effects ramp up over less time than they do now and then ramp back down. You can move keyframes after they're set, and you can even move multiple keyframes over multiple properties, as demonstrated in this step.

---

6 Hold down the **Shift** key, and click to multiple-select the first two keyframes. Press **Cmd+C** (Mac) or **Ctrl+C** (Windows) to copy the keyframes.

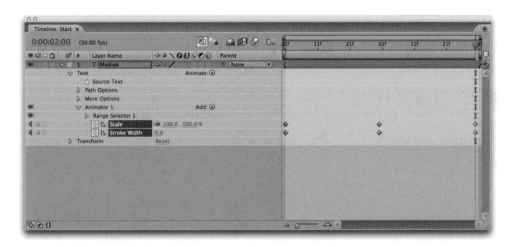

---

7 Press the **End** key to move the **CTI** to the last frame in the **Timeline**. Press **Cmd+V** (Mac) or **Ctrl+V** (Windows). Press the **spacebar** to preview the animation thus far.

This pastes the two keyframes into the last frame. If all worked as planned, your animation should now ramp up to scale and glow and then fade out.

---

8 Move the **CTI** to the beginning of the **Timeline**. Click the **twirly** icon next to **Range Selector 1**. Change the **End** property to **15%** (or to where it brackets the first letter in the **Motion** type layer).

This isolates a section of the type to encompass the approximate width of a single character. If you press the spacebar now, you'll see only the color and scale effects occur within the first letter of the text.

9 Click the **stopwatch** icon for the **Offset** property. Leave it at **0%** on Frame **0:00:00:00**. Move the **CTI** to the last frame, and change **Offset** to **90%**.

Notice the width of the Range selector property's brackets: They still bracket the approximate width of a single character. You have to offset that shape to move the brackets to the end of the lettering.

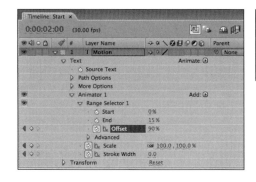

10 Click outside the layer so you don't see the **Range selector** brackets. Press the **spacebar**, or click the **RAM Preview** button to view the results.

The next exercise will reveal even deeper powers found within the Range selector properties.

11 Choose **File > Save**, or press **Cmd+S** (Mac) or **Ctrl+S** (Windows). Choose **File > Close Project**.

Now that you've learned how to use animators and range selectors for your text layers, you'll learn how to combine multiple instances of these techniques in the next exercise.

Introducing Offset

Offset is part of the **Range** selector properties, but it deserves a bit of special attention. The **Offset** value of a selector moves the start and endpoints of the selection relative to the beginning of the text block. For example, an **Offset** property of **0%** leaves the start and end points exactly as you've set them; an **Offset** property of **100%** moves the start and endpoints to the end of the text block.

The advantage of using **Offset** is it gives you the ability to move both start and endpoints at the same time so you can create the effect of a constantly sized selection moving over time. As with the **Start** and **End** properties, you can express **Offset** in terms of percentages or in terms of an index by characters, words, or lines. In the next exercise, you'll use the **Offset** property to apply the same animated effect across different parts of a text block over time.

3 | Applying Multiple Animators and Selectors

In the previous exercise, you used a **Range** selector to isolate an animation within a text block. In this exercise, you'll learn you can use an unlimited number of animation properties and **Range** selector properties on a single text block. The ability to apply multiple animation properties to text gives you a lot of options for achieving the precise look you require and for creating some complex type effects for animated text.

---

1 Choose **File > Open**. Navigate to the **chap_09** folder you copied to your desktop, click **Text_3.aep** to select it, and click **Open**.

---

2 Choose **File > Save As**. In the **Save As** dialog box, navigate to the **AE7_HOT_Projects** folder you created on your desktop. Name the file **Text.aep**, and click **Save**.

---

3 In the **Project** panel, open the **Finished** composition to preview what you'll be doing in this exercise. Press the **spacebar** to view the contents of the composition. Close the **Finished** composition once you've checked it out.

The Finished comp is the result of applying multiple animator and selector settings. You'll be creating the same effects in this exercise as shown in the Finished composition.

---

4 Double-click the **Start** composition to open the **Timeline** and **Composition** panels. Move the **CTI** to the first frame of the **Timeline** before you begin.

The Start composition should be familiar to you: It's where you left off in the previous exercise.

---

5 In the **Timeline** panel, click **Animate**, and choose **Animate > Fill Color > RGB**.

This adds an Animator 2 setting with its own Range selector and properties for Fill Color.

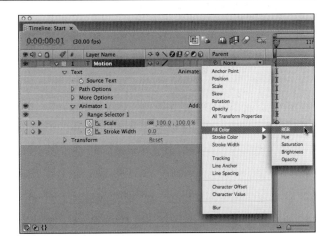

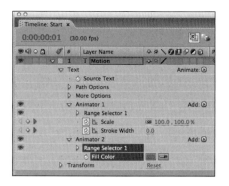
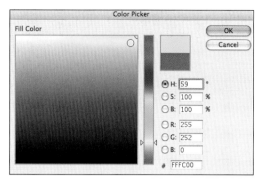

6 Click the **stopwatch** icon next to **Fill Color** to set the keyframe for **0:00:00:00** to its default setting: bright red. Move the **CTI** to the end of the **Timeline**. Click the **Fill Color** box, and select light yellow from the **color picker**. Press the **spacebar** to preview your animation.

This sets two keyframes for a fill color that animates from red to yellow. The fill color changes over the course of the composition; it is not restricted by the Range selector applied to Animator 1 in the previous exercise. Notice Animator 2 has its own Range selector. You'll work with that next.

---

7 Move the **CTI** to the first frame of the composition. Click the **twirly** icons for **Animator 2** and **Range Selector 1** to reveal the **Start**, **End**, and **Offset** properties. Change the **Start** position to **85%**. Leave the **End** position at **100%**. Click the **stopwatch** icon next to **Offset** to set a keyframe in this position.

---

8 Move the **CTI** to the end of the composition. Change the **Offset** position to **-90**. Press the **spacebar** to preview.

Notice how the two animators and Range selectors interact.

Notice also how the Timeline has one Animate menu and two Add menus. What is the difference between them? If you choose a new animation property, you can set up an independent animator property with its own Range selector. Using the Add menu instead adds to the current animator and Range selector. You'll do this next.

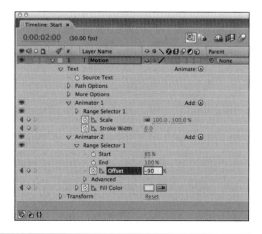

9 Click the **Add** button for **Animator 1**, and choose **Property > Position**.

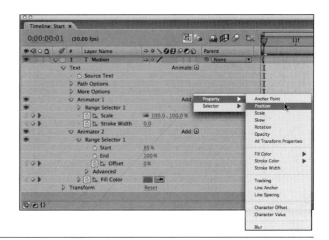

10 For **Position**, change the **Y** property to **15.0**. Press the **spacebar** to watch the position change occur within the existing **Range** selector.

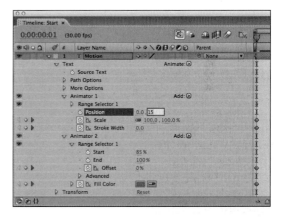

11 Click the **Add** menu for **Animator 2**. Choose **Property > Rotation**. Change the **Rotation** value to **-10**. Press the **spacebar** or click the **RAM Preview** button to preview your animation.

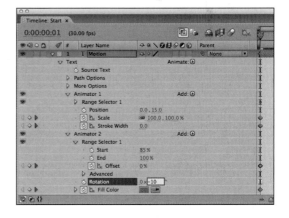

12 Choose **File > Save**, or press **Cmd+S** (Mac) or **Ctrl+S** (Windows). Choose **File > Close Project**.

Congratulations! You just animated multiple animators and Range selectors. The results are pretty interesting. Imagine the endless possibilities you can create with these properties.

Using Advanced Selector Properties

In the previous exercise, you explored the difference between adding a new animator and using the **Add** feature to augment an existing animator. You also worked with the **Range** selector and **Offset** properties. This exercise demonstrates the **Advanced** selector properties you can use to cause text animations to vary in strength over time. You'll play with a couple of ways to create animation via the **Advanced** selector properties without changing the selector's position, start, or endpoints. In fact, you'll create a complex effect by setting only three keyframes.

1   Choose **File > Open Project**. Navigate to the **chap_09** folder you copied to your desktop, click **Advanced.aep** to select it, and click **Open**.

2   Choose **File > Save As**. In the **Save As** dialog box, navigate to the **AE7_HOT_Projects** folder you created on your desktop. Name the file **Advanced.aep**, and click **Save**.

3   In the **Project** panel, double-click the **Finished** composition, and press the **spacebar** to see what you're about to learn in this exercise. When finished, close the **Finished** composition, and double-click the **Start** composition to open it.

4   In the **Timeline**, click the **twirly** icons for the **Power** text layer until you see the **Animate** menu under the **Text** twirly. Click the **Animate** menu in the **Power** text layer, and choose **Fill Color > RGB** from the pop-up menu to add an animator and a **Range** selector to the layer.

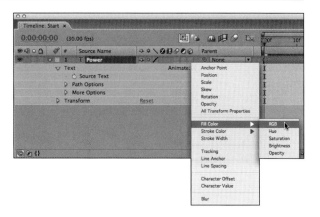

5   Click the **Fill Color** box, and select light yellow to turn the entire word yellow.

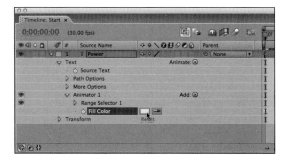

6 Click the **Range Selector 1** twirly, and then click the **Advanced** twirly to reveal the **Advanced** selector properties.

---

7 Make sure the **CTI** is at the beginning of the **Timeline (0:00:00:00)**. Click the **stopwatch** icon next to the **Amount** property (within the **Advanced** properties of **Range Selector 1**). Change the value of the **Amount** property to **0%**.

You have just set a keyframe for the start of the Fill Color property, which will begin at a value of 0 and gradually get stronger, once you set the next keyframe.

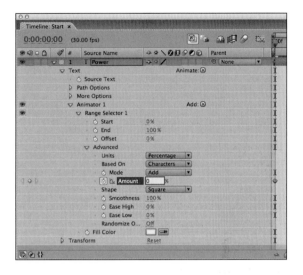

---

8 Move the **CTI** to halfway through the animation **(0:00:01:00)**. Change the value of the **Amount** property to **100%**.

This makes the Fill Color effect get stronger (more visible) over the course of this 1 second, until it is at full strength.

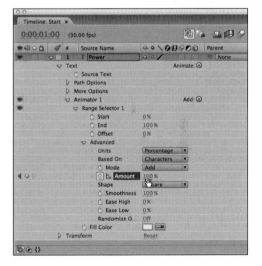

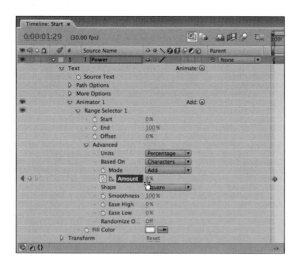

9 Move the **CTI** to the end of the **Timeline**. Change the value of the **Amount** property to **0%**. Press the **spacebar** to preview the animation.

At this point, if you preview the composition, it should look somewhat like the one from the first exercise in this chapter: The entire word gradually changes color and fades out to its initial state. When the Amount property is set to less than 100%, it applies the property changes at a proportionally reduced strength.

10 In the **Advanced** properties of **Range Selector 1**, select the **Shape** property, and choose **Triangle** from the menu. Press the **spacebar** to preview the animation.

Now you should see quite a change to your text animation. Rather than the effect evenly fading in across the entire word, the effect will fade in from the middle to the edges. What's going on here? The Shape property determines how the effect appears across the length of the text. In the next step, you'll see how the triangle shape can influence more than color.

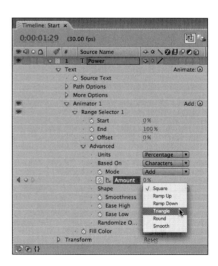

11 From the **Add** menu next to **Animator 1**, choose **Property > Position**. Change the value of the **Y** property to **-100**. Press the **spacebar** to preview the animation.

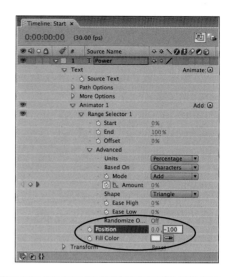

Now you can really see the triangle shape in action. Notice how the highest point in the triangle is also the section glowing the brightest, whereas the lower endpoints of the triangle barely glow at all. Therefore, you can now think of using the Shape property as setting up a graph to plot how much the effect should be applied across the length of the text, with the vertical axis of the graph representing the strength of the effect.

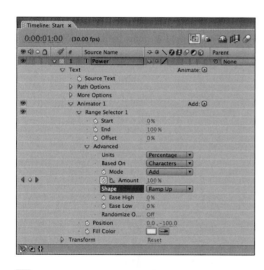

12 Change the **Shape** property from **Triangle** to **Ramp Up**. Preview the animation again, and notice the change in the effect. Try playing with some of the other **Shape** options as well.

The Shape property doesn't have a stopwatch icon because it affects the interpolation of other properties, rather than being an animated effect itself.

13 Choose **File > Save**, or press **Cmd+S** (Mac) or **Ctrl+S** (Windows). Choose **File > Close Project**.

You just learned how to change the shape of your text animation using the Advanced options for animators and a Range selector. Next, you'll learn more about the various Range selector properties.

Working with Range selector properties

The **Range selector** is a powerful animation tool in its own right. The following chart summarizes the properties available when applying a **Range** selector to an animator:

Range Selector Properties		
Property	**Options**	**Function**
Start	Any number	Designates the start point for the text selector. Numbers greater than the length of the text or greater than the **End** property mean the effect won't show up at all.
End	Any number	Designates the endpoint for the text selector. Numbers less than **1** or less than the **Start** property mean the effect won't show up at all.
Offset	Any number	Designates how far from the beginning of the text the selector should be set. An **Offset** property of **0** means no modification to the **Start** and **End** properties.
Units	Percentage	Counts characters, words, or lines by percentage. If the text is lengthened or shortened, the number of characters affected by the selector will also be lengthened or shortened.
	Index	Counts characters, words, or lines using absolute numbers starting with **1**. This is useful if the length of your text may change during the animation.
Based On	Characters	Counts every character and unit of whitespace as a character. When using this option, your animation may seem to pause when it reaches a space.
	Characters Excluding Spaces	Counts individual characters but does not include whitespace (spaces, returns) in the count.
	Words	Counts groups of characters separated by whitespace as a single unit.
	Lines	Counts groups of characters separated by carriage returns as a single unit.
Mode	Add	Adds the characters within this selector to any other active selections within this animator.
	Subtract	Removes the characters within this selector from any other active selections within this animator.
	Intersect	Modifies the selection to allow only characters that appear both within this selector and within any other active selection within this animator.
	Min	Filters out all but the selection closest to the beginning of the word.
	Max	Filters out all but the selection closest to the end of the world.
	Difference	Filters out any characters that appear both within the selector and within any other active selection within this animator.

continues on next page

Range Selector Properties *continued*		
Property	**Options**	**Function**
Amount	**-100%** to **100%**	Determines how much influence the animator properties associated with the current selector have on the overall text.
Shape	**Square**	Applies the **Amount** property from left to right across the text.
	Ramp Up	Applies the **Amount** property from right to left, weighting the effect toward the right.
	Ramp Down	Applies the **Amount** property from left to right, weighting the effect toward the left.
	Triangle	Applies the **Amount** property from the center outward, weighting the effect toward the center.
	Round	Applies the **Amount** property in a gradually increasing and then decreasing amount, describing a half circle.
	Smooth	Applies the **Amount** property from the center outward but in a smoother arc than when you use the **Triangle** shape.
Smoothness	**0%** to **100%**	Determines the gradation with which the effect applies across individual characters; **100%** is the most gradual effect; **0%** applies the full strength of the effect to each character in turn.
Ease High	**-100%** to **100%**	Determines the weighting of influence of the text properties over time, decreasing the rate of change in an effect as its strength increases.
Ease Low	**-100%** to **100%**	Determines the weighting of influence of the text properties over time, increasing the rate of change in an effect as its strength decreases.
Randomize Order	**On** or **Off**	Randomizes the order of characters as determined by the **Range** selector.

Working with Text Boxes and the Wiggly Selector

In the previous four exercises, you changed the properties of a single word over time. In this exercise, you will work with a longer piece of text and will explore not only transforming the "look" of the text but also transforming the text itself.

---

1 Choose **File > Open Project**. Navigate to the **chap_09** folder you copied to your desktop, click **Text_4.aep** to select it, and click **Open**.

---

2 Choose **File > Save As**. In the **Save As** dialog box, navigate to the **AE7_HOT_Projects** folder you created on your desktop. Name the file **Text.aep**, and click **Save**.

---

3 In the **Project** panel, double-click the **Finished** composition to see what you're about to learn in this exercise. When you're finished, close the **Finished** composition, and double-click the **Start** composition to open it.

---

4 In the **Timeline** panel, click the **twirly** icon next to the text layer to reveal the **Source Text** property. With the **CTI** at **0** seconds (**0:00:00:00**), click the **stopwatch** icon next to the **Source Text** property.

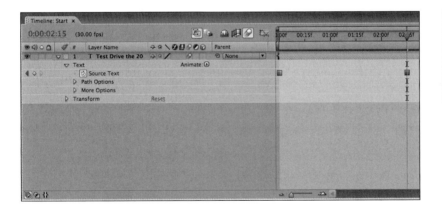

Now with Better Speed and Performance!

---

5 Move the **CTI** to **0:00:02:15**. In the **Composition** panel, double-click the text. If the text is not all automatically selected, drag across the text to select it all. Replace it with the following text: **Now with Better Speed and Performance!**

This automatically creates the Source Text keyframes as Hold keyframes, which are represented by a different icon than keyframes for other properties. This means the text won't morph or transform itself letter by letter between keyframes.

Why Did the Text Just Fit into Place?

The text you just typed fits into the same space filled by the initial text automatically because you created this text using a text box. Just as in Illustrator, you can create a text box instead of a line of text by clicking and dragging a box-shaped area using the **Type** tool. Text boxes are a great way to keep your text aligned across multiple screens of any presentation—from a public service announcement to film credits!

6 From the **Animation** menu, choose **Animate Text > All Transform Properties**.

This option simultaneously assigns all the basic text transformations to a single animator, which provides you with the greatest number of options to adjust this particular animator.

7 Modify the properties underneath **Animator 1** as follows: Set **Position** to **142** horizontal and to **22** vertical. Set **Scale** to **212** horizontal and **212** vertical. Set **Rotation** to **10 x 0.0** (10 complete rotations). Do *not* click the **stopwatch** icons for these properties.

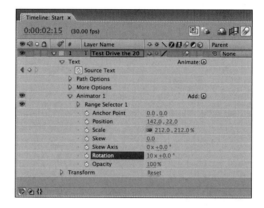

At this point, you should have kind of a mess on your screen. Don't worry—the next steps will clean up this mess.

8 In the **Timeline**, delete **Range Selector 1** by selecting it and pressing the **Delete** (Mac) or **Backspace** (Windows) key.

Next, you'll add a new kind of selector called a Wiggly selector.

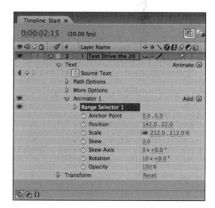

9 From the **Add** menu, next to **Animator 1**, choose **Selector > Wiggly**.

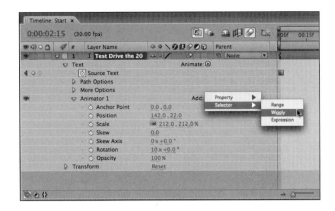

10 Click the **twirly** icon next to the newly created **Wiggly Selector 1**. Move the **CTI** to **0:00:01:00**, and click the **stopwatch** icons for the **Max Amount** and **Min Amount** properties. Make sure both properties are set to **0%**.

The 0% setting essentially turns off all the wild settings you created in the previous step. Setting this keyframe at 0% allows the craziness to animate gradually rather than popping on.

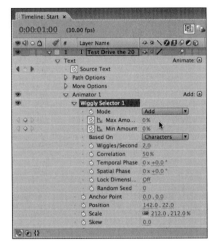

11 Move the **CTI** to **0:00:01:15**. Change the **Max Amount** property to **10%** and the **Min Amount** property to **-10%**.

The Wiggly selector modifies the current selection (and the strength of text animators on the selection) by the given percentages. In this case, you're starting with no selection (because you deleted the original selector), and you're gradually increasing the influence of the Wiggly selector until it affects all of the text.

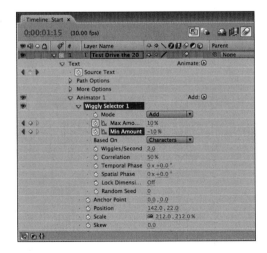

12 Move the **CTI** to **0:00:02:00**. Change the **Max Amount** property to **100%** and the **Min Amount** property to **-100%**.

Now the Wiggly selector can modify as much or as little of the text with each wiggle.

---

13 Move the **CTI** to **0:00:02:15**. Change the **Max Amount** property to **0%** and the **Min Amount** property to **0%**.

Now the text will appear to rearrange itself into the new words.

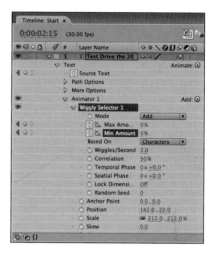

---

14 Change the **Wiggles/Second** property to **5.0**.

This means the text affected by the transformations will change every 5 frames (30 frames/second divided by 5 wiggles/second).

---

15 Change the **Correlation** property to **100%**. In the **Time Controls** panel, click the **RAM Preview** button to preview the animation. Alternatively, press **0** on your keyboard.

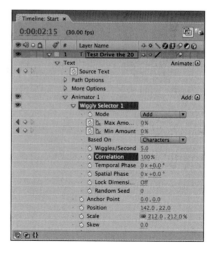

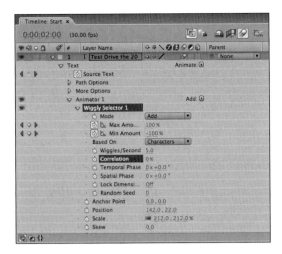

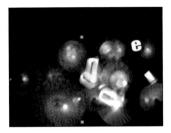

16 Change the **Correlation** property to **0%**. Turn on **Motion Blur** for the layer in the **Timeline**. Click the **RAM Preview** button to view the animation again.

This adds a little more chaos and an added touch of excitement to the piece.

The Correlation property tells the Wiggly selector how much to vary its randomization between characters (or words or lines, if you choose those units). The value 100% causes all the characters in the selection to vary in unison; the value 0% causes each character to do its own thing. For more details about the Wiggly selector, see the "Wiggly Selector Properties" chart following this exercise.

17 Choose **File > Save**, or press **Cmd+S** (Mac) or **Ctrl+S** (Windows). Choose **File > Close Project**.

In this exercise, you learned how to use the Wiggly selector to create random motion with a dynamic text effect. In the next exercise, you will learn about using character offset to randomize text in a different way.

Working with Wiggly selector properties

You can use the **Wiggly** selector on its own or to enhance the power of a **Range** selector, as you'll see in the upcoming exercises. The following chart summarizes the properties unique to the **Wiggly** selector; we haven't included the properties that work the same as they do with **Range** selectors:

Wiggly Selector Properties		
Property	Options	Function
Max Amount	-100% to 100%	Determines the maximum amount the **Wiggly** selector can randomly expand or contract the selection to which it is applied.
Min Amount	-100% to 100%	Determines the minimum amount the **Wiggly** selector will randomly expand or contract the selection to which it is applied.
Wiggles/Second	Any number	Determines how many times per second the **Wiggly** selector changes the size of the selector; a number greater than the frame rate or less than **0** will have no visible effect.
Correlation	0% to 100%	Determines the random individuality of characters (or words or lines, depending on your setting for the **Based On** property). For example, **0%** modifies each character randomly; **100%** modifies all characters within the selection in unison.
Temporal Phase	Revolutions + degrees	Causes slight variations in the animation over time, based on the phase of the animation.
Spatial Phase	Revolutions + degrees	Causes slight variations in the animation per character.
Lock Dimension	On or Off	Instructs the **Wiggly** selector to apply itself equally to both dimensions of multidimensional properties. For example, with this property set to **On**, the **Wiggly** selector will equally modify the horizontal and vertical components of the **Scale** property.

6 | Using Character Offset

In this exercise, you will apply multiple animators to a single text layer to create a complex effect. If you've seen any recent heist movies, you'll recognize the gadget "readout" you'll be simulating. It runs through all the possible numbers for each part of a safe combination until it "hears" the right combination. You could use this same effect as the countdown to a sales date in a car commercial, as a speed readout on a vehicle, as the detonation sequence on a bomb, or as an interesting background detail in a larger animation. In fact, animators used an extension of this technique to create the "falling numbers" effect in the opening titles of *The Matrix* movies.

---

1 Choose **File > Open Project**. Navigate to the **chap_09** folder you copied to your desktop, click **Readout.aep** to select it, and click **Open**.

---

2 Choose **File > Save As**. In the **Save As** dialog box, navigate to the **AE7_HOT_Projects** folder you created on your desktop. Name the file **Readout.aep**, and click **Save**.

---

3 Double-click the **Finished** composition in the **Project** panel to see what you're about to learn in this exercise. Double-click the **Finished 2** composition to see what the project looks like with a different font. When you're finished inspecting these compositions, double-click the **Start** composition to open it.

The font in the Finished composition is Courier, and the font in the Finished 2 composition is Impact. Do you notice how the numbers seem to jump around a bit when set in Impact versus in Courier? In Courier, they seem to work in perfect registration. Courier is a monotype font; Impact is not. **Monotype** means every character in the font is allotted the same width of space, including blank spaces. In other words, the letter *w* takes up the same amount of space as the letter *i*. For effects such as this safe-cracking effect, using a monotype font is more effective because it has better registration throughout the animation.

---

4 Press the **spacebar** to preview the **Start** composition.

We've already created the text layer for you, and we've set the keyframes in the Source Text property to change the numbers from the "unsolved" combination (all zeros) to the "solved" combination.

5 Move the **CTI** to the first frame of the composition. Click the **twirly** for the text layer, click the **Animate** menu, and choose **Character Offset**.

Even though Character Offset is a new property, using it employs the same techniques you've been using throughout this chapter.

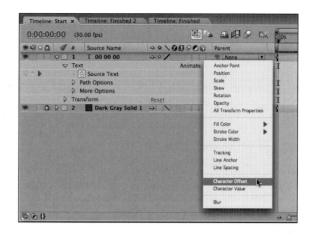

6 Make sure **Character Range** is set to **Preserve Case & Digits**.

This ensures numbers remain numbers and letters remain letters so your animation will seem random within limits.

The Full Unicode property allows you to randomize with letters and numbers.

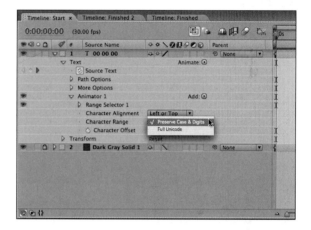

7 Increase the value of the **Character Offset** property to **9** to change all the digits in the readout from **0** seconds to **9** seconds.

This sets the threshold for how the numbers will randomize. After you set the randomization, which you will do next by using a Wiggly selector, the values will never go beyond 9.

You now have new numbers but no randomness. In the previous exercise, you learned about a great force of chaos: the Wiggly selector. You'll use this selector to set the randomness in this exercise.

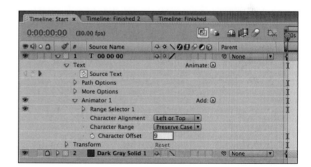

8 From the **Add** pop-up menu next to **Animator 1**, choose a **Wiggly** selector to add to **Animator 1**.

Note: You can have a Range selector and a Wiggly selector in the same animator.

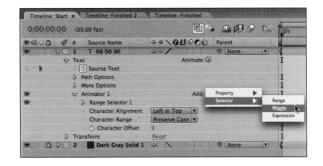

9 Click the **twirly** icon next to **Wiggly Selector 1**. Make sure **Min Amount** is set to **-100%** and **Max Amount** is set to **100%**. Change **Wiggles/Second** to **7**. Make sure **Mode** is set to **Intersect**.

Setting Wiggles/Second to 7 ensures the randomization happens at a speed of seven changes per second.

When a selector is in Intersect mode, only the parts of its selection intersecting another selection will be affected. Right now, because you haven't made any changes to Range Selector 1, the Wiggly selector can randomly change any part of the text layer. Later, you'll constrain the Wiggly selector using Range Selector 1.

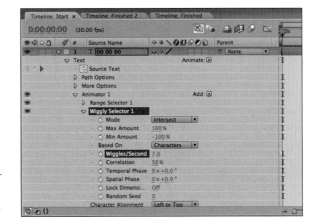

10 Press the **spacebar** to preview the animation.

All the numbers run randomly through the length of the animation, and the combination never gets solved. The numbers randomly increment, which is better than the unison increase you observed in Step 4, but now there's no sense of an ordered solving sequence. You'll fix this next.

Wouldn't it be nice if you could have randomness and order at the same time? This is where multiple selectors come in.

11 Click the **Range Selector 1** twirly, and click the **Advanced** twirly to display its properties. Choose **Index** from the **Units** pop-up menu, and make sure the **Based On** property is set to **Characters**.

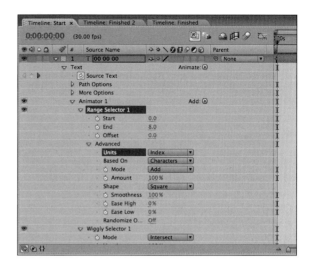

The Units property lets you specify how you want to measure your selection: by characters or by percentages. The Based On property lets you specify whether you want to include spaces in your measurements or whether you want to count by words or lines instead of characters. By changing Units to Index, you're telling After Effects to treat each letter as a unit.

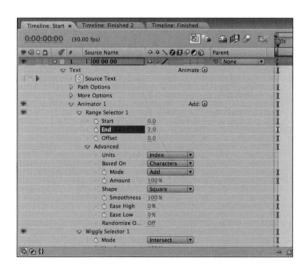

12 Notice the **End** property of **Range Selector 1** is set to **8**. Change the **End** value to **2** in the **Timeline**.

The value of 8 means After Effects recognizes the text block has eight characters (six numbers and two spaces).

We'll now take a moment to summarize what has happened so far: You created a set of six numbers in a text block. You established keyframes to change the source text three times to the final safe-cracking numbers. You applied a Character Offset animator to the entire text block, allowing it to offset to nine numbers away from its origin. You applied a Wiggly selector to randomize the numbers from 0 to 9. Then you set a Range selector to a two-character width to limit the Wiggly selector's effect to only two numbers.

The effect takes a lot of steps, but it is worth it. The next objective is to move the randomization away from each set of two letters so they can end on the real numbers set in the original source text.

13 Make sure the **CTI** is still at **0:00:00:00**. Click the **stop-watch** icon for the **Offset** property of **Range Selector 1**. Set its initial value to **-2**. Choose **Animation > Toggle Hold Keyframe**.

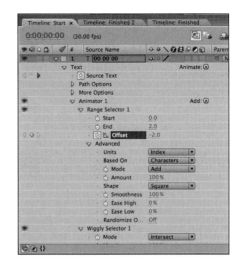

This moves the Range selector, which is set to the width of two characters, completely off the text to the left. The pause makes it appear as if the computer is trying to solve the problem. Choosing Animation > Toggle Hold Keyframe causes the Offset property to hold at its offscreen position until the next time you want it to change. If you don't set a Hold keyframe, the changes in the Offset value will gradually interpolate over time. Because you want the offset value to jump from keyframe to keyframe, you should use a Hold keyframe.

14 Next to the **Source Text** property, click the **Keyframe Navigator** arrows once to advance the **CTI** to the first **Source Text** keyframe (**0:00:01:28**). Set the **Offset** property to **0**.

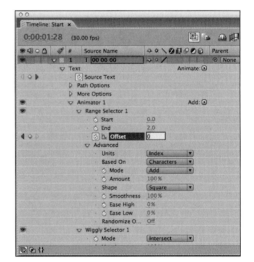

The keyframe icon is for a Hold interpolation type, which is the only kind of keyframe allowed for source text. Moving the Offset property to 0 causes the Range selector to cinch in on the first two numbers of the text block.

Because you set the initial keyframe to a Hold keyframe, all subsequently created keyframes for the Offset property will be set up as Hold keyframes automatically, which is exactly what you want in this case. This causes the Offset value to jump from keyframe to keyframe rather than gradually move over time from keyframe to keyframe. You learned about Hold keyframes and keyframe interpolation in Chapter 6, *"Playing with Time."* Do these features make more sense now that you have a bit more experience? Every keyframe from now on will be a Hold keyframe, unless you toggle your last Hold keyframe to an interpolated keyframe.

15 Click the **Keyframe Navigator** arrow again for **Source Text** to advance the **CTI** to the next **Source Text** keyframe (**0:00:03:28**). Set the **Offset** property to **3**. Click the **Keyframe Navigator** arrow again for **Source Text** to advance the **CTI** to the next **Source Text** keyframe (**0:00:06:00**), and set the **Offset** property to **6**. Click the **Keyframe Navigator** arrow again for **Source Text** to advance the **CTI** to the next **Source Text** keyframe (**0:00:08:01**), and set the **Offset** property to **9**.

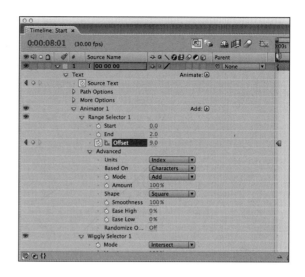

At each source keyframe location, you've moved the Offset value. It started offscreen to the left and then cinched in on the first two numbers, then the second two numbers, then the third two numbers, and then offscreen to the right of the text block.

16 Press the **spacebar** to preview the composition.

At this point, the combination appears to solve itself, but it's a little difficult for the casual viewer to tell what's happening. How about if the solved parts of the combination turn orange? You'll use a second animator to create this effect.

Why use a second animator and not just a second selector? You need a second animator because you will be modifying both the selection and the attributes being applied to the selection for this next effect. If you were changing only one of these, you could just add the new selector or the new property to be changed to this animator. But because they're both changing independently of this animator, you'll need a second animator to do the work.

17 Next to the **Text** property, click the **Animate** menu, and choose **Fill Color > RGB**.

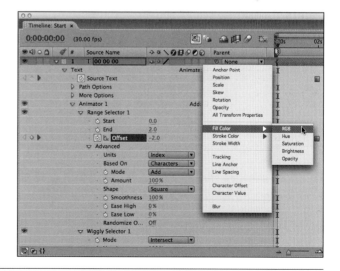

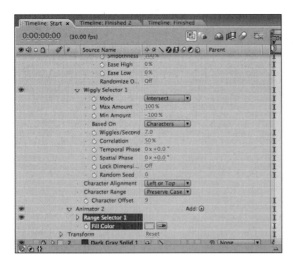

18 Click the **Fill Color** box beneath **Animator 2**, and change its color to bright orange.

All your text in the Composition panel will turn orange as well.

19 Click the **Range Selector 1** twirly beneath **Animator 2**.

If you're running out of room on your Timeline, you can click the Animator 1 twirly; you're done with it.

20 Click the **twirly** icon next to **Advanced**. Change **Units** to **Index**, and notice the **End** property in **Range Selector 1** changes to **8** for the eight characters in the text block (including spaces). In the **Timeline**, drag the **CTI** to **0:00:00:00**, and click the **stopwatch** icon next to the new **Range** selector's **End** property.

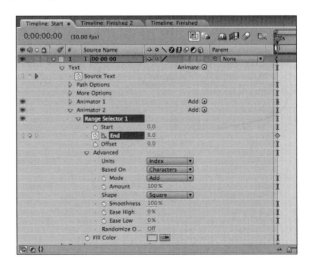

21 In the **Composition** panel, drag the **Range** selector's **End** marker to the left until it matches the selector **Start** marker. All the text returns to red.

Dragging is an alternative to typing values in the Timeline panel. In fact, dragging is a lot more intuitive.

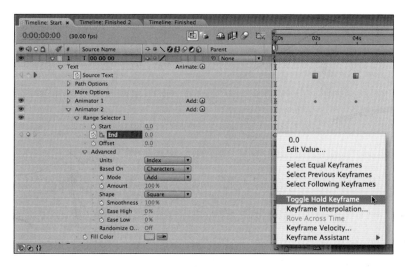

22 Ctrl+click (Mac) or **right-click** (Windows) the keyframe you just created, and choose **Toggle Hold Keyframe** from the contextual menu.

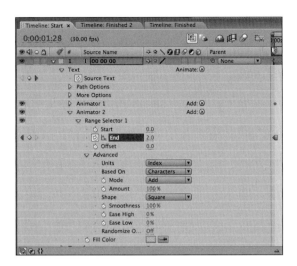

23 Using the **Keyframe Navigator** arrows next to the **Source Text** property of the text layer, advance to the first text change (the second keyframe). In the **Composition** panel, drag the selector **End** marker to the right until the first set of numbers turns orange.

24 Using the **Keyframe Navigator** arrows next to the **Source Text** property, move to the next three keyframes. On the second keyframe, drag the selector **End** marker to the right until the second set of numbers turns orange. Do the same for the third set of numbers at the keyframe.

25 Press the **spacebar** to test the animation one last time.

26 Choose **File > Save**, or press **Cmd+S** (Mac) or **Ctrl+S** (Windows). Choose **File > Close Project**.

After this marathon exercise, where you learned to animate a randomized sequence of numbers, you probably need a little breather. The following exercise is a nice, quick effect to put text on a path, allowing you to animate the text along the outline of a shape.

7 | Putting Text on a Path

After Effects 7 allows you to easily animate text along the outline of a shape. This is a great way to move your text along a predefined course. For example, you can create text that follows the shape of a race-course. However you choose to use this feature, it's a good technique to know because it allows you to move your text quickly in something other than an ordinary, straight line.

---

1 Choose **File > Open Project**. Navigate to the **chap_09** folder you copied to your desktop, click **Path_Text.aep** to select it, and click **Open**.

---

2 Choose **File > Save As**. In the **Save As** dialog box, navigate to the **AE7_HOT_Projects** folder you created on your desktop. Name the file **Path_Text.aep**, and click **Save**.

---

3 In the **Project** panel, double-click the **Finished** composition to see what you're about to learn in this exercise. When you're finished, close the **Finished** composition, and double-click the **Start** composition to open it.

We've created a text layer and a mask (a path defined by the Pen tool, as discussed in more detail in Chapter 13, "*Creating Masks*") for you. The mask is partially clipping the text layer, but you'll fix this soon.

4 If they are not already open, click the **twirly** icon next to the text layer, click the **twirly** icon next to **Text**, and then click the **twirly** icon next to **Path Options**. Choose **Mask 1** from the **Path** pop-up menu.

This step links the text and Mask 1 layers (where the path resides).

You can create a mask on a text layer just like any other layer by selecting the text layer and then simply drawing in the layer with After Effects 7 masking tools. You'll learn how to draw masks in Chapter 13, "*Creating Masks.*"

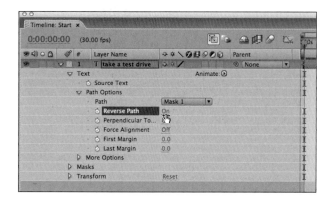

5 In the Composition panel, notice that the text is currently running along the inside of the path. In the new options beneath the **Path** property, change the **Reverse Path** value to **On** if it is not already set.

Note: If your text disappears, don't panic. To fix the disappearing text, click the Masks twirly. If it's not already, change the Mode property of Masks 1 to None by using the pop-up menu next to the mask name. Now the mask will not affect the layer except to serve as a path for the text.

The default behavior of a mask is to reveal only what is contained in the closed path, and you've just asked the text to attach itself to the outside of the path. This applies only to closed paths; open paths do not mask any part of the image.

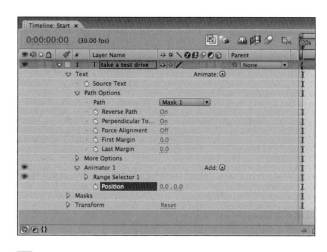

6 Add a **Position** animator to the text layer using any of the techniques you've learned already, such as clicking the **Animate** menu next to the **Text** property and choosing **Position**.

7 Make sure the **CTI** is at **0:00:00:00**, and click the **stopwatch** icon next to the **Position** property of **Animator 1**.

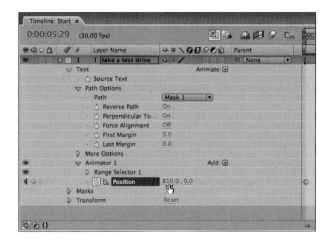

8 In the **Timeline**, drag the **CTI** to **0:00:05:29**. Drag across the first value of the **Position** property (the horizontal value) until the text makes its way one time around the mask shape (the value will be approximately **810**).

When attaching text to a path, the horizontal component of the position controls the text's movement parallel to the path, and the vertical component of the position controls the text's movement perpendicular to the path.

---

9 Press the **spacebar** to preview your animation.

---

10 Choose **File > Save**, or press **Cmd+S** (Mac) or **Ctrl+S** (Windows). Choose **File > Close Project**.

Animating text along a path is simple to do, as you've just seen. If you'd like to experiment further with text animation options, proceed to the next exercise, where you'll see some of the text presets in After Effects 7.

Applying Text Animation Presets

After Effects 7 comes with several text presets to help you quickly animate your text in all sorts of interesting ways. You might think of using presets as "cheating," but they can save you a considerable amount of time and are also a good way to learn about the many possibilities for animating text. In this exercise, you'll apply a text animation preset. You'll also experiment by trying some of the other available presets.

---

1 Choose **File > New > New Project**, and then choose **File > Save As**. In the **Save As** dialog box, navigate to the **AE7_HOT_Projects** folder you created on your desktop. Name the file **Text_Preset.aep**, and click **Save**.

---

2 Click the **Create a new Composition** button in the **Project** panel, name the composition **Speed** in the **Composition Settings** dialog box, and click **OK**.

---

3 In the **Tools** panel, select the **Type** tool. In the **Composition** panel, click near the center of the composition, and type **SPEED**.

---

4 In the **Effects & Presets** panel, click the **twirly** icons next to **Animation Presets**, **Presets**, and **Text** to display the **Text** options.

The Text folder contains all the animation presets for type. As you can see, other folders appear within the Animation Presets folder; you can use them for a variety of purposes besides text.

---

5 Click the **twirly** icon next to the **Blurs** folder, and locate the **Bullet Train** preset.

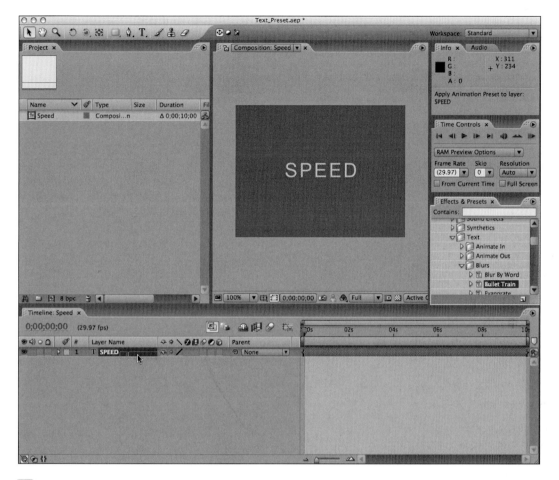

6 Drag and drop the **Bullet Train** preset onto your text layer in the **Timeline**.

You can apply animation presets easily by simply dragging and dropping them onto a layer in the Timeline panel or even in the Composition panel.

---

7 Press the **spacebar** to preview your animation.

This particular animation is fairly short and animates on the screen rather quickly.

8 Click the **twirly** icon to open your text layer, and click the **twirly** icon next to the **Text** property.

Notice this applies a text animator to this layer. You have worked with animators throughout this chapter, although this one was created automatically when you applied the animation preset to your text layer. At this point, you can open the Bullet Train Animator preset and adjust its settings as you would any other animator. You can also modify the Range selector in the same way or add other animators and Range selectors to create an even more complex animation.

As you can see, animation presets can either do the job for you or simply give you a good starting point for further modification.

---

9 Click the **Bullet Train Animator** preset to select it, and then press **Delete** (Mac) or **Backspace** (Windows) to remove it from the text layer.

---

10 Using the same technique, drag and drop other text animation presets from the **Effects & Presets** panel one at a time onto your text layer. Press the **spacebar** to preview the results.

---

11 Choose **File > Save**, or press **Cmd+S** (Mac) or **Ctrl+S** (Windows). Choose **File > Close Project**.

You just learned how to save a lot of time setting keyframes manually by applying animation presets to your text layers in After Effects 7. In the next exercise, you'll import and edit Photoshop text layers without leaving After Effects 7.

---

9 | Importing Text from a Photoshop File

In this exercise, you'll import a graphic with a text layer attached to it, and then you'll correct a typo without leaving After Effects 7. This is important if you want to modify text layers created in Photoshop or Illustrator, rather than those created directly in After Effects 7.

1 Choose **File > New > New Project**, and then choose **File > Save As**. In the **Save As** dialog box, navigate to the **AE7_HOT_Projects** folder you created on your desktop. Name the file **Text_Import.aep**, and click **Save**.

2 Double-click an empty area of the **Project** panel to open the **Import File** dialog box. Navigate to the **chap_09** folder you copied to your desktop, and click (but don't double-click) the **Experience.psd** file.

3 From the **Import As** pop-up menu, choose **Composition – Cropped Layers**. Click **Open** to complete the import process.

This step imports all the Photoshop layers as a single composition.

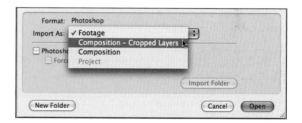

4 In the **Project** panel, double-click the **Experience** composition to open its **Timeline** and **Composition** panels.

Note: If you do not have the same fonts (in this case, a font called Futura) on your machine as in this project, a dialog box warns you of the missing fonts. After Effects 7 will convert the text to editable text, but it changes the text to a font you do have.

5 In the **Timeline** panel, click the **XPERIENCE** layer. From the **Layer** menu, choose **Convert to Editable Text**.

As we just mentioned, if you have the same font used to create this text (Futura), this step changes the text to a text layer without a problem. If you don't, After Effects 7 will alert you about the missing font and will change the text to the default font.

6 In the **Tools** panel, select the **Type** tool, and highlight the word **XPERIENCE**. Type **EXPERIENCE** in its place.

This editing process works great with any Photoshop or Illustrator text that has not already converted to outlines or rasterized in another program. Once you've taken the extra step, you can't go back, so be sure to tell any designers you're working with that they should leave their text unrasterized, as long as you have the same fonts on your system.

---

7 Choose **File > Save**, or press **Cmd+S** (Mac) or **Ctrl+S** (Windows). Choose **File > Close Project**.

Creating Outlines

In the previous exercise, you might have noticed the **Create Outlines** option beneath **Convert to Editable Text**. This option is similar to the options found in Illustrator and Macromedia Flash and is the only way to share an After Effects 7 file containing a specific font with another After Effects 7 user who doesn't have the same font. Unfortunately, this technique has a catch: When you create outlines from text in After Effects 7, you lose all of the text's animated properties. Instead, you end up with a layer with a bunch of masks (one per shape in each letter), which you can then animate separately, but most of the values of the new text layers disappear with the conversion.

In this chapter, you learned a lot about the text features in After Effects 7. Take a break before continuing to the next chapter—you deserve it! In Chapter 10, *"Applying Effects,"* you will explore how to use some of the exciting effects available in After Effects 7.

10

Applying Effects

You might be familiar with the terms **filters** and **layer effects** from using Adobe Photoshop. These are mini-applications, called **plug-ins**, and you can use them to change the appearance of footage, such as the brightness, contrast, color, blur, and so on. After Effects 7 contains plug-in filters, just as Photoshop does, only you can animate them over time, and they have many keyframe settings for visually altering your animations.

In this chapter, you'll learn to apply a variety of effects to modify the look of your animations and control their settings. You'll see the interaction among multiple effects, and you will learn how to control this interaction. Although you will explore several effects in this chapter, such a wide range is available to use in After Effects 7 that we can't come close to covering them all. In fact, the number of variations of parameters for effects plug-ins is practically endless. This chapter will open your eyes to the power of effects so you become inspired to try more of them on your own.

Introducing Plug-Ins

You can think of plug-ins as little programs that work within After Effects 7. After Effects 7 allows these external programs to "plug in" to After Effects 7 and work their magic.

All effects are actually plug-ins, or special add-ons augmenting the capabilities of the application. They reside in the **Plug-ins** folder within the **After Effects** application folder on your hard drive.

Adobe supplies a great number of plug-in effects with After Effects 7. Other companies also create

plug-in effects for use in After Effects 7. In fact, you can add countless effects to your **Plug-ins** folder. Check Appendix B, *"After Effects 7 Resources,"* for plug-in suppliers.

Many Photoshop plug-ins also work with After Effects 7. If you are interested in learning more about plug-ins, consult your After Effects 7 user guide, or choose **Help > After Effects Help**.

1 | Applying Effects

After Effects 7 includes a wide variety of effects for you to use—more than we could possibly discuss in this book. Effects are useful for a variety of purposes, but you will begin by looking at a couple of common effects that produce rather obvious results. In this exercise, you will create a new project and apply four effects: **Find Edges** (creates a sketched look), **Posterize** (reduces the tonal range and creates bold color patterns), **Hue/Saturation** (changes the overall color of the composition), and **Bulge** (distorts the shape of the image). As you work through this exercise, notice how After Effects 7 arranges the effects for easy identification. After Effects 7 groups the various effects to speed the selection process.

1 Copy the **chap_10** folder from the **After Effects 7 HOT CD-ROM** onto your desktop.

2 Choose **File > Open Project**. Navigate to the **chap_10** folder you copied to your desktop, select the file named **Effects.aep**, and click **Open**. Choose **File > Save As**. In the **Save As** dialog box, navigate to the **AE7_HOT_Projects** folder on your desktop. Name the file **Effects.aep**, and click **Save**.

3 In the **Project** panel, click the **twirly** icon next to **Effects Folder** to display the contents of the folder. Locate the **Effects Finished** composition, and double-click to open it. Press the **spacebar** to preview the composition.

It's not necessarily pretty, but this animation does show how dynamic even simple effects can be.

4 In the **Timeline**, click the *f* icon, located in the **Layer Switches** panel, and then view your footage in the **Composition** panel.

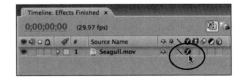

The *f* icon turns on and off all the Effects properties for a layer, regardless of how many you have applied. That's quite a difference, right? Of course, how far you take effects is your own decision. You can easily create garish, over-the-top styles, or you can make subtle changes to trick the eye into not knowing what is real or unreal.

5 In the **Timeline** panel, click the **twirly** icon next to **Seagull.mov**, and then click the **twirly** icons next to its **Effects** properties to display the effects.

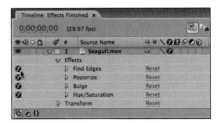

You'll see four effects applied to this layer. If you click their twirly icons, you'll see more properties, and you will start to appreciate the number of options effects offer.

6 With the **Seagull.mov** layer selected, choose **Effect > Effect Controls**.

This opens an auxiliary panel—the Effect Controls panel—showing the effects applied to any layer. If you click any of the *f* icons here, you can selectively turn on or off individual effects.

---

7 In the **Effect Controls** panel, click all the *f* icons to turn on the effects if they are not already on, and then practice moving the order of effects around by dragging the names above or below each other.

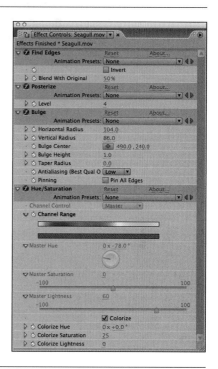

You can also reorder the effects in the Timeline as well as turn on or off individual effects. It might seem confusing to know when to use the Timeline panel and when to use the Effect Controls panel to change effect settings. These panels are similar and present essentially the same information in slightly different layouts. Choosing one or the other is a personal choice. You'll get to work both with the Timeline panel and with the Effect Controls panel in this chapter, so you will be able to develop your own preferences based on your particular working method.

---

8 In the upper-left corner of the **Composition** panel, choose **Close Effects Finished** from the pop-up menu to close the current composition. In the **Project** panel, double-click the **Effects Start** composition, located in the **Effects Folder**, to open it.

Now that you've had a chance to preview a few effects, it is time to re-create these effects yourself.

---

9 In the **Timeline** panel, select the **Seagull.mov** layer. Choose **Effect > Color Correction > Hue/Saturation**.

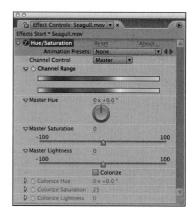

This opens the Effect Controls panel automatically with all the Hue/Saturation properties visible. Hue specifies a particular color value, or gradation of color, and Saturation determines the intensity, or how much of the color to include.

10 In the **Effect Controls** panel, change **Master Hue** to **66** degrees and **Master Lightness** to **64**.

You should see a change in color take place in your layer. Notice the stopwatch icon next to Channel Range. You can animate any of these effect properties, although you won't do that yet.

---

11 Choose **Effect > Distort > Bulge**.

The Bulge effect, which distorts your image around a point, will appear below the Hue/Saturation effect in the Effect Controls panel. Notice the large number of choices available for this particular effect, such as Horizontal Radius, Vertical Radius, Bulge Center, Bulge Height, Taper Radius, and others. You can adjust these properties to change the look of the effect, such as making it fill a larger portion of the screen while distorting your video in different directions. Each effect comes with its own set of properties. Some effects have a large number of properties you can set; others have just a few.

---

12 Change the **Horizontal Radius** setting to **96.0**, the **Vertical Radius** setting to **102.0**, and the **Bulge Height** setting to **0.5**. Move the **x** value for **Bulge Center** to the right on the screen, until it is centered over the bird, at about **490**.

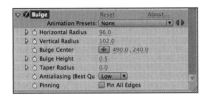

View the adjustments you make in the Composition panel to accurately achieve the desired result. The bird should appear larger over the area where the center point appears, as though it were bulging out toward the surface of the screen.

Try some of the other properties on your own. Ideally, you'll explore each effect and its individual properties to understand what the effect does. In fact, experimenting with each After Effects 7 effect can provide hours of diversion.

---

13 Choose **Effect > Stylize > Find Edges**. Change the **Blend With Original** property to **63%**.

Adjusting the Blend With Original property modifies the effect's transparency and reintroduces more of the original footage underneath. The effect is a little intense on its own.

---

14 Choose **Effect > Stylize > Posterize**. Change the **Level** property to **4**. Click the **spacebar** to preview, and press it again to stop playback.

The Posterize effect reduces the amount of color information in the image. A low value, such as 4, will simplify the look of your video, resulting in a "graphic" look.

---

15 Choose **File > Save**, or press **Cmd+S** (Mac) or **Ctrl+S** (Windows). In the upper-left corner of the **Composition** panel, choose **Close Effects Start** from the pop-up menu. Leave **Effects.aep** open for the next exercise.

This exercise has given you a small inkling of what's in store with effects. You learned how to apply effects and how to view them in the Effect Controls and Timeline panels. You can use keyframes to animate any property of these effects using the stopwatch icon, which you have done many times already in this book.

That's all for this exercise. If you want to create some animation or experiment with other properties or effects before continuing to the next exercise, feel free. In the next exercise, you will learn about other effects you can apply to create interesting results.

NOTE:

Resetting and Deleting an Effect

If you are ever unhappy with settings you've created, you can reset the effect to clear all your settings. To the right of every effect in the **Effect Controls** panel is a **Reset** button. Click this button, and your settings will magically disappear. If you ever want to delete an effect, simply select it in the **Effect Controls** panel, and press the **Delete** key.

---

2 | Adding a Drop Shadow Effect

The **Drop Shadow** effect, which adds a shadow behind a layer, is one of the most commonly used effects in many graphics programs. It is often used to add depth to a composition with flat graphics or text because it adds another dimensional quality to the images. In this exercise, you will add a **Drop Shadow** effect to a composition and learn to animate it.

---

1 If you followed the previous exercise, **Effects.aep** should still be open in After Effects 7. If it's not, choose **File > Open Project**. Navigate to the **chap_10** folder you copied to your desktop, click **Effects_2.aep** to select it, and click **Open**.

---

2 In the **Project** panel, open **Dropshadow Folder**, and double-click **Dropshadow Finished** to open the composition. Press the **spacebar** to preview the composition. When you're finished previewing, close the composition, and double-click **Dropshadow Start** from the same folder.

Notice the drop shadow animates closer to the background as it gets smaller, giving a natural effect of the lighting changes that occur when something gets closer to the ground.

---

3 Select the **Cycle.psd** layer in the **Timeline**, and choose **Effect > Perspective > Drop Shadow**.

When you apply this effect, the Effect Controls panel opens automatically. You have a choice to set the stopwatch icon in this panel or in the Timeline panel. In general, the Timeline panel is often the most convenient place to set keyframes because you can animate other properties there besides effects properties.

---

4 Move the **CTI** (Current Time Indicator) to the beginning of the composition by pressing the **Home** key. In the **Timeline** panel, click the **twirly** icon next to **Cycle.psd** and the **twirly** icon next to **Transform** to view their properties. Click the **Scale** property's **stopwatch** icon.

The Scale property is already set to 75% on both X and Y, which is where you want it to begin its animation.

---

5 Move the **CTI** to the last frame by pressing the **End** key. Change the **Scale** value to **19%**.

Your layer animation now starts at 75% and scales to 19%, which creates the illusion of receding into the background. If you preview the animation now, the drop shadow looks pretty flat and unrealistic. You will change this in the next few steps.

---

6 Move the **CTI** to the beginning of the composition by pressing the **Home** key. In the **Timeline** panel, click the **twirly** icons next to **Effects** and **Drop Shadow** to reveal the properties. Click the **stopwatch** icons for **Opacity**, **Distance**, and **Softness**. Change **Opacity** to **34%**, **Distance** to **96.0**, and **Softness** to **44.0**.

At this point, you are simply adjusting the appearance of the Drop Shadow effect over time. The drop shadow will start less transparent and gradually become more visible, the distance from the drop shadow to the foreground image will become closer, and the softness of the effect becomes harder in appearance.

7 Move the **CTI** to the end of the composition by pressing the **End** key. Change **Opacity** to **60%**, **Distance** to **14.0**, and **Softness** to **9.0**. Press the **spacebar** to watch the animation.

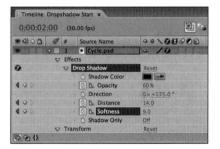

You have now animated a few properties for your Drop Shadow effect, which illustrates the variety of ways you can customize the look of the effect, even changing its appearance over time.

8 Choose **File > Save**, or press **Cmd+S** (Mac) or **Ctrl+S** (Windows). In the upper-left corner of the **Composition** panel, choose **Close Dropshadow Start** from the pop-up menu. Leave **Effects.aep** open for the next exercise.

The Drop Shadow effect, which you just learned about, is often used for text and logos. In the next exercise, you will learn about applying transition effects, which can be useful if you want to create transitions from one clip (or layer) to another in After Effects 7, rather than in a nonlinear editing application such as Adobe Premiere Pro or Apple Final Cut Pro.

TIP:

Using Best Quality for Illustrator Files

When using Adobe Illustrator files or other types of vector graphics in your compositions, set the **Quality** setting to **Best** to ensure the preview image is as detailed as possible. If you want to speed up the rendering of previews, return to the **Draft** setting. You can also use the **Continuous Rasterization** setting on vector files that have effects applied.

EXERCISE

3 | Using Transition Effects

Transition effects are so commonly used they deserve a mention in this chapter. You are probably familiar with transitions from other video applications, such as Premiere Pro or Final Cut Pro. However, transition effects in After Effects 7 are not entirely intuitive upon first glance. Transition effects always require at least two layers because the purpose is to "transition" from one layer to another, such as fading out one layer to reveal another beneath it. A simple fade or dissolve between two different shots in a movie is a basic example of this technique in action. In this exercise, you will learn how to set up and apply transition effects.

---

1 If you followed the previous exercise, **Effects.aep** should still be open in After Effects 7. If it's not, choose **File > Open Project**. Navigate to the **chap_10** folder you copied to your desktop, click **Effects_3.aep** to select it, and click **Open**.

---

2 In the **Project** panel, click the **twirly** icon next to **Wipe Folder**. Double-click the **Gradient_Wipe Finished** and **Radial_Wipe Finished** compositions to open them. Preview these two compositions.

You'll find the effects you see in these two compositions in the Transition category of the Effect menu. You'll get to practice learning how to create transitions in this exercise, and you can apply the techniques you learn here to other transition effects.

---

3 In the **Project** panel, double-click **Radial_Wipe Start** to open the composition.

This is a simple composition with two layers, one hiding the other.

---

4 In the **Timeline**, select the top layer, called **Seagull.mov**.

It's important to note you'll always want to apply the effect to the top layer in a composition when creating transitions. This causes the top layer to wipe off (or gradually disappear from left to right, from top to bottom, in a clockwise direction, or in a variety of other ways) to reveal the bottom layer. If you were to put the wipe effect on the bottom layer, you wouldn't see anything happen because the top layer would be hiding it.

---

5 Choose **Effect > Transition > Radial Wipe**. In the **Timeline**, click the **twirly** icon next to the **Seagull.mov** layer as well as the **twirly** icon next to **Effects** to reveal the properties for the **Radial Wipe** effect.

The Effect Controls panel automatically opens, revealing settings for the clocklike motion properties of the Radial Wipe transition. We prefer to set this effect in the Timeline because we can see the CTI and the keyframes. However, you can work in the Effect Controls panel if you choose.

---

6 Make sure the **CTI** is on the first frame of your composition by pressing the **Home** key. Click the **twirly** icon next to **Radial Wipe**, and click the **stopwatch** icon for **Transition Completion**.

This sets a keyframe on Frame 0:00:00:01 to 0%, which means the transition has not yet occurred but may begin at this point. At the start of a transition, you will set Transition Completion to 0, and at the end, you will set it to 100, which is when it has been fully completed.

---

7 Move the **CTI** to the last frame by pressing the **End** key. Change the **Transition Completion** value to **100%**.

You should see the bottom layer (Blue_Sky.psd) appear in the Composition panel.

8 Drag the **CTI**, and scrub through the **Timeline** to view the **Radial Wipe** effect.

Notice the edge looks rough. This particular transition might look better with a softer edge.

---

9 Change the **Feather** property for the **Radial Wipe** effect to **25**. If you prefer, you can choose another setting you find pleasing.

Because you didn't click the stopwatch icon for the Feather property, this change applies to the entire composition. The only time you want to set keyframes is when you want something to change over time. To leave the feather set the same for the duration of this composition, just change the value, and you're done.

Next, you'll try another transition effect: Gradient Wipe.

---

10 In the **Project** panel, double-click the **Gradient_Wipe Start** composition in **Wipe Folder**.

---

11 In the **Timeline** panel, select the **Seagull.mov** layer, and choose **Effect > Transition > Gradient Wipe**. In the **Effect Controls** panel, which opens automatically, click the **About** link. When you are done reading the message, click **OK**.

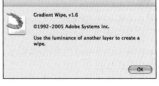

The About link (located in the Effect Controls panel) describes the chosen effect and what it does. This is useful for effects without obvious names, such as Gradient Wipe (which creates a transition using the luminance values of a second, gradient layer to define the shape of the effect), for example.

---

12 In the **Timeline** panel, click the **twirly** icon next to the **Seagull.mov** layer to reveal the **Effects** properties for the **Gradient Wipe** effect. Make sure the **CTI** is on the first frame of your composition. Click the **stopwatch** icon for the **Transition Completion** property.

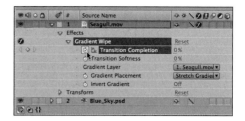

This sets the first keyframe for the Transition Completion property.

13 Move the **CTI** to the last frame of the composition. In the **Transition Completion** value field, type **100%**. Drag the **CTI**, and scrub through the **Timeline**.

Note: If you do not see anything happen when you scrub through your Timeline, it is because this particular effect requires you to assign a layer to it. In this instance, After Effects 7 should have assigned the layer for you automatically (After Effects 7 will sometimes make a "best guess" based on the most common settings). For some effects, you may need to manually set this option by choosing a layer from a pop-up list of available layers in your composition. If necessary, for this particular effect, you can click the Gradient Layer menu and choose Seagull.mov (or another available layer) to see the effect.

14 Increase the **Transition Softness** property for **Gradient Wipe** to **37%**. Press the **spacebar** to preview the effect, and press it again to stop the playback.

Once you've seen the effect in action, you might decide it is too hard-edged and could use a bit of softness applied to it. In this case, increase the Transition Softness property.

15 Choose **File > Save**, or press **Cmd+S** (Mac) or **Ctrl+S** (Windows). In the upper-left corner of the **Composition** panel, choose **Close All** from the pop-up menu. Leave **Effects.aep** open for the next exercise.

This exercise demonstrated how to work with radial and gradient transition effects. Be sure to look in the Effect > Transition menu for other effects you might want to try. In the next exercise, you'll learn about different types of effects called Lens Blur.

4 | Using a Lens Blur Effect

After Effects 7 includes a variety of blur effects, which make images hazy, although one of the more interesting ones is the **Lens Blur** effect. Using **Lens Blur**, you can create the illusion your video footage or animation was "shot" with a camera lens using selective focus or a narrow depth of field. To produce the desired result most accurately, you need to use a special gradient image (created in an application such as Photoshop) to define which areas of the frame will be in "focus" and how much blur will apply to the image. In this exercise, you will learn how to apply this effect and what pieces you use to create it.

1 If you followed the previous exercise, **Effects.aep** should still be open in After Effects 7. If it's not, choose **File > Open Project**. Navigate to the **chap_10** folder you copied to your desktop, click **Effects_4.aep** to select it, and click **Open**.

2 In the **Project** panel, click the **twirly** icon next to **Lens Blur Folder**. Double-click **Lens Blur Finished** to open the composition, and observe the effect you are about to create. When you have finished previewing the effect, double-click **Lens Blur Start** in the **Project** panel.

You can use the Lens Blur effect to make certain areas of the frame look "out of focus." Oftentimes, this appears as the inverse of what is shown in the illustration here, with objects in the foreground sharp and a defocused background. This creates a narrow depth of field not present in the original footage or animation. You can use this selective-focus effect in interesting ways to simulate the look of the effect produced by a film or video camera to direct the viewer's attention.

3 In the **Lens Blur Start** composition, click the **Solo** button for the **Radial_Gradiant.psd** layer to view it by itself. Observe the circular pattern created in Photoshop. When you are finished viewing this layer, click the **Solo** button for **Radial_Gradient.psd** again, and then click the **Solo** button for the **Linear_Gradient.psd** layer to view it. Notice the linear pattern of lines on this graphic, which was also created in Photoshop. Click the **Solo** button for **Linear_Gradient.psd** when you are finished viewing it.

The Lens Blur effect uses black, white, and gray areas in a separate graphic layer (called a **depth map**) to determine the amount of blur it should apply to an image. By default, black areas in the depth map are considered to be close to the fictional camera lens, or less blurred. White areas of the depth map are considered further away, or more blurred. You define the actual appearance of the Lens Blur effect by setting its special Effect properties. You will see each gradient layer in action as you work through this exercise.

4 In the **Timeline** panel, select the top **Sunset_Drive.psd** layer.

5 In the **Effects & Presets** panel, type the word **lens** in the **Contains** field at the top of the panel. (If the **Effects & Presets** panel is not visible, choose **Window > Effects & Presets**.)

Search results are returned immediately as you type. You can use the Effects & Presets panel to quickly locate an effect based on a keyword in the name, rather than manually searching for it through multiple pop-up menus. Depending on your working style, you may find yourself using this panel exclusively to locate and apply effects.

6 In the **Effects & Presets** panel, double-click the **Lens Blur** effect, located in the **Blur & Sharpen** category.

This applies the effect to the currently selected layer in the Timeline (Sunset_Drive.psd).

You can find the same effect by choosing Effect > Blur & Sharpen > Lens Blur. The Effects & Presets panel just easily found it for you.

Note: In addition to double-clicking, you can drag the effect from the Effects & Presets panel and drop it directly on a layer in the Timeline panel or on an object in the Composition panel.

7 In the **Effect Controls** panel, choose **Linear_Gradient.psd** from the **Depth Map Layer** pop-up menu. In the **Composition** panel, observe the results.

Notice the black areas in the Linear_Gradient.psd layer are sharp, and the white areas are blurred. Black areas are usually reserved for those places nearest to the camera (although no "real" camera was used to record this scene), and white areas are reserved for those further away. The gray gradiant in between creates a smooth transition between the two.

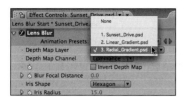

8 In the **Effect Controls** panel, choose
Radial_Gradient.psd from the **Depth Map Layer** pop-up
menu. In the **Composition** panel, observe the results.

Notice the black areas in the Radial_Gradient.psd layer
are sharp, and the white areas are blurred. In this instance,
the subject in focus isn't necessarily nearest to the camera,
although you used the Lens Blur effect to highlight, or draw
attention to, a specific area of the frame in a dramatic way.

---

9 In the **Effect Controls** panel, set **Specular Brightness** to **90** and **Specular Threshold** to **250**.

The Specular Brightness and Specular Threshold properties adjust the amount of specular highlights, which
are the glow created by the reflection of light off a bright source, such as sunlight bouncing off the chrome
on a motorcycle or the bloom around the edges of the sun.

You can adjust additional properties as desired and experiment with the other properties for this particular effect. A bit of experimentation and playful exploration will reveal even more possibilities.

---

10 Choose **File > Save**, or press **Cmd+S** (Mac) or **Ctrl+S** (Windows). In the upper-left corner of the
Composition panel, choose **Close All** from the pop-up menu. Leave **Effects.aep** open for the next exercise.

Each effect you apply in After Effects 7 has its own, and often unique, set of properties you can use. In
this exercise, you worked with the Lens Blur effect, using gradient layers to define the specific appearance of the effect. In the next exercise, you'll learn a few ways to adjust the colors in your composition
using a new set of effects.

NOTE:

Understanding the Effects & Presets Panel

The **Effects & Presets** panel (not to be confused with the **Effect Controls** panel you
used previously) is a great tool for locating effects. To display the **Effects & Presets**
panel, choose **Window > Effects**. This panel contains an organized list of all the
effects (and presets) available in your copy of After Effects 7. Simply click the **twirly**
icons to display the individual effects available under each category.

Best of all, you can type letters in the **Contains** field to display the name of any effect
with matching letters. As you continue typing, the panel will instantly update with
search results for the keywords or letters you have typed. As you've begun to see,
After Effects 7 has many effects, and it can be difficult to remember where each one
is located or even to remember the name of an effect. Using the **Effects & Presets**
panel to search for effects makes it easy to find exactly what you are looking for quickly.

5 | Making Color Correction Adjustments

Even carefully shot footage may require some color correction. In fact, the majority of video and film projects use color correction as a major element of the post-production process. **Color correction** allows you to fix uneven lighting or color elements in your footage; it also allows you to experiment with different looks, which can evoke interesting moods. This exercise introduces just a few of the color correction effects built into After Effects 7, such as **Brightness & Contrast**, **Exposure**, and **Color Balance**. The next time your project requires a bit of color adjustment, you'll know where to find the effects you need.

1 If you followed the previous exercise, **Effects.aep** should still be open in After Effects 7. If it's not, choose **File > Open Project**. Navigate to the **chap_10** folder you copied to your desktop, click **Effects_5.aep** to select it, and click **Open**.

2 In the **Project** panel, click the **twirly** icon next to **Color Correction Folder**, and double-click **Color_Correction Start** to open the composition. In the **Timeline** panel, select the **Seagull.mov** layer.

This footage is a bit dark, and its color palette is a bit dull. You'll apply some effects to improve its overall appearance.

3 Choose **Effect > Color Correction > Brightness & Contrast**.

Notice the wide array of Color Correction effects available to you in After Effects 7. If you are a Photoshop pro, you should already recognize many of these names. Two of the simplest ways to adjust the look of an image are brightness and contrast, available here in a single effect item.

4 In the **Effect Controls** panel, increase both values for the **Brightness** and **Contrast** properties to about **40**. In the **Effect Controls** panel, click the *f* symbol repeatedly to see the "before" and "after" results. When you are done, click the *f* symbol to turn off the effect.

Notice the dramatic difference in the Composition panel. Although brightness and contrast adjustments can go a long way, they are rather imprecise and do not allow for a great deal of flexibility or options for correcting specific ranges of color. They may also remove some important details from the image. In the next step, you will try a different effect to achieve more precise results.

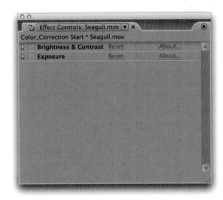

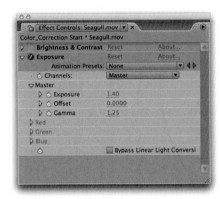

5 Choose **Effect > Color Correction > Exposure**. Under **Master**, change **Exposure** to **1.40** and **Gamma** to **1.25**.

You can use the Exposure effect to adjust an image in terms of **f-stops**, which are the light levels utilized by cinematographers in the "real world." A few simple exposure adjustments can go a long way toward correcting dimly lit images and improving the tonal characteristics of the footage.

Gamma adjustments within the Exposure effect reintroduce more color, which is often lost when brightening an image. If you choose Individual Channels (instead of Master) from the Channels pop-up menu, you can make exposure adjustments for the red, green, and blue color channels of the image independently for maximum control (color images are composed of varying amounts of these three colors).

6   Choose **Effect > Color Correction > Color Balance**. Turn on **Preserve Luminosity**, and change **Shadow Blue Balance** to **15**, **Midtone Red Balance** to **12**, and **Hilight Blue Balance** to **-50**.

The Color Balance effect adjusts the amount of each color channel (red, green, and blue) for an image. Dragging a slider to the right, or raising the numbers toward +100, increases the amount of that color in the image; dragging a slider to the left, or lowering the numbers toward -100, removes that particular color. This is a great effect for focusing adjustments on the particular range of color, whether within Shadow, Midtone, or Hilight luminance values.

Turning on Preserve Luminosity allows you to keep the brightness of your image constant while allowing you to use the color balance controls. This is especially useful if you have already made adjustments with an effect such as Exposure and want to maintain those settings while fine-tuning color.

In this step, adjust the colors to achieve whatever effect you desire, whether subtle or exaggerated (large increases in color balance values will produce dramatic results).

---

7   Choose **File > Save**, or press **Cmd+S** (Mac) or **Ctrl+S** (Windows). In the upper-left corner of the **Composition** panel, choose **Close Color_Correction Start** from the pop-up menu. Leave **Effects.aep** open for the next exercise.

In addition to Brightness & Contrast, Exposure, and Color Balance, many more color correction effects exist. Use this exercise as a starting point to explore the many adjustments you can make. If you are color correcting video, you might also consider an application such as Premiere Pro or Final Cut Pro. Additionally, Exercise 7 later in this chapter covers adjustment layers, which are great to use in combination with color correction effects. But first, you will explore creating presets for your favorite effects in the next exercise.

Creating Favorite Effects or Animation Presets

In After Effects 7, **animation presets**, sometimes referred to as **favorites** or (as described in the actual After Effects 7 file information) **After Effects Favorite Effects**, offer a way to save an effect and its keyframes for use on another composition. If you plan on using a particular effect again at some point in the future, you can save a lot of time and frustration by saving it as a favorite. Once you've saved it, you can use it on any composition you create in After Effects 7. In this exercise, you'll make an animation preset based on a transition effect you worked on previously in this chapter, and then you'll apply this favorite to another composition.

1 If you followed the previous exercise, **Effects.aep** should still be open in After Effects 7. If it's not, choose **File > Open Project**. Navigate to the **chap_10** folder you copied to your desktop, click **Effects_6.aep** to select it, and click **Open**.

2 In the **Project** panel, open **Wipe Folder**, and double-click the **Gradient_Wipe Start** composition, which you completed in Exercise 3.

You will learn how to take the effect you produced in this particular composition, save it, and then reapply it to new sequences.

3 If necessary, in the **Timeline** panel, click the **twirly** icon for the **Seagull.mov** layer if the effects aren't already visible. Double-click the **Gradient Wipe** effect.

Double-clicking the Gradient Wipe effect in the Timeline opens the Effect Controls panel for the layer (if it was closed).

4 In the **Effect Controls** panel, click the **Animation Presets** pop-up menu, and choose **Save Selection as Animation Preset**.

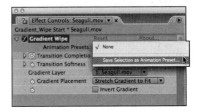

5 In the **Save Animation Preset as** dialog box, name the file **Gradient.ffx**, navigate to the **Presets** folder (located in the main After Effects 7 application folder), and open the **Transitions – Wipes** folder. Click **Save**.

This saves the effect, with all of its settings and animation properties, to an animation preset, which means you can now easily access it in any composition.

6 In the **Project** panel, open **Wipe Folder**, and double-click the **Favorites Start** composition. In the **Timeline** panel, select the **Sky1.tif** layer. Choose **Animation > Apply Animation Preset**.

You will now be able to select a preset, such as the one you just made, and apply it to the selected layer.

---

7 In the **Open** dialog box, select the **Gradient.ffx** prefix in the **Transitions – Wipes** folder, and click **Open**.

---

8 Drag the **CTI**, and scrub through the **Timeline** to preview the results. Click the **twirly** icon for **Sky1.tif** to reveal the **Effects** settings.

Notice keyframes have been set, and the Gradient Wipe effect has been applied to this layer.

---

9 Choose **File > Save**, or press **Cmd+S** (Mac) or **Ctrl+S** (Windows). In the upper-left corner of the **Composition** panel, choose **Close All** from the pop-up menu. Leave **Effects.aep** open for the next exercise.

Favorites are a great way to store your Effects settings for later use. They can save lots of time, especially on a project that reuses the same effects repeatedly. On a different note, the next exercise will introduce you to adjustment layers, which allow you to apply effects to several layers at once.

---

7 | Using Adjustment Layers with Effects

Adjustment layers are special layers you can place in a composition to affect other layers. You did not learn about these in Chapter 8, *"Working with Layers,"* because they are difficult to demonstrate without applying effects. If you apply an effect to an adjustment layer, the effect applies to all layers below it. This is particularly useful for making global changes to a composition, such as changing its overall color or appearance. Adjustment layers give you the flexibility you need to apply effects in ways not otherwise practical, such as blurring an entire composition, rather than blurring all layers individually.

---

1 If you followed the previous exercise, **Effects.aep** should still be open in After Effects 7. If it's not, choose **File > Open Project**. Navigate to the **chap_10** folder you copied to your desktop, click **Effects_7.aep** to select it, and click **Open**.

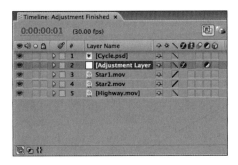

2 In the **Project** panel, double-click the **Adjustment Finished** composition in **Adjustment Folder** to open it.

This is a finished composition, which includes an adjustment layer containing a Gaussian Blur effect.

Notice the stacking order of the layers in the Timeline. The adjustment layer has a Blur filter attached to it, and its Effects settings affect all the layers below it. If you move the adjustment layer below Star1.mov and Star2.mov, you'll see those layers are no longer blurry. If you move the adjustment layer to the top of the stack, you'll observe this affects all the layers in the composition, including Cycle.psd. This is the power of an adjustment layer. It's an easy way to apply one effect to multiple layers.

---

3 In the upper-left corner of the **Composition** panel, choose **Close Adjustment Finished** from the pop-up menu. In the **Project** panel, double-click the **Adjustment Start** composition.

This composition contains unaltered footage but does not yet contain an adjustment layer.

---

4 Choose **Layer > New > Adjustment Layer**.

This adds an adjustment layer to this composition, but nothing will have changed yet because you haven't associated an effect with it. In the next step, you will apply an effect to the layer.

---

5 With the adjustment layer selected, choose **Effect > Blur & Sharpen > Gaussian Blur**. In the **Effect Controls** panel, change **Blurriness** to **6.0**.

Notice all the layers in the composition become blurry. The Gaussian Blur effect affects any layer, which is below the adjustment layer, containing an effect. Although we're demonstrating this with the Gaussian Blur effect, it works with any effect! This is particularly useful with color correction effects.

---

6 In the **Timeline** panel, drag the adjustment layer to beneath **Cycle.psd** so it is above the **Star1.mov** layer.

Notice the layers above the adjustment layer are unaffected, and the layers below it are still affected. In essence, anytime you want to apply the same effect to multiple layers, use an adjustment layer.

---

7 Choose **File > Save**, or press **Cmd+S** (Mac) or **Ctrl+S** (Windows). Leave **Effects.aep** and the **Adjustment Start** composition open for the next exercise.

In this exercise, you saw how to use adjustment layers to apply effects to several layers at once. In the next exercise, you will look at another way to manage layers and effects, called **precomposing**, or placing one composition inside another.

---

8 | Using Precompose with Effects

In the previous exercise, you learned how to use an adjustment layer with an effect. In this exercise, you'll see how to combine what you've learned with another technique called **precomposing**. This means you can use a composition as a footage item inside another composition (compositions placed within other compositions, or **nesting**). You might want to use precomposing to apply special effects or to simplify the animation of large groups of layers. This exercise will provide a good example of why you might want to use a precomp.

---

1 If you followed the previous exercise, **Effects.aep** should still be open in After Effects 7. If it's not, choose **File > Open Project**. Navigate to the **chap_10** folder you copied to your desktop, click **Effects_8.aep** to select it, and click **Open**.

---

2 In the **Timeline** panel, drag the adjustment layer to the top position in the **Adjustment Start** comp.

As you saw in the previous exercise, this blurs all the layers below it. But what if you want to blur the motorcycle and star animations in this composition but not the background movie? How do you accomplish this? Well, you can put the star layers (Star 1.mov and Star2.mov) and the adjustment layer in their own composition, and then place that composition inside this composition. You'll learn to do this next.

---

3 Click the adjustment layer, hold down the **Shift** key, and click **Star2.mov** to multiple-select the top four layers.

4 Choose **Layer > Pre-compose**.

The Pre-compose dialog box appears, with the "Move all attributes into the new composition" option selected. Basically, this option moves layers, effects, masks, and keyframes to the new composition and places it in the existing composition.

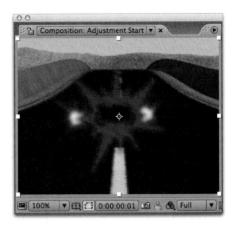

5 In the **Pre-compose** dialog box, click **OK**.

The name Pre-comp 1 automatically appears in the dialog box, but you can change it if you want. For now, keep this default name.

The four layers you selected in Step 3 disappeared and were replaced by a composition layer called Pre-comp 1. You may be scratching your head right now, but read on.

When you choose Pre-compose, After Effects 7 takes those layers, places them in their own composition, and places this new composition inside the original. The result is that the adjustment layer that affected all the layers now affects only the layers in Pre-comp 1. The Highway.mov layer is unaffected by the adjustment layer because it is in its own composition.

The note at the end of this exercise explains all the settings in the Pre-compose dialog box.

---

6 In the **Project** panel, hold down **Opt** (Mac) or **Alt** (Windows), and double-click the **Pre-comp 1** composition in the **Timeline**.

Pre-comp1 opens, and you can view it in the Timeline and Composition panels. Notice the adjustment layer is affecting all the layers below it (these are the layers you originally selected for making the precomp).

---

7 In the **Timeline** for **Pre-comp 1**, drag the adjustment layer below the **Cycle.psd** layer, and look in the **Composition** panel to see the result.

Notice the adjustment layer now does not affect the Cycle.psd layer.

---

8 In the **Timeline** panel, select the **Adjustment Start** tab, and look in the **Composition** panel to see the result.

Notice the Adjustment Start composition reflects the change you made in Pre-comp 1. This is the nature of a nested composition, which is what the precompose feature allows you to do.

---

9 Choose **File > Save**, or press **Cmd+S** (Mac) or **Ctrl+S** (Windows). Choose **File > Close Project**.

If you're wondering about some of the other options in the Pre-compose dialog box, read the following note.

NOTE:

Working with the Pre-compose Dialog Box

The following are the features in the **Pre-compose** dialog box:

Leave all attributes in "Adjustment Start": This option works with a single layer only. Because you selected multiple layers before choosing **Pre-compose** in the previous exercise, this option was dimmed. It places the single layer in its own composition and places that new composition in the original composition.

Move all attributes into the new composition: This feature is chosen most often. It moves layers, effects, masks, and keyframes to the new composition and places it in the existing composition.

Open New Composition: You can use this setting with either of the other choices. It simply means the new composition will open. If you don't turn on this option, you stay in the existing composition, and the new composition is nested in the original composition.

Be sure to experiment with effects on your own—we have barely scratched the surface. A great way to learn about effects is to visit discussion boards and learn from other After Effects 7 users. The combinations of effects are endless, so don't stop with this chapter! In the next chapter, you'll explore parenting, which will help you create relationships between layers.

11

Parenting Layers

If you have worked with a program such as Adobe Photoshop or Adobe Illustrator, you're probably familiar with the concepts of **grouping**, **linking**, and **nesting** objects. These features allow you to treat multiple objects as a single object to edit, move, or organize them as a unit. Although After Effects 7 doesn't use any of these terms, it does offer some of these same functions in its parenting features.

Parenting allows one layer to inherit the **Transform** properties of another. This means you can animate the **Anchor Point**, **Position**, **Scale**, and **Rotation** properties of one parent object, and the attached child object's properties will animate in the same way. For example, you could animate a car and then have all the wheels inherit the settings automatically. The only **Transform** property that parenting doesn't affect is **Opacity**.

This chapter covers how to use the After Effects 7 parenting features and gives some examples of why you would want to use them. Achieving similar effects without the parenting feature requires nesting compositions within compositions (covered in Chapter 10, *"Applying Effects"*). Suffice it to say, the tasks you'll learn to do easily with parenting take much longer and are much harder to perform when using nested compositions.

Parenting Layers

In parenting, you assign one layer as a parent and assign another layer or multiple layers as the child (or children). Any layer assigned as a **child** inherits the **Transform** properties of its **parent** layer. For example, if a parent layer had a **Rotation** property set to **30** degrees, the child layer would also rotate 30 degrees from its initial position, even though you hadn't specifically set the child's **Transform** properties to do so.

A child layer can have only one parent, but a parent layer can have any number of child layers within the same composition. Also, a composition can have multiple parent layers, each controlling a different set of children.

In this chapter's first exercise, you will learn how to assign parenting to a layer. You'll also learn how to fine-tune the child layer to work appropriately with the parent. These are all techniques to save you a lot of time and headaches when trying to animate groups of objects, such as a car with wheels or a character with arms and legs that must stay grouped with the body.

1 | Attaching Children to a Parent

Assigning a parent layer to a child layer is easy in After Effects 7. However, once you've attached a child layer to a parent, you may need to adjust the child layer's position with respect to the parent. For example, if you want an arm (child) to attach to a body (parent), you need to position the arm at the shoulder point. In this exercise, you will attach exhaust smoke to the back of a moving motorcycle by using parenting and by changing the layer position. You will also learn about the **Interpret Footage** dialog box, which will allow you to loop the smoke footage.

1 Copy the **chap_11** folder from the **After Effects 7 HOT CD-ROM** onto your desktop.

2 Choose **File > Open Project**. Navigate to the **chap_11** folder you copied to your desktop, click **Motorcycle_Project.aep** to select it, and click **Open**. Choose **File > Save As**. In the **Save As** dialog box, navigate to the **AE7_HOT_Projects** folder on your desktop. Name the file **Motorcycle_Project.aep**, and click **Save**.

3 If necessary, double-click the **Motorcycle** composition in the **Project** panel to open it.

In this exercise, you will assign the motorcycle layer as the parent and the smoke footage as the child. Setting the motorcycle layer as the parent will allow the smoke to follow the motorcycle's animation path. As you'll see, the motorcycle layer's Transform properties will affect the Position, Scale, and Rotation properties of the smoke layer.

The smoke footage is an Apple QuickTime movie about 4 seconds long. It is too short to play for the entire duration of the composition. However, we have designed the smoke to play as a continuous loop, and After Effects 7 provides a way to loop movies.

Before assigning the parenting, you will first use the Interpret Footage dialog box to loop the smoke movie. This dialog box provides options for each footage item in the Project panel.

4 In the **Timeline**, click the **Video** switch for **Smoke.mov** to display the smoke footage if it is not already on. Scrub the **CTI** (**C**urrent **T**ime **I**ndicator), and notice the smoke footage has fewer frames represented in the **Timeline** than the motorcycle footage.

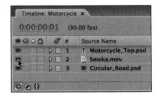

In the next steps, you'll learn how to loop the smoke for the duration of the shot by using the Interpret Footage dialog box.

5 In the **Project** panel, select the **Smoke.mov** footage from the **Movies** folder.

In the following steps, you'll learn how to make this footage loop last longer. This process has to start in the Project panel, where you select the footage you want to loop.

6   Choose **File > Interpret Footage > Main**.

You can also launch the Interpret Footage dialog box by Ctrl+clicking (Mac) or right-clicking (Windows) the file name in the Project panel and choosing Interpret Footage > Main. You can also press Cmd+F (Mac) or Ctrl+F (Windows) to open the Interpret Footage dialog box.

7   At the bottom of the **Interpret Footage** dialog box, type **2** in the **Loop** field, and click **OK**.

Note: The value 2 makes the approximately 4-second movie last about 8 seconds. We will explain the options in the Interpret Footage dialog box in the chart following this exercise.

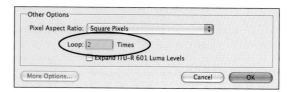

8   Notice the duration of the **Smoke.mov** layer now matches the length of the other layers. Scrub the **CTI**, and notice the footage now stretches for the duration of the shot.

It does this by looping (repeating) itself twice. In the next steps, you'll assign the Motorcycle_Top.psd layer as the parent of the Smoke.mov layer.

9   If necessary, in the top-right corner of the **Timeline** panel, click the **arrow** icon, and choose **Columns > Parent** to display the **Parent** column.

Depending on the way you have your Timeline set up from previous projects, the Parent column may already be displayed.

10   Locate the **Pick Whip** icons (the spirals) in the **Parent** column. Click the **Pick Whip** icon for **Smoke.mov**, drag the resulting line from the **Smoke.mov** layer to the **Motorcycle_Top.psd** layer, and then release the mouse.

This method of dragging the Pick Whip icon from one layer to another is an easy way to create a parent-child relationship. Everything in the child layer (Smoke.mov) takes on the Transform properties (except Opacity) of the parent layer (Motorcycle_Top.psd). You establish which layer is the parent and which is the child through this method. You always drag the child to the parent to establish this relationship.

Notice the Parent pop-up menu now lists the 1.Motorcycle_Top.psd layer as the parent for the Smoke.mov layer.

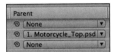

Note: The *1.* in 1.Motorcycle_Top.psd indicates the layer's stacking order in the Timeline. Layers are numbered from top to bottom.

NOTE:

Understanding the Pick Whip Icons

You might wonder what the heck a **Pick Whip** icon is and why Adobe chose to use this funny term. The **Pick** in **Pick Whip** stands for picking a relationship between layers. Adobe chose the **Whip** part of the term because of how the line behaves between the layers if you change your mind and don't select anything. It animates, kind of like a whip at a rodeo.

---

11 Scrub the **CTI**, and notice the smoke movie now moves with the motorcycle animation.

The Position, Scale, and Rotation properties of the motorcycle's layer now apply to the smoke layer's properties! That's what happens when you "parent" something—the Transform properties (except Opacity) apply to the child layer. You'll properly position the smoke and motorcycle in the following steps.

NOTE:

Why Not Opacity?

It may seem odd that After Effects 7 does not support the **Opacity** property in its parenting feature. This probably has to do with the traditional uses of parenting features in animation. The other four **Transform** properties—**Position**, **Scale**, **Rotation**, and **Anchor Point**—all affect the movement of your layers in one way or another, but **Opacity** affects the layer's appearance. Because artists traditionally use parenting to create movement hierarchies, **Opacity** doesn't really fit in.

---

12 Move the smoke below the motorcycle by clicking and dragging it in the **Composition** panel, as shown in the illustration here.

---

13 Press the **spacebar** to play your animation.

The smoke should now track the motorcycle perfectly. By making the Smoke.mov layer a child of the Motorcycle_Top.psd layer, you avoided having to animate the smoke to make it match the motion of the motorcycle.

---

14 Choose **File > Save**, or press **Cmd+S** (Mac) or **Ctrl+S** (Windows). Choose **File > Close Project**.

In this exercise, you learned how to loop footage and create a parent-child relationship between two simple objects. Next, you'll investigate the Interpret Footage dialog box a bit further and then learn more about parenting, including how to use the Pan Behind tool to adjust an anchor point.

TIP:

Changing or Removing a Parent

To specify a different layer as a child's parent, click the **Pick Whip** icon for the child layer, and drag the line to another layer. The new layer will be selected as the parent. Alternatively, click the **Parent** pop-up menu to choose another layer. To remove a child's parent, choose **None** from the **Parent** pop-up menu.

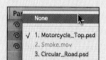

Understanding the Interpret Footage Dialog Box

In the previous exercise, you learned to loop the smoke footage to make it last longer. You did this using the **Interpret Footage** dialog box, which you will use when you want to change footage from the way it was imported originally. Specifically, you can use it to change the number of times footage repeats, or **loops**; the frame rate; or the way After Effects 7 interprets an alpha channel.

You don't need to use this dialog box all the time—only when you want to change your footage in some way. Often you'll use it to make a change while you're in the middle of a project, as you did in the previous exercise when the footage wasn't long enough to last the duration of the composition (although in some projects you may not be lucky enough to have a seamlessly looping piece of footage from which to start).

You can access the **Interpret Footage** dialog box by selecting any footage item in the **Project** panel and pressing **Cmd+F** (Mac) or **Ctrl+F** (Windows) or by **Ctrl+clicking** (Mac) or **right-clicking** (Windows) it and choosing **Interpret Footage > Main**. The following chart describes the options in this dialog box:

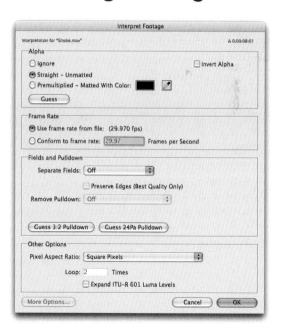

The Interpret Footage Dialog Box

Category	Option	Description
Alpha	Ignore	When you import a partially transparent image or movie, that transparency information is stored in the footage's alpha channel. If you select **Ignore**, After Effects 7 will ignore the transparent parts of the image or movie, and those parts will appear as a solid color (generally the background color defined in the program used to create the image).
	Straight – Unmatted	After Effects 7 treats footage files containing alpha channels in two ways: straight or premultiplied. When you import footage, After Effects 7 makes a guess, and it almost always guesses right. The only time you need to use this option is when you want to alter the way After Effects 7 has treated your alpha channel—for example, you don't like the way your footage looks once it's in a composition, and you want to change it. For footage with a straight alpha channel, the program you used to generate the footage must have built a straight alpha channel. Few 2D programs use this kind of alpha channel. Many 3D programs generate straight alpha channels because these kinds of alphas can be placed over any background color without predisposition.
	Premultiplied – Matted With Color	Most alpha channels created in common graphics applications such as Photoshop and Illustrator are premultiplied. With a **premultiplied alpha channel**, a footage item keeps the transparency information in the alpha channel. A premultiplied alpha channel is also known as a **matted alpha with a background color**. The colors of semitransparent areas, such as feathered edges, shift toward the background color in proportion to their degree of transparency. The background color, in this instance, is defined in the authoring program, such as Photoshop or Illustrator.
	Invert Alpha	This option inverts the alpha channel mask, so everything originally masked out will show, and everything not masked will be hidden.
Frame Rate	Use frame rate from file	This setting applies only to movie footage. It uses the original frame rate of the footage.
	Conform to frame rate	This setting applies only to movie footage. It changes the original frame rate of the movie to any new frame rate you enter. A higher frame rate than the original causes the footage to play faster (the same number of frames in less time).

continues on next page

The Interpret Footage Dialog Box *continued*

Category	Option	Description
Fields and Pulldown	Separate Fields: Off	When footage is transferred to video or originates from video, it contains two fields for every frame: an upper field and a lower field. So, every frame of video has two fields. These two fields are **interlaced**, meaning they are blended and combined in a single frame during the video-recording process. During playback on NTSC- and PAL-capable televisions, the fields are rendered sequentially but sufficiently quickly so the viewer sees a blended image. Sometimes you'll want to separate one interlaced frame of video into two separate fields. The **Separate Fields: Off** setting does not separate the fields; it leaves them untouched.
	Separate Fields: Upper Field First	When importing video footage, After Effects 7 tries to guess which of the fields came first in the interlacing process. If the footage looks funny, use this option to reverse the field order (lower first or upper first) of the interlacing process. This problem is most often obvious when motion in video does not appear smooth.
	Separate Fields: Lower Field First	This is the same as the **Upper Field First** option, except this places the lower field first.
	Preserve Edges (Best Quality Only)	This increases the quality of rendered footage that has its fields separated.
	Remove Pulldown: Off	Pulldown becomes an issue with footage originating as film (35 mm, 16 mm, or 8 mm shot at 24 frames per second) and transferred to video using a Telecine process at 29.97 frames per second. If you choose **Off** from the **Remove Pulldown** pop-up menu, After Effects 7 converts the video footage into 60 separate frames per second (each frame representing one video field). This setting is useful for **rotoscoping** live action (drawing on top of or tracing video footage). The choices in this pop-up menu determine which frames in the pulldown will be whole frames and which frames will be split-field frames. Because of the uneven division involved in 3:2 pulldown, two out of every five frames are built from fields spanning two different frames; these are the **split-field frames**.
	Guess 3:2 Pulldown	This option is important when your footage originated on film and was transferred to video using a Telecine process. Clicking the **Guess 3:2 Pulldown** button converts every four film frames into 10 video fields, making the math for the transition from film to video work.
	Guess 24Pa Pulldown	Similar to the **Guess 3:2 Pulldown** button, clicking this button converts progressive scan (a mode used to more closely simulate film on video) imagery recorded at 23.976 frames per second to the correct number of interlaced video fields to make the video sync with footage brought in by other means.

continues on next page

The Interpret Footage Dialog Box *continued*

Category	Option	Description
Other Options	Pixel Aspect Ratio	You have these options for the **Pixel Aspect Ratio** pop-up menu: **Square Pixels, D1/DV NTSC (0.9), D1/DV NTSC Widescreen (1.2), D1/DV PAL (1.07), D1/DV PAL Widescreen (1.42), HDV 1080 / DVCPRO HD 720 (1.33), DVCPRO HD 1080 (1.5), Anamorphic 2:1 (2).** Your computer graphics files produce images composed of square pixels, but many video formats use nonsquare pixels. Sometimes you may incorporate live action into your After Effects 7 project originally produced with a nonsquare format. That's OK—After Effects 7 can mix square and nonsquare pixels, but you have to tell it what footage is not square during the import process. You do that with this option. By importing the footage with the proper setting (you must know how the footage was originally shot), you allow After Effects 7 to preserve its pixel aspect ratio. When you output to a final movie, you can also choose whether to output square or nonsquare pixels, depending on the setting you use in the **Time Sampling** area of the **Render Settings** dialog box, accessed from the **Render Queue** panel. You'll learn about the rendering settings in Chapter 20, *"Rendering Final Movies."*
	Loop	You can set the number of times footage will repeat. The footage will become longer in the **Timeline** as a result.

2 | Preparing for Parenting

In the previous exercise, you practiced how to connect a child layer (**Smoke.mov**) to a parent (**Motorcycle_Top.psd**) layer. The child took on all the **Transform** properties (except **Opacity**) specified for the parent. It's also possible to animate children independently from their parents. You will learn how to do this in the following exercises. First, however, some preparation work has to go into this process.

When planning this type of animation, you have to think about how the pieces of artwork fit and move together. This often involves changing the anchor point of some of the pieces so they rotate, scale, or move in the correct manner. In this exercise, you'll learn how to import a layered Photoshop file, and you will practice changing anchor points and parenting. Once you've prepared the document properly, you'll learn to animate the parent and children independently in Exercise 3.

---

1 Choose **File > New > New Project**. Choose **File > Save As**. In the **Save As** dialog box, navigate to the **AE7_HOT_Projects** folder on your desktop. Name the file **Waving.aep**, and click **Save**.

---

2 Double-click the empty **Project** panel. In the **Import File** dialog box, navigate to the **chap_11** folder you created on your desktop, and select **Waving.psd**. From the **Import As** pop-up menu, choose **Composition – Cropped Layers**. Click **Open**.

NOTE:

Differentiating Between the Composition and Composition – Cropped Layers Options

Importing a Photoshop or Illustrator document by choosing **Composition** from the **Import As** pop-up menu in the **Import File** dialog box brings in the layers at a uniform size and roots all the anchor points to the center of the composition. This is the best mode for keeping nonmoving elements aligned. The **Composition – Cropped Layers** option, on the other hand, imports each layer at the smallest possible size, with the anchor point rooted to the center of the artwork on each layer. This is the better mode for quickly manipulating layers for animation, because After Effects 7 has less material to composite, and you have a smaller layer to move around the screen.

---

3 In the **Project** panel, select the **Waving** composition, and choose **Composition > Composition Settings**. In the **Composition Settings** dialog box, set the duration to **4** seconds (**0:00:04:00**). Click **OK**. Double-click the **Waving** composition in the **Project** panel to open the composition's **Timeline** and **Composition** panels.

Tip: Press Cmd+K (Mac) or Ctrl+K (Windows) to quickly open the Composition Settings dialog box.

---

4 In the **Timeline** panel, select the **Arm** layer, and click the **Solo** switch.

This causes all the other layers to turn off so you can see the Arm layer by itself. You need to move the anchor point to align with the shoulder of the driver. You'll do this next.

NOTE:

Why Move the Anchor Point?

In the previous exercise, you did not have to change the anchor point because the smoke never moved independently from the motorcycle. It seemed the smoke was "rigidly" attached to the motorcycle's base and followed its exact path. In this exercise, you will see how carefully positioning anchor points can create the illusion of a hinged or jointed connection.

5 In the **Tools** panel, select the **Pan Behind** tool, and then click and drag the **anchor point** in the **Composition** panel as shown in the illustration here.

Note: You must select the layer for the anchor point to be visible in the Composition panel. Moving the anchor point will affect future animations, because the Transform properties—specifically Rotate, Scale, and Position—all use the anchor point position as a reference point. This is why it is important to set the anchor points properly before animating; later changes to your anchor points will shift entire sections of your animation in ways you may not have intended.

6 Click the **Solo** switch for the **Arm** layer to turn on all the other layers again.

Clicking the Solo switch makes it easier to isolate this layer so you can see and move its anchor point.

7 Select the **Forearm** layer, click its **Solo** switch, and then move its anchor point, using the **Pan Behind** tool, as shown in the illustration here. Click the **Solo** switch again to turn the other layers on once you complete this task.

8 Select the **Hand** layer, click its **Solo** switch, and move its anchor point, using the **Pan Behind** tool, as shown in the illustration here. Click the **Solo** switch again to turn the other layers on once you complete this task.

You've finished changing the anchor points on the objects. If you think about your own shoulder, arm, forearm, and hand, and where those joints pivot, you'll see you've just created the anchor points to mimic human anatomy. Soon you'll animate the hand of the human driver, and you'll see how the anchor point adjustments play an important role in the success of your movie.

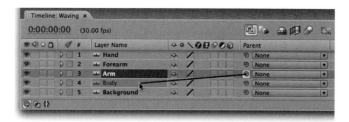

9 In the **Timeline**, click the **Pick Whip** icon for the **Arm** layer, and attach the **Arm** layer to the **Body** layer.

Next, you'll attach the Forearm layer to the Arm layer. Alternatively, you can click the Parent pop-up menu and choose an option instead of clicking the Pick Whip icon.

10 Click the **Parent** pop-up menu for the **Forearm** layer, and choose **3. Arm** from the pop-up menu.

The *3.* indicates this is the third layer in the stack. This tells the Arm layer to be the parent for the Forearm layer.

11 Attach the **Hand** layer to the **Forearm** layer. Do this using the **Pick Whip** icon or the **Parent** menu item—both methods achieve the same result.

12 Choose **File > Save**, or press **Cmd+S** (Mac) or **Ctrl+S** (Windows). Leave **Waving.aep** open for the next exercise.

In Exercise 1 of this chapter, you had only one parent (the motorcycle) and one child (the smoke). Now you know a layer can be the child of one layer and the parent of another. You'll see this come together in the next exercise.

EXERCISE

3 | Animating Children and Parents

In Exercise 1, you saw how animating a parent affected the child. In Exercise 2, you created a more complicated set of relationships. You've already done the hard part of setting the anchor points and parenting. The anchor points allow you to properly position the joints, and creating a parent-child relationship between the layers ensures all the parts move as a unit. You can think of this process as creating a digital puppet. Now it's time to enjoy the fun of making it all move.

1 If you followed the previous exercise, **Waving.aep** should still be open in After Effects 7. If it's not, choose **File > Open Project**. Navigate to the **chap_11** folder you copied to your desktop, click **Waving_2.aep** to select it, and click **Open**.

2 In the **Timeline** panel, click the **Lock** switch next to **Background**.

This prevents you from accidentally moving the background layer during the animation you are about to create.

3 In the **Timeline**, make sure the **CTI** is at **0:00:00:00**.

The easiest place to see this is in the Current Time display in the upper-left corner of the Timeline.

4 Select the **Body** layer, and press **Opt+P** (Mac) or **Alt+Shift+P** (Windows) to set a **Position** keyframe.

You can set a keyframe in many ways. You can click all the twirly icons and click the stopwatch icon, or you can press Opt+P (Mac) or Alt+Shift+P (Windows), as in this step. This keyboard shortcut sets the stopwatch and clicks the twirly icon for the Position property.

5 In the **Tools** panel, select the **Selection** tool, and drag the biker to the left side of the screen, as shown in the illustration here.

This sets the start position for the driver to a different place. Notice the Body layer and all the child layers move at the same time. Even though you set only the Body layer as the parent for the Arm layer, the Forearm and Hand layers moved as well. That's because they're all indirectly linked to the Body layer through the hierarchy of parenting. Specifically, the Arm layer is a child of the Body layer. The Forearm layer is a child of the Arm layer, which is a child of the Body layer. The Hand layer is a child of the Forearm layer, which is a child of the Arm layer, which is a child of the Body layer. In other words, all the layers ultimately relate to the main Body layer as the master parent.

6 In the **Timeline**, drag the **CTI** to **0:00:01:00** (which may appear as **1s** depending on how far you are zoomed in). Drag the **Body** layer to the middle of the screen, as shown in the illustration here.

You should now see two keyframes in your Timeline.

TIP:

Moving to an Exact Time

With the **Zoom** control, you can see rulers in your **Timeline** broken down into single frames, or you can see an overview in seconds (or minutes, if your composition is long enough). This is one visual way of finding the exact place you want to put your keyframe.

Another, even faster way, if you know exactly when in the composition you want something to occur, is to click the **Current Time** display and type a new time in the format **seconds:frames**.

7 Drag the **CTI** to **0:00:00:00**. Select the **Arm** layer, and press **Opt+R** (Mac) or **Alt+Shift+R** (Windows) to set a **Rotation** keyframe.

Notice this Rotation keyframe is at 0:00:00:00 as well. Remember, a keyframe is always set at whatever frame the CTI was on when you set it.

8 Drag the **CTI** to **0:00:01:20** (**1s, 20f** on the Timeline). In the **Tools** panel, select the **Rotation** tool. In the **Composition** panel, click and drag the arm so it looks like the illustration shown here.

The Arm child will now animate independently from its parent, taking all its children with it. As you rotate the arm, notice all the children attached to it rotate as well. The parent doesn't move because you haven't told it to do so. You can animate children separately from their parents, but if the parent moves, so do the kids.

9 Drag the **CTI** to **0:00:00:00**. Select the **Forearm** layer, and press **Opt+R** (Mac) or **Alt+Shift+R** (Windows) to set a **Rotation** keyframe.

This sets a start keyframe for the rotation of the forearm at Frame 0.

10 Drag the **CTI** to **0:00:01:20**, and turn on the **Keyframe** check box.

Placing a keyframe at this point holds the start position for the Forearm layer so it stays still from 0:00:00:00 to 0:00:01:20.

11 Drag the **CTI** to **0:00:01:25**, and with the **Forearm** layer selected, use the **Rotation** tool to place it as shown in the illustration here.

As you rotate the forearm, notice it rotates all the children attached to it. The parents don't move because you haven't told them to do so.

---

12 Drag the **CTI** to **0:00:0:00**. Select the **Hand** layer, and press **Opt+R** (Mac) or **Alt+Shift+R** (Windows) to set a **Rotation** keyframe.

---

13 On the **Forearm** layer, press the **right arrow** icon twice next to the **Keyframe** check box to advance the **CTI** to **Frame 0:00:01:25**. On the **Hand** layer, turn on the **Keyframe** check box.

This is an easy way to advance the CTI through the keyframes on an already animated layer to ensure the keyframes of the next layer you're animating will be accurately aligned. Turning on the Keyframe check box on the Hand layer sets the rotation so it will not move at all from 0:00:00:00 to 0:00:01:25.

---

14 Drag the **CTI** to **0:00:02:10**. Select the **Rotation** tool, and drag the **Hand** layer as shown in the illustration here.

This is the last child in the hierarchy. It can move all by itself without moving the other parents.

---

15 Drag the **CTI** to **0:00:02:15**. With the **Rotation** tool, drag the **Hand** layer as shown in the illustration here.

---

16 On the **Hand** layer, select the keyframe at **0:00:02:10**. Hold down the **Shift** key, and select the keyframe at **0:00:02:15** to multiple-select the in-between frame. Copy the keyframes by pressing **Cmd+C** (Mac) or **Ctrl+C** (Windows).

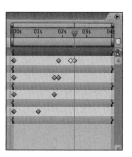

If necessary, use the Zoom slider to zoom into the Timeline so you can get a closer look at your keyframes.

17 Drag the **CTI** to **0:00:02:20**, and press **Cmd+V** (Mac) or **Ctrl+V** (Windows) to paste the copied keyframes. Drag the **CTI** to **0:00:03:00** to paste them again. Keep advancing the **CTI** by 10 frames and pasting until you've pasted a few more times.

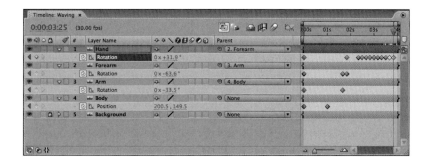

18 Press the **Home** key to move to the beginning of the **Timeline**. Click the **RAM Preview** button to test your work. Click the **Continuous Rasterization**, **Best Quality**, and **Motion Blur** switches to see a big improvement in appearance.

When you use RAM preview to test again, you'll see it takes much longer to render but looks much better. You can also press the spacebar to see whether the playback quality or speed are different (depending on your computer setup).

19 Choose **File > Save**, or press **Cmd+S** (Mac) or **Ctrl+S** (Windows). Choose **File > Close Project**.

You can find a finished version of this project, called Waving_3.aep, in the chap_11 folder on your desktop, if you want to look at it. In the next exercise, you will learn how to use null layers to expand your parenting techniques.

Deciding Between Parenting and Precomposing

You already learned about precomposing in Chapter 10, *"Applying Effects,"* and you just learned about parenting. You might wonder when to use each technique. The following comparison chart should help you decide:

Parenting Versus Precomposing	
Parenting	**Precomposing**
Parenting can affect all **Transform** properties except **Opacity**.	All **Transform** properties can be precomposed. However, parenting may prove more effective than precomposing much of the time.
Parenting is not useful for all effects or mask properties.	Effects and mask properties can be precomposed for selected layers.
Parenting is useful for creating complex, dependent animation such as orbiting planets in a solar system or moving parts of a marionette.	Precomposing is not always useful for anchor point–based animation. For example, linking the parts of a marionette would not be an effective use of precomposing.
Parenting does not affect the rendering order.	You can use precomposing to change the rendering order. You learned about the rendering order in Chapter 10, *"Applying Effects."* In that chapter, you used the **Transform** properties to render the rotation before the drop shadow. You could also have used precomposing to create a composition that rotated and then nested that composition in the composition with the **Drop Shadow** effect. This is an important use of precomposing.
Parenting does not affect adjustment layers.	Precomposing can control adjustment layers.
You cannot do this with parenting.	You can reuse precomposing items in other compositions.
You cannot do this with parenting.	You can update precomposed animations in one step by editing the original composition.

Use this chart to help you identify where you might use parenting rather than precomposing. Parenting affects only the **Transform** properties (except **Opacity**). For this reason, use parenting for animating the motion of objects. As its major strength, parenting provides an effective way to create animation that depends on the motion of other objects within a composition.

Precomposing, on the other hand, provides the most effective means of applying complex changes to a multitude of properties and layers. Effects, masks, adjustment layers, and prerendering are all excellent reasons to use precomposing on a group of layers. Many people also use precomposing as a way to organize groups of layers in complicated projects.

4 | Using a Null Object as a Parent

Null object may seem like a strange term for an invisible object. Even the concept of an invisible object is a bit hard to comprehend. Why would anyone need something not visible? Well, with null objects, you can use **Position** keyframes to control the movement of the already animated visible objects. Adding the null object's movement to the already animated children achieves a compound movement that is otherwise incredibly difficult to achieve (before parenting, animators would create similar effects using nested compositions). For example, you can have a null object control the overall movement of a complex human figure or a vehicle with several moving parts, causing all the parts to move in unison.

In this exercise, you will create a **null layer**, a layer with an invisible object in it. The visible objects will be attached to the null layer, making them the children and the null layer the parent. You will tell the parent to move, and the children will follow.

---

1 Choose **File > Open Project**. Navigate to the **chap_11** folder you copied to your desktop, click **Event.aep** to select it, and click **Open**. Choose **File > Save As**. In the **Save As** dialog box, navigate to the **AE7_HOT_Projects** folder on your desktop. Name the file **Event.aep**, and click **Save**.

---

2 In the **Project** panel, double-click the **Event** composition to open the **Composition** and **Timeline** panels.

---

3 In the **Timeline**, press **Cmd+A** (Mac) or **Ctrl+A** (Windows) to select all the layers, and then press the **U** key to show all the animated properties. Deselect the layers so you don't see the motion paths. Press the **spacebar** to play the composition to see what it looks like, and then click the **Home** key to return to **Frame 0:00:00:00**.

Pressing the U key shows all the animated properties in the composition. In the Event composition, we have already set the Position, Scale, Rotation, and Opacity properties.

---

4 Press **Cmd+A** (Mac) or **Ctrl+A** (Windows) to select all the layers again, and press the **U** key to hide the properties.

This collapses all the properties so your layers take up less space.

---

5 Choose **Layer > New > Null Object**.

This puts a new layer called Null 1 in the Timeline. Notice an outlined box appears in the Composition panel. This is your null object. In other words, the box appears only in the Composition panel. If you use RAM preview or make a movie (which you'll learn to do in Chapter 20, *"Rendering Final Movies"*), this outlined box disappears. Meanwhile, however, the outlined box is important because you need to see the null object even though you don't want anyone else to see it.

6 Attach the layers **MOTORCYCLE**, **SPECIAL EVENT**, and **2006** to the **Null 1** layer by clicking the **Pick Whip** icon for each layer and dragging it to the **Null 1** layer.

Alternatively, you can choose Null 1 from the Parent pop-up menu on each layer.

7 Click the **Lock** switch next to the **Yellow Background** layer to lock it so you don't accidentally move it.

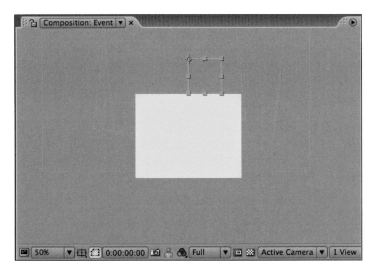

8 In the **Timeline** panel, select the **Null 1** layer, and move it upward in the **Composition** panel, as shown in the illustration here.

Because other layers are assigned to be children of the Null 1 layer, they will move too. Keep moving the box upward until the text is off the stage.

---

9 Press **Opt+P** (Mac) or **Alt+Shift+P** (Windows) to set a **Position** keyframe for **Null 1** at **0:00:00:00**.

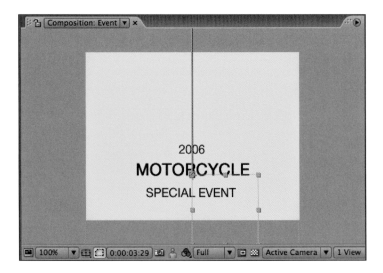

10 Drag the **CTI** to the last frame of the animation (**0:00:03:29**). Move the **Null 1** layer to the bottom of the **Composition** panel, as shown in the illustration here.

---

11 Press the **RAM Preview** button or the **spacebar** to watch the animation.

The null object has allowed you to create compound motion. The type has its own motion (such as scaling and rotating), and the null object offers the opportunity to add another motion path to the animation, treating the various text layers as a unit. This would be hard to do any other way. You can probably imagine how useful this would be for title sequences, type treatments, and other kinds of artwork.

---

12 Choose **File > Save**, or press **Cmd+S** (Mac) or **Ctrl+S** (Windows). Choose **File > Close Project**.

That concludes this chapter. We hope you've seen the tremendous possibilities the parenting features offer, from both practical and aesthetic perspectives. In the next chapter, you'll learn about working with the powerful paint features of After Effects 7.

12

Painting on Layers

If you've ever used Adobe Photoshop's paint tools, you might expect to feel right at home with them in After Effects 7. However, it's much more complex to paint over time, throughout the course of an animation or video. After Effects 7's paint tools have many new functions to learn, and many of these are not intuitive at first glance, such as using a paint stroke to reveal the contents of a layer over time or cloning the contents of one area in a frame to another area of the frame.

Painting in After Effects 7 takes place as vector artwork (similar to Adobe Illustrator) instead of bitmap artwork (such as in Photoshop). Painting with vectors has advantages and drawbacks. With the new paint tools, After Effects 7 records each stroke and each erasure separately (even if you are drawing only a single frame); therefore, you can modify the properties over time: from the color to the brush style to the shape of the stroke. In addition, with the time-enhanced **Clone Stamp** tool, you can copy parts of an image across space or time—or even do both at once. This chapter covers all these topics.

Working with Paint

The paint features in After Effects 7 are considered effects, but you access them through the **Paint** tools interface rather than the **Effects** menu. The paint tools include the **Brush**, **Clone Stamp**, and **Eraser** tools. All three have their own icons in the **Tools** panel, and all three share options in the **Paint** and **Brush Tips** panels. You can use the paint tools only in the **Layer** panel. To access the **Layer** panel, double-click any layer in the **Timeline** or **Composition** panel. The **Composition** panel will change to display the selected layer, with the title of the layer and the name of the composition in which you're currently working.

Once you're in the **Layer** panel, you can use any of the paint tools (and the modifiers in the **Paint** and **Brush Tips** panels) to modify the layer. Once you've set the initial stroke, you can use the main **Timeline** to modify the **Paint** properties just as you would with any other effect. The paint tools are **nondestructive**, meaning they don't make any permanent changes to your original image. This also means all changes are recorded as individual modifications you can change over time.

1 | Creating a Write-on Effect

This exercise introduces you to using the paint tools and using a write-on effect to animate the creation of brush strokes. A **write-on** effect is used to generate brush strokes that are applied over time. The result is similar to watching someone draw on a canvas or piece of paper.

It's necessary to learn the principles of how to use the paint tools before you begin any truly interesting projects. Learning how to adjust the brush and stroke options are some of the other techniques you will be playing with in this exercise. Once you get the hang of how the paint tools work, you can apply them to your own, more complex projects.

---

1 Copy the **chap_12** folder from the **After Effects 7 HOT CD-ROM** onto your desktop.

---

2 Choose **File > Open Project**, navigate to the **chap_12** folder you copied to your desktop, select the file named **Paint.aep**, and click **Open**. Choose **File > Save As**. In the **Save As** dialog box, navigate to the **AE7_HOT_Projects** folder on your desktop. Name the file **Paint.aep**, and click **Save**.

---

3 At the bottom of the **Project** panel, click the **Create a new Composition** button.

---

4 In the **Composition Settings** dialog box, name the comp **Write On**, and set **Duration** to **0:00:01:00** (1 second). Click **OK**.

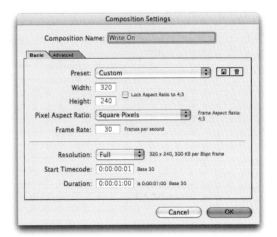

5 Choose **Layer > New > Solid** to create a new solid layer. In the **Solid Settings** dialog box, click the **color swatch**. In the **Color Picker** dialog box, select a light color, and click **OK**. In the **Solid Settings** dialog box, click **OK**.

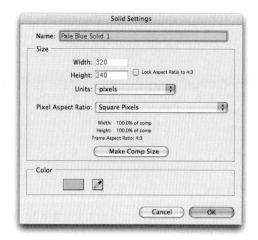

To use the paint tools, you must have a layer in which to work. Any layer will do—a movie, a still image, or a solid. In this exercise, you created a solid so you have a layer on which to paint.

6 In the **Timeline** panel, double-click the solid layer.

This opens the Layer panel where you can apply changes and edit an individual layer, rather than the composition as a whole. Notice it appears docked next to the Composition panel? This makes it easy to confuse it with the Composition panel, but you'll learn how to switch between the Layer and Composition panels in the upcoming steps.

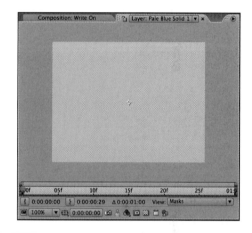

You might be wondering why you opened the Layer panel. You did this so you can paint; you can't paint in any other panel in After Effects 7.

7 In the **Tools** panel, select the **Brush** tool.

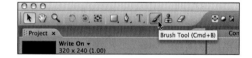

8 Choose **Window > Paint** to open the **Paint** panel, and choose **Window > Brush Tips** to open the **Brush Tips** panel.

Depending on the layout of your After Effects 7 workspace and the amount of screen space you have, you may need to rearrange or change the size of panels to make room for the Paint and Brush Tips panels. You can also choose Window > Workspace > Paint to automatically set up the After Effects 7 workspace for painting tasks.

9 In the **Paint** panel, click the **Set Foreground Color** swatch. In the **Color Picker** dialog box, select a dark color, such as black, and click **OK**. In the **Paint** panel, choose **Write On** from the **Duration** pop-up menu.

You'll learn about the duration types throughout this chapter. The Write On duration type memorizes the stroke you create and records it in real time as you draw with it. If you draw your artwork quickly, it will occupy fewer frames in the Timeline than if you take a long time to carefully create your stroke. You'll learn more about controlling the duration of the Write On duration type in the upcoming steps.

10 Click the **Brush Tip Selector** button, and in the **Brush Tips** panel, click the **Hard Round 9 pixels** brush.

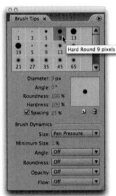

11 In the **Layer** panel, click and drag your cursor to create a spiral shape like the one shown in the illustration here.

Once you release the mouse, the shape will disappear. Don't worry; it isn't really gone.

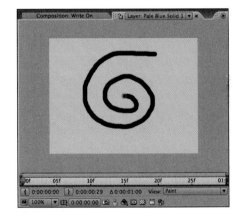

12 In the **Composition** panel, select the **Composition: Write On** tab, if it's not already visible. Press the **spacebar** to play the composition and see the stroke of the spiral appear.

Selecting the Composition: Write On tab switches you from the Layer panel to viewing the actual Composition panel content. Most likely, the spiral won't finish drawing itself onscreen. Why? Well, the composition was set for only 1 second and you probably took longer than 1 second to draw the shape (when you paint with a duration of Write On, your painting is recorded in real time). You'll remedy that next.

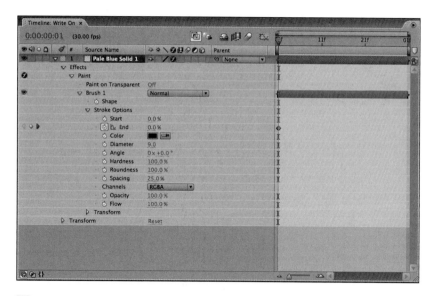

13 Make sure the **CTI** (Current Time Indicator) is set to the first frame. In the **Timeline**, click the **twirly** icon to open the **Pale Blue Solid 1** layer, and then click the **twirly** icons for **Effects**, **Paint**, and **Brush 1**. Locate **Stroke Options** for **Brush 1**, and click its **twirly** icon as well.

See the keyframe for the End property? Note the stopwatch icon has been turned on even though you never touched it. Also, note it is set to 0.0%. These are automatic settings created when you choose the Write On duration type in the Paint panel.

---

14 Click the **Keyframe Navigator** to the left of the **End** property to locate the second keyframe that was automatically created when you drew the spiral.

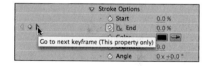

How do you know another keyframe is hidden from view? You'll see a right arrow in the Keyframe Navigator. Arrows appear only when keyframes appear to the right or left of where the CTI resides. The Current Time display in this example shows a value of 0:00:05:18; your Current Time display will vary according to how long it took you to draw your spiral.

---

15 In the **Project** panel, click the **Write On** composition to select it. Choose **Composition > Composition Settings**.

---

16 In the **Composition Setting** dialog box, change **Duration** to match whatever value was in your **Current Time** display when you checked the last keyframe for the **End** property in the previous step. Click **OK**.

Because the Current Time in this example was set to 0:00:05:18, we typed 0:00:05:18 in the Duration field in the Composition Settings dialog box. Once you're done, you won't be able to see the entire Timeline. You'll fix this in the next step.

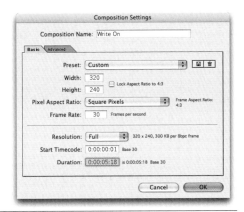

17 In the **Timeline** panel, drag the **Time Navigator End** handle to the end of the composition to view the entire **Timeline**.

Notice the keyframe in the last frame. You won't be able to see it play, however, because the duration of the Pale Blue Solid 1 layer and the Brush 1 layer are too short.

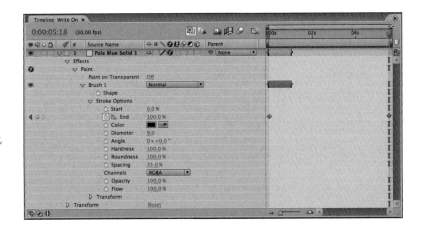

18 Drag the layer handles until they reach to the end of the composition. Press the **spacebar**, or click **RAM Preview** to preview the animation.

You will see the spiral draw onscreen before your eyes.

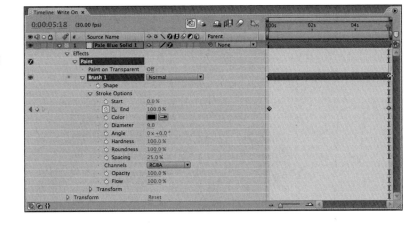

19 Choose **File > Save**, or press **Cmd+S** (Mac) or **Ctrl+S** (Windows). Leave **Paint.aep** and the **Write On** composition open for the next exercise.

In this exercise you learned how to create paint strokes that write onto the screen. The Write On duration type depends on how fast or slow you draw. Keyframes are automatically set to a start and end frame for the End property located under Stroke Options. Every stroke becomes its own brush, which can easily get daunting if you create more than a simple spiral shape! That's because the Paint effect treats every stroke as its own brush. There's power in that, which will soon be revealed to you, but it can also be cumbersome. You'll find yourself longing for the brushes you use in Photoshop, but those are bitmap brushes, not vector brushes. The beauty of vector brushes is that you can edit and animate them easily. In the next exercise, you'll learn how to edit paint strokes.

NOTE:

Exploring the Duration Options

The **Duration** pop-up menu resides in the **Paint** panel. It dictates how long a stroke remains onscreen by default. Here are the four choices:

Constant: This paints the entire stroke at the current time. The stroke will remain on the screen for the duration of the layer's existence.

Write On: This paints the stroke in real time, beginning at the current time and finishing in approximately the same amount of time it took you to create the stroke.

Single Frame: This paints the stroke only in the current frame. Use this mode for traditional frame-by-frame tracing, often called **rotoscoping**.

Custom: This paints the stroke beginning at the current time; the stroke will remain onscreen for the number of frames specified in the field next to the **Duration** pop-up menu.

NOTE:

Understanding Pressure Sensitivity with Paint Tools

You need to access the **Brush Dynamics** settings to get pressure sensitivity to work. You must also own a pressure-sensitive tablet and stylus. Tablets are great—you will want one if you do a lot of paint work in Illustrator, Photoshop, or After Effects 7. The most popular tablets are from Wacom (**www.wacom.com**).

Brush strokes inside the **Layer** panel can have thick and thin strokes and varying amounts of ink and opacity. You set this through the **Brush Dynamics** settings in the **Brush Tips** panel. If you want to use pressure sensitivity in After Effects 7, set **Size, Angle, Roundness, Opacity,** or **Flow** to **Pen Pressure** in the **Brush Dynamics** area of the **Brush Tips** panel to get this pressure sensitivity to work. (Don't forget the tablet, though—this won't work with a regular mouse!)

Exploring the Stroke Options Properties

The following chart describes the **Stroke Options** properties found in the Timeline panel:

Stroke Options Properties	
Setting	Description
Start	Specifies the timing (measured by percent) where the brush begins.
End	Specifies the timing (measured by percent) where the brush ends.
Color	Is where you set or animate color settings.
Diameter	Sets the size of the brush.
Angle	Sets the angle of the nib of the brush. Different angle settings are visible only on noncircular brush nibs (tips).
Hardness	Specifies the rigidity of the brush. **100%** indicates a hard brush. Decreasing the percentage creates a feathered brush.
Roundness	Specifies the stoutness of the brush. **100%** indicates a round brush. Decreasing the setting creates an elliptical brush tip.
Spacing	Affects the spacing of the stroke. With a round brush, changing this setting can create a dotted line.
Channels	Limits the channel to one of these settings: **RGB**, **RGBA** (which is RGB plus alpha), or **Alpha**.
Opacity	Affects the transparency or opacity of a stroke.
Flow	Specifies how much the flow of brush marks varies in a stroke. (This works with the pressure-sensitive tablet; see the note preceding this chart.)

2 | Editing a Paint Stroke

It's possible to edit paint strokes you've created by accessing an existing brush and changing its attributes using the **Stroke Options** properties. This is important if you want to modify a paint stroke you have already created without having to delete it and create a new one. This exercise will help you understand the basic principles of editing a paint stroke, which you should be able to apply to your own, more complex work in the future.

---

1 If you followed the previous exercise, **Paint.aep** should still be open in After Effects 7. If it's not, choose **File > Open Project**. Navigate to the **chap_12** folder you copied to your desktop, click **Paint_2.aep** to select it, and click **Open**. Double-click **Write On** to open the composition if it's not already open.

---

2 In the **Timeline** panel, make sure **Brush 1** is selected for the solid layer and the **Stroke Options** properties are visible. Drag the **CTI** to the first frame.

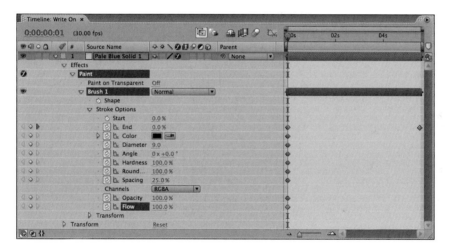

3 Click the **stopwatch** icons for **Color**, **Diameter**, **Angle**, **Hardness**, **Roundness**, **Spacing**, **Opacity**, and **Flow** to set the start keyframes.

Read the previous chart to learn what each of these settings does. You don't have to be in the Layer panel to make the following edits, but you can be.

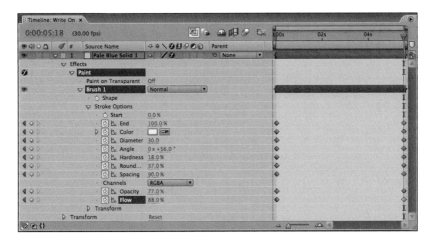

4 Drag the **CTI** to the last frame in the **Timeline**. Change the values for **Color** to light yellow, change **Diameter** to 30, change **Angle** to **56.0** degrees, change **Hardness** to **18%**, change **Roundness** to **37%**, change **Spacing** to **90%**, change **Opacity** to **77%**, and change **Flow** to **88%**.

Each change you make alters the appearance of the paint stroke. You can animate these properties by setting keyframes, or you can change them throughout the composition by altering them and not clicking the stopwatch icon. Whether you animate or change these settings, it's good to know they're there and you can change them at any time.

5 Press the **spacebar** to play the animation for your **Write On** composition.

You'll see the stroke write itself on the screen and also change its visual characteristics based on the settings you made.

6 Choose **File > Save**, or press **Cmd+S** (Mac) or **Ctrl+S** (Windows). In the top-left corner of the **Composition** panel, choose **Close Write On** from the **Composition** pop-up menu to close the current composition. Leave **Paint.aep** open for the next exercise.

Having learned a bit about modifying paint strokes using the usual controls, you'll learn about a method to change the shape of a paint stroke over time.

3 | Morphing Paint Strokes over Time

In the previous exercise, you controlled the placement, duration, and initial timing of paint strokes. In this exercise, you will modify the shape of a paint stroke over time. After Effects 7 lets you **morph** (interpolate) shapes that have been created with its paint tools, such as changing a circle into a square.

---

1 If you followed the previous exercise, **Paint.aep** should still be open in After Effects 7. If it's not, choose **File > Open Project**. Navigate to the **chap_12** folder you copied to your desktop, click **Paint_3.aep** to select it, and click **Open**.

---

2 In the **Project** panel, click the **Create a new Composition** button. In the **Composition Settings** dialog box, name the composition **Morphing**, and set **Duration** to **0:00:05:00**. Click **OK**.

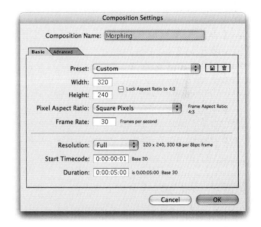

---

3 Choose **Layer > New > Solid** to create a new solid layer. Keep the same color you chose in the previous exercise, or select another color of your liking.

---

4 In the **Tools** panel, select the **Brush** tool.

---

5 In the **Paint** panel, click the **Brush Tip Selector** button, and in the **Brush Tips** panel, click the **Hard Round 5 pixels** brush. In the **Paint** panel, choose **Constant** from the **Duration** pop-up menu.

6 In the **Timeline** panel, double-click the solid layer to open the **Layer** panel. Make sure the **CTI** is set to the first frame. Draw a star.

It's a bit hard to control the brush in After Effects 7 because you're drawing vector artwork. This is a limitation of the program. A stylus and tablet, such as those Wacom offers, can help you gain better control. For now, a crude star will work to teach you how to morph brush strokes.

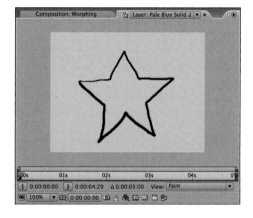

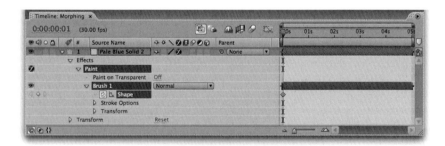

7 In the **Timeline** panel, click the **twirly** icons next to the solid layer until you see the **Shape** property under the **Brush 1** property. Click the **stopwatch** icon for the **Shape** property to set a keyframe.

This sets a starting keyframe for the Shape property. This step is important and easily overlooked. By selecting an existing paint stroke in the Timeline, you are telling After Effects 7 you want to modify the stroke rather than create a new one.

8 Drag the **Time Marker** in the **Layer** panel to some-where around **2** seconds.

Moving the Time Marker in the Layer panel also moves the CTI in the Timeline.

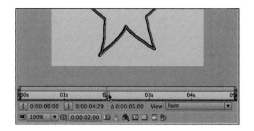

9 Draw a cloud surrounding the star.

When you release the mouse, the star disappears. The cloud in this frame has replaced the star. The star is still in the first keyframe.

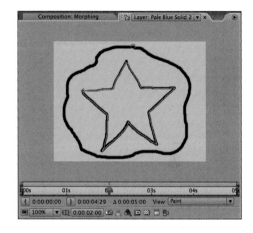

10 In the **Timeline** panel, drag the **CTI** to the last frame. Draw a star inside the cloud.

This adds the third keyframe once you release the mouse, and the cloud shape disappears. The cloud shape is still in the second keyframe, however.

11 In the **Composition** panel, select the **Composition: Morphing** tab, which returns you to the composition and takes you out of **Layer** panel. Press the **spacebar**, or click the **RAM Preview** button; you'll see the three shapes morph from one keyframe to another.

12 Choose **File > Save**, or press **Cmd+S** (Mac) or **Ctrl+S** (Windows). In the top-left corner of the **Composition** panel, choose **Close Morphing** from the **Composition** pop-up menu to close the current composition. Leave **Paint.aep** open for the next exercise.

Although the paint and animation results are a little crude, this should give you an idea of how to morph from one shape to another using the paint features. In the next exercise, you will learn how to reveal a shape using the Eraser tool to create a write-on effect. As you'll see, the Eraser tool functions similarly to the Brush tool.

4 | Creating a Write-on Effect with the Eraser Tool

The **Eraser** tool provides a great way of gradually hiding or revealing a layer over time. With this capability, you can create a write-on effect for text or graphics in your animation—a popular effect for creating dynamic title sequences for film and television. You could attempt a similar effect with the **Brush** tool, as you did in Exercise 1, but you could never paint each stroke as precisely as you can with the method you are about to learn. In this case, you will start with finished artwork, hide it, and then instruct After Effects 7 to remove the eraser strokes over time.

---

1 If you followed the previous exercise, **Paint.aep** should still be open in After Effects 7. If it's not, choose **File > Open Project**. Navigate to the **chap_12** folder you copied to your desktop, click **Paint_4.aep** to select it, and click **Open**.

---

2 In the **Project** panel, double-click **Eraser Finish**, and press the **spacebar** or click **RAM Preview** to view its contents. After you've viewed this composition, close the **Eraser Finish** composition. In the **Project** panel, double-click **Eraser Start** to open the starting composition.

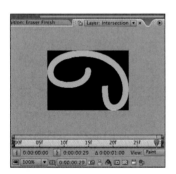
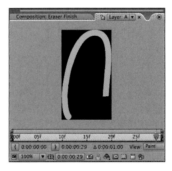
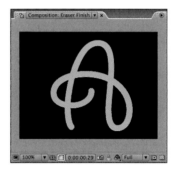

This finished composition shows the goal of this exercise. The letter A appears to draw itself on the screen. In this exercise, you'll be working with an image that includes some text created in Photoshop, rasterized there, and broken into two pieces. You will make it appear one stroke at a time. Notice the composition includes two layers.

---

3 In the **Timeline** panel, double-click the **Intersection** layer to open its **Layer** panel. Double-click the **A** layer to open its **Layer** panel. At the top of the **Composition** panel, click the **Layer: A** pop-up menu to view its contents. When you are finished, select the **Composition: Eraser Start** tab.

This pop-up menu allows you to switch between the two open layers (without creating a lot of clutter with new tabs), as well as the composition, which combines the two layers causing them to appear as a single letter A. Why separate

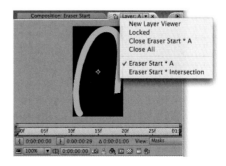

the cross-strokes from the main strokes of the letters? The reason will become apparent as you work through the exercise.

4 In the **Tools** panel, select the **Eraser** tool.

5 In the **Paint** panel, make sure the **Duration** pop-up menu is set to **Constant** and the **Erase** pop-up menu is set to **Layer Source & Paint**. Leave all the other settings alone that you set in the previous exercise.

6 In the **Brush Tips** panel, change **Diameter** to **25**.

7 In the **Timeline**, make sure the **Time Marker** is at **0:00:00:00**. In the **Layer** panel, choose **Eraser Start * Intersection** from the **Layer** pop-up menu to open the **Layer** panel for the **Intersection** layer (**Layer: Intersection**). Click and drag to start erasing the image from the left side to the right side, following the shape.

After Effects 7 is recording your stroke, so it's important to make this stroke perfect—it may take you several tries. If you make a mistake, press Cmd+Z (Mac) or Ctrl+Z (Windows) to immediately undo the stroke, or select the Paint effect in the Timeline (use your twirly icons to find it), and press the Delete key. It's important to make the stroke follow the shape and do so with one brush stroke. When you come to the end of the shape, don't go beyond the end of the visible shape. Your next brush stroke will pick up where this one leaves off.

8 In the **Layer** panel, choose **Eraser Start * A** from the **Layer** pop-up menu to open the **Layer** panel for the **A** layer (**Layer: A**). Click and drag to start erasing the image from the right side to the left side, following the shape.

Again, After Effects 7 is recording your stroke, so it's important to make this stroke perfect. Make sure you completely erase the shape on the screen.

---

9 In the **Timeline** panel, click the **twirly** icons for the **Intersection** layer until you see the **Stroke Options** properties for **Eraser 1**. Click the **twirly** icon for **Stroke Options**, and then click the **stopwatch** icon next to **Start** to set a keyframe at the beginning of the composition.

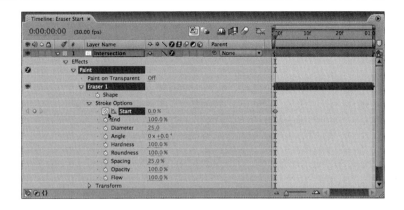

---

10 In the **Composition** panel, click the **Eraser Start** tab. In the **Timeline** panel, drag the **CTI** to **Frame 0:00:00:13**. Change the value of **Start** to **100%** to set a second keyframe. You'll see the stroke appear in the **Composition** panel.

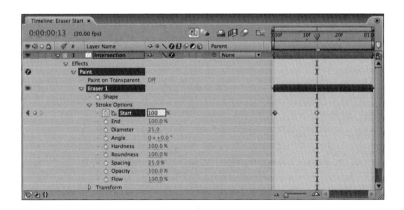

---

11 Make sure the **CTI** is still set to **0:00:00:13**. Click the **twirly** icons for the **A** layer until you see the **Stroke Options** properties for **Eraser 1**. Click the **stopwatch** icon next to **Start** so you see a keyframe appear for this layer at **Frame 13** in the **Timeline**.

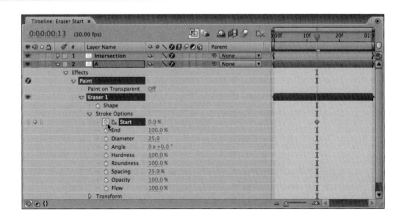

---

12 Drag the **CTI** to **0:00:00:24**. Change the **Start** value to **100%**.

---

13 Preview the animation by pressing the **spacebar** or by clicking **RAM Preview**.

You should see the text appear as if it is writing itself on the movie. If you were to create an entire word using this technique, you might get a sense of how many layers and eraser strokes you would need. It is time-consuming to make and plan paint effects as you see here, but the results are pretty nice. We chose a single letter for this exercise to teach you the technique. Feel free to try something on your own that is more complicated, and be sure to allot yourself extra time.

---

14 Choose **File > Save**, or press **Cmd+S** (Mac) or **Ctrl+S** (Windows). In the top-left corner of the **Composition** panel, choose **Close Eraser Start** from the **Composition** pop-up menu to close the current composition. Leave **Paint.aep** open for the next exercise.

In the next exercise, you'll learn to use the Clone Stamp tool, which is a different type of Paint tool than you've used thus far.

VIDEO:

eraser.mov

To view this exercise being performed, watch **eraser.mov** from the **videos** folder located on the **After Effects 7 HOT CD-ROM**.

NOTE:

Understanding Cumulative Eraser Effects

Did you figure out why it was important to separate the intersecting strokes into two layers? Intersecting strokes make the write-on effect impossible to create in a single layer because the **Eraser** tool is a paintbrush that, like all the other paint tools, layers its effect with each new stroke. The problem is that any area where your strokes overlap won't show up until you have removed both strokes. However, because eraser effects are cumulative only *per layer*, two erasures on different layers won't "hide" the contents of both layers. By hiding the intersecting strokes on one layer and the "main" strokes on another, you can fully hide each stroke and then fully reveal them without interference between the two.

5 | Using the Clone Stamp Tool

The **Clone Stamp** tool, which samples pixels from one part of a frame or layer and applies them to another, has been a staple of Photoshop for a long time. You can use a **Clone Stamp** tool to create amusing effects, such as putting a third eye on a face, or you can use it to remove objects or clean up and fill in portions of an image by duplicating objects from other areas in the frame. Animators often use cloning to remove the wires in special-effects movies, such as the cables used to suspend the actors in *Crouching Tiger, Hidden Dragon*. In After Effects 7, unlike in Photoshop, the **Clone Stamp** tool includes a time dimension, so in this exercise you will see the objects that you clone actually move.

---

1 If you followed the previous exercise, **Paint.aep** should still be open in After Effects 7. If it's not, choose **File > Open Project**. Navigate to the **chap_12** folder you copied to your desktop, click **Paint_5.aep** to select it, and click **Open**.

---

2 In the **Project** panel, double-click **Clone Finish** to open the composition, and press the **spacebar** to preview the end result of this exercise. When you're done inspecting it, close this composition, and double-click **Clone Start** to get started.

Note the two birds sitting on the beach? The original source footage has only one bird. In this exercise, you'll create a set of identical bird "twins" from a movie layer containing a single bird on the beach.

---

3 Press the **spacebar** to preview the **Clone Start** composition. Drag the **CTI** to the first frame. Double-click the **Beach.mov** layer to open the **Layer** panel.

As you preview the movie, you'll see the bird is alone for the entire length of the layer.

---

4 In the **Tools** panel, select the **Clone Stamp** tool.

---

5 In the **Brush Tips** panel, click the **Soft Round 65 pixels** brush.

This changes the brush to a feathered brush. It's best to choose a large feathered brush for this cloning exercise, because it will be more forgiving than a small, precise, hard-edged brush.

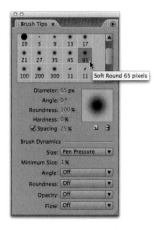

6 Make sure the **CTI** is on the first frame. **Opt+click** (Mac) or **Alt+click** (Windows) the bird's head.

This sets the clone source point.

7 In the **Layer** panel, drag your cursor to the left side of the frame, and start painting where you want the duplicate bird's head to appear, lining up the reference frame with the original movie layer. Keep painting with one stroke until you get the entire figure drawn at the left.

It's important you complete the clone with a single stroke; otherwise, you'll have multiple clone brush objects in the end, and they'll be harder to control than a single object.

The large feathered brush creates a soft edge to the image, which helps it blend better with the background.

8 Select the **Composition: Clone Start** tab, and press the **spacebar** or click the **RAM Preview** button to view the results.

9 Choose **File > Save**, or press **Cmd+S** (Mac) or **Ctrl+S** (Windows). In the top-left corner of the **Composition** panel, choose **Close Clone Start** from the **Composition** pop-up menu to close the current composition. Leave **Paint.aep** open for the next exercise.

This was a quick introduction to cloning with After Effects 7. You can animate the clone layer as well, to follow your source layer better, which is particularly important when working with moving-camera footage or objects changing their position within the frame. In the next exercise, you'll learn how to create a special painterly look with the Scribble effect.

VIDEO: | **clone.mov**

To view this exercise being performed, watch **clone.mov** from the **videos** folder located on the **After Effects 7 HOT CD-ROM**.

NOTE: | **Aligning Clones and Locking the Source Time**

By default, when you **sample** an area to be cloned, you are setting up a "virtual line" between the area you sample (when holding down the **Opt** or **Alt** key) and the area you begin painting. This line moves with your painting so the sampled area moves in alignment as you work across the area you're painting.

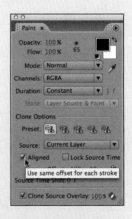

Turning off the **Aligned** check box in the **Clone Options** area in the **Paint** panel "locks" the source area so all your destination painting is based on the single sample from where you first clicked. This is useful when you're trying to spread out a small, regular area of color across a wider area.

By default, the **Lock Source Time** check box is not turned on, so the clone source is sampled for each video frame. This means if something changes in the source area of your clone, the change will be reflected in the destination area of your clone as well. This is generally what you want when you're copying an area of action over time. However, if you're doing "cover-up" cloning to remove an unwanted object from a scene, you may want to sample all the material from a single frame—perhaps a frame in which the offending object does not appear. In those cases, turn on the **Lock Source Time** check box so the part of the image being sampled does not change as the video changes.

Faking Painting with the Scribble Effect

Although this final exercise doesn't actually use any of the new paint tools in After Effects 7, it does introduce a technique you can use to produce the "look" of an image being painted on the screen. You achieve the result by tracing the transparent alpha channel of a layer to create a mask and then applying the **Scribble** effect to the layer. You can also use this effect for a variety of custom transitions, but one of its simplest and most powerful uses is to make an object look like it's made entirely from animated paint strokes.

1 If you followed the previous exercise, **Paint.aep** should still be open in After Effects 7. If it's not, choose **File > Open Project**. Navigate to the **chap_12** folder you copied to your desktop, click **Paint_6.aep** to select it, and click **Open**.

2 In the **Project** panel, double-click **Scribble Finish** to view the result of this exercise. Once you are finished looking at the "painterly" effect, close the composition. Double-click **Scribble Start** to get started.

In this exercise, you will "paint" a picture of a motorcycle on the screen by varying the strength of the Scribble effect over time. The Scribble effect requires absolutely no brushwork to create.

3 In the **Timeline** panel, select **Cycle.psd**. Choose **Layer > Auto-trace**. In the **Auto-trace** dialog box, leave the settings as shown in the illustration here, and click **OK**.

This creates a mask from the transparency information of the layer. You require a mask to define the outline of the shape you want to "draw" using the Scribble effect.

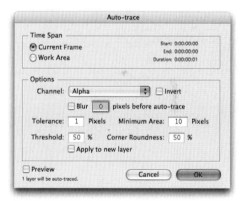

4 In the **Composition** panel, repeatedly click the **Toggle View Masks** button to turn on and off the yellow outlines of the mask. When you are finished, make sure the button is in the **off** position (no masks visible).

The Toggle View Masks button allows you to preview and edit your mask shapes in the Composition panel. You will learn more about masks in Chapter 13, *"Creating Masks."*

5 Choose **Effect > Generate > Scribble**.

The motorcycle should turn into a loose, white scribble.

6 In the **Timeline**, click the **twirly** icon next to **Cycle.psd** and the **twirly** icon next to the **Masks** property (if the icons are visible). Click the **twirly** icon next to **Effects** and then the **twirly** icon next to **Scribble** to reveal the effect's properties. Change the **Angle** property to **49%** and the **Stroke Width** property to **1.5**.

The Angle property affects the direction the stroke is drawn. The Stroke Width property affects how thick the stroke is.

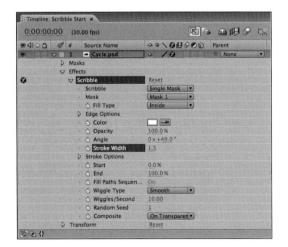

7 On the **Cycle.psd** layer, click the **twirly** icon next to **Stroke Options** (beneath the **Stroke Width** property). Change **Curviness** to **20%** and **Curviness Variation** to **10%**.

The Curviness property affects how "loopy" the stroke is; Curviness Variation determines whether the stroke appears uniform and controlled or wild and varied.

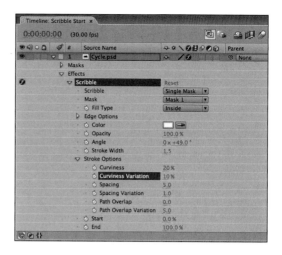

8 From the **Composite** pop-up menu, choose **Reveal Original Image**.

You should now see a rough, squiggly version of the motorcycle on the screen.

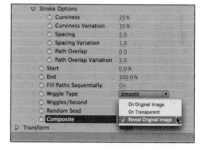

9 Make sure the **CTI** is on the first frame, and then click the **stopwatch** icon next to the **End** property of the **Scribble** effect. Change the value of the **End** property to **0%**.

This sets the start value for the Scribble effect, which you will increase over time once you've set the end keyframe in the next step.

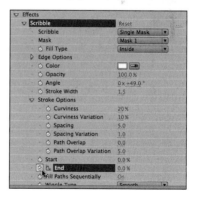

10 Drag the **CTI** to **0:00:02:00**, and change the value of the **End** property to **100%**.

11 Press the **spacebar** to preview the animation.

Notice how even after you've drawn the motorcycle, the lines continue to wiggle as if the drawing were alive. The Wiggle property determines how the lines change over time; change Wiggle Type to Static if you want the effect to appear to be a single, smooth line drawing.

Now you will make the drawing appear to "fill in" a bit more after the initial scribble is in place.

---

12 Drag the **CTI** to **0:00:03:00**, and click the **stopwatch** icon next to **Curviness**.

This creates a keyframe at 0:00:03:00.

Clicking the stopwatch icon in midanimation means the property value set in the first keyframe will apply from the beginning of the animation through the first keyframe.

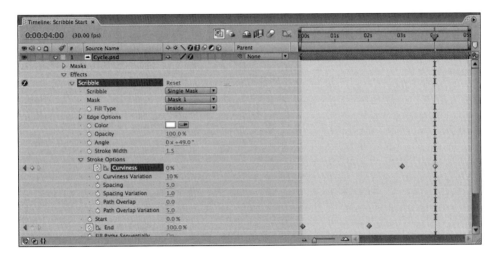

13 Drag the **CTI** to **0:00:04:00**, and change **Curviness** to **0%**.

This brings your lines together into a more solid motorcycle.

---

14 Drag the **CTI** to **0:00:02:00**, and click the **stopwatch** icon for the **Spacing** property. Change **Spacing** to **13.1**.

This changes your motorcycle into a loose line again.

---

15 Drag the **CTI** to **0:00:03:00**, and change **Spacing** to **3.1**.

This tightens up the motorcycle's lines again while still leaving them broadly curved.

---

16 Press the **spacebar** to preview your animation. The motorcycle should now appear to be formed from a single scribble, which gradually resolves itself into a shimmering motorcycle form.

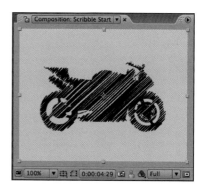

17 Choose **File > Save**, or press **Cmd+S** (Mac) or **Ctrl+S** (Windows). Choose **File > Close Project**.

With this chapter and the text layer chapter under your belt, you've experienced two of the most customizable, built-in, and nondestructive tools After Effects 7 has to offer. In the next chapter, you will learn how to use masks, a feature you glimpsed briefly in this chapter when you used the Auto-trace function.

13

Creating Masks

Masks allow you to define transparent areas for footage items, and they play an important role in motion-graphics design. You have already imported Adobe Photoshop and Adobe Illustrator images with transparent, masked regions into After Effects 7. This chapter will show you how to produce masks directly in After Effects 7, which is often more efficient. Masks are useful for all kinds of visual effects; in fact, professional animators use them often.

In this chapter, you'll learn several practical methods for creating, editing, and animating masks. You'll often find these masking skills used in professional work—no After Effects 7 animator's training would be complete without these skills.

1 | Creating Simple Masks

A **mask** defines the boundary between the transparent and opaque areas of a composition, such as the outline separating the motorcycle image (in the previous chapter) from the empty background. When you draw a mask in After Effects 7, the area inside the boundary is visible, and the area outside the mask boundary is transparent. In addition to setting masked regions, you can use After Effects 7 to set masked areas to different levels of opacity. You can use masks on still or movie footage.

After Effects 7 allows you to create simple masks using the **Rectangular** and **Rectangular Mask** tools or complex, irregularly shaped masks using the **Pen** tool, similar to the one in Illustrator and Photoshop. This exercise will focus on making simple mask shapes, such as an elliptical-shaped mask.

---

1 Copy the **chap_13** folder from the **After Effects 7 HOT CD-ROM** onto your desktop.

---

2 Choose **File > Open Project**. Navigate to the **chap_13** folder you copied to your desktop, select the file named **Mask_Project.aep**, and click **Open**. Choose **File > Save As**. In the **Save As** dialog box, navigate to the **AE7_HOT_Projects** folder on your desktop. Name the file **Mask_Project.aep**, and click **Save**.

Warning: If you get an error message saying you don't have a particular font, don't worry. This project will still work properly; After Effects 7 will simply substitute a font you do have.

In the following steps, you will learn to draw a simple mask and adjust its size. You will also learn to invert a mask. **Inverting** a mask reverses the transparent and opaque areas defined by the mask boundary. This is particularly useful for cutting out shapes in a layer to composite over another layer, such as a shape with video playing underneath.

---

3 In the **Project** panel, double-click the **Simple Masks** composition to open it.

---

4 Press the **spacebar** to preview the motorcycle animation.

In the following steps, you'll place the motorcycle footage inside the camera image, which is currently turned off in the Timeline panel. You will turn on the camera layer and draw a circular mask you will use to make the lens transparent.

---

5 In the **Timeline** panel, move to **Frame 1**, and click the **Video** switch to display the **Camera.psd** layer in the **Composition** panel.

We have set up the animation for the purposes of this masking exercise. Observe the solid camera lens, which is where you will draw the mask to reveal the motorcycle animation underneath.

6 Make sure your **CTI** (Current Time Indicator) is on **Frame 0:00:00:01** and the **Camera.psd** layer is selected. If the **Tools** panel is not visible, choose **Window > Tools**.

7 In the **Tools** panel, click and hold the **Mask** tool to display the **Rectangular Mask** and **Elliptical Mask** tools. Choose **Elliptical Mask Tool**.

In the following steps, you will draw the mask in the Composition panel and adjust the size of the mask. Go slowly with each step. If you want to undo something, choose Edit > Undo. Alternatively, press Cmd+Z (Mac) or Ctrl+Z (Windows). The After Effects 7 default Preferences settings give you 32 undos—which should be sufficient for any exercise in this book.

8 Hold down the **Shift** key, and in the **Composition** panel, click just above and to the left of the camera's lens; then drag to create a circular matte shape around the lens of the camera.

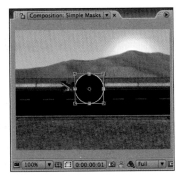

It will look as though the camera has just disappeared, but don't worry! The mask immediately makes everything outside the mask path transparent. You'll fix this in the next steps. Too, don't worry if your circle doesn't perfectly match the shape of the lens. You'll fix this soon as well.

Tip: Holding down the Shift key creates a perfect circle when you draw with the Elliptical Mask tool. Likewise, when using the Rectangular Mask tool, hold down the Shift key to create a perfect square.

9 To the left of the **Camera.psd** layer, click the **twirly** icon to display the layer's mask-related properties. Click the **twirly** icon next to the **Masks** property.

In the Timeline panel, notice this adds a mask (Mask 1) to the camera layer.

---

10 In the **Switches** panel, locate the **Inverted** switch, and turn on the **Inverted** check box to invert the mask.

Notice this inverts the mask, and it is now transparent inside the mask boundary and completely opaque outside the boundary. This allows you to see through the camera lens. If the mask you drew doesn't fit properly, don't worry. You'll learn how to adjust its size and position next.

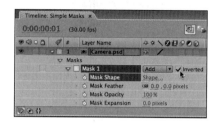

---

11 In the **Tools** panel, select the **Selection** tool.

---

12 In the **Composition** panel, click the **Magnification ratio popup** pop-up menu, and choose **200%**. In the **Composition** panel, double-click the yellow mask shape to display the mask bounding box, which allows you to resize and manipulate the mask.

---

13 Hold down the **Shift** key, and drag a **corner scale handle** to adjust the size of the circle mask until it fits the lens on the camera. When finished resizing, click an empty part of the **Timeline** panel to deselect and hide the bounding box.

If you need to reposition the mask, click inside the mask, and use the Selection tool to move it around the screen. You can also use the arrow keys on your keyboard to move the mask 1 pixel at a time in any direction. If you want to readjust the size of the mask, double-click any mask shape to display the bounding box and repeat the scale adjustment process.

14 Click the **Magnification ratio popup** pop-up menu at the bottom of the **Composition** panel, and choose **100%**. Click the **RAM Preview** button, or press the **spacebar** to view the properly masked animation.

Notice the motorcycle, background, and camera move together. We animated them with parenting to do this for you.

---

15 Choose **File > Save**, or press **Cmd+S** (Mac) or **Ctrl+S** (Windows). In the top-left corner of the **Composition** panel, choose **Close Simple Masks** from the **Composition** pop-up menu to close the current composition. Leave **Mask_Project.aep** open for the next exercise.

Drawing a circular or rectangular mask using the masking tools is rather easy once you get the hang of it. Inverting a mask layer is simple as well. In the next section, you'll learn how to use the Pen tool, which is useful when making masks for unusual shapes.

Drawing Masks with the Pen Tool

In the previous exercise, you learned to create an elliptical mask using the **Elliptical Mask** tool. You can also draw custom masks using the **Pen** tool, which uses Bézier points to define a mask path with smooth, curved geometry. Masks drawn with the **Pen** tool can be either closed or open paths.

A **closed path** has no definite beginning or end. A closed path is continuous; for example, a circle is a closed path.

An **open path** has different beginning and end points. For example, a straight line is an open path. You'll get to create an open path in the next exercise.

Specifically, in the next exercise you will learn to use the **Pen** tool to draw a free-form Bézier mask, which (since you can create smooth curves) can be very precise. The mask you'll create will have an open path.

TIP:

Importing Masks from Illustrator

If you don't want to make masks in After Effects 7, you can copy and paste paths from Illustrator. Simply create your mask in Illustrator, select it there, and copy it. In After Effects 7, select the layer in which you want the mask applied, and paste it there. The shape from Illustrator will not only paste in the **Composition** panel, but the artwork in the selected layer will also appear within the mask. It's that simple, and it can save you the time and aggravation of having to re-create complex masks for an object you've already designed in Illustrator.

Working with the Selection Tool

The **Selection** tool has a great deal of functionality when used with paths. One of the tricks to using After Effects 7 effectively is to understand how the **Selection** tool works.

What might not be obvious when working with the **Selection** tool is that it performs different functions depending on what is currently selected. For example, if the entire mask is selected, the **Selection** tool will move the mask in the **Composition** panel. However, if only a single point or a group of points of the mask is selected, using the **Selection** tool will change the shape of the mask. This can be a bit frustrating when you're adjusting a path.

Here's a possible scenario: The entire mask is selected, and you click a point to select it individually, but After Effects 7 won't let you select that single point. This behavior can cause a bit of frustration. You can develop a system, however, to make these frustrations disappear.

The first step to take is to identify whether the entire mask or just individual points are selected before you attempt to drag a mask path. In a certain respect, this is the hardest part. Once you've trained yourself to become aware of the selection "state," the rest is easy.

The answer to the **Selection** tool dilemma lies in using keyboard commands that modify **Selection** tool functionality. Three techniques can help you when using the **Selection** tool, and luckily they're easy to remember because you use the three keys all the time. The keys are **Cmd**, **Opt**, and **Shift** (Mac) or **Ctrl**, **Alt**, and **Shift** (Windows).

The first technique to learn is what to do if your entire mask is already selected and you want to change the state of the mask so you can select single points. Before you begin, make certain your mask is selected in the **Timeline** panel by opening the **Mask** property for the layer.

Hold down the **Shift** key and, with the **Selection** tool, draw a **marquee** (a selection box) around any point(s) you want to select, as shown in the illustration here. After that, the mask will be in the "individual point" selection state. You can just

click any point within the marquee you want to select directly. Holding down the **Shift** key allows you to click unselected points and add them to your selected group.

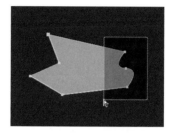

The second technique covers what to do if individual points are selected and you want to select the entire mask. Press **Opt** (Mac) or **Alt** (Windows), and click the mask. After that, the entire mask will be selected, and you can reposition it anywhere you want in the **Composition** panel.

The third technique is to hold down the **Cmd** (Mac) or **Ctrl** (Windows) key to toggle between the **Selection** tool and the current **Pen** tool. For example, if the **Convert Vertex Point** tool (whose cursor looks like an inverted **V**) is visible in the **Tools** panel, it will become active if you hold down the **Cmd** (Mac) or **Ctrl** (Windows) key while using the **Selection** tool, as shown in the illustration here. This can be handy when you are adjusting Bézier points and you want to convert their types from straight points to curved ones, or vice versa.

Finally, remember to double-click to display or hide the mask bounding box.

Knowing these techniques will make working with masks much less frustrating. You'll get some hands-on practice in the following exercises; also, feel free to revisit this section as you gain more experience with masking in After Effects 7.

2 | Drawing Bézier Masks Using the Pen Tool

In Chapter 5, *"Creating Keyframes and Animation in the Timeline,"* you learned to use the **Pen** tool to adjust spatial keyframes in motion paths. You can use the **Pen** tool to draw Bézier mask paths directly in the **Composition** panel, which can help you create smooth motion paths or masks for complex shapes. In this exercise, you will open the **Effects Mask** composition, select the **Pen** tool, and draw a Bézier mask. Not only is this technique helpful for defining an open path for an effect, such as a text placement, but it is also useful when trying to mask a specific shape in a layer with a closed path, which we will discuss later in this chapter.

---

1 If you followed the previous exercise, **Mask_Project.aep** should still be open in After Effects 7. If it's not, choose **File > Open Project**. Navigate to the **chap_13** folder you copied to your desktop, click **Mask_Project_2.aep** to select it, and click **Open**.

---

2 In the **Project** panel, double-click the **Effects Mask** composition to open it.

---

3 In the **Tools** panel, select the **Pen** tool.

In the following steps, you will draw the mask path and save it for later. In the next exercise, you will combine that mask path with the text effect.

---

4 In the **Timeline** panel, select the **Text Effect** layer. In the **Composition** panel, using the **Pen** tool, start on the right side, and click and then drag from point to point to draw the mask path shown in the illustration here; end the path by placing your last point on the left side.

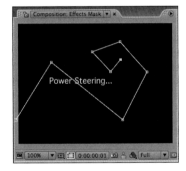

The Text Effect layer is a solid layer with the Text effect applied to it. When you click from point to point using the Pen tool, you create a straight path. You don't have to follow exactly what's shown in the illustration here; just do something basically resembling this path, and it'll be fine.

Note: Open mask paths, like the one you just drew, are used only with effects. They act as boundaries for effects, or they can define a path for an effect.

In the following steps, you will smooth the mask path by converting each point from a straight path to a curved path.

---

5 With the **Pen** tool still selected, **Opt+click** (Mac) or **Alt+click** (Windows) over the second point from the right. Notice the cursor changes to a caret (^) shape. Click this same point again, and notice the point changes to a curved path.

This caret shape is the icon for the Convert Vertex tool.

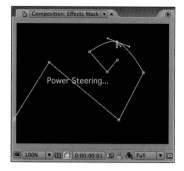

6 Using the method discussed in the previous step, convert each point except the beginning and ending points to a curved path point.

7 In the **Tools** panel, select the **Selection** tool, and adjust any points you like (by clicking a point and adjusting its Bézier handle) until you get a pleasing shape.

Your finished mask path should be fairly smooth, so the text will flow nicely along the path when you animate it.

8 Choose **File > Save**, or press **Cmd+S** (Mac) or **Ctrl+S** (Windows). Leave **Mask_Project.aep** and the **Effects Mask** composition open for the next exercise.

So far, you've learned how to create straight and curved paths, which will aid you in creating better motion for your animations, in addition to helping later when you need to mask complex shapes. The **upcoming** exercises will build on these skills.

NOTE:

Locking Masks

Knowing how to lock and unlock a mask is a nice skill to have so you don't accidentally edit a mask after going to the trouble of creating it. To display the **Lock** switch for a mask, you must first display the mask properties by clicking the **twirly** icons for a layer.

Tip: You can display the **Mask Shape** property by pressing the **M** key one time. This will also display the **Lock** switch for the mask.

The **Lock** column and the **Lock** switch for the mask are in the **Switches** panel on the far left. Click the column with the **Lock** icon to lock the mask. The icon changes to a lock to indicate the mask is now locked and cannot be edited.

3 | Using Masks with Text Effects

In the following exercise, you'll apply a **Path Text** effect to the mask path you created in the previous exercise. A **Path Text** effect allows you to animate text along the mask path. Using a mask path with the **Path Text** effect combines techniques you learned from the previous chapter with some you learned in this one.

---

1 If you followed the previous exercise, **Mask_Project.aep** should still be open in After Effects 7. If it's not, choose **File > Open Project**. Navigate to the **chap_13** folder you copied to your desktop, click **Mask_Project_3.aep** to select it, and click **Open**. Double-click the **Effects Mask** composition to open it, if it is not already visible.

The Effects Mask composition should still be open from the previous exercise.

---

2 In the **Timeline** panel, select the **Text Effect** layer.

To make this exercise more efficient, we've already applied the text effect to this solid layer.

Tip: You can add a text effect to any kind of layer—a solid layer, a still footage, or a movie.

---

3 Choose **Effect > Effect Controls** to display the **Effect Controls** panel. Alternatively, press **Cmd+Shift+T** (Mac) or **Ctrl+Shift+T** (Windows).

---

4 In the **Effect Controls** panel, click the **twirly** icon for **Path Text**, and then click the **twirly** icon for **Path Options** if they are not already open.

---

5 Locate the **Custom Path** option, click the pop-up menu, and choose **Mask 1**.

Notice the text conforms to the path.

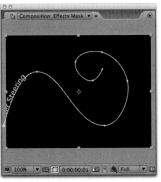

Note: After Effects 7 automatically assigns the name Mask to the mask you made in the previous exercise. You can change the mask's name to anything you want by selecting Mask 1 in the Timeline panel, pressing Return (Mac) or Enter (Windows), and renaming it. For this exercise, you can leave it named Mask 1.

In the following step, you'll see how to reverse the orientation of the text by reversing the path.

6 In the **Effect Controls** panel, turn off the **Reverse Path** check box (after you do this, it should be unselected), which should reorient the text.

The text should be oriented right side up.

Reversing the path affects the text in two ways. First, it reverses the vertical orientation of the text. Second, it reverses the first and last points of

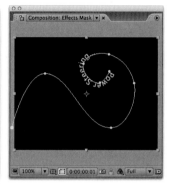

origin of the text. In the following steps, you'll learn to animate the text along the custom path you created, using the Left Margin option.

7 In the **Timeline** panel, make sure the **CTI** is set to **Frame 1**.

8 In the **Effect Controls** panel, click the **twirly** icon for **Path Options** to hide those properties. Click the **twirly** icon for **Paragraph** to display the **Paragraph** properties.

9 In the **Effect Controls** panel, click the **stopwatch** icon **Left Margin** to turn on keyframes. Set **Left Margin** to **0**.

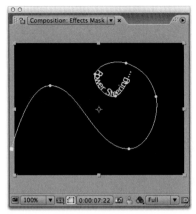

10 In the **Timeline** panel, drag the **CTI** to the last frame by pressing the **End** key. Position your mouse over the **Left Margin** value so you can see the arrows, as shown in the illustration here. Click the value field and drag to the right, causing the number to increase to approximately **600** until the text makes its way all the way to the right end of the path.

The value (in this case 600) relates to the relative position of the artwork, so it will be different for every path.

---

11 Scrub the **CTI**, click **RAM Preview** in the **Time Controls** panel, or press the **spacebar** to see the results of the animation.

---

12 Choose **File > Save**, or press **Cmd+S** (Mac) or **Ctrl+S** (Windows). In the top-left corner of the **Composition** panel, choose **Close Effects Mask** from the **Composition** pop-up menu to close the current composition. Leave **Mask_Project.aep** open for the next exercise.

You just learned how to work with an open mask path in conjunction with an effect. In the next exercise, you will learn how to work with feather properties on closed mask paths, like the one you created in Exercise 1.

---

4 | Creating Feathered Masks

So far, you've created a closed path (using the **Elliptical Mask** tool in Exercise 1) and an open path (using the **Pen** tool in Exercise 2). You can create closed paths using the **Elliptical Mask** tool, **Rectangular Mask** tool, or **Pen** tool. One of the benefits of creating a closed path is that it can be **feathered** (to help it blend better within your composition), which creates a soft-edged mask. That's what you'll learn to do in this exercise.

1 If you followed the previous exercise, **Mask_Project.aep** should still be open in After Effects 7. If it's not, choose **File > Open Project**. Navigate to the **chap_13** folder you copied to your desktop, click **Mask_Project_4.aep** to select it, and click **Open**.

2 In the **Project** panel, double-click the **Feathered Masks** composition to open it.

3 In the **Timeline** panel, select the **Solid Yellow BG** layer. In the **Tools** panel, select the **Elliptical Mask** tool.

You must always select the layer in which you want the mask applied before you create a mask. In fact, the masking tools in the Tools panel are dimmed unless you select a layer in the Timeline first.

Tip: Press the Q key to switch between the Elliptical Mask and Rectangular Mask tools.

4 With the **Elliptical Mask** tool, draw an oval mask similar to the one shown in the illustration here.

If you want to adjust the position of the mask, drag it with the Selection tool; alternatively, use the arrow keys on your keyboard.

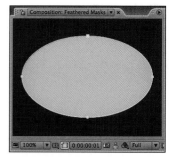

5 Press the **M** key two times to display all the masking properties for the selected layer. Set the **Mask Feather** property to **30** pixels.

Note: The two values in this property represent the X axis and Y axis of the mask shape (horizontal and vertical directions). They are locked by default, which is probably how you'll want to keep them for most feathering purposes. Because you haven't clicked the stopwatch icon, this change will last for the duration of the composition. The only reason to click the stopwatch icon is if you want to animate a property over time.

6 In the **Composition** panel, notice the mask path is in the center of the feathered transition.

You can control the feathering along the mask path by using the Mask Expansion property. In the following steps, you will reduce the mask expansion. This will move the area from which the feathering originates.

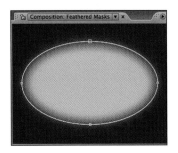

7 In the **Timeline** panel, set the **Mask Expansion** property to **–10** pixels.

Positive numbers increase the mask expansion; negative numbers decrease it.

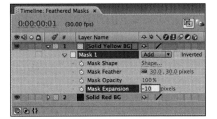

8 Choose **File > Save**, or press **Cmd+S** (Mac) or **Ctrl+S** (Windows). In the top-left corner of the **Composition** panel, choose **Close Feathered Masks** from the **Composition** pop-up menu to close the current composition. Leave **Mask_Project.aep** open for the next exercise.

In this exercise, you learned how to apply feathering to a mask, which will help you eliminate harsh edges and create more pleasing masks. If you want to experiment more, you could set keyframes for the Mask Feather or Mask Expansion properties and change the values over different keyframes. You can animate any of the masking properties by clicking the stopwatch icon, just as you can with any other After Effects 7 property. In the next exercise, you'll learn how to work with mask modes, which change the way multiple layer masks interact.

TIP:

Deleting a Mask

How do you delete a mask? It's simple, really. Select the mask by clicking its name in the **Timeline** panel, and then press the **Delete** key. This will delete only the mask, not the layer.

---

5 | Using Mask Modes

You can apply more than one mask to a single layer. Although you probably wouldn't use, say, more than 127 masks on a layer, you can get some interesting effects from using multiple masks. When you use multiple masks on a single layer, you can work with **mask modes**, which change the appearance of the different mask shapes in relation to each other and which can create beautiful effects. In this exercise, you will learn to apply multiple masks and to use mask modes. You'll also learn to use mask opacity with mask modes.

This exercise works with a solid layer. It's amazing how many different looks you can create with a solid layer, especially when you're working with masking, feathering, and opacity. You might even use Photoshop and Illustrator less, once you see the power of combining solid layers and masks within After Effects 7.

---

1 If you followed the previous exercise, **Mask_Project.aep** should still be open in After Effects 7. If it's not, choose **File > Open Project**. Navigate to the **chap_13** folder you copied to your desktop, click **Mask_Project_5.aep** to select it, and click **Open**.

---

2 In the **Project** panel, double-click the **Mask Modes** composition to open it.

This is an empty composition, although you will add content to it.

---

3 Choose **Layer > New > Solid** to create a new solid layer. In the **Solid Settings** dialog box, select yellow, and click **Make Comp Size**. When you are finished, click **OK**.

You should see a solid yellow layer that fits perfectly in the Composition panel.

---

4 With the solid layer selected in the **Timeline** panel, press **Return** (Mac) or **Enter** (Windows), and rename the layer **Solid Yellow BG**. In the **Tools** panel, select the **Elliptical Mask** tool.

---

5 With the **Elliptical Mask** tool selected, press the **Shift** key, and then draw a circle on the screen, like the one shown in the illustration here.

Remember, if you hold down the Shift key while clicking and dragging with the Elliptical Mask tool, you can create a perfect circle.

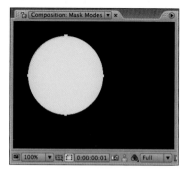

6 In the **Tools** panel, select the **Rectangular Mask** tool. Hold down the **Shift** key, and draw a square mask overlapping the circle.

Note: The Shift key constrains the rectangle mask to a perfect square. Don't worry too much about getting the positions to match exactly; the idea for this exercise is to simply create two masks like the ones shown in the illustration here.

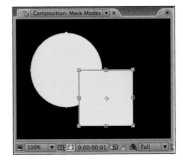

7 Press the **M** key to display the **Mask Shape** property for your layer.

Notice the Solid Yellow BG layer has two mask-related properties (Mask 1 and Mask 2), each with a Mask Shape property. Multiple masks on a layer appear in the order you create them.

8 Select **Mask 1**, press **Return** (Mac) or **Enter** (Windows), and type **Circle Mask** to rename the mask. Repeat this process for **Mask 2**, and type **Square Mask** as the new name.

9 In the **Layer Switches** panel, click the **Mask Mode** pop-up menu for the **Square Mask** (which is set to **Add** by default), and choose **Subtract** to change the mode.

Notice this subtracts the square mask from the area of the circle in which the masks overlap. This is the opposite of Add, which displays the combination of the two layers.

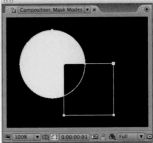

The Mask Mode pop-up menu is automatically available in the Timeline as soon as you create a mask. Like many things in the Timeline, the Mask Mode menu in After Effects 7 is context sensitive. Simply add a mask, and the menu appears.

10 For **Square Mask**, click the **Mask Mode** pop-up menu, and choose **Intersect**.

Notice this displays only the intersecting area of the masks.

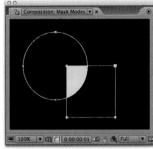

11 Click the **Mask Mode** pop-up menu, and choose **Difference**.

In Difference mode, only the areas of the masks *not* overlapping appear.

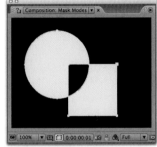

12 Click the **Mask Mode** pop-up menu, and choose **Add**. Click the **Mask Mode** pop-up menu again, and choose **Lighten**. Compare the two modes.

Notice the results are the same.

Some modes work identically on the same artwork. Even though you used a solid layer for this exercise, you could have used a photograph or a movie as your source layer for the mask. If, instead of these solid shapes, you had photographic content that wasn't at full opacity, you would see a different effect when you selected Lighten.

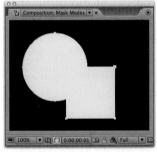

13 Click the **Mask Mode** pop-up menu, and choose **Intersect**. Click the **Mask Mode** pop-up menu again, and choose **Darken**. Compare the two modes.

The results of these modes also appear the same.

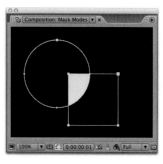

The Lighten and Darken modes take on greater significance when acting on masks with opacities of less than 100 percent. In the following steps, you will draw a triangular Bézier mask and then adjust the opacity of all three masks. After that, you will reapply the Lighten and Darken modes and observe the new results.

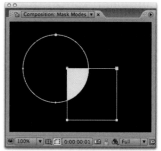

---

14 Click the **Mask Mode** pop-up menu, and choose **Add**. Make sure the **Solid Yellow BG** layer is selected, and then in the **Tools** panel, select the **Pen** tool.

You'll start with a basic Add mode and then throw another shape into the mix.

---

15 In the **Composition** panel, draw a triangle overlapping both the circle and the square, as shown in the illustration here. Create this shape by clicking the three points to form the triangle and clicking one last time on the first point to close the shape.

When you are creating a mask shape by using the Pen tool, you can close the mask by returning to the point where you began the shape, positioning the cursor (the Pen tool) over that point until a circular icon appears next to it, and then clicking with your mouse one last time.

You'll notice it's a bit difficult to see the outline of your triangular mask layer. In the next step, you'll select a new color for its bounding box.

---

16 In the **Timeline** panel, to the left of the new **Mask 1** shape, click the **color swatch**. In the **color picker**, select a new color, such as red.

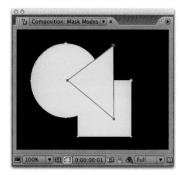

The edges of your triangular mask should be easier to identify now. If you want, you can choose a different color for each of your masks to make them easier to identify, which is helpful for layers with several overlapping masks.

---

17 In the **Timeline** panel, select **Mask 1**, and then press **Return** (Mac) or **Enter** (Windows). Type **Triangle Mask**, and press **Return** (Mac) or **Enter** (Windows) to rename the mask.

---

18 Press the **M** key two times to display the mask-related properties for all the masks.

Feel free to adjust the size of your Timeline panel if you want to see all the mask-related properties without scrolling.

---

19 For **Circle Mask**, set the opacity to **80%**. For **Square Mask**, set the opacity to **60%**. For **Triangle Mask**, set the opacity to **40%**.

After setting the opacity values (which will make the results of your chosen mode a little more dramatic), click the twirly icon next to each of the masks to hide the properties but still display the mask names. Readjust the height of your Timeline panel if you want.

---

20 Click anywhere in the **Timeline** except in a layer to deselect everything.

Tip: You also can choose Edit > Deselect All or press Cmd+Shift+A (Mac) or Ctrl+Shift+A (Windows) to deselect.

---

21 In the **Timeline** panel, click the **Mask Mode** pop-up menu for the **Triangle Mask**, and choose **Lighten** to change its mode from the default (**Add**). Compare the results.

The Add and Lighten modes display opacity values differently. In the Add mode, where multiple masks intersect, After Effects 7 adds the opacity values of all intersecting masks together. In the Lighten mode, where multiple masks intersect, After Effects 7 uses the highest opacity value.

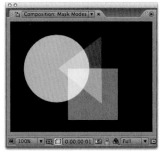

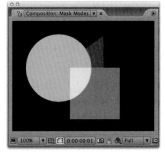

22 Click the **Mask Mode** pop-up menu for the **Triangle Mask**, and change its mode to **Intersect** and then to **Darken**. Compare the results.

Here again, After Effects 7 processes and displays the opacity values differently. In Intersect mode, After Effects 7 adds the opacity of all the intersecting masks together. In Darken mode, After Effects 7 doesn't add the opacity values together; instead, After Effects 7 uses a single opacity value for intersecting multiple masks.

23 Choose **File > Save**, or press **Cmd+S** (Mac) or **Ctrl+S** (Windows). In the top-left corner of the **Composition** panel, choose **Close Mask Modes** from the **Composition** pop-up menu to close the current composition. Leave **Mask_Project.aep** open for the next exercise.

You don't need to worry about memorizing how each mode works. With experience you will intuitively understand the results you get from each mode.

Right now, it's primarily important to see what the Add, Subtract, Intersect, and Difference modes do. Of secondary importance is to realize the Lighten and Darken modes won't do anything for you unless you are using masks with opacities of less than 100 percent.

Now that you've seen the modes and you have some firsthand experience, you'll be able to experiment and incorporate mask modes into your own work.

In the next exercise, you'll not only take a look at more mask shapes but you will also learn how to animate the masks over time.

TIP:

Changing the Color of a Mask Outline

As you saw in the previous exercise, when working with multiple masks, it can be a good idea to change the color of mask outlines so you can easily identify each one in the **Composition** panel.

To change the color, locate the mask in the **Timeline** panel, and click the **color swatch** to the left of the mask name. Select a new color, and click **OK**.

---

6 | Animating and Changing Mask Shapes

You can animate mask shapes. The result creates the impression of one shape morphing into another. This is particularly useful for revealing different areas of your layer over time or for **rotoscoping** an object in a motion layer (manually cutting out a shape in moving video or film). In this exercise, you'll learn to animate mask shapes and to change mask types.

1 If you followed the previous exercise, **Mask_Project.aep** should still be open in After Effects 7. If it's not, choose **File > Open Project**. Navigate to the **chap_13** folder you copied to your desktop, click **Mask_Project_6.aep** to select it, and click **Open**.

2 In the **Project** panel, double-click the **Animate Mask Shape** composition to open it.

3 With **Cycle.psd** selected in the **Timeline**, select the **Pen** tool in the **Tools** panel. Click around the motorcycle image to create a mask showing the vehicle without the starburst, as shown in the illustration here.

You may need to zoom into your Composition panel to work more easily when setting points with the Pen tool. You can press Cmd++ (Mac) or Ctrl++ (Windows)—in other words, hold down Cmd (Mac) or Ctrl (Windows) and then press the plus key—when you have the Composition panel selected, or you can choose 200% or 400% from the Magnification ratio popup pop-up menu.

Note: Click an empty part of the Timeline to get rid of the mask selection so you can see whether you're happy with the mask. If you're not, using the Selection tool, double-click the motorcycle in the Composition panel to see the mask handles. Using the Pen tool, you can modify the points from straight lines to curves; using the Selection tool, you can move the mask. Keep up this process of clicking an empty part of the Timeline to see it and fixing it until you're happy with its shape. This often takes some massaging—few people get it right without a little extra effort.

4 Make sure you are in **Frame 1** of your **Timeline**. With the **Cycle.psd** layer selected, press the **M** key to reveal the **Mask Shape** property. Next to the **Mask Shape** property, click the **stopwatch** icon.

This sets a keyframe for the Mask Shape property in the first frame.

Note: The shortcut M reveals only the property you have set (Mask Shape), whereas the shortcut MM reveals all the mask-related properties. Because you are animating only the Mask Shape property, the shortcut key M is sufficient to show you what you need to see.

5 Drag the **CTI** to the end of the **Timeline** by pressing the **End** key or the **K** key.

---

6 In the **Tools** panel, select the **Selection** tool. In the **Layer Viewer** panel, double-click the motorcycle artwork to open the **Layer: Cycle.psd** panel.

See the "Using the Layer Viewer Panel for Better Control" sidebar after this exercise for more information about working in this particular panel.

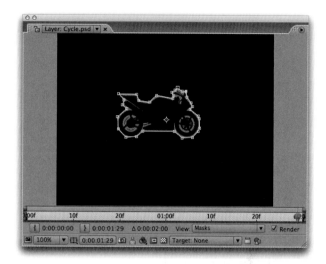

---

7 With the **Selection** tool, move the points of the mask outward, revealing the entire starburst. Close the **Layer: Cycle.psd** panel when you're finished.

If you look in the Timeline, you'll see this change sets another keyframe. That's because you clicked the stopwatch icon for the Mask Shape property. Any change you make to the mask creates a keyframe as long as you move the CTI to a new location. If you think about it, this is how all keyframes are created in After Effects 7—click the stopwatch icon, move the CTI, make a change, and *voilà*! You have a new keyframe.

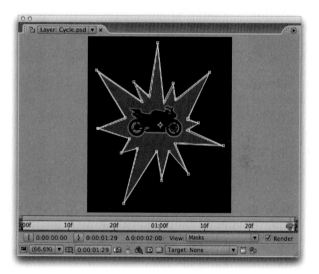

8 Click an empty part of the **Timeline** panel to deselect the **Cycle.psd** layer. In the **Composition** panel, turn off the mask shape outline. Scrub the **CTI** or press the **spacebar** to view the mask shape animation.

9 Choose **File > Save**, or press **Cmd+S** (Mac) or **Ctrl+S** (Windows). Choose **File > Close Project**.

In this exercise, you learned how to animate a mask shape over time, which can be useful for creating transitions and revealing parts of your composition, as well as for following shapes that change over time. Before you move to the next chapter about creating track mattes, refer to the tips and other short-cuts discussed next.

TIP:

Using the Layer Viewer Panel for Better Control

Sometimes for really detailed and complex masking jobs, it's easier to view the mask in the **Layer Viewer** panel. You access this panel by double-clicking the artwork with the **Selection** tool in the **Composition** panel.

Double-clicking with the **Selection** tool launches the **Layer Viewer** panel for that particular graphic. It is more intuitive to move anchor points in this view, but you must close the view (or switch from one tab to another) to see the results of your work in the **Composition** panel, so it's a little inconvenient.

Masks are great tools for adding transparent areas to a layer, hiding or revealing certain objects, and creating transitions. You certainly have the experience now to create a vast array of masks for your projects. Practice on some footage of your own—don't stop with the examples in this chapter. Try masking all kinds of footage, and you'll be amazed by the effects you can achieve.

TIP:

Exploring the Tools Panel's Keyboard Commands

Drawing and adjusting masks often requires many trips to the **Tools** panel. You can streamline your work process by using keyboard commands instead to access every tool in the **Tools** panel. Use these shortcut keys in the following chart, and you'll spend less time clicking the **Tools** panel and more time making creative decisions:

Tools Panel Shortcut Keys	
Key	**Tool**
V	**Selection** tool
H	**Hand** tool
Z	**Zoom** tool
W	**Rotation** tool
C	**Camera** tools (works only when a 3D layer is selected, which you'll learn more about in Chapter 16, "*Working with 3D Layers*")
Y	**Pan Behind** tool
Q	**Elliptical Mask/Rectangular Mask** tools (works only when a layer is selected)
G	**Pen** tool

14

Creating Track Mattes

Track mattes are often new to those who have never used After Effects 7. Even experienced After Effects 7 users may be unfamiliar with track mattes. The concept is slightly abstract and is best explained by seeing it in action, which is what you will do in this chapter. Basically, a **track matte** is a special type of matte that is used to place video or graphics inside a cutout shape. A track matte effect is a perfect solution when you want to play a movie inside text. In this scenario, you would separate the text and movie into two layers and use a track matte to tell After Effects 7 to use the shape (or alpha channel) of the text as a mask for the movie. The cool feature of a track matte is you can still animate the associated layers independently. This means you could have a movie that scales (for example) to different sizes, which also appears inside moving text letters. This isn't just restricted to moving images inside text; it can work with any artwork containing an alpha channel, which you'll learn more about in this chapter.

Introducing Alpha Channels

Alpha channels are critical to working with track mattes. Why? Well, a track matte has to use the alpha channel of footage in the **Timeline** in order to work. Not all footage items contain an alpha channel, but this chapter will help you identify when one exists and how to use it.

The simple explanation is that an **alpha channel** works invisibly to mask areas of a digital image created from Adobe Photoshop, Adobe Illustrator, and other programs supporting this feature. If you've worked with Photoshop, you've probably created documents with alpha channels, even if you weren't aware you were doing so. Any Photoshop or Illustrator layer containing artwork employing transparent pixels uses an invisible alpha channel.

An image or movie containing an alpha channel is considered a **32-bit** graphic. This stands for 8 bits of red, 8 bits of green, 8 bits of blue, and 8 bits of 256 shades of gray making up the masking channel. When you add all the bits from the RGB and alpha channels, you get 32 bits. A 32-bit image or movie has the extra value of the alpha channel.

Whenever you create a layer in Photoshop that has visible and transparent pixels, such as text, the program generates an invisible mask called an **alpha channel**, or **transparency channel**. The checkerboard background in Photoshop, shown in the illustration here, denotes this type of transparency.

If you could see the alpha channel, it would look like the image shown in the illustration here. It works much like a film negative does. If you were to shine a light through it, the white areas would expose the content, and the black areas would mask it.

When you import a still image file into After Effects 7, you can choose to merge layers, import a single layer, or import a Photoshop document as a composition. All these methods preserve the alpha channel.

If you don't want to preserve the alpha channel, you must do a little bit of work. If you want to turn off an image's alpha channel, select the image in the **Project** panel, choose **File > Interpret Footage > Main**, and then select **Ignore**.

Masks and mattes in After Effects 7 work in conjunction with alpha channels. The track matte feature in After Effects 7 uses the alpha channel residing in artwork created by Photoshop, Illustrator, or other software supporting this feature.

Importing Alpha Channels from Photoshop Documents

Knowing that alpha channels are essential to your track matte workflow, you might wonder how to prepare Photoshop artwork and alpha channels properly. Because this is an After Effects 7 book and not a Photoshop or Illustrator book, we have created the artwork in the following exercises for you. When you work on your own, however, you will be preparing artwork in other programs.

Photoshop and Illustrator files can contain layers making up a complete image. The illustration shown here contains an image in Photoshop consisting of four layers, each with its own alpha channel. The Photoshop **Layers** palette lists each layer from top to bottom: **Line**, **Motorcycle**, **Starburst**, and **Circle**.

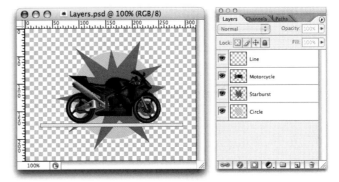

When you import the Photoshop file as footage, you can choose to merge the layers or import each one individually. Selecting the **Merged Layers** radio button will combine all the Photoshop layers and their alpha channels into a single footage item. Selecting an individual layer will import only that layer as a footage item.

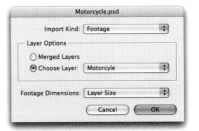

Individually imported Photoshop layers show up in the **Project** panel with their original layer names followed by the name of the Photoshop file. Notice the information for this footage states it contains **Millions of Colors+ (Straight)**. In other words, this footage contains a straight alpha channel, which is the most common type. We list the different types of alpha channels later in this chapter, along with more complete definitions.

You can also choose to import a Photoshop or Illustrator file choosing **Composition** or **Composition – Cropped Layers**. You've worked with both these types of import options in previous chapters.

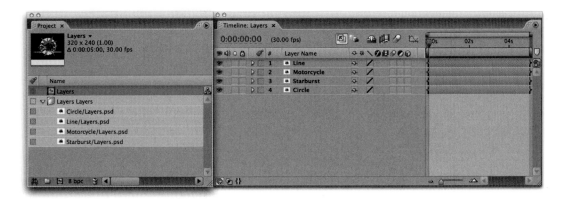

When you import a file as a composition, After Effects 7 automatically creates a new composition in the **Project** panel and places the layers in the original stacking order. This is a real time-saver.

In all cases, After Effects 7 imports the alpha channel transparency from Photoshop and Illustrator files appropriately without you having to do anything special.

In this exercise, you will learn to create a simple track matte that places a photograph inside some text. This represents one of the most common uses of track mattes, and it is a technique you can use with alpha channels in your artwork to create more interesting titles for your next movie.

---

1 Copy the **chap_14** folder from the **After Effects 7 HOT CD-ROM** onto your desktop.

---

2 Choose **File > New > New Project**, and then choose **File > Save As**. In the **Save As** dialog box, navigate to the **AE7_HOT_Projects** folder on your desktop. Name the file **Track_Mattes.aep**, and click **Save**.

---

3 Double-click the empty **Project** panel. In the **Import File** dialog box, navigate to the **chap_14** folder. Click **Clouds.tif** to select it. Hold down **Cmd** (Mac) or **Ctrl** (Windows), and then click **Sale.psd** and **Sky.tif** to multiple-select the files. Click **Open**, and then click **OK** to merge the layers when prompted.

---

4 In the **Project** panel, click the **Create a new Composition** button. In the **Composition Settings** dialog box, name the new composition **Sale**, and make sure your settings match those shown in the illustration here. Click **OK**.

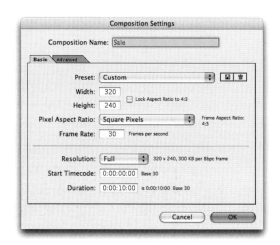

5 Drag the **Clouds.tif** and **Sale.psd** files, and drop them in the **Timeline** panel. Make sure the type layer, **Sale.psd**, is on top.

6 In the **Timeline** panel, click the **Expand or Collapse the Transfer Controls pane** switch to open the **Transfer Controls** pane, where you'll see track matte information. Notice the column headings **Mode**, **T**, and **TrkMat** appear.

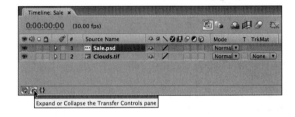

As you may recall, you learned what modes do in Chapter 8, *"Working with Layers."* You'll work with the T and TrkMat settings shortly, when we'll reveal their meanings. Toward the end of this chapter, you'll also learn about stencil modes, which you did not learn about in Chapter 8 because they work only with artwork containing alpha channels.

7 In the **Clouds.tif** layer, click the **TrkMat** pop-up menu, and choose **Alpha Matte "Sale.psd"**.

Notice the red sky photograph now appears inside the type. The color you see behind the type is whatever color you have set your composition background color to be. The track matte layer is using the alpha channel from the layer directly above it. This is how track mattes work—you put the layer from which you want to pull the matte above the layer you want to be affected.

8 In the **Project** panel, drag **Sky.tif** in the **Timeline** panel below **Clouds.tif**.

This layer's TrkMat option is automatically set to None, which means it is unaffected by the type. Because the Sky.tif file is now at the bottom of the layer stack, you see it instead of the background color.

9 In the **Timeline** panel, change the **TrkMat** option (short for **Track Matte**) for **Sale.psd** from **Alpha Matte "Sale.psd"** to **Alpha Inverted Matte "Sale.psd"**. Be sure to change it back to **Alpha Matte "Sale.psd"** when you're finished seeing the change.

The type mask is now inverted.

Whether you select Alpha Matte "Sale.psd" or Alpha Inverted Matte "Sale.psd" as your TrkMat option is a creative decision that depends on the kind of look you want. This feature is so flexible you can try both settings. You'll learn about the luminance TrkMat settings

in a later exercise. The artwork you used in this exercise (the type) has an alpha channel, so it doesn't need to rely on the Luma (luminance) option in the TrkMat pop-up menu, which is not as precise.

10 Choose **File > Save**, or press **Cmd+S** (Mac) or **Ctrl+S** (Windows). Leave **Track_Mattes.aep** and the **Sale** composition open for the next exercise.

In this exercise, you learned how to create a basic track matte using a graphic with an alpha channel. In the next exercise, you will learn how to animate these layers separately to create movement within the image.

2 | Animating a Track Matte

Because you can animate anything and everything in After Effects 7, you can't really harness the power of track mattes until you combine them with some keyframes and set some properties in motion. You'll see in this exercise how you can animate the matte, animate the contents of the matte, and do both at the same time.

---

1 If you followed the previous exercise, **Track_Mattes.aep** should still be open in After Effects 7. If it's not, choose **File > Open Project**. Navigate to the **chap_14** folder you copied to your desktop, click **Track_Mattes_2.aep** to select it, and click **Open**. Double-click the **Sale** composition to open it.

---

2 With the **Sale.psd** layer selected, press the **P** key, and then press **Shift+S** to reveal the **Position** and **Scale** properties.

---

3 Make certain you are in **Frame 1** in the **Timeline**. Click the **stopwatch** icon for both the **Position** and **Scale** properties. Change the **Position** setting to approximately **74.0, 25.0** and the **Scale** setting to approximately **40%**.

You'll set some keyframes next.

If you don't want to set the position in the Timeline panel, you can click the word *SALE* and just move it in the Composition panel. This is the easiest way to set a position without thinking in numbers.

---

4 Drag the **CTI** (**C**urrent **T**ime **I**ndicator) to the end of the **Timeline**. Change **Scale** to **100.0%** and **Position** to **160.0, 165.0**, as shown in the illustration here. Press the **spacebar** to see the effect of moving and scaling the type over time.

Tip: Press the **K** key to move to the end of the Timeline.

In all, you should set four keyframes.

It's nice to see the type move through the cloud image of the track matte. Next, you'll animate the photo of the clouds for an even better effect.

5 Drag the **CTI** to the beginning of the **Timeline**, or press the **J** key. Select **Clouds.tif**, and press the **P** key to reveal the **Position** property. Click the **stopwatch** icon to set a keyframe. Change the **Y** position to **–45**.

This moves the image inside the type on the screen.

6 Drag the **CTI** to the end of the **Timeline**, or press the **K** key. Change the **Position** property for **Clouds.tif** to **160.0, 165.0**. Press the **spacebar** to preview the results of your work.

Now, not only is the type moving, but the clouds are moving inside the type.

You could also put movie footage inside the type, if you used an Apple QuickTime movie instead of a still photo. The variations are endless.

7 Choose **File > Save**, or press **Cmd+S** (Mac) or **Ctrl+S** (Windows). In the top-left corner of the **Composition** panel, choose **Close Sale** from the **Composition** pop-up menu to close the current composition. Leave **Track_Mattes.aep** open for the next exercise.

As you have seen in this exercise, it's possible to animate layers within a track matte separately, just like any other layers. In the next exercise, you'll learn how to use luminance information, rather than an alpha channel, to create a track matte.

3 | Using Luminance-Based Track Mattes

So far, you've had a chance to work with alpha channels and track mattes. This exercise will demonstrate when and why to use a luminance-based track matte. The term **luminance** in After Effects 7 refers to footage measured in grayscale values. Source footage can originate in Photoshop, Illustrator, or QuickTime and can be in color or grayscale.

If the artwork is in color, After Effects 7 will convert the color values to grayscale values automatically for you behind the scenes. Basically, After Effects 7 treats the grayscale value as it would an alpha channel—black in the grayscale image represents full masking, white represents full transparency, and gray shades take on varying degrees of transparency.

Why would you use luminance track mattes? Artists generally use them when they want to make a mask from artwork that doesn't contain an alpha channel. It's convenient to be able to choose from source artwork containing either grayscale information or an alpha channel.

---

1 If you followed the previous exercise, **Track_Mattes.aep** should still be open in After Effects 7. If it's not, choose **File > Open Project**. Navigate to the **chap_14** folder you copied to your desktop, click **Track_Mattes_3.aep** to select it, and click **Open**.

---

2 In the **Project** panel, click the **Create a new Composition** button. Name the new composition **Luma**, and click **OK**.

Your composition settings should match those from the previous project. After Effects 7 remembers the last settings you made and applies them to new compositions you create.

---

3 Double-click an empty area of the **Project** panel. In the **Import File** dialog box, navigate to the **chap_14** folder, and select **Luma.psd**, **Pattern1.psd**, and **Pattern2.psd**. Click **Open**, and then click **OK** to accept the merged layers for all the files.

---

4 In the **Project** panel, drag **Luma.psd**, **Pattern1.psd**, and **Pattern2.psd** to the **Timeline** panel. Place the layers in the order shown in the illustration here.

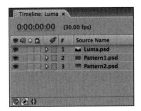

Notice the Luma.psd artwork has some areas of pure black, some areas of pure white, and some areas of mixed grays.

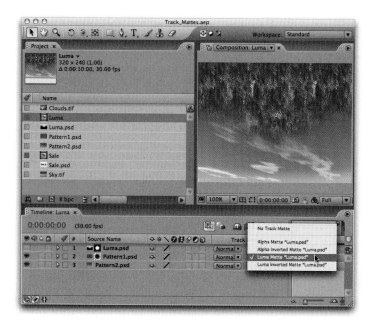

5 Click an empty area of the **Timeline** panel to make sure your layers are deselected. In the **Timeline panel,** click the **TrkMat** pop-up menu for **Pattern1.psd**, and choose **Luma Matte "Luma.psd"**.

Observe the Luma.psd artwork. Notice the areas that were pure black completely knock out Pattern1.psd to reveal Pattern2.psd. Also, the areas that were pure white fully reveal Pattern1.psd and hide Pattern2.psd. The gradient gradually causes one pattern to reveal the other, proving the luminance mask is doing its job.

---

6 Click the **TrkMat** pop-up menu for **Pattern1.psd**, and choose **Luma Inverted Matte "Luma.psd"**. Observe the mask changes to the opposite of what it was before.

---

7 Choose **File > Save**, or press **Cmd+S** (Mac) or **Ctrl+S** (Windows). In the top-left corner of the **Composition** panel, choose **Close Luma** from the **Composition** pop-up menu to close the current composition. Leave **Track_Mattes.aep** open for the next exercise.

To summarize, luminance mattes are based on grayscale values. Use them when you have source artwork containing lights and darks and you want to use the artwork as a mask. Remember, you can use movie footage as well as still footage as your mask source.

---

4 | Using a Soft-Edged Track Matte with a Masked Solid Layer

This track matte stuff gets even better. You can combine the masking skills you learned in Chapter 13, *"Creating Masks,"* with what you've learned in this chapter. In this exercise, you'll create a soft-edged matte from a solid layer and feather its edges. Then you'll use that layer to mask another layer for an interesting window effect, which you can animate to reveal parts of the underneath layers. It's easier than it sounds!

---

1 If you followed the previous exercise, **Track_Mattes.aep** should still be open in After Effects 7. If it's not, choose **File > Open Project**. Navigate to the **chap_14** folder you copied to your desktop, click **Track_Mattes_4.aep** to select it, and click **Open**.

---

2 In the **Project** panel, click the **Create a new Composition** button, name the new composition **Soft**, and click **OK**.

---

3 In the **Project** panel, drag **Clouds.tif** and drop it in the **Timeline** panel, where it will be centered automatically.

---

4 Choose **Layer > New > Solid** to create a new solid layer. In the **Solid Settings** dialog box, name the solid layer **Glow**, and click **OK**.

The layer color doesn't really matter because ultimately the solid layer won't be visible. However, you can practice using the color picker and choose a different color.

5 In the **Timeline** panel, select the **Glow** layer if necessary. In the **Tools** panel, select the **Elliptical Mask** tool, and draw an oval in the solid layer.

The result is a solid layer with a mask in the shape of an oval.

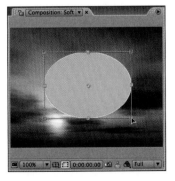

6 With the **Glow** layer still selected, press **MM** (press the **M** key twice) to reveal all the mask-related properties. Change **Mask Feather** to **48** pixels, and click an empty area of the **Timeline** panel to deselect the shape, which turns off the bounding box around the circle.

---

7 In the **Clouds.tif** layer, click the **TrkMat** pop-up menu, and choose **Alpha Matte "Glow"**.

The Clouds.tif layer appears inside the glow.

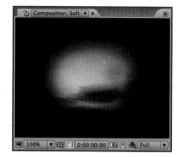

When you create a mask on a solid layer, you also create an alpha channel without probably realizing it. In this instance, the track matte is using the alpha channel from the masked solid layer. This is a useful technique because it's so convenient to make masks from solid layers. You don't have to leave After Effects 7 and go to Photoshop to make the glow artwork this way.

Now it is time to animate.

---

8 With the **Glow** layer selected, press **M** to hide the mask-related properties. Click the **Lock** switch for **Clouds.tif** so you don't accidentally move it.

---

9 With the **Glow** layer selected, press **S** to open the **Scale** property. Change **Scale** to **50%**.

The mask on your solid layer scales as well. Optionally, you may want to adjust the mask feather for the layer because the feathering will also scale.

---

10 Make sure you're in **Frame 1** of the **Timeline**. Press **Opt+P** (Mac) or **Alt+Shift+P** (Windows) to set a keyframe for the **Position** property. In the **Composition** panel, drag the artwork to the top-left corner of the panel, as shown in the illustration here.

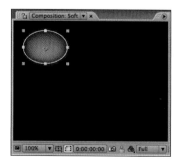

11 Drag the **CTI** to **0:00:03:00**, then to **0:00:06:00**, and then to the end of your **Timeline**, moving your artwork accordingly to create a motion path similar to the one shown in the illustration here.

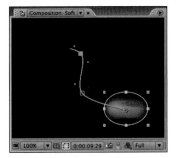

This is a good refresher on how to set multiple keyframes, as discussed in Chapter 5, *"Creating Keyframes and Animation in the Timeline."*

12 Press the **spacebar** to preview your animation.

The glow passes over the static cloud image, panning the image as it moves. Sometimes this is what you want, but other times you want the artwork to move with the glow. You can do that too, as you'll learn in the following steps.

13 In the **Timeline** panel, unlock the **Clouds.tif** layer by clicking the **Lock** switch again. In the **Timeline** panel's **Options** menu, choose **Columns > Parent** to display the **Parent** panel, if it is not already visible.

The Timeline's Options menu sits in the upper-right corner of the Timeline panel.

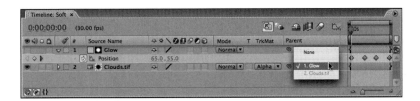

14 Drag the **CTI** to **0:00:00:00**. From the **Parent** column for **Clouds.tif**, select **1. Glow**. Press the **spacebar** to play the animation.

15 Choose **File > Save**, or press **Cmd+S** (Mac) or **Ctrl+S** (Windows).

You just learned how to create and animate a soft mask for use as a track matte. In the next section, you will learn a bit about other masking modes for creating different results when using graphics with alpha channels and luminance information.

Working with Other Masking Modes

You learned about layer modes in Chapter 8, *"Working with Layers."* With layer modes, you can composite two or more images to create interesting artistic effects. You may recall a few layer modes weren't discussed in Chapter 8 because they dealt specifically with masking. Animators tend to use masking modes less frequently than track mattes, but sometimes they are useful. Although the following examples are not hands-on exercises, you have all the artwork shown in this section based on the projects you created in this chapter, so experiment with these masking modes if you want. You can find definitions of the masking modes later in this section.

Modes appear next to the **T** and **TrkMat** columns of the **Transfer Controls** pane. A **Mode** pop-up menu appears for each layer in the **Timeline**, and its default setting is **Normal**. For the most part, modes have nothing to do with masks or alpha channels. A few modes do, however, and they appear toward the bottom of the **Mode** pop-up menu.

The stencil modes, in general, cut through multiple layers so you can see all the layers beneath the layer containing the stencil. The source artwork sits on top in the stacking order of layers in the **Timeline**, and the mode applies to this source layer. The following are the stencil modes:

Stencil Alpha mode: Cuts through all the layers beneath it (the source footage must contain an alpha channel). Shown in the illustration here, the top layer is set to **Stencil Alpha**, and the bottom two layers show through.

Stencil Luma mode: Cuts through all the layers beneath it. (The source footage will be treated as grayscale; if it's in color, it will be converted.) Shown in the illustration here, the top layer is set to **Stencil Luma**, and the bottom two layers show through.

The silhouette modes, in general, block all the layers beneath the layer containing the silhouette, allowing you to cut a hole through several layers at once. The source artwork sits on top in the stacking order of layers in the **Timeline**, and the mode applies to this source. The following are the silhouette modes:

Silhouette Alpha mode: The artwork with an alpha channel punches a hole all the way through to the background color of the composition. It cuts through every layer below it in the composition. Shown in the illustration here, the top layer is set to **Silhouette Alpha**, and the two bottom layers are set to Normal.

Silhouette Luma mode: The grayscale artwork (source artwork in color will be converted to grayscale) punches a hole all the way through to the background color of the composition. It cuts through every layer below it in the composition. Shown in the illustration here, the top layer is set to **Silhouette Luma**, and the two bottom layers are set to Normal.

The modes **Alpha Add** and **Luminescence Premul** require complex compositions and are not detailed in this book because only advanced artists use them, and even then only rarely (refer to the After Effects 7 user manual for more information).

We hope you enjoyed the techniques you learned in this chapter. Feel free to experiment and try other combinations of artwork for your track mattes. We suggest you use track mattes with QuickTime movies as source footage or practice working with masked solid layers as your source for track mattes. With a little imagination and some experimentation, you can create an infinite number of results using track mattes with your own footage. In the next chapter, you will learn about working with color keys, a technique for removing solid-colored backgrounds from your footage for compositing.

Using the Preserve Underlying Transparency Option

The **Transfer Controls** pane contains another option: the **Preserve Underlying Transparency** check box. Locate the option by finding the letter **T** at the top of the column. (Think **T** for transparency in this case.)

With the **Preserve Underlying Transparency** check box turned on for the top layer, After Effects 7 uses the alpha channel from the layer beneath to mask the artwork. The **Preserve Underlying Transparency** option works only if the artwork below the layer with the **T** option checked contains an alpha channel.

To use the **Preserve Underlying Transparency** option, just turn on the check box. This option produces the same effect as alpha channel–based track mattes; it just accomplishes it differently. We usually use whichever method is most convenient based on the stacking order (although it's also easy to move the stacking order!).

15

Working with Color Keys

Up until now, you've used masks, mattes, and layer modes to create composites and complex layer interactions. In this chapter, you'll work with keying to composite video footage over new background images, which is particularly useful for footage shot against a blue- or green-screen backdrop.

Introducing Color Keying

Keying simply refers to the **key**, or primary, color that is selected and removed from a shot. Keying is a popular technique used in film and television to place an actor or prop into a new (and sometimes entirely synthetic) environment. This is also the same technique used to place a meteorologist in front of a weather map. The process begins by lighting and shooting your subject in front of a solid-colored backdrop (usually blue or green) and then using an application such as After Effects 7 to remove that key color. This leaves only the subject remaining onscreen—so the subject is available for compositing with other material. This process is also called **chroma keying**.

In essence, keying quickly and easily generates a complex matte (a matte that would be difficult to create with a manual process), placing a transparent alpha channel around your subject. If you remember from Chapter 13, *"Creating Masks,"* and Chapter 14, *"Creating Track Mattes,"* **alpha channels** are invisible masks or transparency channels, such as those created in Adobe Photoshop. Using these alpha channels, you can place footage (graphics or video) on top of other layers to create more complex compositions. For example, you might shoot video footage of an actor in front of a green screen, use color keying in After Effects 7 to remove all the green from the shot, and then place the actor on top of a new background, such as an animation you created in After Effects 7. On occasion, it is also advantageous to isolate an area of the screen using masks so your color key focuses its effect on a smaller region of the shot.

Before beginning the first keying exercise, it's important to understand a few principles necessary for achieving a successful key. As with any project, preparation is essential and should help you eliminate potential headaches when working with this unique type of footage in After Effects 7.

Working with blue and green screens

Although the uses for blue- and green-screen footage are nearly endless, setting up a shot for proper keying requires the proper care and preparation. The best approach to setting up any color key shot for use in an After Effects 7 project starts with good lighting.

Make certain your background is evenly and brightly illuminated, removing as many shadows or other areas of discoloration—no matter how minor they may appear through your camera's viewfinder. Creases and seams in the fabric of a screen are frequent culprits (creating shadows), as are uneven placement of lights and mismatched fabrics. Cobbling together a screen from different pieces of fabric, paper, or painted surfaces is not recommended.

Additionally, **spill**, or color that is reflected off a screen and onto your subject, creates a halo of color around the edges or fringes of your subject. To avoid spill, make certain your subject is placed at an adequate distance from your screen, or at least six feet in many instances (often, the farther the better).

Also, make certain the key color you are using is not present in your subject's clothing or the props you are using. For example, if you are shooting in front of a green screen, make certain the talent is not wearing a green shirt. In fact, even the smallest areas of matching color can be problematic. When applying your key, you may notice some of these problem areas right away because they will leave "holes" anywhere the color is keyed.

A complete course in setting up a blue- or green-screen shoot is outside the scope of this book. However, with some common sense and a little practice, you can set up a simple shoot in no time by using an inexpensive screen and a basic lighting kit. To locate more information about this subject, check out Appendix B, *"After Effects 7 Resources."*

1 | Choosing a Key Color

Once you possess footage shot in front of a solid-colored screen or rendered in a graphics application, you can import it into After Effects 7 and begin the process of removing color, or **keying**, which must occur to remove the background and generate a matte around your subject. Although After Effects 7 includes several tools for performing and manipulating keys (including **Keylight**, which we'll discuss later in this chapter), you'll begin by working with the simplest of these options: the **Color Key** effect.

In this exercise, you'll begin by importing a new green-screen shot, as well as a separate file to be used as a background image in the final composite. You'll finish by applying a **Color Key** effect and adjusting some of its most important properties.

NOTE:

Choosing Between the Color Key Effect and the Keylight Effect

If you are working with the After Effects 7 Professional edition, you may choose to skip these first two exercises and go directly to Exercise 3, which shows how to use **Keylight**. Of course, your choice may depend on the complexity of the shot or effect you are trying to achieve. In general, a basic **Color Key** will not be as effective as a specialized filter, such as **Keylight**, which is designed specifically for blue- and green-screen footage originating on video or film. The properties for each are not the same, and the difference in results can be dramatic. The basic **Color Key** effect often works best for graphics or still images, where areas of solid color exist, whereas **Keylight** and similar professional effects are best for moving images containing greater complexity, such as differing shades of color, video noise, and grain.

---

1 Copy the **chap_15** folder from the **After Effects 7 HOT CD-ROM** onto your desktop.

---

2 Choose **File > New > New Project**, and then choose **File > Save As**. In the **Save As** dialog box, navigate to the **AE7_HOT_Projects** folder on your desktop. Name the file **Color_Key.aep**, and click **Save**.

---

3 Double-click the empty **Project** panel. In the **Import File** dialog box, navigate to the **chap_15** folder on your desktop. Select the **Highway.mov** and **Moto_Front.mov** files, and click **Open**.

4 In the **Project** panel, drag the **Moto_Front.mov** file onto the **Create a new Composition** button.

This creates a new composition matching the settings (frame size, frame rate, duration, and so on) of the video footage you imported.

The video appearing in the Composition panel contains a green background, which you'll remove in a moment. Ideally, if you shot your footage properly, the background color should appear as a single shade of color, most likely bright green or blue. If your background is too dark or the color and lighting is uneven, it will be difficult to achieve a perfect key. However, in Exercise 2, we'll discuss a few methods for fixing a problematic shot.

---

5 In the **Timeline** panel, select the **Moto_Front.mov** layer. Choose **Effect > Keying > Color Key** to apply the **Color Key** effect to this layer.

You will need to select a specific key color to notice any change take effect, which you will do next.

---

6 If the **Effect Controls** panel is not visible, press the **F3** key. In the **Effect Controls** panel, click the **eyedropper** icon for **Key Color**, as shown in the illustration here.

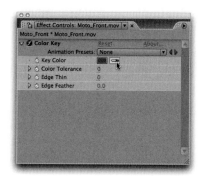

Tip: You can make the Effect Controls panel for the currently selected layer appear or disappear by pressing the F3 key.

Note: If you need to use a function key such as F3 while on a laptop or PowerBook, hold down the Fn key and then press the appropriate function key. By default, function keys on a laptop are usually assigned to various system operations, such as volume or brightness controls, in order to save space on the keyboard.

7 With the **eyedropper** icon selected, click the bright green area in the **Composition** panel.

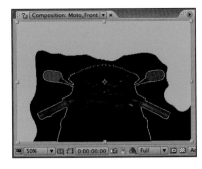

As soon as you click the green-screen background, you should notice a large portion of the background disappear or turn black (without other footage underneath), indicating you have removed this particular shade of green from the shot.

Tip: If you remove only a small area of color with your first click, click the Key Color eyedropper icon again and try clicking a different area of the screen. Click the background until you find the dominant shade of green in your shot, which should remove the majority of your background. If using the eyedropper to select a single color is not accomplishing a great deal, you may want to try a different keyer, such as Keylight (discussed later in the chapter), to assist with difficult shots, or you may want to use the Color Range effect to select a range or multiple areas of color. You can also apply multiple Color Key effects to the same layer, which you'll do in the next exercise.

8 In the **Effect Controls** panel, click the **twirly** icon for the **Color Tolerance** property. Drag the slider to adjust the amount of **tolerance**, or range, until the majority of green has disappeared from the image, without destroying the foreground object.

Color tolerance determines the range of similar color to include along with your original Key Color selection. Assuming your initial color selection is close to finished, only a slight increase in tolerance is necessary to include other, minor gradations in color. If your initial Key Color selection does not remove the majority of your green-screen background, then you will need a higher Color Tolerance setting in order to expand the selection to include a wider range of colors. This leaves a slight ring of green around portions of your subject, which you will attempt to remove in the next series of steps.

9 In the **Effect Controls** panel, click the **twirly** icon for the **Edge Thin** property. Drag the slider to adjust the amount you want your selection area to reduce, or "cut into," your subject.

Edge Thin brings the keyed-out area closer toward your subject, removing any additional green edges that may (and usually do) surround them.

Too much edge thinning is undesirable and is particularly noticeable in parts of an image with fine detail, such as hair. Only apply as much edge thinning as you can without removing important information from the subject you are keying. Often, a low value, such as 1 or 2, is all you need.

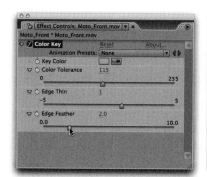 

10 In the **Effect Controls** panel, click the **twirly** icon for the **Edge Feather** property, and increase the feathering slightly to soften the harshness of the edge around your keyed-out subject.

The Edge Feather property is particularly effective when you use it in combination with Edge Thin. Feathering can return some of the detail removed by other keying properties, such as Edge Thin, and make the mask shape more pleasing. However, it can also reintroduce more green **fringing** (uneven bands of color around edges). You will work on removing this unwanted green color in the next exercise.

11 In the **Project** panel, drag the **Highway.mov** file to beneath the **Moto_Front.mov** layer in the **Timeline** to add a background image and complete the shot setup. Press the **spacebar** to preview the animation with your newly keyed footage.

12 Choose **File > Save**, or press **Cmd+S** (Mac) or **Ctrl+S** (Windows). Leave **Color_Key.aep** and the **Moto_Front** composition open for the next exercise.

In this exercise, you used a simple Color Key effect to remove a solid-colored background from one layer, which allowed you to composite it over another layer. If your composition includes green jagged edges, a green halo, or areas of the background showing through where they shouldn't, it may require some careful adjustment. You will take care of this in the next exercise.

2 | Adjusting and Fixing Color Key Selections

Even the best keying effects require adjustment to eliminate problem areas in the shot. For example, if your shot contains shadows or color spill from your green screen, you can't easily fix these without applying additional techniques. To finesse your final result, you'll start by applying a garbage matte, or mask, around your subject to eliminate other areas of the screen from showing through in the final color selection. Next, you'll apply additional **Color Key** effects to expand your original selection, and then you'll finish by using the **Spill Suppressor** feature to remove some of the more noticeable color fringing around the subject.

---

1 If you followed the previous exercise, **Color_Key.aep** should still be open in After Effects 7. If it's not, choose **File > Open Project**. Navigate to the **chap_15** folder you copied to your desktop, click **Color_Key_2.aep** to select it, and click **Open**.

---

2 Double-click the **Color Key** composition to open it.

---

3 In the **Timeline** panel, click the **Video** switch for your **Highway.mov** layer to turn it off. Make certain the **Moto_Front.mov** layer is selected in the **Timeline**.

---

4 In the **Effect Controls** panel for the **Moto_Front.mov** layer, click the *f* icon (the **Effects** switch) for **Color Key** to turn off the **Color Key** effect.

You can easily turn an effect on or off in this way, which helps you preview the "before" and "after" results of the effect you're applying. In this particular exercise, it will help you see the original background and outline of the subject as you create a mask.

---

5 With the **Moto_Front.mov** layer selected in the **Timeline**, select the **Pen** tool from the **Tools** panel. Click around your subject in the green-screen footage, as shown in the illustration here.

This creates a mask to isolate the object, and the green color immediately surrounding it, from the rest of the shot.

Using a mask (or garbage matte) helps narrow the focus of the keying effect, removing unnecessary portions of the picture and focusing its attention on the most important shades of color immediately surrounding your subject. Make certain to

select an area large enough to include any movement your subject makes during the course of the shot, such as moving their arms, walking, or turning their head. For more complex shots with lots of motion, you might choose to animate the mask shape over time, as described in Chapter 13, *"Creating Masks."*

---

6 In the **Effect Controls** panel, click the *f* icon to turn on the **Color Key** effect. Click **Reset**.

This resets the Color Key effect you originally created in the previous exercise. For this exercise, you'll start the keying process over at this point.

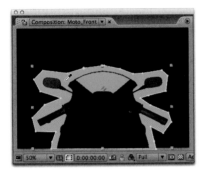 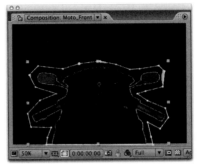

7 With the subject better isolated with a mask, click the **eyedropper** icon for the **Key Color** property, and then click the green area remaining in the shot.

Applying a mask around your subject prior to keying almost always helps eliminate other problem areas on the screen (particularly those areas near the edges of the frame). If your shot contains a lot of movement, this approach may not be ideal, although it often helps achieve the most satisfactory results.

8 Choose **Effect > Keying > Color Key** to add another **Color Key** effect to your **Moto_Front.mov** video layer.

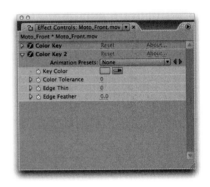

You can stack up as many Color Key effects as necessary to create a satisfactory keying result. In fact, many professional color key jobs, like those created for feature films, involve several keying effects stacked upon each other (especially for those tricky keying shots).

Tip: At this point, you may want to click the twirly icon for your first Color Key effect in the Effect Controls panel to turn it off to see your second effect without scrolling.

9 Click the **eyedropper** icon for the **Key Color** property for the **Color Key 2** effect you just added, and choose another shade of green to add to your previous selection.

If you cannot adequately select from the thin ring of green, you may need to zoom in on your footage in the Composition panel.

10 Adjust the **Color Tolerance**, **Edge Thin**, and **Edge Feather** properties for each instance of the **Color Key** effect, as discussed in the previous exercise.

This is where you may need to do a lot of tweaking to get the best result. It's not always easy to find the absolute best balance of controls, but even a small adjustment may go a long way toward achieving a suitable key.

---

11 Choose **Effect > Keying > Spill Suppressor**.

Although your subject may be separated from the green-screen backdrop in your footage, still a slight halo of green may have spilled off the screen. Choosing Spill Suppressor replaces green or blue spill toward the edges of a keyed-out subject with another, more complementary color.

12 Click the **eyedropper** icon for the **Color to Suppress** property, and choose a green color at the edge of your subject that you want to subdue.

If the effect is too extreme, use the slider controls for the Suppression property to decrease the effect. You can see the results of the spill suppression by zooming in on the edges of your keyed subject in the Composition panel, as shown in the illustration here. Make certain to not overapply spill suppression because it can lead to an unnatural halo or color cast around your subject. The spill suppression applied to a green-screen shot, for example, may appear purple.

---

13 In the **Timeline** panel, click the **Video** switch for the **Highway.mov** layer to turn it on again. Click an empty area of the **Timeline** panel to deselect the **Moto_Front.mov** layer, hiding the outline of its mask, and view the final results of your color keying exercise. Press the **spacebar** to preview the composited video.

14 Choose **File > Save**, or press **Cmd+S** (Mac) or **Ctrl+S** (Windows). In the top-left corner of the **Composition** panel, choose **Close Color Key** from the **Composition** pop-up menu to close the current composition. Leave **Color_Key.aep** open for the next exercise.

The Color Key effect is useful for a wide variety of keying tasks, regardless of the key color you are trying to extract. Once you have mastered using a basic Color Key effect, you'll be equipped to move on to more advanced filters and plug-ins, which allow for greater control over selecting colors and manipulating the matte you're creating.

In this exercise, you learned how to finesse the results of a simple color key a bit, using masks and some other effects specific to keying. In the following exercise, you will learn about an effect to pull high-quality keys, particularly those shot in front of a traditional blue or green screen. In fact, if you are working with After Effects 7 Professional, the following effect, called Keylight, is the best solution for working with footage shot against a blue or green screen.

EXERCISE

3 | Using Keylight and Viewing Key Results

Keylight is a keying effect plug-in that ships with the Professional edition of After Effects 7. It is the preferred plug-in for any blue- or green-screen keying tasks, especially those shot on video or film that are particularly difficult to extract. A difficult blue- or green-screen shot usually stems from poor lighting or other factors related to the setup for shooting the footage.

Using the **Keylight** effect (licensed from The Foundry, **www.thefoundry.co.uk**, a high-end, visual-effects software company), you can quickly and easily achieve excellent results. In fact, sometimes it takes only a couple clicks to produce the desired effect. However, for difficult jobs, **Keylight** also has many powerful, professional properties, a few of which you will explore in this exercise.

1 If you followed the previous exercise, **Color_Key.aep** should still be open in After Effects 7. If it's not, choose **File > Open Project**. Navigate to the **chap_15** folder you copied to your desktop, click **Color_Key_3.aep** to select it, and click **Open**.

2 Double-click an empty area of the **Project** panel. In the **Import File** dialog box, navigate to the **chap_15** folder you copied to your desktop, click the **Green_Screen.mov** file to select it, hold down **Cmd** (Mac) or **Ctrl** (Windows), and then click **Sky_Backdrop.tif** to multiple-select the files. Click **Open**.

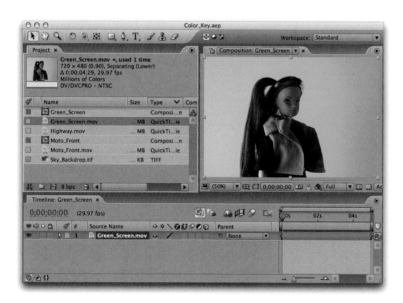

3 In the **Project** panel, drag the **Green_Screen.mov** file onto the **Create a new Composition** button.

The video appearing in the Composition panel contains a green-screen background, which you'll remove. Assuming your footage was shot properly, the background color should appear as a single shade of bright green or blue. In this example footage, the background is a bit brighter on the left side of the

Chapter 15 : **Working with Color Keys** | 375

screen than on the right. The variation in shades of green would make this shot particularly difficult to work with using the standard Color Key effect. This looks like a job for the Keylight effect.

As with any keying effect, before you begin using the Keylight plug-in, you may choose to create a garbage matte, or mask, around your subject by using the Pen tool or by cropping the edges of the frame. (You did this in the previous exercise for the Color Key effect.) This will eliminate unwanted areas of the frame and save you some time and effort as you adjust properties to achieve the desired effect. To demonstrate the results of a general Keylight effect and the matte it generates, you will not create a garbage matte in this exercise. However, it is advisable to use a garbage matte for your own project, especially when the shot contains little movement.

---

4 In the **Timeline** panel, select the **Green_Screen.mov** layer if it is not already selected. Choose **Effect > Keying > Keylight** to apply the **Keylight** effect to this layer.

Note: To use the Keylight effect, you must be working with After Effects 7 Professional and have installed the plug-in from the After Effects 7 installation discs.

---

5 In the **Effect Controls** panel, click the **eyedropper** icon for the **Key Color** property.

---

6 In the **Effect Controls** panel, click the **eyedropper** icon for the **Screen Colour** property.

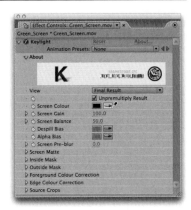

---

7 With the **eyedropper** icon selected, click a bright green area in the **Composition** panel.

As soon as you click the green-screen background, you should notice a large portion of the background disappear or turn black (without other footage

underneath), indicating you have removed this particular shade of green from the shot, as you saw in Exercise 1. Areas appearing as shades of gray, rather than pure black, are semitransparent; you need to remove them as well. You will work on improving the results of your key in the next steps.

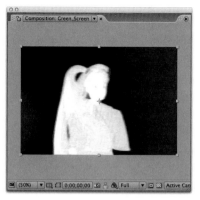

8 In the **Effect Controls** panel, choose **Screen Matte** from the **View** pop-up menu, which currently displays **Final Result**.

Screen Matte displays the alpha channels in your keyed footage as a grayscale image, which indicates areas that are transparent (black), opaque (white), or semitransparent (varying shades of gray). The idea is to keep your subject totally white while the background is completely black. Areas of the image requiring varying degrees of transparency, such as hair and the edges of a subject, may require a little bit of gray. As you adjust the properties to create your key effect, switch back and forth between Final Result and Screen Matte underneath it. If your Screen Matte view looks correct, you are close to achieving the final result you want.

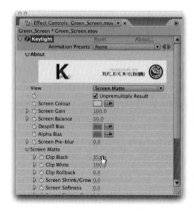
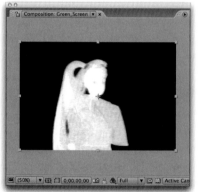

9 With the **View** pop-up menu set to **Screen Matte**, click the twirly for the **Screen Matte** property in the **Effect Controls** panel. Position your mouse over the **Clip Black** property, and drag to increase the value until the background of your matte turns completely black.

The Clip Black property increases the black levels in your matte, decreasing the contrast and causing darker gray areas to shift toward black. As you adjust the black levels in your matte, make sure you watch the edges of your subject. Increasing the Clip Black value too much may have an adverse effect on any gray or black values in your foreground subject.

You'll fix the light gray areas inside your subject in the next step.

10 In the **Effect Controls** panel, position your mouse over the **Clip White** property, under the **Screen Matte** property, and drag to decrease the value until the gray areas in your foreground subject turn completely white, or opaque.

The Clip White property increases the white levels in your matte, decreasing the contrast and causing light gray areas to shift toward white. Once again, as you adjust the white levels in your matte, make sure you watch the edges of your subject and avoid clipping the white value too much. Increasing the Clip White value too much will cause the edges around your subject to expand and become jagged.

Optionally, you can increase the Screen Pre-blur property. You would do this before clipping your white values; this can help further simplify the areas of differing color in your matte. The result is a smoother image allowing you to pull an easier key. Screen Pre-blur will also help eliminate some jagged edges, although it may expand the borders of your matte a bit, so apply carefully. A fine amount of Screen Pre-blur is usually all you need.

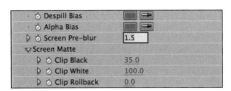

In the next steps, you will test the results of your key with some actual footage, adjusting a few settings if necessary.

---

11 Make sure you are in the first frame of your **Timeline**. In the **Project** panel, drag the **Sky_Backdrop.tif** file to beneath the **Green_Screen.mov** layer in the **Timeline**.

---

12 In the **Effect Controls** panel, choose **Final Result** from the **View** pop-up menu. Inspect the results in the **Composition** panel.

At this point, you should see your subject keyed out in front of the new background you've added to the composition. If everything worked well with the settings you made earlier, your foreground subject should be neatly keyed and separated from the green screen in the original footage. Usually, a little adjustment of the properties set earlier, or a few new settings, is necessary to achieve a perfect key.

13 With your **Green_Screen.mov** layer selected and while viewing your composite image in the **Composition** panel, drag your mouse over the field to the right of the **Screen Shrink/Grow** property in the **Effect Controls** panel. Change this value to −**1.5** to trim the edges of your matte slightly.

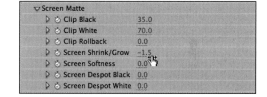

It's best to avoid using the Screen Shrink/Glow property whenever possible. However, in this case, you've opted to reduce the matte slightly to remove a bit of the excess screen showing through around the edges of your subject. Be careful not to remove too much from the edges of your subject.

14 Choose **File > Save**, or press **Cmd+S** (Mac) or **Ctrl+S** (Windows). Choose **File > Close Project**.

You just learned how to use some of the basic properties for a professional color keyer in After Effects 7. Using Keylight is actually simple and intuitive, although the results will depend on the quality of the footage you are working with and (when dealing with difficult keying jobs) how much you tweak the effect's various properties. Now that you've had experience creating masks and mattes, you can continue to the next chapter, which covers a rather exciting feature of After Effects 7: 3D layers.

16

Working with 3D Layers

Working with 3D layers in After Effects 7 can inspire creativity. Seeing your images move in 3D space—complete with effective lighting, shadows, and camera work—is exciting for anyone using After Effects 7. However, we have a lot of new territory to cover if you have never worked in a 3D environment. In fact, getting to know your way around different views and looking at artwork from the top, left, right, bottom, and front can be awkward at first. Likewise, actions such as moving artwork along a new axis and dealing with cameras and lights aren't intuitive. Fortunately, you'll get to try everything firsthand in this chapter, which will demystify the process.

Using 3D in After Effects 7

At its core, After Effects 7 is a program designed to combine 2D images. As you've seen, you can import a variety of digital image formats as footage into After Effects 7. All these footage files have an **X axis** (for the ability to move from side to side) and a **Y axis** (for the ability to move up and down). These axes represent the primary directions of movement for an image.

Artwork in After Effects 7 is 2D and has no depth. However, by activating the **3D Layer** switch, you can allow your 2D objects to reside within a special 3D space in After Effects 7. In 3D space, the **X axis** (the horizontal dimension) and the **Y axis** (the vertical dimension) define 2D space, and a third axis—the **Z axis**—defines the distance, or depth. With this coordinate system, you can place objects in the After Effects 7 3D space and use the axis values to define their exact positions.

You can designate a layer as 3D by selecting the layer and clicking the **3D Layer** switch in the **Timeline** or by choosing **Layer > 3D Layer**. When you select the layer, you'll see three arrows extending from the anchor point in the **Composition** panel. Each arrow is color coded. The red arrow is the X axis, the green arrow is the Y axis, and the blue arrow is the Z axis.

Within this unique 3D environment, you can move, rotate, and otherwise manipulate 2D layers, just like a piece of paper you can turn and view from all sides. Still, you should not confuse After Effects 7 with 3D programs, such as Maya (by Autodesk) and CINEMA 4D (by MAXON Computer). The main difference between After Effects 7 and true 3D programs is the lack of a modeling application. This means you can't create true 3D objects in After Effects 7 with thickness and depth (at least not without special plug-ins); you can create only 2D artwork and then move it in a 3D space. As a result, when a 2D object has its side toward the viewer, it will disappear. That's because 2D objects have no depth.

What does all this mean? Well, as you design your 3D work in After Effects 7, you have to keep in mind you are working with 2D objects. A 2D object has no thickness when viewed in perspective. However, the realistic perspective results you can create in the 3D environment are quite astounding. As well, the 3D lighting and shadows provide benefits you can only fully appreciate when you see them in action. You can do amazing work in After Effects 7. By understanding the way its 3D layers work, you can create striking images with unique styles.

EXERCISE

1 | Making 3D Layers

In this exercise, you'll work with a composition containing two layers, and you'll learn how to convert the layers to 3D layers. After you've created the 3D layers, you will animate them by adding movement along the Z axis. You'll also get the chance to use the **Position** and **Rotate** properties for each layer. Feel free to take your time and become comfortable with each step.

1 Copy the **chap_16** folder from the **After Effects 7 HOT CD-ROM** onto your desktop.

2 Choose **File > Open Project**. Navigate to the **chap_16** folder you copied to your desktop, select the file named **3D_Project.aep**, and click **Open**. Choose **File > Save As**. In the **Save As** dialog box, navigate to the **AE7_HOT_Projects** folder on your desktop. Name the file **3D_Project.aep**, and click **Save**.

3 In the **Project** panel, double-click the **Making 3D Layers** composition to open it.

This composition has two simple layers: a Photoshop file called Cycle.psd and a solid layer named Gray Solid 1.

4 In the **Timeline** panel, locate the **3D Layer** switch in the **Switches** pane, whose icon looks like a cube. Click the **3D Layer** switch for the **Cycle.psd** layer.

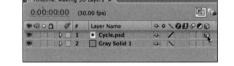

This designates the layer as 3D and turns on the additional 3D layer properties, such as Z Rotation and Material Options.

Note: If you do not see the Switches pane, click the Expand or Collapse the Layer Switches Pane button in the lower-left corner of the Timeline panel.

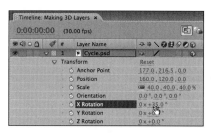

5 In the **Timeline** panel, click the **twirly** icon for the **Cycle.psd** layer to display its properties. Click the **twirly** icon to display the **Transform** properties, if necessary. Place your cursor on the **X Rotation** value, and click and drag your cursor back and forth to see the effect on the composition. When you are done, set the **X Rotation** property to **0** degrees.

Notice the layer rotates around the X axis as you change the X Rotation value. The rotation is measured in degrees.

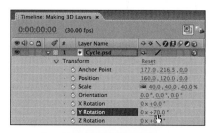

6 Place your cursor on the **Y Rotation** value, and click and drag your cursor back and forth to see the effect on the composition. When you are done, set the **Y Rotation** property to **0** degrees.

Notice the layer rotates around the Y axis as you change the Y Rotation value.

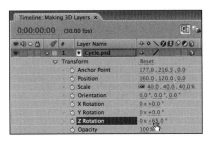

7 Drag the **Z Rotation** value, and observe the image as it rotates around the Z axis. When you are done, set the **Z Rotation** value to **0** degrees.

Notice the layer rotates around the Z axis. Next, you'll set keyframes to animate the 3D layer.

NOTE: | **Using the Orientation Property**

Another property in the **Transform** group you can use to rotate a 3D layer is the **Orientation** property. However, it can get confusing if you start using the **Orientation** property in conjunction with the **X Rotation**, **Y Rotation**, and **Z Rotation** properties to rotate layers.

For this reason, we recommend using the **X Rotation**, **Y Rotation**, and **Z Rotation** properties for animating 3D rotation while learning After Effects 7. That way, you'll develop a consistent approach to working in 3D.

Later, after you've had a fair amount of experience with 3D, use the **Orientation** property when you need to set an object in 3D space but do not need to use keyframe animation. The **Orientation** property moves your object along the shortest rotational path in 3D space. For this reason, **Orientation** is best for setting a position and leaving it, rather than for animating a keyframe. If you attempt to use keyframe animation with **Orientation**, the layer may move in ways you do not intend.

8 In the **Timeline**, make sure the **CTI** (Current Time Indicator) is in the first frame of the composition. Click the **stopwatch** icon for the **X Rotation** and **Y Rotation** properties to set keyframes at **Frame 0**. Accept the default value of **0** for both properties.

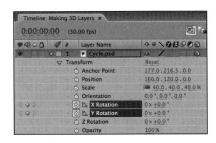

The keyframes you set in these steps create rotation for the 3D layer on multiple axes.

9 Move the **CTI** to **0:00:00:29**. Change the **X Rotation** property to **–30** degrees, and set the **Y Rotation** property to **30** degrees.

---

10 In the **Timeline** panel, scrub the **CTI** (or in the **Time Controls** panel, click the **RAM Preview** button) to view your 3D layer in action.

By setting the X Rotation and Y Rotation values, you have created a simple animation causing the Cycle.psd layer to rotate around its X and Y axes. In the following steps, you'll turn the Gray Solid 1 layer into a 3D layer and set its properties.

---

11 In the **Timeline** panel, click the **twirly** icon for the **Cycle.psd** layer to hide its properties. Click the **3D Layers** switch for the **Gray Solid 1** layer.

---

12 Click the **twirly** icon for the **Gray Solid 1** layer to display its properties, and then click the **twirly** icon next to **Transform** to display its properties as well. For **Position**, set the **Z** value to **100**.

Note: 2D layers do not have a Z axis for the Position property. This extra field appears only when you click the 3D Layers switch for a layer.

In the Composition panel, the Gray Solid 1 layer gets smaller because you moved it away from Active Camera view, which you'll learn more about in future steps. In After Effects 7, you view 3D layers from several angles. In the following steps, you'll switch the 3D view to see your layers from another viewpoint.

---

13 In the **Timeline** panel, make sure the **CTI** is set at **Frame 0**. In the **Composition** panel, click the **3D View** pop-up menu, and choose **Left**.

Note: If you can't locate the pop-up menu, it's likely hidden. In the Composition panel, click and drag the bottom-right corner to make the panel wider, which should reveal the 3D View menu. Alternatively, you can access the 3D view settings anytime by choosing View > Switch 3D View.

Observe the Left view of your 3D layer in the Composition panel. The Gray Solid 1 layer is selected and appears 100 pixels along the Z axis behind the Cycle.psd layer. Because the Cycle.psd and Gray Solid 1 layers are 2D objects without depth, you will see only a line representing each object's position.

---

14 From the **3D View** pop-up menu, choose **Active Camera** to return to the default view.

Active Camera view is the most important view because it is what After Effects 7 will render if you preview or make a movie.

15 In the **Timeline** panel, click the **stopwatch** icon for the **X Rotation** and **Y Rotation** properties to set keyframes at **Frame 0** of the **Gray Solid 1** layer. Accept the default value of **0** for both properties.

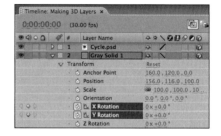

You will now make the Gray Solid 1 layer rotate around two different axes in 3D space.

16 In the **Timeline** panel, move the **CTI** to **0:00:00:29**. Change the **X Rotation** property to **–30** degrees, and change the **Y Rotation** property to **30** degrees.

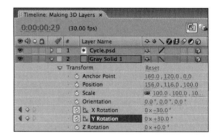

17 In the **Time Controls** panel, click the **RAM Preview** button to view your 3D animation.

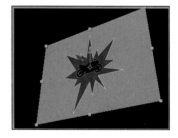

Although this result may look just like a simple "skew" effect, After Effects 7 is actually moving this flat artwork in true 3D space. More realistic 3D results come later in this chapter, when you'll learn to animate the lighting and camera.

18 Choose **File > Save**, or press **Cmd+S** (Mac) or **Ctrl+S** (Windows). Leave **3D_Project.aep** and the **Making 3D Layers** composition open for the next exercise.

In this exercise, you learned how to turn ordinary 2D layers into 3D layers. You also learned to animate some simple properties (Position and Transform) for the layers in 3D space. Next, you'll learn how to use a variety of 3D views in After Effects 7 to help you preview the results of your 3D animations.

2 | Using 3D Views

The previous exercise introduced you to 3D views, which allow you to see 3D layers from different angles in your **Composition** panel. When you first start working with 3D layers, it can be a little disorienting to see any 3D view other than the default view, which is **Active Camera**. With a little experience, though, you'll quickly get comfortable with using different 3D views.

In this exercise, you'll check out all the 3D views. The purpose of doing this is to become familiar with each view and how they show object relationships in the **Composition** panel. By the end of this exercise, you'll be able to relate your objects' positions to each view and understand the view options. You can position the three custom views anywhere you like. You'll learn to create your own views at the end of the exercise.

You'll also learn to move and position layers in space using 3D views. This is one of the main tasks when working in 3D. For most people who are new to 3D, positioning objects in 3D space is one of the hardest concepts to master. Take your time with this exercise!

---

1 If you followed the previous exercise, **3D_Project.aep** should still be open in After Effects 7. If it's not, choose **File > Open Project**. Navigate to the **chap_16** folder you copied to your desktop, click **3D_Project_2.aep** to select it, and click **Open**.

---

2 The **Making 3D Layers** composition should still be open. If it's not, double-click the composition in the **Project** panel to open it now.

---

3 In the **Timeline** panel, make sure the **CTI** is at **Frame 0** and the **Gray Solid 1** layer is selected. In the **Composition** panel, from the **3D View** pop-up menu, choose **Front**. Compare this view to **Active Camera** view.

 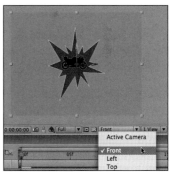

In Active Camera view, the Gray Solid 1 layer looks smaller than it does in Front view. That's because Front view doesn't show any perspective. When you take away the perspective, the width (the X axis) and the height (the Y axis) appear at their full values.

Active Camera view is the view that will be rendered when you preview or create a final movie; this is the view you should use to evaluate your work. The other 3D views are available to aid you in positioning your layers accurately in 3D space.

---

4 From the **3D View** pop-up menu, choose **Back**.

You are looking at the back of the Gray Solid 1 layer, so you can't see the Cycle.psd layer. Again, the width and the height of the Gray Solid 1 layer appear without perspective.

The Front, Left, Top, Back, Right, and Bottom views are orthogonal views. An **orthogonal view** shows the position of your layers but does not show perspective. This can take some practice to understand. With a little experience, you'll feel comfortable with these views.

As you work, you'll see orthogonal views (without perspective) are useful because they give you a good idea of object relationships, proportions, and positions. Perspective changes the apparent size of objects, which can be a hindrance at times. For these reasons, the orthogonal views are valuable.

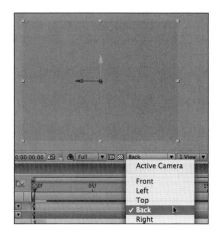

5 From the **3D View** pop-up menu, choose **Top**.

You are looking down on the Cycle.psd and Gray Solid 1 layers. Note the Gray Solid 1 layer is selected, so its axis handles are visible. Those handles appear only on selected layers.

6 From the **3D View** pop-up menu, choose **Bottom**.

Now you are looking up at the two layers. The Gray Solid 1 layer is still selected, so its axis handles are visible.

7 From the **3D View** pop-up menu, choose **Left**.

You will see the side of the graphics again. The Gray Solid 1 layer is still selected, so its axis handles are visible.

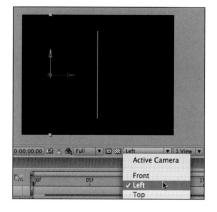

8 From the **3D View** pop-up menu, choose **Right**.

This is another side view, from the right side. The Gray Solid 1 layer is still selected, so its axis handles are visible.

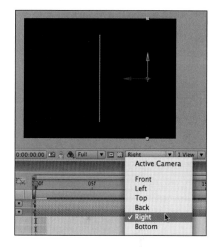

9 From the **3D View** pop-up menu, choose **Custom View 1**.

Notice this view has perspective. This is the default Custom View 1 in After Effects 7. You will learn to create your own views soon.

You can use three custom views for showing your layers in perspective. These views look more natural because they use perspective. They are also quite useful because you can adjust each view position to your liking.

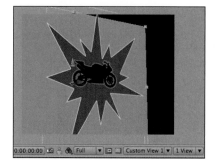

10 From the **3D View** pop-up menu, choose **Custom View 2**.

The default Custom View 2 view looks down from the center of the 3D world.

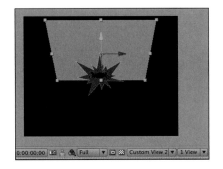

---

11 From the **3D View** pop-up menu, choose **Custom View 3**.

The default Custom View 3 view sits above and to the right of center.

At this point, you've looked at all the possible views for this composition. These views are available to compositions containing 3D objects. You'll use them only when viewing 3D layers, but they are helpful when you're positioning your objects in 3D space.

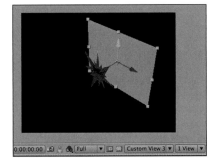

---

12 Choose **File > Save**, or press **Cmd+S** (Mac) or **Ctrl+S** (Windows). Leave **3D_Project.aep** and the **Making 3D Layers** composition open for the next exercise.

At this point, you should be able to make some sense of each view. If you are having trouble with this, it's OK. Understanding the 3D views is the hardest part of learning how to work with 3D layers in After Effects 7. With repetition, you'll be able to understand where you are in the 3D world using each view.

3 | Changing Custom Camera Views

In the previous exercise, you became familiar with views and learned how they can help you see the 3D environment. You can also easily change any of the custom camera views while you are working. By setting a custom view, you can effortlessly return to a particular angle on your composition, which may be useful when checking the positioning of layers. This exercise will show you how to set up a custom view.

1 If you followed the previous exercise, **3D_Project.aep** should still be open in After Effects 7. If it's not, choose **File > Open Project**. Navigate to the **chap_16** folder you copied to your desktop, click **3D_Project_3.aep** to select it, and click **Open**.

2 The **Making 3D Layers** composition should still be open. If it's not, double-click the composition in the **Project** panel to open it.

3 From the **3D View** pop-up menu in the **Composition** panel, choose **Custom View 1**.

4 In the **Tools** panel, select the **Orbit Camera** tool. In the **Composition** panel, click and drag the cursor across the panel to orbit your view (rotate around your composition in 3D space).

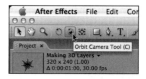

Note: This tool is simply changing the 3D view you see in the Composition panel, not moving the artwork!

5 In the **Tools** panel, click the **Orbit Camera** tool, hold the mouse down, and choose **Track XY Camera Tool** from the pop-up menu. Click and drag in the **Composition** panel to change your view in the X axis or the Y axis.

As stated previously, this tool is simply changing the view. The artwork remains in the same position.

6 In the **Tools** panel, click the **Orbit Camera** tool, and choose **Track Z Camera Tool** from the pop-up menu. Experiment with changing your view in the Z axis by dragging.

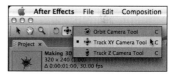

The Z axis controls how close or far the camera view is from your artwork. Once again, note this tool changes only the view of the artwork, not its position.

That's all there is to it. If you switch between Custom View 2 and Custom View 1, you'll see Custom View 1 is just where you left it. It will be set to the last view you created until you change it.

7 Choose **View > Reset 3D View** to reset the view to the default.

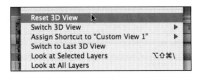

Note: Any change you make to a custom view is permanent until you change it. Resetting the view will return it to the default, unless you change it again.

---

8 Choose **File > Save**, or press **Cmd+S** (Mac) or **Ctrl+S** (Windows). In the **Composition** panel, choose **Close Making 3D Layers** from the pop-up menu at the top of the panel.

As you've seen in this exercise, you are able to adjust and customize the preview of 3D layers shown in the Composition panel. In the next exercise, you'll learn about applying lights to your 3D layers.

---

4 | Working with Lighting in 3D

The power of 3D really becomes evident once you start adding lights to a scene. Light adds shadows, depth, and in general just more visual interest to a composition. In After Effects 7, a **light** is a special type of layer. When you add a light, it shows up in the **Timeline** panel, just as any other layer does. However, lights have their own set of properties, all of which you can keyframe for animation.

After Effects 7 offers several types of lights, but in general you'll probably use the **Spot** light most often. **Spot** provides many options and the greatest range of control. In the following exercise, you'll learn how to add lights, adjust the options, and position lights within your compositions.

---

1 If you followed the previous exercise, **3D_Project.aep** should still be open in After Effects 7. If it's not, choose **File > Open Project**. Navigate to the **chap_16** folder you copied to your desktop, click **3D_Project_4.aep** to select it, and click **Open**.

---

2 In the **Project** panel, double-click the **3D Lighting** composition to open it. Notice it already contains three layers, two of which have 3D layers turned on. Press the **spacebar** or click the **RAM Preview** button in the **Time Controls** panel, and observe the **7** layer has already been animated in 3D.

---

3 In the **Timeline** panel, select the **7** layer, and press the **U** key to see which properties have been animated for this layer. When you're finished observing the animation, return the **CTI** to **0:00:00:00** in the **Timeline** panel.

You'll see keyframes have been set for the Y Rotation property.

You should already know how to do this kind of animation based on Exercise 1. If you want to practice, turn off the 3D Layers switch in the Timeline panel, and then turn it back on to reanimate this layer on your own. Because this exercise focuses on lighting, we've chosen to do the animation work for you, but don't let that stop you from gaining more practice.

---

4 In the **Timeline** panel, deselect the **7** layer by clicking an empty space. Choose **Layer > New > Light**.

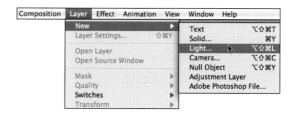

5 In the **Light Settings** dialog box, click the **Light Type** pop-up menu.

Notice you can choose from four types of lights:

Parallel light is directional, unconstrained light from an infinitely distant source. This type is best when you want light to fall evenly on all objects and you want the light to come from a specific direction.

Spot light is constrained by a cone. The Spot type is the most useful because you can control all aspects of the light.

Point light is unconstrained, omnidirectional light. This type is best when you need something such as a bare lightbulb to light whatever is nearby.

Ambient light has no source and casts no shadows. It contributes to the overall brightness of your composition. It is best as a secondary light to raise the general lighting level for all objects. Use it sparingly, if at all.

---

6 From the **Light Type** pop-up menu, choose **Spot**. Make sure the **Casts Shadows** check box is turned on. Click **OK**.

As soon as After Effects 7 creates the light, notice it affects the two layers with 3D turned on. You must turn on 3D on a layer for the light to have an effect. Also notice that even though you turned on the Casts Shadows check box, no shadow is cast on the background. You'll fix this next.

---

7 In the **Timeline** panel, select the **7** layer, and press the **U** key to hide the properties. Manually click the **twirly** icons for the **7** layer until you see the **Material Options** properties. Set the **Casts Shadows** property to **On**.

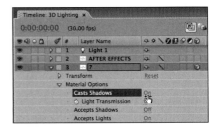

---

8 Click the **twirly** icons for the **Turquoise Solid 1** layer to display its **Material Options** properties. Set the **Accepts Shadows** property to **On**.

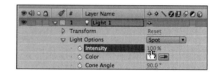

In the Composition panel, notice the 7 layer now casts a shadow. The shadow is quite hard edged and not very attractive yet. You'll fix this soon.

Note: You have not turned the layer named AFTER EFFECTS into a 3D layer, so it does not cast any shadows. Only 3D layers cast shadows in After Effects 7. You can control whether some layers are 3D and some are not by clicking the 3D Layers switch for each layer, as you did in Exercise 1. For this exercise, leave the AFTER EFFECTS layer alone—do not convert it to 3D.

---

9 In the **Timeline** panel, click the **twirly** icon to display the **Light 1** layer properties, and then click the **twirly** icon to display the **Light Options** properties. Click and drag across the **Intensity** value to see the effect of changing the intensity. When you're done experimenting with this property, set the **Intensity** property to **100%**.

The Intensity property sets how bright you want the light to be.

---

10 Click and drag across the **Cone Angle** value to see the effect of changing it. When you're done, set the **Cone Angle** property to **90%**.

The Cone Angle property constrains the light in terms of degrees.

---

11 Click and drag the **Cone Feather** value to see the effect of changing it. When you're done, set the **Cone Feather** property to **50%**.

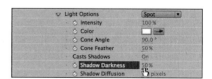

The Cone Feather property determines how soft or hard the edges of the light should be.

---

12 Change the **Shadow Darkness** property to **50%**. In the **Composition** panel, observe the results. In the **Timeline** panel, move the **CTI** to **0:00:01:22** to see the effect the lighting has on the 7 as it animates.

The Shadow Darkness property determines how light or dark the shadow appears.

13 In the **Light 1** layer properties, set the **Shadow Diffusion** property to **7** pixels to soften the edges of the shadow. If the shadow still looks too hard, make sure the **Quality** pop-up menu for the **Turquoise Solid 1** layer is set to **High**. Leave the **CTI** at **0:00:01:22** to see the position of the **7** layer at this point in its animation.

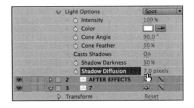

So far, you haven't set any keyframes, meaning you're making a global change to the Shadow Diffusion property over the entire composition. This property softens the edges of the shadow.

Because the layer is turned toward the camera view, you can see the lighting changes better. In the following steps, you will learn to position the light using the axis arrow handles.

14 Leave the **CTI** at **0:00:01:22**. In the **Composition** panel, click and drag the red **X axis** handle to move the light to the far left of the composition.

15 Locate the **Point of Interest** control. (It's the round icon with the crosshairs extending from the center of the light.) Drag this control to the right to fully illuminate the **7**.

The default position of the light is center screen. Lighting effects are always more interesting if they are set to an angle, like you just learned how to do.

16 In the **Time Controls** panel, click the **RAM Preview** button to play the animation. When you are finished viewing the results of your light and shadow settings, press the **RAM Preview** button again to stop playback. Move the **CTI** to the beginning of the **Timeline**.

Lights can be colors other than white. In the following steps, you'll change the color of Light 1 to purple.

17 In the **Timeline** panel, click the **color swatch** for **Light 1**. In the **Color Picker** dialog box, change the color to **purple** and click **OK**.

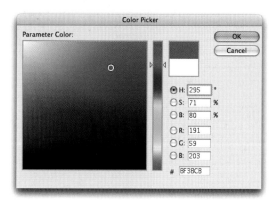

18 Press the **spacebar** to preview your animation. When you are finished previewing, press the **spacebar** again to stop playback.

In this exercise, you merely set the lights in a single position and did not set keyframes for them. Notice every light has properties and every property has a stopwatch icon. Anytime you see a stopwatch icon, it means you can animate a property.

19 In the upper-left corner of the **Composition** panel, choose **Close 3D Lighting** from the pop-up menu.

20 Choose **File > Save**, or press **Cmd+S** (Mac) or **Ctrl+S** (Windows). Leave **3D_Project.aep** open for the next exercise.

This exercise was just a starting point to help you begin learning about light layers and Light Options properties. Take some time on your own to set up some lighting animation to better understand the feature.

NOTE:

Using the Intensity Property with Lights

Intensity is a rather unique property. You can adjust most properties based on percentages from 0 to 100. However, you can adjust the **Intensity** property to values greater than 100 percent. You can also type negative values, which will actually subtract light from your scene, something like a black hole. Used judiciously, both high values and negative values can be beneficial ways of controlling light in your scene.

5 | Adding and Animating a Camera

So far in this chapter, you have been working with **Active Camera** view, a camera view set up by After Effects 7. All compositions containing 3D layers employ a single, default **Active Camera** view. After you add 3D layers to your composition, this **Active Camera** view appears and displays 3D perspective on 2D objects, including the capability to control lights and cast shadows.

You probably didn't realize it is possible to add a new camera to your composition. This may sound odd at first. Why would you want or need to have more than one camera? The most common reason to add a camera is because you cannot animate the default camera. In other words, you *can* move the artwork or lights in 3D, but you *cannot* animate the point of view of those objects with the default camera. When you add a new camera layer manually, it contains properties you can keyframe. Setting keyframes for the camera layer makes it possible to create animations with camera views, not just by moving artwork and lights.

In the following exercise, you'll learn to add a camera, position it in your 3D world, set keyframes on its position, and animate it through the 3D capabilities within After Effects 7.

---

1 If you followed the previous exercise, **3D_Project.aep** should still be open in After Effects 7. If it's not, choose **File > Open Project**. Navigate to the **chap_16** folder you copied to your desktop, click **3D_Project_5.aep** to select it, and click **Open**.

---

2 In the **Project** panel, click the **Create a new Composition** button to create a new composition. In the **Composition Settings** dialog box, name the composition **Basic Camera Comp**, and use the settings shown in the illustration here.

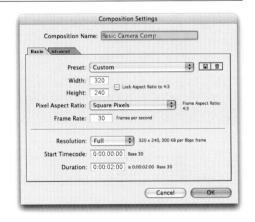

---

3 In the **Project** panel, drag the **Cycle.psd** graphic from the **Footage** folder, and drop it in the **Timeline** of this new composition.

---

4 Press the **S** key to display the **Scale** property, and set **Scale** to **30%**. Click the **3D Layer** switch for the layer to set it to 3D.

---

5 Choose **Layer > New > Camera** to open the **Camera Settings** dialog box.

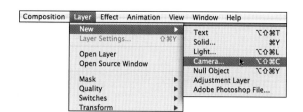

Just as you added a light to your composition in the previous exercise, you can add a camera to your composition, which appears as its own layer in the Timeline.

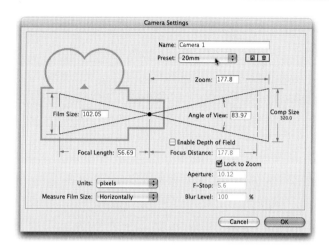

6 In the **Camera Settings** dialog box, click the **Preset** pop-up menu, choose **20mm**, and click **OK**.

When you add your own camera, you can access a lot of new controls that affect the outcome of the movie.

The Camera Settings dialog box might seem intimidating. It's different from most dialog boxes because of the picture and all the new terminology. A chart describing the options in this dialog box appears later in this chapter. The 20mm lens preset you chose in this step provides a wide-angle lens view, which will look like a fish-eye lens. Basically, setting the lens to a lower number will produce a more dramatic perspective that will be more obvious when you get close to objects.

If you are not familiar with photography or cameras, that's OK. If you are, you will probably marvel at these settings, which emulate those of conventional movie cameras.

7 In the **Composition** panel, click the **3D View** menu, and choose **Custom View 1**.

This view allows you to see the camera you just added within your composition.

Note: You must have the camera layer selected in the Timeline panel to see the new camera in the Composition panel. You cannot see the outline of the camera if you are in Active Camera view, which is why you changed the view to Custom View 1.

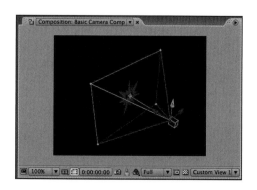

8 In the **Timeline** panel, click the **twirly** icon for the **Camera 1** layer, and then click the **twirly** icon for **Transform** to display the camera properties.

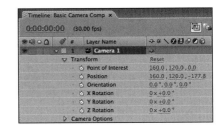

This exercise focuses on ways to move the camera while getting feedback from the view in the Composition panel and from the property values in the Timeline.

---

9 In the **Timeline** panel, click and drag back and forth over the **Position X axis** value. As you drag, watch the **Composition** panel, and notice the camera appears to pivot and rock from side to side. In the **Timeline** panel, click and drag over the **Position Y axis** value, and notice the camera appears to pivot while rocking up and down.

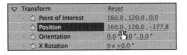

The camera is pivoting on the point of interest, which has been set by default on the center of the Composition panel.

Anytime you add a new camera to a 3D composition, the new camera will place its point of interest in the center of the screen, just as it has done here. You had a little experience with the Point of Interest property when you worked with lighting in the previous exercise. This setting tells a camera (or a light) where to point itself. The **point of interest** is the origin point on the Camera layer from which all X, Y, and Z values are based. It is what causes the camera to pivot.

---

10 In the **Composition** panel, click the **3D View** menu, and choose **Active Camera**. As you did in the previous step, move the **X** and **Y** values for the **Camera 1** layer's **Position** property in order to see how the pivot effect looks from this view.

You won't see the outline of the camera any longer because After Effects 7 doesn't show you the camera in Active Camera view. What you will see, which is almost more important, is how this movement will appear in the final rendering or preview of this composition.

The custom view lets you see the camera while you set up your composition, whereas Active Camera view shows you what the camera is seeing. It's extremely important to be aware of this distinction so not only can you position the camera properly but also so you can accurately gauge what the camera will see. For this reason, you will change views often when staging camera animations.

NOTE:

Using Active Camera Versus New Cameras

In this exercise, you have added a new camera, called **Camera 1**. When you choose **Active Camera** view, you are seeing what **Camera 1** sees. If you added more than one camera to this composition, **Active Camera** view would show the results of whatever camera was selected in the **Timeline**. Because you have only one camera in this **Timeline**, whenever you choose **Active Camera** view, you see the point of view of **Camera 1**.

11 Make sure you are in the **Active Camera** view and the **CTI** is set to **Frame 0** in the **Timeline** panel. In the **Camera 1** layer, click the **stopwatch** icon for the **Position** property to set a keyframe. Change the **X** value for **Position** to **0.0**, and move the **Y** value for **Position** to **277.0**. Leave the **Z** value for **Position** as is.

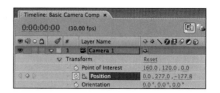

12 In the **Timeline** panel, click the **Lock** switch for the **Cycle.psd** layer so you don't accidentally move it while you animate the camera.

13 In the **Timeline** panel, move the **CTI** to **Frame 59** (0:00:01:29). Change the **X** value for **Position** to 272.0 and the **Y** value for **Position** to **0.0**. Preview the animation. When you are finished previewing the camera animation you created, press the **spacebar**.

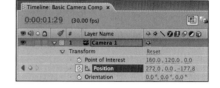

As you can see, you can animate the cameras just like any other layer.

14 In the upper-left corner of the **Composition** panel, choose **Close Basic Camera Comp** from the pop-up menu.

15 Choose **File > Save**, or press **Cmd+S** (Mac) or **Ctrl+S** (Windows). Leave **3D_Project.aep** open for the next exercise.

You could have made the animation you just created by using a camera instead of moving the object. Once you've had some experience with animating a camera, you will see it is often easier to leave your object layers stationary and move the camera instead. In the next exercise, you'll explore working with the point of interest in a little more detail.

6 | Animating the Point of Interest

The previous exercise contained only a single 3D object. However, you will rarely create a camera animation to view a single object. Camera animations are much better suited for flying by multiple layers in a 3D environment because the camera creates a sense of space and depth you can't achieve simply by moving the objects themselves.

This exercise builds on the previous one, adding complexity as it deals with handling multiple objects and animating the point of interest. The first part of the exercise shows you how to set up a composition containing multiple objects set at different depths along the Z axis of the 3D environment. The second part deals with getting your camera to fly by the objects along a path you control.

---

1 If you followed the previous exercise, **3D_Project.aep** should still be open in After Effects 7. If it's not, choose **File > Open Project**. Navigate to the **chap_16** folder you copied to your desktop, click **3D_Project_6.aep** to select it, and click **Open**.

---

2 At the bottom of the **Project** panel, click the **Create a new Composition** button to create a new composition. In the **Composition Settings** dialog box, name the composition **Tree Comp**, and use the settings shown in the illustration here.

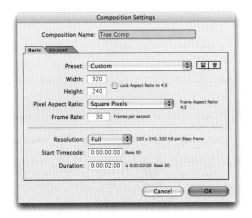

3 In the **Project** panel, drag four instances of the **Palm_Tree.psd** graphic from the **Footage** folder, and drop them in the **Timeline** panel. Select the first **Palm_Tree.psd** layer, press **Return** (Mac) or **Enter** (Windows), rename the layer **Palm_Tree 1**, and press **Return** (Mac) or **Enter** (Windows) again to accept the change. Repeat the renaming process for the remaining layers, naming them **Palm_Tree 2**, **Palm_Tree 3**, and **Palm_Tree 4**, as shown in the illustration here.

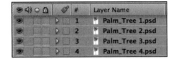

When you drag these images to the Timeline panel, each image is automatically centered in the Composition panel. It will look as though only one image is in the Composition panel because all the trees are the same size and appear stacked on top of one another, obscuring all the layers but the top one. You'll soon fix this by moving them in 3D space.

---

4 In the **Timeline** panel, click the **3D Layers** switch for each layer to turn it into a 3D object.

5 In the **Timeline** panel, click **Palm_Tree 1.psd**, hold down the **Shift** key, and then click **Palm_Tree 4.psd** to multiple-select all the palm-tree layers. Press the **S** key to display the **Scale** property, and change the **Scale** property to **33%**.

The graphics you are using happen to be a little large, so in this step you scaled them down a bit before proceeding.

6 In the **Composition** panel, click the **3D View** pop-up menu, and choose **Left**.

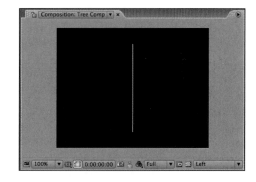

This view shows the artwork from the left side. Again, this shows the four layers stacked on top of one another, which causes them to look like a single line.

You'll next move the layers to position them farther apart on the Z axis. (Remember, the Z axis represents depth.) By moving the objects on their Z axes, you will be spreading them apart in 3D space, as you might see with a grove of trees, for example.

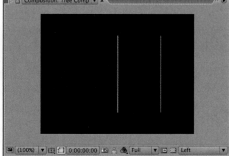

7 In the **Timeline** panel, select the **Palm_Tree 1.psd** layer. Notice the layer's axis handles appear in the **Composition** panel. Click the blue **Z axis** handle (your cursor arrow will show a small **z**, indicating this is the Z axis), and drag the artwork to the right, as shown in the illustration here.

Selecting the image in the Timeline first causes its selection handles to appear, making it easier to isolate in the composition. This is a great technique for positioning artwork in 3D space because all artwork, by default, is on the same Z axis until you move it. You will often encounter overlapping artwork, and this technique helps you isolate it in order to move it. You may need to click somewhere other than the layer in order to see it once you have moved it with the handles in the Composition panel.

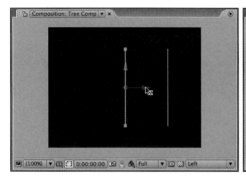 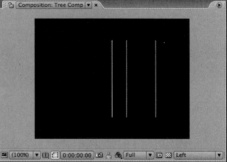

8 In the **Timeline** panel, select the **Palm_Tree 2.psd** layer to display its selection handles in the **Composition** panel. Click and drag the layer's blue **Z axis** handle, and move it to the right, as shown in the illustration here.

9 Repeat this process with the **Palm_Tree 3.psd** and **Palm_Tree 4.psd** layers, spacing them somewhat evenly until your **Composition** panel looks like the one shown in the illustration here.

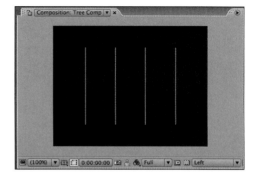

10 In the **Composition** panel, click the **3D View** pop-up menu, and choose **Top**. Drag your artwork into the positions shown in the illustration here.

Tip: If you cannot see the gray work area around the screen, drag the edges of the Composition panel to make it larger.

Changing the view to Top allows you to view the art-work from above. Your artwork is now positioned so a camera can fly around the objects and display them. That's what you'll learn to do next.

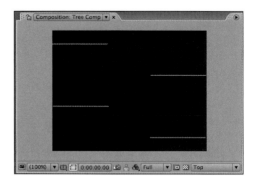

11 Choose **Layer > New > Camera**. In the **Camera Settings** dialog box, make sure the **Preset** option is set to **20mm**, and click **OK**.

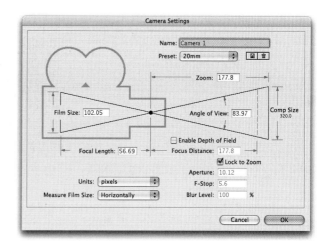

This step creates a new camera and opens the Camera Settings dialog box. We'll describe the settings in this dialog box in the chart later in this chapter.

Camera 1 appears in the Timeline and also in the Composition panel. Adding a camera to your composition is the only way to animate a camera.

---

12 In the **Composition** panel, click the **Magnification ratio** pop-up menu, and choose **50%** to better see the arrangement of your layers.

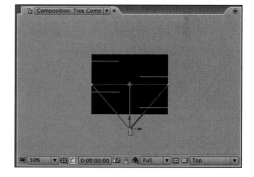

As you can see, the camera has handles similar to the ones 3D objects have. However, it also has a triangular shape attached to it simulating the field of view from the lens. The point of interest is circled in the illustration shown here. It indicates which way the camera is pointing—currently straight ahead.

---

13 In the **Timeline** panel, click the **twirly** icon next to the **Camera 1** layer. Click the **twirly** icon next to **Transform**, and then click the **stopwatch** icon for the **Point of Interest** and **Position** properties.

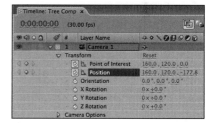

You have now set the first keyframes for these properties. Next, you'll move the camera and create new keyframes for an animated camera.

---

14 In the **Composition** panel, move the **Point of Interest** handle so it points toward the **Palm_Tree 1.psd** layer, as shown in the illustration here.

You have moved the camera to face the Palm_Tree 1.psd layer.

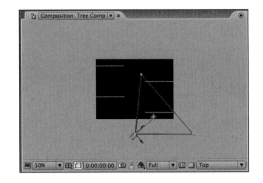

15 Move the **CTI** to **Frame 15**, and change the point of interest to roughly match what's shown in the illustration here. Move the camera's position as well by clicking and dragging the rectangular, camera icon closer to the **Point of Interest** handle.

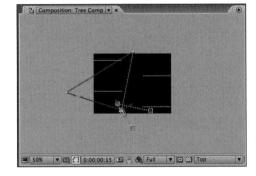

16 Move the **CTI** to **Frame 30**. Move the camera to roughly match the illustration shown here by moving the point of interest and camera position.

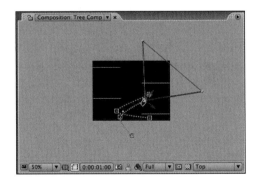

17 Move the **CTI** to **Frame 45**. Move the point of interest and camera position to roughly match what's shown
in the illustration here.

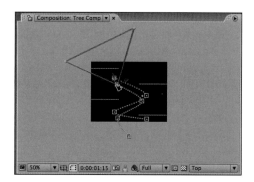

18 Move the **CTI** to **Frame 59**. Move the point of interest and camera position to roughly match what's shown
in the illustration here.

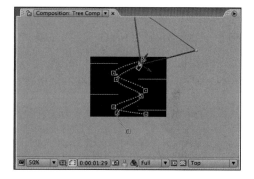

19 Move the **CTI** to the first frame of the **Timeline**. In the **Composition** panel, click the **3D View** menu,
and choose **Active Camera**. Press the **spacebar** to preview your animation.

When you preview the animation, your camera should fly through the path of trees. The only problem
is the trees look like cardboard cutouts. In addition, the animation (based on the initial composition
settings) is rather fast. To help make the animation look a little smoother, you'll use Auto-Orient, as
described in the following steps. Also, you'll use Time Stretch to change the length of the animation.

20 In the **Timeline** panel, click the **Palm_Tree 1.psd** layer to select it. Hold down the **Shift** key, and then
click **Palm_Tree 4.psd** to multiple-select the layers.

21 Choose **Layer > Transform > Auto-Orient**. In the **Auto-
Orientation** dialog box, click the **Orient Towards Camera** radio
button to select it, and click **OK**.

The Orient Towards Camera option tells each object to face the
camera as it passes.

22 With the palm-tree layers still selected, hold down the **Shift** key, and click the **Camera 1** layer to select it also. Choose **Layer > Time > Time Stretch**. In the **Time Stretch** dialog box, change **New Duration** to **0:00:08:00**. Leave the **Layer In-point** option set at the default, and click **OK**.

This step isn't related to 3D layers, but it allows you to achieve a smoother animation by slowing down the animation.

---

23 Choose **Composition > Composition Settings**. In the **Composition Settings** dialog box, change **Duration** to **0:00:08:00**, which matches your newly stretched layers, and click **OK**.

---

24 Preview your movie by pressing the **spacebar**. When you are finished, press the **spacebar** again to stop playback.

---

25 Choose **File > Save**, or press **Cmd+S** (Mac) or **Ctrl+S** (Windows). Choose **File > Close Project** to close the project.

You have just learned a method for animating a camera through 3D space in After Effects 7. Before finishing this chapter, take a moment to review the chart in the next section, which covers the majority of settings in the Camera Settings dialog box you encountered in this exercise.

Exploring the Camera Settings Dialog Box

In the previous exercise, you had a chance to add a camera to your composition, and you briefly worked with the **Camera Settings** dialog box. As promised, the following handy chart describes the numerous features in this dialog box:

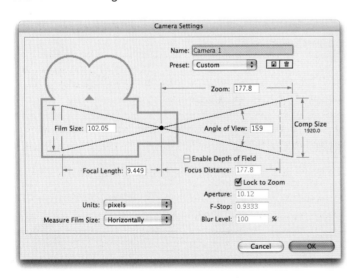

Camera Settings

Setting	Description
Name	After Effects 7 can automatically name your camera, or you can give your camera a name. This name appears in the **Timeline** layer representing the camera object.
Preset	The camera ships with a menu of different presets, which emulate different 35mm lens settings with different focal lengths. The angle of view, zoom, focus, distance, focal length, and aperture are all stored with each preset. You can create your own camera presets by changing the settings and clicking the **Disk** icon to save them.
Zoom	This specifies the distance from the position of the camera to the image plane.
Film Size	This relates directly to the composition size. When you specify a new value for film size, the zoom changes to match the perspective of a real camera.
Angle of View	The focal length, film size, and zoom settings all determine the angle of view. You can create wide-angle lens settings or more narrow lens settings, depending on what value you type.
Enable Depth of Field	This affects the distance range in which the image is in focus. Images outside the distance range are blurry. You can use this setting to create realistic camera-focusing effects.
Focal Length	This is the distance from the film plane to the camera lens. The camera's position represents the center of the lens. When you specify a new value for the focal length, the zoom changes to match the perspective.
Focus Distance	This specifies the distance from the camera's position at which objects appear in focus.
Aperture	This increases or decreases the size of the lens. This setting affects depth-of-field blur as well as f-stop positions.
F-Stop	This indicates the ratio of focal length to aperture. Most cameras specify aperture size using the f-stop measurement. If you specify a new value for this setting, the value for **Aperture** changes dynamically to match it.
Blur Level	This indicates the amount of depth-of-field blur in an image. A setting of **100%** creates a natural blur as dictated by the camera settings. Lower values reduce the blur.
Units	This indicates the units of measurement in which the camera setting values are expressed.
Measure Film Size	These are the dimensions used to depict the film size.

If this was a hard chapter for you, don't worry. The subject of 3D has a steep learning curve, but the more you practice, the easier it will become. Take a break, and get ready for the next chapter about expressions.

17

Using Expressions

The word **expression** is a mathematical and programming term describing the creation of a new value based on an old value. As an After Effects 7 user, you can use expressions to take the value from one property and apply it to another property. One example of this, which you'll learn to do in this chapter, is making some lettering get blurrier as the letters become spaced farther apart. You can change the reaction of one property based on the transformation of another only by using expressions.

Expressions are written in JavaScript, but the beauty is you don't have to know how to write any code at all to use them because After Effects 7 will automatically write them for you. However, to make expressions more than minimally useful, you will want to know how to modify the expressions After Effects 7 creates, which is fairly easy once you learn a few rules. This chapter shows you some practical examples of using expressions and also teaches you how to modify them.

1 | Adding Expressions and Creating Relationships

Chapter 11, *"Parenting Layers,"* introduced you to the **Pick Whip** tool for creating parent-child relationships. You can also use the **Pick Whip** tool to create relationships for expressions—simply drag from one property to another. In this exercise, you'll learn how to add an expression to a property on a layer (in this case, **Scale**) and create a one-to-one relationship with another layer's property, which automates the process of animating both layers (one layer follows the other).

---

1 Copy the **chap_17** folder from the **After Effects 7 HOT CD-ROM** onto your desktop.

---

2 Choose **File > Open Project**. Navigate to the **chap_17** folder you copied to your desktop, select the file named **Expression_Project.aep**, and click **Open**. Choose **File > Save As**. In the **Save As** dialog box, navigate to the **AE7_HOT_Projects** folder on your desktop. Name the file **Expression_Project.aep**, and click **Save**.

---

3 In the **Project** panel, double-click the **Creating Expressions** composition to open it.

This composition contains two layers with distinct names yet identical artwork and no keyframes. You will animate one layer and learn to apply an expression to the other layer.

---

4 In the **Timeline** panel, click the **Motocycle_1** layer. Hold down the **Shift** key, and then click the **Motorcycle_2** layer to multiple-select the layers. Once both layers are selected, press the **S** key to display the **Scale** property for both layers.

---

5 Click the **Scale** property for **Motorcycle_2**. Choose **Animation > Add Expression**.

This doesn't set a keyframe; instead, it sets an expression.

A new set of icons appears in the Switches panel of the Timeline. The most useful one is the Pick Whip icon. You can identify it by the spiral icon (which looks like a coiled whip). The button to the left of the Pick Whip icon is the Post-Expression Graph switch, which turns on a value graph for the expression (not demonstrated in this chapter, but this tool is useful for seeing the velocity of changes to the property). To the right is the Expression language menu arrow, which you will learn about later in this chapter.

Tip: Alternatively, press Opt+Shift+= (Mac) or Alt+Shift+= (Windows), and click the stopwatch icon to create an expression.

---

6 Click the **Pick Whip** icon for the **Motorcycle_2** layer's **Scale** property, and drag it to the **Motorcycle_1** layer's **Scale** property.

Once you've done this, notice After Effects 7 automatically writes a JavaScript expression in the Motorcycle_2 Expression field, to the right in the Timeline.

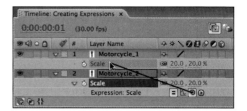

7 Drag the **Scale** value for the **Motorcycle_1** layer back and forth to change it while you observe the results.

Notice both motorcycles now scale equally when the Motorcycle_1 value changes. This is because the Motorcycle_2 value is tied to the Motorcycle_1 value via the expression.

This is pretty neat, but couldn't you achieve the same effect with parenting? Yes! This is a simple example of creating an expression, but it doesn't really reveal the power of expressions. In the following exercises, the technique will get more exciting—we promise!

8 Set the **Scale** property for the **Motorcycle_1** layer to **20%**, which will be the starting point for the next exercise.

9 Choose **File > Save**, or press **Cmd+S** (Mac) or **Ctrl+S** (Windows). Leave **Expression_Project.aep** and the **Creating Expressions** composition open for the next exercise.

Congratulations! You just created your first expression. Having learned how to create a simple expression that ties similar properties together (both Scale properties in this exercise), you will next learn how to create an expression that ties together two different properties, such as Scale and Rotation.

WARNING:

Assigning Unique Layer Names

Expressions use a layer's name to refer to layer objects. Without unique layer names, expressions can refer to the wrong layer object. Rename layers, if necessary, to ensure all layers have unique names. To rename a layer, simply select the layer name, press **Return** (Mac) or **Enter** (Windows), enter the new name, and then click off of the layer.

2 | Creating Property Relationships

In this exercise, you'll continue to work with the same layers and composition to build on what you've learned so far. The first expression you created borrowed the **Scale** property from one layer and applied it to another. In fact, you could have achieved this same result with parenting. Now, however, you will tell After Effects 7 to take the value of the **Scale** property from one layer and apply it to the **Rotation** property of another layer. Once completed, if you scale the original layer to 30 percent, the other layer will rotate 30 degrees. That is something you cannot do with parenting!

1 If you followed the previous exercise, **Expression_Project.aep** should still be open in After Effects 7. If it's not, choose **File > Open Project**. Navigate to the **chap_17** folder you copied to your desktop, click **Expression_Project_2.aep** to select it, and click **Open**.

2 Double-click the **Creating Expressions** composition to open it.

3 Select the **Motorcycle_2** layer, and press the **R** key to display the **Rotation** property.

4 Make sure you are in **Frame 1**. **Opt+click** (Mac) or **Alt+click** (Windows) the **stopwatch** icon for **Rotation**.

Notice an expression is turned on for the Rotation property in the Motorcycle_2 layer. You can tell the expression is active because the words *transform.rotation* appear within the Expression field in the layer.

5 Click the **Pick Whip** icon for the **Motorcycle_2 Rotation** property, and drag it to the **Motorcycle_1 Scale** property.

Using the Pick Whip tool links the two properties together so the Rotation property of the Motorcycle_2 layer will draw its values from the Scale property of the Motorcycle 1 layer.

6 Click and drag back and forth over the **Motorcycle_1 Scale** value, and observe the results.

Notice the Motorcycle_2 layer scales and rotates but the Motorcycle_1 layer just scales. You have linked a property from one layer to another using expressions without affecting the original layer.

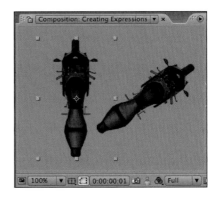

7 Choose **File > Save**, or press **Cmd+S** (Mac) or **Ctrl+S** (Windows). Leave **Expression_Project.aep** and the **Creating Expressions** composition open for the next exercise.

This exercise demonstrated the basic principle of linking two different properties through an expression. Next, you'll learn how to modify the expression you just created.

3 | Multiplying Expression Values

As you've seen, once you use the **Pick Whip** tool to create property relationships, After Effects 7 automatically writes some JavaScript code in the **Expression** field. If you want, you can edit and modify this code. This allows you to create fairly sophisticated relationships between properties based on mathematical equations and if-then statements.

In this exercise, you will learn a simple way of modifying an expression by multiplying the values it generates. For example, you can scale a layer at twice the rate as the layer it is linked to by multiplying the expression by two. You can use this same method to add, subtract, multiply, or divide the value of an expression. Although it might sound intimidating to write your own code, you'll soon see this method is quite straightforward.

1 If you followed the previous exercise, **Expression_Project.aep** should still be open in After Effects 7. If it's not, choose **File > Open Project**. Navigate to the **chap_17** folder you copied to your desktop, click **Expression_Project_3.aep** to select it, and click **Open**.

2 Double-click the **Creating Expressions** composition to open it.

3 Make sure the **CTI** is at **Frame 1 (0:00:00:01)** and the **Scale** property shows for the **Motorcycle_1** layer. Set **Scale** to **20%**. Click the **stopwatch** icon for **Scale** to set a beginning keyframe. Move the **CTI** (Current Time Indicator) to **0:00:01:00**, and set a keyframe for the **Scale** property by changing **Scale** to **100%**.

You are doing this so you can see how the expressions you've created interact with keyframes and with properties that change over time. Once you set the second keyframe, you'll see both motorcycles increase in size. The expression is doing its job!

4 Move the **CTI** to **Frame 1 (0:00:00:01)**, click the **Motorcycle _2 Rotation Expression** field, and place your cursor at the end of the line of code. Type ***4**, and then either press **Return** (Mac) or **Enter** (Windows) on your numeric keypad or click outside the **Expression** field to activate the expression.

In this example, you are multiplying the expression by a specified value (the asterisk key means multiply), although you can add (+), subtract (-), or divide (/) as well to get the desired result—in this case, more or less rotation.

5 Scrub the **CTI** and notice the rotation of **Motorcycle _2** quadruples.

6 Choose **File > Save**, or press **Cmd+S** (Mac) or **Ctrl+S** (Windows). In the top-left corner of the **Composition** panel, choose **Close Creating Expressions** from the **Composition** pop-up menu to close the current composition. Leave **Expression_Project.aep** open for the next exercise.

You have just seen a simple way to modify an expression you created, without needing to know JavaScript. This is a useful method for adjusting the results of an expression you've applied. In the next exercise, you will learn how to apply expressions to properties other than Transform properties.

N O T E :

Performing Math Operations Using Expressions

In the previous exercise, you added an asterisk and a value at the end of the line of JavaScript code to multiply the value for the **Rotation** property by four. This method allows you to easily modify the automatically generated JavaScript code. The following chart lists the keys you can use for other simple math operations in JavaScript expressions; as you can see, they are just standard math symbols:

Simple Math Operations	
Key	**Operation**
+	Add
–	Subtract
*	Multiply
/	Divide

Use these keys to perform simple math operations on expression values. You can also change an action to its opposite by using a negative number. For example, to change the rotation from clockwise to counterclockwise, use *–1 (or any other value).

4 | Using Text, Effects, and Expressions

You can use expressions to control the values of **Effects** properties, as well as those of **Transform** properties. This is useful for a wide range of desired results, such as linking the position of an object to the intensity of an effect. In this exercise, you will see an example of using a text layer and the **Fast Blur** effect.

---

1 If you followed the previous exercise, **Expression_Project.aep** should still be open in After Effects 7. If it's not, choose **File > Open Project**. Navigate to the **chap_17** folder you copied to your desktop, click **Expression_Project_4.aep** to select it, and click **Open**.

---

2 In the **Project** panel, click the **Create a new Composition** button. In the **Composition Settings** dialog box, name the composition **Blur**, and set **Duration** to **0:00:02:00**.

3 Choose **Layer > New > Text** to create a new text layer. When you see your cursor blinking in the **Composition** panel, type **Speed**. Make sure the text is center-aligned by clicking the **Center** button in the **Paragraph** panel.

A new text layer appears in the Timeline called Speed (once you click somewhere other than the text).

---

4 In the **Timeline** panel, make sure the **CTI** is in the first frame. Click the **twirly** icons for the text layer until you see the **Text** properties.

---

5 In the **Timeline** panel, choose **Tracking** from the **Animate** pop-up menu for the **Speed** layer.

The properties for Animator 1 will appear, including a Tracking Amount property (**tracking** is the amount of space between letters and words).

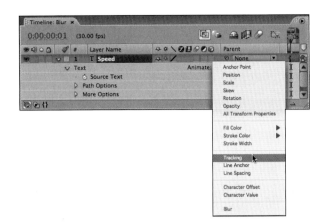

6 Next to the **Tracking Amount** property, click the **stopwatch** icon to activate it.

This creates a keyframe at Frame 0:00:00:01.

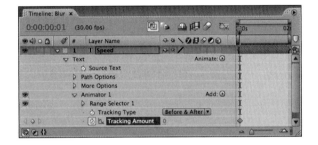

7 Drag the **CTI** to the last frame by pressing the **End** key. Change **Tracking Amount** to **46**.

Your screen should look like the one shown in the illustration here.

8 Choose **Effect > Blur & Sharpen > Fast Blur**.

This adds the Fast Blur effect to the basic Text effect, although it won't look any different yet. That's because you haven't applied any settings to the Fast Blur effect. That will come in a later step.

9 In the **Timeline**, click the **twirly** icon next to **Effects**. Click the **twirly** icon next to **Fast Blur** to reveal its properties.

Next, you'll create an expression.

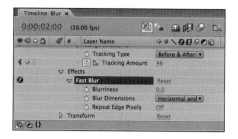

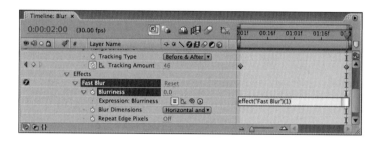

10 Drag the **CTI** to **Frame 0:00:00:01**. **Opt+click** (Mac) or **Alt+click** (Windows) the **stopwatch** icon for **Blurriness** to add an expression.

You'll see JavaScript code appear immediately for the Blurriness value.

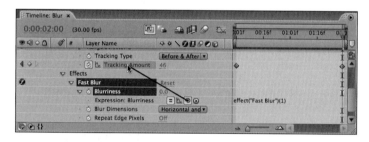

11 Drag the **Pick Whip** icon for **Blurriness** to the **Tracking Amount** property.

This adds more code to the JavaScript field.

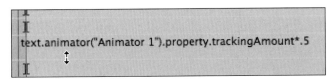

12 At the end of the JavaScript code, type ***.5**.

This multiplies the Tracking Amount property by .5 and applies the resulting blur to the Blurriness property. You won't see any change at first because the value in the first keyframe of the Tracking Amount property is 0.

```
text.animator("Animator 1").property.trackingAmount*.5
```

If you have trouble getting to the end of the JavaScript code, you can expand the text field by placing your cursor at the bottom of the field. The cursor will change to a double-headed arrow. Dragging the text field with this cursor will expand what it shows.

13 Drag the **CTI** to a frame in the middle of the composition, and you'll see the amount of tracking directly affects the amount of blur.

Tip: Try changing the Tracking Amount value to something else, such as .2 or .7, and scrub the Timeline to see the result. You'll be able to pick a value that is pleasing to you this way.

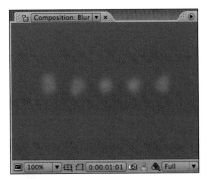

14 Choose **File > Save**, or press **Cmd+S** (Mac) or **Ctrl+S** (Windows). In the top-left corner of the **Composition** panel, choose **Close Blur** from the **Composition** pop-up menu to close the current composition. Leave **Expression_Project.aep** open for the next exercise.

What's nice is that you didn't use any keyframes for the Fast Blur effect. After Effects 7 is collecting values for the blur based on how much the Tracking Amount values are. This makes for perfectly synchronized motion; the Blurriness amount directly relates to the Tracking Amount property. You can use expressions to control all types of Effects properties and values; this is just a sample of the sorts of results you can achieve with this kind of programming. In the next exercise, you'll learn how to turn off an expression.

EXERCISE

5 | Turning Off an Expression

After Effects 7 will sometimes turn off an expression if that expression contains an error. You can also choose to turn off an expression manually. You may want to turn off a complex expression to speed up your previews. Or you may have several expressions chained together and want to debug the chains. Or you may simply be unsure as to whether you want to use an expression, in which case you can choose to turn it off until you decide.

1 If you followed the previous exercise, **Expression_Project.aep** should still be open in After Effects 7. If it's not, choose **File > Open Project**. Navigate to the **chap_17** folder you copied to your desktop, click **Expression_Project_5.aep** to select it, and click **Open**.

2 Double-click the **Disable and Delete** composition to open it.

In this exercise, you'll learn how to turn off an expression. Turning on an expression is equally easy.

3 Scrub the **CTI**, and notice the starbursts rotate as the motorcycle position animates.

All the starburst layers have expressions chained to the first starburst's Rotation property. In the following step, you will turn off the first expression in the chain. This will turn off all rotations of the starburst layer.

4 Select the **Starburst_1** layer, press the **R** key to open the **Rotation** property for the layer, and click the **twirly** icon to reveal the **Expression: Rotation** property. Click the **Enable Expression** switch next to the **Starburst_1 Rotation** property.

The Enable Expression switch looks like an equal sign. Notice it changes to an equal sign with a slash through the center when turned off.

5 Scrub the **CTI**, and in the **Composition** panel, notice the starburst images no longer rotate.

The chain of expressions is **disabled**, which means it is temporarily turned off; the good news is it doesn't mean the work is lost forever, as if it were deleted. Turning on the expression again is easy, as you'll see in the next step.

Chapter 17 : *Using Expressions* | 421

6 To turn on the expression, click the **Enable Expression** switch so it appears as an equal sign.

---

7 Choose **File > Save**, or press **Cmd+S** (Mac) or **Ctrl+S** (Windows). In the top-left corner of the **Composition** panel, choose **Close Disable and Delete** from the **Composition** pop-up menu to close the current composition.

In this exercise, you learned that turning off and on an expression is as simple as clicking the Enable Expression switch. In the next exercise, you'll learn how to convert expressions into keyframes to speed up previews and gain access to individual keyframes for animation purposes.

NOTE:

Deleting Expressions

Deleting an expression, rather than turning it off, is simple. You can accomplish this in three ways: You can choose **Animation > Remove Expression**, you can **Opt+click** (Mac) or **Alt+click** (Windows) the **Enable Expression** switch, or you can **Opt+click** (Mac) or **Alt+click** (Windows) the **stopwatch** icon.

Using the JavaScript Expression Language Menu

If you know JavaScript, you can use the **Expressions language menu** to write your own JavaScript expressions.

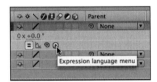

To access the menu, click the **Expression language menu** arrow for an expression.

You can select from the entire library of JavaScript language elements used by After Effects 7. An experienced JavaScript programmer could have a blast with all these options. If you don't know JavaScript, you can ignore these options or learn what they mean by reading a book about JavaScript.

If you don't want to type them manually, you can select from a wide variety of JavaScript items from the library in the **Expressions language menu** pop-up menu, such as the options shown in the illustration here for a composition.

6 | Converting Expressions to Keyframes

After Effects 7 obtains the values for an expression frame by frame during the rendering process. In essence, After Effects 7 calculates expressions "live." If you have a particularly complex expression, this can slow down rendering time; therefore, you can convert expressions to keyframes to speed up rendering. You might also convert expressions to keyframes if you want to access the keyframes to manually animate them.

1 If you followed the previous exercise, **Expression_Project.aep** should still be open in After Effects 7. If it's not, choose **File > Open Project**. Navigate to the **chap_17** folder you copied to your desktop, click **Expression_Project_6.aep** to select it, and click **Open**.

2 Double-click the **Convert to Keyframes** composition to open it.

In this exercise, you'll select a property that already has an expression, and you'll learn to use the Convert Expression to Keyframes option.

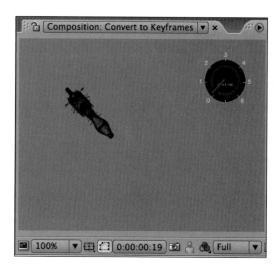

3 Press the **spacebar**, or click the **RAM Preview** button in the **Time Controls** panel. Notice the motorcycle moves through the **Composition** panel as the dial makes a complete rotation.

The motorcycle layer has an expression referencing the dial layer. In the following steps, you will convert the motorcycle expression to keyframes.

4 Select the **Motorcycle_Top.psd** layer, and click its **twirly** icon until you see the **Position** property and its expression. Click the **Position** property to select it.

For this step, it doesn't matter where your CTI is in the Timeline.

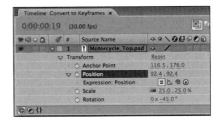

5 Choose **Animation > Keyframe Assistant > Convert Expression to Keyframes**.

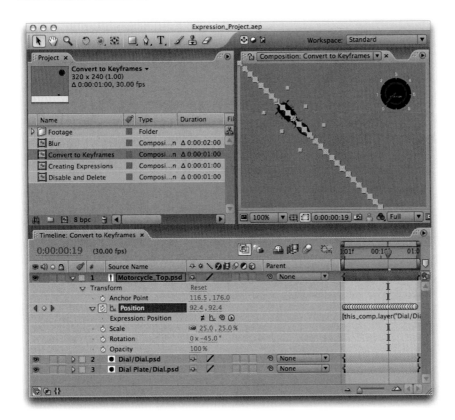

6 In the **Composition** and **Timeline** panels, notice the keyframes created by the expression.

In particular, observe the motion path created by the keyframes in the Composition panel and the keyframe marks indicating the motorcycle's position over time. Also notice the expression is now turned off, as demonstrated by the Enable Expression switch with the slash through it.

7 Choose **File > Save**, or press **Cmd+S** (Mac) or **Ctrl+S** (Windows). Choose **File > Close Project**.

That's it for this chapter! You have sampled the power of expressions. If you like working with expressions, you have endless possibilities. They are truly boundless tools you can combine in infinite new ways. In the next chapter, you'll learn how to simply stabilize and track footage in After Effects 7.

18

Tracking Motion and Stabilizing Footage

Shaky video footage is the inevitable result of most handheld camera work. To "fix" these erratic motions or (even more intriguing) to "pin" video or graphics onto a moving layer, you'll use a technique called **motion tracking**, which analyzes the movement of pixels in one layer and, using that data, applies the same motion to another layer. This technique, which is available in the After Effects 7 Professional edition only, allows you to match the movement from one shot of video to another, which is particularly useful when trying to attach a graphic or effect to a moving object within the scene.

After Effects 7 animators use this technique of pinning one layer to another quite often, and it usually goes unnoticed. For example, you can use this approach to put a new picture within a television screen, even if the camera used to shoot the footage was moving. You can also use motion tracking to place a logo on a moving car or match a lens flare to the direction of your camera. Additionally, you can use the data generated by analyzing your video's motion to stabilize your footage, correcting the majority of unwanted horizontal and vertical motion. In this chapter, you'll learn how to use the motion-tracking and stabilization features in After Effects 7.

Introducing Motion Tracking

As explained, motion tracking is the automatic analysis and tracking of specific objects, or points, in your video, which you can use to match the motion of one layer to another or to stabilize the footage by using position, rotation, and scale information derived from the tracking process.

By applying tracking points to a feature in your video footage, such as the corner of a television screen, After Effects 7 will follow that feature over the course of the entire clip, adding keyframes to describe the path of that particular object. Once After Effects 7 has generated these keyframes, you can easily apply them to another layer, causing that layer to move in tandem with the tracked layer. When one layer accurately matches the motion of another, it looks like the two layers are actually part of the same footage. Using motion tracking in this way allows you to seamlessly combine elements that were shot or generated separately. If done correctly, the viewer won't even suspect they are separate layers.

How does After Effects 7 actually track motion, and what tools do you have to accomplish this magical feat? You first need to establish a **track point** to determine what feature the motion tracker is actually following. After Effects 7 allows you to set an unlimited number of track points, although you'll probably use only a few, unless you need to track multiple, complex objects. A track point consists of an attach point, a feature region, and a search region.

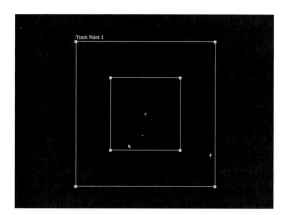

The **attach point** (the cross shown in the illustration here) is where you want the target layer to appear on your footage once you apply the motion-tracking data (the object, on a separate layer, that will follow your track). Generally, you will place the attach point in the center of the location to which you will eventually attach the new layer.

The **feature region** (the inside box shown in the illustration here) simply defines the primary area in your footage you want to track, at the center of which should be the most prominent feature. As long as the object you want to track remains fairly consistent within the feature region you've selected (in terms of light and shape), After Effects 7 should be able to find and track it.

The **search region** (the outside box shown in the illustration here) is a bit broader than the feature region and serves to provide a limited area within the frame that After Effects 7 may search in case it starts to lose sight of the target. The search region can be large, but the larger it is, the more time it will take After Effects 7 to analyze your footage. This also applies to the feature region, so keep both of these regions relatively small at first.

You can use the **Tracker Controls** panel to set up the necessary parameters for motion tracking and stabilization. This panel includes options for setting a **motion source** (the layer whose motion you want to analyze), the **current track** (the track point currently selected for editing), and the **track type** (the options to select, depending on what you are tracking). In this panel, you can turn on check boxes to determine what kind of motion you want to track and apply to another layer, such as **Position**, **Rotation**, and **Scale**, as well as click playback-style controls for analyzing motion in forward or backward directions.

As mentioned, the motion-tracking technique is perfect for placing a new image within a television or computer screen, which you will do in Exercise 1. Later, you will see how you can use a similar process to stabilize motion in your video. Although these are only simple examples of how you can use motion tracking, you will surely think of many others as you become familiar with this feature. Sky replacements and set extensions (such as adding a city skyline outside a window), as well as special effects that follow the trail of a moving object, are just a few examples.

1 | Tracking Motion in a Video Clip and Applying It to Another Layer

This exercise introduces you to the techniques needed to use the motion tracker in After Effects 7. A common scenario, where motion tracking can really help, is when you need to take a shot of a video screen and replace its contents with something new. You'll use the motion tracker to accomplish this task in a couple of ways. First you'll track the motion with a couple of track points, and then you'll track the motion with several track points.

1 Copy the **chap_18** folder from the **After Effects 7 HOT CD-ROM** onto your desktop.

2 Choose **File > Open Project**. Navigate to the **chap_18** folder you copied to your desktop, select the file named **Motion_Tracking.aep**, and click **Open**. Choose **File > Save As**. In the **Save As** dialog box, navigate to the **AE7_HOT_Projects** folder on your desktop. Name the file **Motion_Tracking.aep**, and click **Save**.

3 In the **Project** panel, double-click the **Tracking** composition to open it.

This composition contains three layers. The bottom layer, Monitor_1.mov, contains the video footage whose motion you will track. The middle layer, Screen.psd (which is currently turned off), contains an artificial video-screen image you will have follow the motion of your video layer. You will also track the top text layer, 2007, to follow the footage. When you're finished, it should appear as if Screen.psd is actually displayed within the video screen on the Monitor.mov layer, and 2007 should appear in the white bar at the bottom of the monitor.

4 In the **Timeline** panel, make sure the **CTI** (Current Time Indicator) is at **0;00;00;00**, and select the **Monitor_1.mov** layer.

The layer you select should be video or contain some sort of motion you can track. In this example, you will be tracking the motion of the monitor object on this layer of video. You will use this tracking data to pin the 2007 text to the white bar at the bottom of the screen. Later in this exercise, you will apply a new image to fill its screen, following every motion of the unsteady camera used to shoot the footage.

5 Choose **Animation > Track Motion** to open the **Tracker Controls** panel.

When you choose Track Motion, the Track Controls panel opens in After Effects 7. Notice in the Tracker Controls panel the Monitor_1.mov layer is selected as the motion source. If you changed your mind and wanted to choose another layer's motion to track, you could select it from this pop-up menu.

Also, notice a new track point appears in the Layer panel, which opens in place of the Composition panel. As you probably remember, you can use the Layer panel to edit properties of a single layer without affecting the overall composition.

If the Track Controls panel is already open, you can click the Track Motion button to apply a track point, rather than choosing Animation > Track Motion. No matter how you set this option, it performs the same task.

---

6 In the **Tracker Controls** panel, click the **Edit Target** button. In the **Motion Target** dialog box, choose **2007** from the **Layer** pop-up menu. Click **OK**.

The Motion Target dialog box allows you to assign the layer to which you will apply the tracked motion. The first item you will apply this tracking data to is the 2007 text layer in your Timeline.

---

7 In the **Tracker Controls** panel, make sure the **Position** and **Rotation** check boxes are turned on.

As soon as you select Rotation, another track point, Track Point 2, appears in the Layer panel. To determine the amount of rotation, you need two track points for measuring the angle.

The majority of motion in this video clip is side to side or up and down. If your original video footage has any degree of rotation (such as the camera tilting or rolling), you should make sure to turn on the Rotation check box, as you did in this step. If you're tracking a moving object from a tripod-mounted camera, this wouldn't be a problem, and you'd most likely need to turn on only Position. Also, if the object you are tracking moves toward or away from the camera, you will probably want to turn on the Scale check box.

This example is pretty simple, although the needs of your footage can vary widely. Often, if you are working with footage shot from a stationary position (and the object you're tracking doesn't move by itself), you can just turn on Position. However, a little bit of experimentation with both the Position and Rotation check boxes may be necessary to get the best results.

---

8 In the **Layer** panel, locate a unique, clearly defined feature you want to track, such as the lower-left corner of the white strip at the bottom of the monitor. Click and drag the **feature region** (the innermost box) for **Track Point 1** until it appears directly on the corner you want to track.

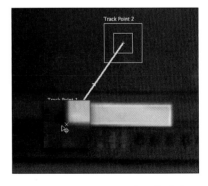

In this case, it's best to click and drag anywhere within the track point except for the attach point because you don't want to move the attach point independent of the feature and search regions. You'll actually keep the attach point where it is, since this also happens to be where you want the text layer to end.

Notice as you drag the track point, it acts as a magnifying glass, allowing you to see a more detailed view of your footage. This makes it easier to find a good place for your track point. Corners, or other sharp angles and features with a lot of contrast, make the best places to place a track point—the corner of a white door frame against a black background, for example.

---

9 After moving **Track Point 1** and centering your feature region, click and drag the **feature region** to make it a little larger. Also, click and drag the corners of the **search region** to make it a little larger as well, as shown in the illustration here.

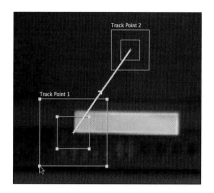

Enlarging the feature and search regions ensures After Effects 7 will be looking at a large enough area when it attempts to find the feature you specified, even if the footage gets a little too bumpy.

10 As you did with your first track point, click and drag **Track Point 2** until it's located directly on the opposite lower corner of the white strip at the bottom of the monitor. Click and drag its **feature region** and **search region** to make them a little bit larger as well, ensuring you achieve better tracking results.

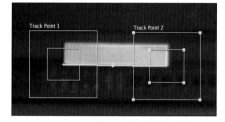

It doesn't necessarily matter where you place this second track point, as long as it's on a recognizable feature and not close to Track Point 1. After Effects 7 will use this track point to determine the angle of change occurring when the two points move. You'll be able to visualize this when you see the line connecting these two track points pivot slightly, like a seesaw, when the motion-tracking analysis takes place.

11 In the **Tracker Controls** panel, click the **Analyze forward** button.

After Effects 7 analyzes the entire duration of your clip and tracks its motion, based on the points you set.

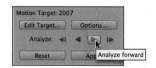

12 After the program is done analyzing your video, click the **Apply** button in the **Tracker Controls** panel.

When you click Apply, After Effects 7 automatically adds keyframes to the tracked layer to define the positions of the tracker points you set. Notice these keyframes are currently visible in the Layer panel.

13 In the **Motion Tracker Apply Options** dialog box, leave the **Apply Dimensions** pop-up menu set to **X and Y** to apply motion in both the horizontal and vertical directions. Click **OK**.

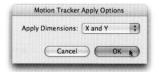

14 In the **Timeline** panel, click the **Video** switch for the **2007** text layer, and look at it in your **Composition** panel. In the **Timeline** panel, click somewhere other than the **2007** layer to deselect it.

Make certain you are looking at your Composition panel and not the Layer panel you were working in previously. Also, deselecting the layer will help you view it better without all the keyframes in the Composition panel covering it.

Notice the 2007 layer is not centered exactly where you want it in the composition. You'll fix this in the next step.

---

15 Click the **twirly** icons for the **2007** layer so you can view the **Anchor Point** property. For **Anchor Point**, change the **X** and **Y** values until your text is properly positioned (offset) at approximately −**50, 5**.

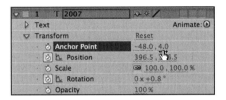

While you are looking in the Timeline, also notice the keyframes set for the Position and Rotation properties of the 2007 text layer. These are based on the applied tracking data you created by setting the tracking points previously. Also, notice the Monitor_1.mov layer has some new Motion Tracker properties, which are simply another place to view the properties for the track points you set.

---

16 Press the **spacebar** or click the **RAM Preview** button in the **Time Controls** panel to preview the results so far. Notice the **2007** text follows the motion of your **Monitor_1.mov** video layer. When you are finished previewing, press the **spacebar** to stop playback.

Next, you will set tracking points to place the Screen.psd layer in the video screen image.

---

17 In the **Timeline** panel, select the **Monitor_1.mov** layer. In the **Timeline** panel, make certain the **CTI** is at **0;00;00;00**.

In the next steps, you will place tracking points to specifically pin the Screen.psd layer to the corners of the video screen. This process is referred to as **corner pinning**.

---

18 In the **Tracker Controls** panel, choose **Perspective corner pin** from the **Track Type** pop-up menu.

This automatically places four new track points in the Layer panel. Each track point corresponds to a corner to which you want to pin another layer.

19 In the **Tracker Controls** panel, click the **Edit Target** button. In the **Motion Target** dialog box, choose **Screen.psd** from the **Layer** pop-up menu, and click **OK**.

In this instance, you are selecting a new layer to which to apply the motion-tracking data.

20 In the Composition panel, click and drag each track point (**Track Point 1**, **Track Point 2**, **Track Point 3**, and **Track Point 4**) until it is in its corresponding corner of the video monitor, as shown in the illustration here. Expand the **feature region** and **search region** for each to account for any uneven motions in the video.

The track points you are placing correspond to the corners in the target layer you want to pin.

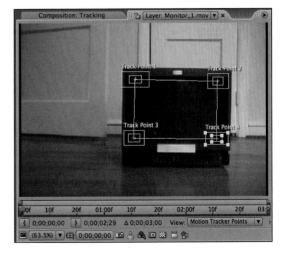

21 In the **Tracker Controls** panel, click the **Analyze forward** button. When After Effects 7 is done analyzing your video, click the **Apply** button in the **Tracker Controls** panel.

22 In the **Timeline** panel, click the **Video** switch for the **Screen.psd** layer to make it visible. In the **Time Controls** panel, click the **RAM Preview** button to preview the results of your motion tracking and corner pinning. When you are finished previewing, press the **spacebar** to stop playback.

Notice the Screen.psd layer follows the motion of the Monitor_1.mov layer, pinning its four corners against the corners you defined with the track points. Not too difficult, right?

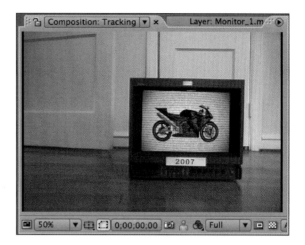

23 Choose **File > Save**, or press **Cmd+S** (Mac) or **Ctrl+S** (Windows). In the upper-left corner of the **Composition** panel, choose **Close Tracking** from the pop-up menu to close the current composition. Leave **Motion_Tracking.aep** open for the next exercise.

Now that you've acquired some simple motion-tracking skills for the purpose of linking multiple layers, you'll learn to use tracking data to help stabilize shaky video footage.

EXERCISE

2 | Stabilizing Video Footage

Everyone with a video camera has wondered how they could get better-looking, more stable images. In this exercise, you'll learn how to use the motion-tracking features in After Effects 7 to help you stabilize your shaky, handheld video footage. Now that you've seen how to work with track points, it's really quite simple.

1 If you followed the previous exercise, **Motion_Tracking.aep** should still be open in After Effects 7. If it's not, choose **File > Open Project**. Navigate to the **chap_18** folder you copied to your desktop, click **Motion_Tracking_2.aep** to select it, and click **Open**.

2 In the **Project** panel, double-click the **Stabilize** composition to open it. Press the **spacebar** to preview the footage you will be using.

3 In the **Timeline** panel, make sure the **CTI** is at **0;00;00;00**, and select the **Monitor_2.mov** layer.

This is the layer of video you want to track and stabilize.

4 Choose **Animation > Stabilize Motion**.

5 In the **Tracker Controls** panel, make sure the **Position** and **Rotation** check boxes are turned on.

Just as in the previous exercise, this footage changes position and has slight rotation.

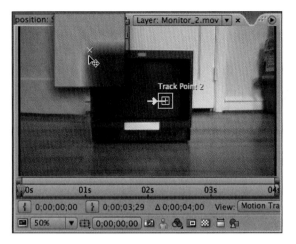

6 In the **Composition** panel, click and drag the first track point, **Track Point 1**, and place its **feature region** on the top-left corner of the monitor in your video. Adjust its **feature region** and **search region** to be a little larger. Repeat this process for **Track Point 2**, placing it on the opposite corner at the top of the monitor.

Selecting a feature to track with high contrast and clearly defined shapes helps the tracker do its job better.

---

7 In the **Tracker Controls** panel, click the **Analyze forward** button. Once After Effects 7 finishes analyzing your video, click the **Apply** button in the **Tracker Controls** panel. In the **Motion Tracker Apply Options** dialog box, leave the **Apply Dimensions** pop-up menu set to **X and Y** in order to apply motion in both the horizontal and vertical directions. Click **OK**.

After Effects 7 analyzes the entire duration of your clip and tracks its motion, based on the points you set.

---

8 In the **Time Controls** panel, click the **RAM Preview** button to preview the results of stabilizing using two tracking points. When you are finished previewing, press the **spacebar** to stop playback.

Notice the video appears to float in the middle of the Composition panel. You'll also notice some black edges around the frame, where the video moves to reveal blank space. When you stabilize footage, the frame shifts left, right, up, and down as necessary to keep the selected features in one place. To fix this, you'll need to enlarge your video so you cannot see the empty black spaces.

9 With the **Monitor_2.mov** layer selected, press the **S** key to reveal the **Scale** property. Increase the value for **Scale** to approximately **140%**, or until you no longer see empty areas outside the frame. Press the **spacebar** to preview your video, and press it again to stop playback.

Depending on how much motion was in your video, you may need to scale by quite a bit, which can affect the quality of your video.

---

10 Choose **File > Save**, or press **Cmd+S** (Mac) or **Ctrl+S** (Windows). In the upper-left corner of the **Composition** panel, choose **Close Stabilize** from the pop-up menu to close the current composition.

You've just completed two exercises that introduced you to the tracking and stabilization features in After Effects 7. Take the time to test these techniques using some of your own video footage. Each piece of video is unique and has its own set of challenges. In the next chapter, you'll learn how to work with the audio features in After Effects 7.

19

Working with Audio

Most professional animation and motion-graphics work contains music, narration, or sound effects—or all of these at once. After Effects 7 is primarily a tool for motion graphics and animation, but it would not be complete if it didn't offer the ability to include audio. You can use audio files simply as "guide tracks" to help you choreograph moving images, or you can use them to create the final audio tracks for your movies.

It's important to understand After Effects 7 is not designed to be an audio-authoring tool. Other programs, such as Adobe Audition or Adobe Premiere Pro, are better equipped to record and process a finished music track.

However, if you want to combine a finished music track with sound effects, narration, and animation, After Effects 7 is a great tool for the job. You can import a prerecorded track, fit it to your image, adjust the volume, and output the final audio track with your movie. You'll learn how to do many of these tasks in this chapter.

Using Audio in After Effects 7

In After Effects 7, you can import audio files into the **Project** panel, just as you import any other file, by choosing **File > Import**.

When you select audio footage in the **Project** panel, rather than seeing the little image preview, you'll see a **waveform** (a visual indicator of the sound's amplitude) indicating the footage is audio only, as shown in the illustration here.

Audio file formats supported by After Effects 7 include Apple QuickTime movies, AIFF (a popular Mac audio file format), and WAV (a popular Windows audio file format). You can import these and other audio files supported by QuickTime, including MP3 and AU, directly into After Effects 7. Once you've imported the audio footage, you can use it as layers in your compositions so you can synchronize music or sound effects to your animation.

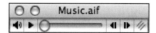

You can preview audio footage by double-clicking the audio files in the **Project** panel. This opens an audio player so you can hear the audio track before placing it in your composition.

To work with and edit an audio file for a project, you need to be able to see it within the context of your animation's **Timeline**. In this exercise, you will learn to use the **Audio** switch and to view audio waveforms in the **Timeline** panel. A waveform can tell you a lot about your audio, including where silence occurs and where a particularly loud sound occurs. Using these visual cues will help you better identify where you might want to synchronize your audio with the visuals.

---

1 Copy the **chap_19** folder from the **After Effects 7 HOT CD-ROM** onto your desktop.

---

2 Choose **File > Open Project**, navigate to the **chap_12** folder you copied to your desktop, select the file named **Audio.aep**, and click **Open**. Choose **File > Save As**. In the **Save As** dialog box, navigate to the **AE7_HOT_Projects** folder on your desktop. Name the file **Audio.aep**, and click **Save**.

---

3 Double-click the **Motorcycle_Rotate** composition to open it, if it's not already open.

---

4 In the **Timeline** panel, click the **Audio** switch for the **Music.aif**, **Passing.aif**, and **Thunder.aif** layers, thus enabling the sound for those layers.

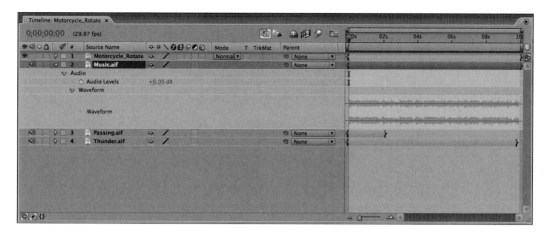

5 Click the **twirly** icon next to the **Music.aif** layer to display the **Audio** properties, and then click the **twirly** icons next to **Audio** and then **Waveform** to reveal the waveform graph.

The waveform is a graphical representation of recorded sound. As mentioned previously, waveforms can tell you a lot about what is happening in your audio at any point in time. If the file contains a loud sound (such as a cymbal crash), you will see a spike in the waveform. If the file contains silence, such as the spaces that occur when you have a pause in a spoken conversation, you will simply notice a flat line. Once you know where a sound occurs, you can pinpoint where to place a corresponding visual component in your composition. As shown in the illustration here, the two squiggly lines represent the left and right stereo tracks. Each squiggly line represents the frequency and volume of the audio track.

Tip: The Audio switch must be on to see the waveform.

6 Choose **File > Save**, or press **Cmd+S** (Mac) or **Ctrl+S** (Windows). Leave **Audio.aep** open for the next exercise.

In this exercise, you simply learned how to turn on layers of audio and view their waveforms. You'll learn how to preview the sound in the next exercise.

2 | Previewing Audio

One of the least intuitive parts of After Effects 7, strangely enough, is previewing sound. In this exercise, you will learn how to preview audio using the **Time Controls** panel and the **Audio Preview** option. This will help you when you want to find a particular portion of audio to synchronize your animations. You will also learn to preview sound in the **Timeline** by dragging the **CTI** (Current Time Indicator).

---

1 If you followed the previous exercise, **Audio.aep** should still be open in After Effects 7. If it's not, choose **File > Open Project**. Navigate to the **chap_19** folder you copied to your desktop, click **Audio_2.aep** to select it, and click **Open**.

---

2 Double-click **Motorcycle_Rotate** to open the composition, if it is not already visible.

---

3 In the **Time Controls** panel, click the **Mute Audio** button to turn it on, and then click the **RAM Preview** button. When you are done previewing, press the **spacebar** to stop the preview.

The Audio button is actually called Mute Audio, which means you have the option of previewing your composition with or without audio by clicking this button. When using RAM preview, you'll preview the first few seconds of your audio with the animation. Notice the audio and image must be rendered first, which causes a slight delay.

Warning: If you have turned down the sound on your computer, you may not hear the audio. If this is the case, locate the Sound Control Panel for your operating system, and check the sound levels.

---

4 Drag the **CTI** to the middle of the composition. Choose **Composition > Preview > Audio Preview (Here Forward)**.

Notice the audio plays immediately from the current CTI position. No prerendering is necessary when using this preview method. The image does not move using this method, so you cannot use it to check synchronization, but it's the quickest way to hear all your audio tracks. You might do this initially when seeing what audio exists, when checking levels, or when your composition is too render intensive to play alongside your audio in real time.

Note: When you want to stop the preview, you can click anywhere or press any key (such as the spacebar).

---

5 Press the **period** key on your numeric keypad to start playback of audio. Press any key to stop the preview.

The period key on your numeric keypad is the keyboard shortcut for the Audio Preview (Here Forward) command and is probably the method you'll use most often, once you've memorized some common shortcuts.

Note: Make certain the Num Lock key is not activated on your keyboard when using this function.

---

6 In the **Timeline** panel, hold down **Cmd** (Mac) or **Ctrl** (Windows), and scrub the **CTI**. Stop scrubbing the **CTI** to stop the preview.

Notice the audio previews while you scrub (drag) the CTI, which allows you to locate a particular sound or portion of your audio quickly, without needing to play it.

Note: Scrubbing audio can result in jerky playback. It's best to use RAM preview with the Audio button turned on for smooth movement and sound. If you stop moving the CTI while holding down the mouse, a short section of audio will loop.

---

7 Choose **File > Save**, or press **Cmd+S** (Mac) or **Ctrl+S** (Windows). Leave **Audio.aep** open for the next exercise.

In this exercise, you looked at a variety of ways to play and preview your audio. In the next exercise, you'll add some markers, which can help you quickly locate an especially important piece of audio.

TIP:

Setting the Audio Preview Duration

You can set the audio preview duration in the **Preferences** dialog box. You might want to limit the audio preview duration if you have a long piece and you want to concentrate on only a small part of the sound and how it synchronizes with your live action or animation.

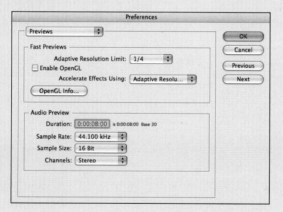

Choose **After Effects > Preferences > Previews** (Mac) or **Edit > Preferences > Preview** (Windows). In the **Preferences** dialog box, set **Duration** to the desired time, and click **OK**. This causes the audio preview to last for a specified length of time. After Effects 7 will cut short the audio preview if the audio footage is longer than the amount of time typed for this setting.

3 | Adding Markers and Comments

When working with audio layers, it's often helpful to add **markers** as references for where you want to emphasize beats in the music or passages of dialogue. These markers help you visualize where beats in the music occur, for example, and you can use them to synchronize sound with motion events.

After Effects 7 offers an easy way to add markers while listening to audio. In this exercise, you will learn to add markers while listening to an audio layer.

---

1 If you followed the previous exercise, **Audio.aep** should still be open in After Effects 7. If it's not, choose **File > Open Project**. Navigate to the **chap_19** folder you copied to your desktop, click **Audio_3.aep** to select it, and click **Open**.

---

2 Double-click **Motorcycle_Rotate** to open the composition, if it is not already visible.

---

3 In the **Timeline** panel, make sure you're in **Frame 1**, and click the **Solo** switch for the **Music.aif** layer to solo the layer.

You learned about the Solo switch in Chapter 8, *"Working with Layers."*

---

4 Select the **Music.aif** layer. If necessary, click the **twirly** icons next to **Audio** and **Waveform** to display their properties.

---

5 Make certain the layer you want to add markers to is currently selected by clicking it first. Press the **period** key on your numeric keypad to preview the **Music.aif** audio track. While listening to the audio track, press the **asterisk** key on the numeric keypad each time you hear a major beat. Press any other key to stop the preview.

Tip: If you want to delete a marker, Ctrl+click (Mac) or right-click (Windows) it to delete.

Notice this adds a marker to the layer at each press of the asterisk key. The markers look like small pyramids in the Timeline. These markers provide a helpful guide when you are setting animation keyframes you want to match up with audio beats.

Tip: If you work on a laptop and don't have a numeric keypad, you can add a marker manually by choosing Layer > Add Marker. Here too, you must select a layer to access this feature. In addition, this process is not useful for synchronizing to the beats of the audio because it is too slow. You can, however, move a marker once you create it.

---

6 Double-click any one of the markers you just added to open the **Marker** dialog box, and create a comment. When you are finished, click **OK**.

Anything you type in the Comment field of the Marker dialog box, such as a description of the marker (such as Bass Beat), shows up in the Timeline as a comment. We explain the other features of this dialog box, such as the creation of chapter markers for a DVD, in the chart after this exercise.

7 Choose **File > Save**, or press **Cmd+S** (Mac) or **Ctrl+S** (Windows). Leave **Audio.aep** open for the next exercise.

In this exercise, you learned how to create markers, which can help you identify important portions of an audio layer. In the next exercise, you'll learn how to adjust volume levels. But first, take a look at the following sections about using the Marker dialog box and working with the Audio panel.

Investigating the Marker Dialog Box

The **Marker** dialog box allows you to do more than simply type a comment for the purpose of adding sound notations. You can access the **Marker** dialog box by double-clicking any marker you've created. Here's a chart explaining the features of this dialog box:

Marker Dialog Box Options	
Setting	**Description**
Comment	Adds a comment to the marker, allowing you to write notes to yourself in the **Timeline**.
Chapter	Offers the capability to jump to a certain part of a movie. You can add the chapter name easily to After Effects 7 by typing in this field. You can add chapters and work with them in a QuickTime movie, or use them in a DVD project, to make navigation easier within a movie.
Web Links	Allows you to insert a Web link that users can click to be transported to the link's destination.
URL	Indicates the Web site you want users to be taken to when they click the Web link.
Frame Target	Allows you to set up the destination Web page in a separate window from the movie containing the Web link. The target naming conventions are part of standard HTML (HyperText Markup Language) targeting.

Working with the Audio Panel

Occasionally, you will need to fix a sound you've chosen to work with in your After Effects 7 project. You can use the **Audio** panel to make changes to your audio files, such as adjusting the volume level. Again, it's important to reiterate that After Effects 7 is not an ideal sound-editing tool. The **Audio** panel is generally reserved for small, simple audio needs.

To access the **Audio** panel, choose **Window > Audio**.

The **Audio** panel has several tools allowing you to work with volume levels. The following chart describes these tools:

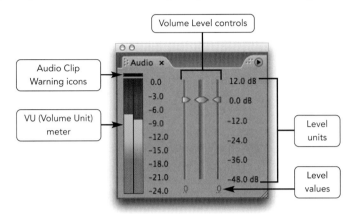

The following chart describes these tools:

	Audio Panel Controls	
Setting	**Description**	
Volume Level controls	Adjusts the volume.	
Level units	Indicates the change of volume in decibels.	
Level values	Indicates the exact value of each **Volume Level** control.	
Audio Clip Warning icons	Indicates when the audio is being **clipped**. When these icons are red, the audio level is loud enough to cause loss of audio data.	
VU (Volume Unit) meter	Offers feedback about the volume of your audio; it displays the volume range as the audio plays.	

While you're previewing audio, the **VU meter** displays green, yellow, and red volume levels. Green audio levels during playback indicate your volume level is perfectly safe and will not be clipped. Yellow peaks indicate caution, but your levels are still safe. Red peaks during playback indicate your audio levels may be in danger of being clipped. If your audio is clipped, the **Audio Clip Warning** icons will turn red.

When After Effects 7 clips audio, you will lose some of the audio frequency data. However, if you are familiar with digital recording techniques, you may be comfortable with some audio clipping. A safe rule is to keep the levels high enough that your audio bounces into the yellow and red zones occasionally but never so high the audio data is clipped. If you follow this guideline, your audio will be safe while maintaining maximum clarity and richness of tone.

If you intend to use After Effects 7 to finish the audio for your final movie, we recommend you learn more about digital audio and work with other tools besides After Effects 7. You'll find a list of audio-related resources in Appendix B, *"After Effects 7 Resources."*

4 | Adjusting Volume Levels

In this exercise, you will learn to adjust the **Master Volume Control** slider for the overall audio levels and to adjust the **left channel** and **right channel** sliders for individual channels.

---

1 If you followed the previous exercise, **Audio.aep** should still be open in After Effects 7. If it's not, choose **File > Open Project**. Navigate to the **chap_19** folder you copied to your desktop, click **Audio_4.aep** to select it, and click **Open**.

---

2 Double-click **Motorcycle_Rotate** to open the composition, if it is not already visible.

---

3 In the **Timeline** panel, make sure the **Music.aif** layer is selected.

---

4 If the **Audio** panel is not already open, choose **Window > Audio**. Drag the **Master Volume Control** slider (the center slider) to **12.0 dB**, thereby increasing the overall levels of your audio.

The center slider is the Master Volume Control slider. It moves both the left and right channels equally from their current positions.

---

5 In the **Timeline** panel, notice the waveforms get larger when you increase the volume.

---

6 Press the **period** key on your numeric keypad to preview the audio.

---

7 In the **Audio** panel, watch the **VU meter** while the audio previews. Click the **Audio Clip Warning** icons to reset them to black.

Both the left and right channels are too loud, which has caused the Audio Clip Warning icons to turn red. You need to reset the icons to black; otherwise, they will stay lit.

Note: Previewing audio does not alter your original audio footage data. Volume settings affect only the preview and output of audio data. It is perfectly safe to preview your audio files with clipping. You will learn how to output a final audio file in Chapter 20, *"Rendering Final Movies."*

8 Drag the **right channel** slider to approximately **–1.0 dB**, which decreases the volume.

Note: You must have the audio layer selected, or you cannot adjust the channel slider.

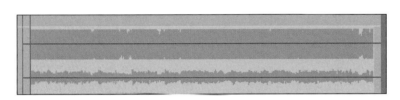

9 Notice the **right channel** waveform gets smaller as the volume decreases, which demonstrates the height of the waveforms corresponds to the volume levels.

10 Drag the **left channel** slider to approximately **0.0 dB**, which reduces the volume for that channel.

Tip: You can also click the Level Values field and type a number.

11 Press the **period** key on your numeric keypad to preview the audio. Both channels are set about as loud as possible without clipping.

12 Choose **File > Save**, or press **Cmd+S** (Mac) or **Ctrl+S** (Windows). Choose **File > Close Project**.

In this exercise, you learned to adjust volume levels for your audio in After Effects 7.

TIP:

Setting Volume Level Keyframes

You can set keyframes for the **Volume Level** controls. Click the **stopwatch** icon for **Audio Levels** to turn on keyframes for the **Volume Level** controls. This is useful if you want to fade sound in or out or animate a sound effect by increasing or decreasing its levels on separate keyframes.

You're all done with this short chapter on working with audio in After Effects 7. Next, you'll learn how to render and output your final movies, with both audio and video.

20

Rendering Final Movies

Throughout this book, you've learned how to preview your movies. This chapter focuses on outputting the final product of your movie. In After Effects 7, you can create many types of movie output from a single composition. For example, you can output a single composition to video, motion-picture film, CD, streaming Web video, GIF (**G**raphic **I**nterchange **F**ormat) animation, HDTV (**H**igh-**D**efinition **Tele**Vision), and so on. The variety of choices available is one of the great strengths of After Effects 7.

The process of outputting your project is called **rendering**. Just as an artist renders a painting, After Effects 7 follows your instructions and renders the final movie. After Effects 7 reads each pixel of your image and each audio signal, it renders them to the output type of your choice.

We saved this chapter until late in the book because it's a complicated subject. Although all the output choices After Effects 7 offers are wonderful, they also require careful explanation. Don't be intimidated, though; this is a necessary step in your After Effects 7 education, and you can always refer to this chapter if you get stuck on a future project.

Outputting to QuickTime Versus AVI/Video for Windows

If you use a Mac, you have likely heard of Apple QuickTime, and if you use Windows, you've probably heard of AVI/Video for Windows. When rendering movies, After Effects 7 defaults to producing QuickTime in its Mac version and AVI/Video for Windows in its Windows version.

It is possible to create movies in many formats using After Effects 7. In the first few exercises of this chapter, you will learn to create movies in your default file type—either QuickTime (Mac) or AVI/Video for Windows (Windows). After that, you'll learn to create movies using any file type. You'll find handy charts throughout this chapter to help you decide which file formats and settings to use for various types of projects.

Understanding Compression and Decompression

When you render a movie in After Effects 7, you are not only creating a final product but you are also creating settings for compression and decompression. The term for this in video production is **codec** (short for **co**mpression/**dec**ompression). Many settings affect the quality of your movies, such as dimensions, colors, and sound. The codec, however, deals specifically with how the video is rendered.

Some codecs compress the size of the movie to be small enough for Web delivery; other codecs are reserved for high-quality film production. Sometimes your client will tell you which codec to use, and sometimes you'll have to figure it out on your own. As a student of After Effects 7, however, you should conduct a lot of your own codec experimentation. Using a Sorenson codec produces better colors than a Cinepak codec, for example. If you want to get an in-depth education about compression, we suggest *QuickTime Compression Principles* by Sean Blumenthal, a video title published exclusively through the **lynda.com Online Training Library**. Visit **http://movielibrary.lynda.com/html/modPage.asp?ID=40** to learn more and watch free sample movies.

Exploring the Render Queue Panel

In this chapter, you'll work with a part of After Effects 7 you haven't learned about yet—the **Render Queue** panel. (The term **queue** means to wait your turn and is pronounced like the letter **Q**.) This panel offers feedback about how you are rendering your final movies. It's possible to render a single composition or to add multiple compositions to the **Render Queue** panel and have After Effects 7 render each composition in the order you specify.

The settings in the **Render Queue** panel do not affect your composition but instead affect how that composition will be published for use outside After Effects 7 (for video, digital video, the Web, and so on). As well, you can turn movies you import as footage items into an After Effects 7 project.

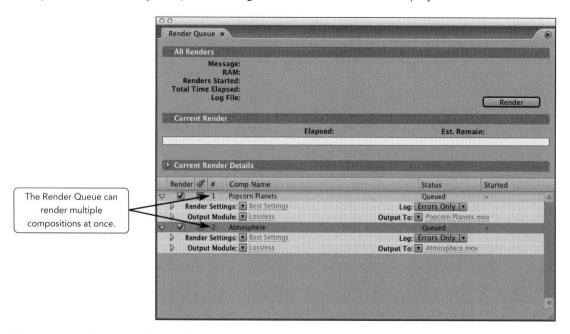

The Render Queue can render multiple compositions at once.

You can set each item in the **Render Queue** panel to the type of output you want. Because many output types are available and each output type has its own set of options, rendering is a fairly substantial subject for those with no experience in producing digital movies.

Sometimes, the best way to learn is by doing, so the hands-on exercises should help you through the learning curve. To begin, you'll learn how to render a single composition. Later in the chapter you'll learn how to render multiple compositions at once.

1 | Using the Render Queue Default Settings

Mac versions of After Effects 7 default to producing QuickTime movies; Windows versions default to producing AVI/Video movies. This exercise walks you through the basics of rendering a movie, using the program's default settings to output a final movie so it can be played outside After Effects 7. Later in this chapter, you'll learn about when and how to change these settings, but for now this exercise will give you the satisfaction of learning the basic rendering steps.

---

1 Copy the **chap_20** folder from the **After Effects 7 HOT DVD-ROM** onto your desktop.

---

2 Choose **File > Open Project**. Navigate to the **chap_20** folder you copied to your desktop, select the file named **Rendering.aep**, and click **Open**. Choose **File > Save As**. Navigate to the **AE7 HOT Projects** folder on your desktop, and click **Save**.

---

3 Double-click the **Popcorn Planets** composition to open it, and then preview the movie.

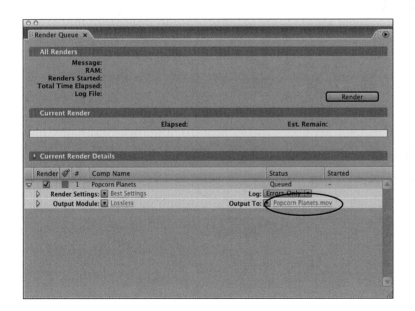

4 Choose **Composition > Make Movie** to open the **Render Queue** panel with the item **Popcorn Planets**. Notice all items in the **Render Queue** panel are set to **Queued** until rendered. Locate the **Output To** field, and click the underlined movie name. You will be prompted to save the movie. On a Mac, After Effects 7 prompts you to save this as **Popcorn Planets.mov** and on Windows as **Popcorn Planets.avi**. Navigate to the **AE7 HOT Projects** folder on your desktop, and click **Save**.

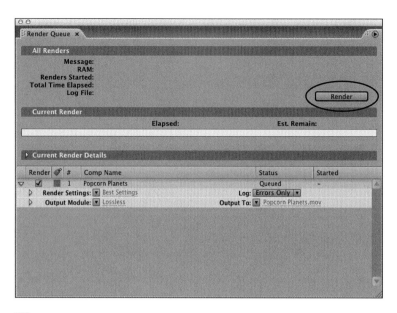

5 In the **Render Queue** panel, observe the available settings. For now, leave these settings as they are. Click the **Render** button.

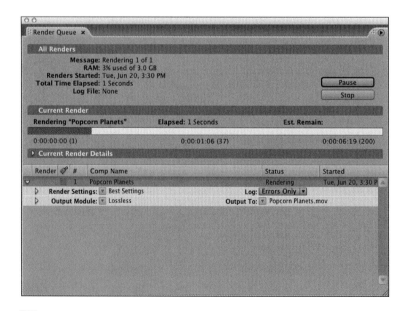

6 In the **Render Queue** panel, notice the **Current Render** status bar becomes active, along with messages showing the elapsed time, the estimated time remaining, and the other information about the rendering process.

This feedback shows you After Effects 7 is rendering the movie!

7 When After Effects 7 has finished rendering the movie, you'll hear a chime, if your sound is turned on. After hearing the sound, locate your **Popcorn Planets.mov** or **Popcorn Planets.avi** movie, and double-click it to open it in QuickTime or Windows Media Player. Click the **Play** button to view the movie.

8 When you're finished watching the movie, return to After Effects 7. In the **Render Queue** panel, select **Popcorn Planets**, and press **Delete** to delete the rendered composition in the **Render Queue** panel. Close the **Render Queue** panel.

Tip: Alternatively, you can delete this composition in the queue by choosing Edit > Clear.

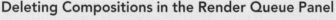

9 Choose **File > Save**, or press **Cmd+S** (Mac) or **Ctrl+S** (Windows). Close the **Popcorn Planets** composition. Leave **Rendering.aep** open for the next exercise.

NOTE:

Deleting Compositions in the Render Queue Panel

It's not necessary to delete the composition in the **Render Queue** panel. We suggested this only because After Effects 7 does not automatically delete compositions for you. It leaves rendered compositions displayed in the queue in the event you need to check the settings or statistics for that render. It's up to you to delete rendered compositions if and when you no longer need to refer to them. It can be confusing to see rendered and unrendered compositions in the same panel. Rendered compositions will not be rendered again, even if you leave them in the queue.

TIP:

Closing the Composition Panel

Although you can view the results in the **Composition** panel while rendering is in progress, this slows down the rendering. Before starting your render, close the **Composition** panel to make the rendering go as fast as possible.

2 | Changing the Render Settings

The settings in the **Render Queue** panel are at the heart of outputting final movies. In this exercise, you'll learn to change some of these settings. The focus will be on making a low-resolution test movie. Many After Effects 7 professionals render movies at small sizes to test their work before outputting a final movie at high-resolution settings. "The Render Settings Dialog Box" chart at the end of this exercise outlines the scope of all the settings and indicates when you should use each one.

1 If you followed the previous exercise, **Rendering.aep** should still be open in After Effects 7. If it's not, choose **File > Open Project**. Navigate to the **chap_20** folder you copied to your desktop, click **Rendering.aep** to select it, and click **Open**.

2 In the **Project** panel, select (but do not open) the **Atmosphere** composition.

3 Choose **Composition > Make Movie**, or press **Cmd+M** (Mac) or **Ctrl+M** (Windows) to open the **Render Queue** panel. In the **Output To** field, click the underlined movie name. You will be prompted to save the movie. On a Mac, After Effects 7 prompts you to save this as **Atmosphere.mov** and on Windows as **Atmosphere.avi**. Navigate to the **AE7 HOT Projects** folder on your desktop, and click **Save**. Choose **File > Save** or press **Cmd+S** (Mac) or **Ctrl+S** (Windows), and save the movie in the **AE7 HOT Projects** folder.

Feel free to open and preview the Atmosphere composition before you render it. However, remember to close the composition before rendering because it takes longer to render an open composition.

4 Click the underlined words **Best Settings** in the **Render Queue** panel to open the **Render Settings** dialog box.

5 In the **Render Settings** dialog box, notice the three groups of settings: **Composition "Atmosphere"**, **Time Sampling**, and **Options**.

To read about these choices, check out the chart at the end of this exercise.

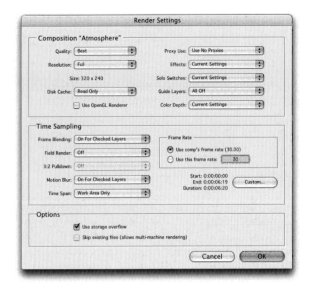

6 In the **Composition "Atmosphere"** section, click the **Quality** pop-up menu, and choose **Draft**.

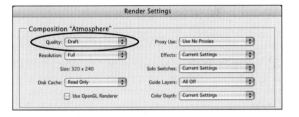

You'll generally use Best quality for final output and Draft quality when you need to do a test movie and don't want to wait for Best quality to render. Wireframe quality will render wireframe outlines of each layer; it is extremely quick but lacks detail.

These are the same settings available in the Quality switch in the composition's Timeline panel. The default is Current Settings, which pulls the setting used in your composition. Therefore, if your composition's Quality switch is set to Best, Current Settings will use that setting, and you don't have to make a change here.

7 In the **Composition "Atmosphere"** section, click the **Resolution** pop-up menu, and choose **Half**. After you make this change, notice **Size** indicates the original composition size, with the half size shown in parentheses.

The Resolution default is Current Settings, which uses the resolution you set for your composition. You would generally choose a smaller size for your resolution when you are making test movies in order to speed up the rendering time and to get a quick sense of what your movie will look like.

8 In the **Time Sampling** section, click the **Time Span** pop-up menu, and choose **Length of Comp**. Click **OK** to close the **Render Settings** dialog box.

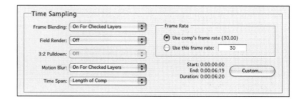

The Time Span setting is an important option. The default is Work Area Only. You learned to set the work area in Chapter 7, *"Previewing Movies."* However, in most cases you'll probably want to output the entire composition. For this reason, you should make it a habit to check this option each time you set up a composition to be rendered.

---

9 In the **Render Queue** panel, click the **Render** button.

---

10 When After Effects 7 is finished rendering, locate the **Atmosphere.mov** (Mac) or **Atmosphere.avi** (Windows) movie, and double-click the file name to open it. Click the **Play** button to view the results.

---

11 In the **Render Queue** panel, select the **Atmosphere** composition, and press **Delete** (or choose **Edit > Clear**) to remove it from the queue.

---

12 Choose **File > Save**, or press **Cmd+S** (Mac) or **Ctrl+S** (Windows). Leave **Rendering.aep** open for the next exercise.

In this exercise, you learned how to set some render settings. The chart on the next page explores the Render Settings dialog box.

The Render Settings Dialog Box

Setting	Description
Composition settings	
Quality	You have the following options: **Current Settings**, **Best**, **Draft**, and **Wireframe**. **Best** quality takes the longest to render; use it for final output. Use **Draft** quality for rendering test movies, when the speed of rendering is more important than quality. **Wireframe** quality renders only wireframe outlines of each layer. It is extremely quick but lacks detail. **Current Settings**, the default, uses the **Quality** setting in your composition.
Resolution	You have the following options: **Current Settings**, **Full**, **Half**, **Third**, **Quarter**, and **Custom**. These terms relate to the original size setting in the composition being rendered. When you choose one of the sizes, the **Size** field displays the dimensions in pixels. The **Custom** setting allows you to type your own settings. After Effects 7 artists generally pick smaller resolution settings when they want the movie to render faster because it takes less time to render a lower-resolution movie.
Proxy Use	You have the following options: **Current Settings**, **Use All Proxies**, **Use Comp Proxies Only**, and **Use No Proxies**. **Proxies** are an advanced feature allowing you to set up dummy footage you can later swap with real footage. Professionals often use proxies as a faster method of creating high-resolution movies. The idea is you make a low-resolution "understudy" of your footage, and once you're happy with how everything looks, you replace the proxy footage with the final footage. To learn more about proxies, refer to the After Effects 7 manual.
Effects	You have the following options: **Current Settings**, **All On**, and **All Off**. **Current Settings** uses the effects you have active in your composition. You can also choose to render with all effects on or with all effects off (overriding the composition settings). Movies render more quickly with effects off, so consider using **All Off** if you need to speed up rendering.
Solo Switches	You have the following options: **Current Settings** and **All Off**. This setting determines whether solo layers are rendered. **Current Settings** leaves all **Solo** switches as they currently are on your layers. This option renders all layers regardless of the status of their **Solo** switch, unless layer visibility is turned off. **All Off** makes all **Solo** switches behave as if they are off.
Guide Layers	You have the following options: **Current Settings** and **All Off**. This setting determines whether guide layers are rendered. Choose **Current Settings** to render guide layers in the current composition or **All Off** (the default setting) to not render guide layers. (Guide layers in nested compositions are never rendered.)
Color Depth	You have the following options: **Current Settings**, **8 bits per channel**, **16 bits per channel**, and **32 bits per channel**. **Current Settings** (the default) uses the project bit depth to render the composition, but you can override it by choosing another setting.

continues on next page

The Render Settings Dialog Box *continued*

Setting	Description
Time sampling settings	
Frame Blending	You have the following options: **Current Settings**, **On For Checked Layers**, and **Off For All Layers**. You can use frame blending only on moving footage, and you set it in the **Switches** area of the **Timeline** panel. It creates an effect of a cross dissolve (one image fading out while another image fades in) and is usually used in time-stretched footage. To learn more about frame blending and time stretching, refer to Chapter 8, *"Working with Layers,"* or the After Effects 7 user manual.
Field Render	You have the following options: **Off**, **Upper Field First**, and **Lower Field First**. You can use **Field Rendering** only in video projects, not for film or the Web, because it deals with video fields that are present only in video footage and output. Use this option if you are outputting to NTSC or PAL video, for example. Before you can accurately set this option, you will need to know whether your video hardware (camera and recording deck) uses upper field first or lower field first. If you are not outputting to video, leave this option set to **Off**.
Motion Blur	You have the following options: **Current Settings**, **On For Checked Layers**, and **Off For All Layers**. The **Motion Blur** setting defines how you want to treat motion blur in the rendered output. You must turn on **Motion Blur** in the **Switches** panel of the **Timeline**. You learned about this panel in Chapter 8, *"Working with Layers."*
Time Span	You have the following options: **Length of Comp**, **Work Area Only**, and **Custom**. The default time span is **Work Area Only**. You learned to set the work area in Chapter 7, *"Previewing Movies."* You will usually want to set this to **Length of Comp** to output the entire composition. The **Custom** setting allows you to specify time spans that aren't tied to the length of the composition or the work area.
Frame Rate	You have the following options: **Use comp's frame rate** and **Use this frame rate**. You can choose to use the composition's frame rate or set a different frame rate. Sometimes you'll choose to increase or decrease the frame rate of your movie to save rendering time or disk space.
Options settings	
Use storage overflow	If your hard drive fills up before the render is complete, this option, when selected, will use another hard drive that you specify as the overflow volume. To specify overflow volumes, choose **Edit > Preferences > Output**.

3 | Working with the Output Module

In the previous exercise, you worked with the settings in the **Render Queue** panel. This time, you'll learn to work with the **Output Module**, which is also located in the **Render Queue** panel. Here you'll learn to choose a format and set the various format options based on the needs of your movie. Although many of the settings remain as is for this exercise, you'll learn how to use these settings for other movies as well.

---

1 If you followed the previous exercise, **Rendering.aep** should still be open in After Effects 7. If it's not, choose **File > Open Project**. Navigate to the **AE7 HOT Projects** folder you copied to your desktop, click **Rendering.aep** to select it, and click **Open**.

---

2 In the **Project** panel, select (but do not open) the **3D Text** composition.

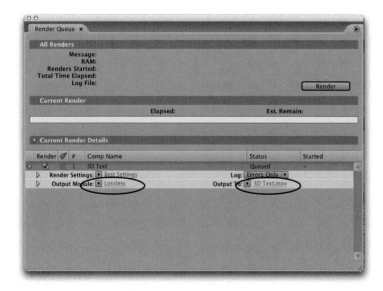

3 Choose **Composition > Make Movie**, or press **Cmd+M** (Mac) or **Ctrl+M** (Windows) to open the **Render Queue** panel. In the **Output To** field, click the underlined movie name. Navigate to the **AE7 HOT Projects** folder on your desktop, and click **Save**. Locate the **Output Module** field, and click the underlined word **Lossless** to open the **Output Module Settings** dialog box.

In the next section, you will find a chart listing the features in this dialog box. For now, you'll learn to change the settings appropriate to the movie in this exercise.

---

4 In the **Output Module Settings** dialog box, click the **Format** pop-up menu, and observe the available output formats. From the **Format** pop-up menu, choose **QuickTime Movie**.

QuickTime Movie is the default format on a Mac; AVI/Video for Windows is the default format in Windows. The "Output Format Types" chart in the following section explains the format types and their uses.

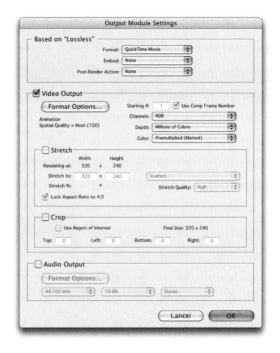

5 In the **Output Module Settings** dialog box, click the **Embed** pop-up menu, observe the available options, and then choose **None** to leave the selection set to **None**.

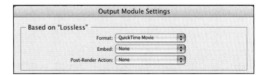

If you are working with other Adobe products, such as Adobe Premiere Pro, you can use the Embed option to create a link to the original After Effects 7 project. The Project Link option embeds a link only. The Project Link and Copy option embeds a link and a copy of the project in the output file. When you use an embedded output file in Premiere Pro, you can use the Edit Original command to easily reopen the project in After Effects 7.

6 In the **Video Output** section of the **Output Module Settings** dialog box, click the **Format Options** button to open the **Compression Settings** dialog box.

If you select a format other than QuickTime, you'll see additional options. After Effects 7 does a great job of providing the appropriate options for all the supported formats.

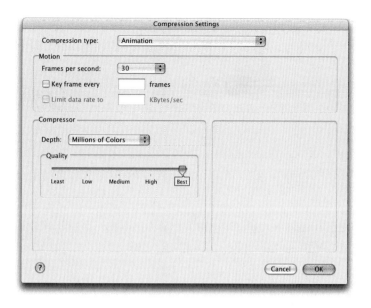

7 In the **Compression Settings** dialog box, click the **Compression type** pop-up menu, and choose **Animation**. Observe all the available compressor types. For this exercise, leave the compressor type set to **Animation**.

The Animation setting represents the Animation compressor. The Animation compressor preserves high-quality visuals, but it can also result in large files, which aren't suitable for certain kinds of output, such as the Web. The "QuickTime Compressors" chart later in this chapter explains all the compressor types and their uses.

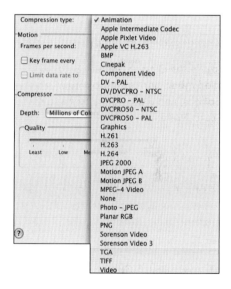

8 In the **Compression Settings** dialog box, observe the **Motion** section. These options allow you to set the number of frames per second, add a QuickTime key frame, and, for streaming video, limit the data rate. For this exercise, leave these settings as they are.

A key frame in QuickTime sets a reference for the compressor. Reference frames are not highly compressed. The more QuickTime key frames you set, the larger your output file.

Note: Keyframes in After Effects 7 are different from key frames in QuickTime.

9 In the **Compressor** section of the **Compression Settings** dialog box, click the **Depth** pop-up menu, and observe all the depth options available. For now, leave the menu set to **Millions of Colors**.

10 In the **Compressor** section of the **Compression Settings** dialog box, drag the **Quality** slider to **High**. Click **OK** when you are done making your settings.

The Animation compressor offers a full range of quality. Best quality results in lossless output, which means you won't lose any image quality. Least quality will probably show image degradation because of the compression. Other compressors may or may not offer a range of quality settings as an option.

11 In the **Video Output** section of the **Output Module Settings** dialog box, click the **Channels** pop-up menu. Notice you can choose **RGB**, **Alpha**, or **RGB + Alpha** for your output. For this exercise, choose **RGB**.

This is the most common setting. If you wanted to export a mask or a movie with a mask, you would choose one of the other settings. You'll get a chance to do this later in this chapter.

12 In the **Video Output** section of the **Output Module Settings** dialog box, click the **Depth** pop-up menu, and notice the color bit depth is set to **Millions of Colors**. Again, leave this menu set to **Millions of Colors**.

This setting is identical to the Colors setting under Format Options. If you change the setting in either place, they both change.

13 In the **Video Output** section of the **Output Module Settings** dialog box, click the **Color** setting, and notice the choices of **Straight (Unmatted)** and **Premultiplied (Matted)**. For this exercise, leave the menu set to **Premultiplied (Matted)**.

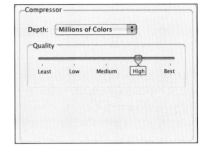

A straight alpha channel is sometimes known as an **unmatted alpha**. With a straight alpha channel, the effects of transparency are not visible until the image is displayed in an application supporting straight alpha. Many 3D programs support straight alpha channels.

Many times, you will want a premultiplied alpha, also known as a **matted alpha**, with a background color. The colors of semitransparent areas, such as feathered edges, are shifted toward the background color in proportion to their degree of transparency. For most purposes, you'll use the Premultiplied option.

14 In the **Stretch** section of the **Output Module Settings** dialog box, observe the various options. For this exercise, leave the **Stretch** options as is.

If you needed to stretch your output to a larger size, you would do it here by turning on the Stretch check box and typing the size you wanted.

Stretching in After Effects 7 scales the movie to be larger or smaller, depending on the values you type. It is not recommended that you stretch your final output because this severely degrades the image quality. If you have to provide a larger output than anticipated for your project, and you must use the Stretch options, be sure to choose High from the Stretch Quality pop-up menu. In general, avoid using the Stretch options, if at all possible.

15 In the **Crop** section of the **Output Module Settings** dialog box, observe the various options. For this exercise, leave the **Crop** options untouched.

If you needed to crop pixels off any side of your composition, you would do it here by turning on the Crop check box and typing the number of pixels you want to crop. For example, typing 10 in each box removes 10 pixels from each side of the output.

16 Observe the options for the **Audio Output** section in the **Output Module Settings** dialog box. In this exercise, leave the **Audio** options untouched. Click **OK** to complete the **Output Module** settings for your render.

If you needed to output audio in your QuickTime movie, you would specify it here by turning on the Audio Output check box and selecting the appropriate options.

You will learn how to use the audio output options in the next exercise.

17 In the **Render Queue** panel, click the **Render** button.

This composition is fairly complex and takes a few minutes to render. Watch the estimated time remaining, and take a short break if you'd like while the rendering completes.

18 When the rendering completes, double-click the saved QuickTime movie to play it in the QuickTime player.

---

19 In the **Render Queue** panel, select the **3D Text** comp name, and press **Delete** (or select **Edit > Clear**) to delete the rendered composition in the **Render Queue** panel.

---

20 Choose **File > Save**, or press **Cmd+S** (Mac) or **Ctrl+S** (Windows). Leave **Rendering.aep** open for the next exercise.

Exploring the Output Module Settings Dialog Box

You worked with the **Output Module** in the previous exercise. This module is an important part of After Effects 7. It is where you choose the type of format you want to output and the options for the format type. For example, you can choose to output a sequence of TIFF (**T**ag **I**mage **F**ile **F**ormat) images, a QuickTime movie, or an animated GIF file, to name just a few of the format choices.

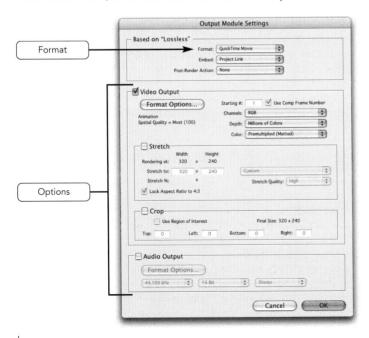

The following chart describes the numerous features in this important dialog box:

\ Output Module Settings Dialog Box	
Setting	**Description**
Format settings	
Format	This allows you to choose the format for your movie. See the following "Output Format Types" chart for a description of the available formats.
Embed	This allows you to set your movie so it can be opened using **Edit Original** in programs that support this feature, such as Premiere Pro. This allows you to launch an After Effects 7 movie from within Premiere Pro by double-clicking the movie file. Any changes made to the movie in After Effects 7 will appear in the Premiere Pro project.
Post-Render Action	The **Import into Project When Done** setting causes the finished movie to be imported into the current project when it's finished rendering.
Video output settings	
Format Options	This opens another dialog box that lets you specify format-specific options. For example, QuickTime will have different options from TIFF.
Channels	This allows you to set how many channels your movie will have. Most movies are rendered in RGB, although you can also render in **RGB + Alpha**, which stores the movie and an alpha channel.
Depth	This sets the bit depth of the movie. This option controls whether the movie is in grayscale, in color, or in color with an alpha channel.
Color	This specifies how colors are treated in the alpha channel. The options are **Straight (Unmatted)** and **Premultiplied (Matted)**. You'll use the **Premultiplied** option for most purposes. We discussed these options in Chapter 11, *"Parenting Layers."*
Stretch	This group of options specifies the dimensions of your final movie. If you enter dimensions that differ from the composition settings, you can choose to do so at **Low** or **High** quality.
Crop	This determines how many pixels to **crop**, or trim, from your rendered movie.
Audio output settings	
Format Options	This opens a **Sound Settings** dialog box, which lets you specify options for your movie's audio. Options in the **Sound Settings** dialog box include **Compressor, Rate, Size,** and **Use.** Apart from **Compressor,** the other options are available directly from the pop-up menus in the **Audio Output** section of the **Output Module Settings** dialog box.

The following chart describes the format choices in the **Format** pop-up menu:

Output Format Types	
Format	**Use**
Animated GIF	This is a popular Web file format, often used for Web banners, cartoons, buttons, and simple animated graphics.
BMP Sequence	This is the Microsoft Windows bitmap format.
Cineon Sequence	Kodak developed the Cineon file format, which is the standard file format used for professional motion-picture visual effects.
ElectricImage IMAGE	Electric Image is a 3D animation package. You can use IMAGE files as texture maps or cards within Electric Image.
FLC/FLI	Autodesk designed the "Flic" animation format for Autodesk Animator and Autodesk Animator Pro.
Filmstrip	This is the Adobe Photoshop filmstrip format developed to contain a series of animated images for importing into Photoshop. This single file can contain many images.
IFF Sequence	Electronic Arts created the IFF (Interchange File Format) to make transferring files between different systems easier. Currently, software such as Autodesk Maya produces IFF files.
JPEG Sequence	JPEG is the popular Web file format used for continuous-tone images such as photographs. Use this format if you need to output a single image or group of images to the Web.
MP3	MP3 is an audio file format used extensively on the Web and in personal audio players.
OMF	You can use the OMF (Open Media Framework) format to create special media files for Avid systems.
OpenEXR Sequence	This 32-bits-per-channel format (floating point), released by ILM (Industrial Light & Magic), supports the exchange of image files with extremely high dynamic ranges, which are ideal for film and special-effects work.
PCX Sequence	This is the PC Paintbrush format. You might choose this format if you need to get a sequence of images from After Effects 7 into another program that supports PCX.
PICT Sequence	PICT is a Mac image file format. You might choose this format if you need to get a sequence of images from After Effects 7 into another program that supports PICT.

continues on next page

Output Format Types *continued*

Format	Use
PNG Sequence	PNG is a cross-platform image file format utilizing lossless compression. Images can include an alpha channel. It is a public domain format used to transport images between computers or to store images with good compression. You might choose this format if you needed to get a sequence of images from After Effects 7 into another program that supports PNG.
Photoshop Sequence	Use this format to output a single file or a sequence of images to Photoshop.
Pixar Sequence	The Pixar format is sometimes used in professional motion-picture and television work with proprietary software applications. You might choose this format if you needed to get a sequence of images from After Effects 7 into another program that supports Pixar.
QuickTime Movie	The QuickTime format is a cross-platform standard for distributing movies. QuickTime is a container file that holds various types of audio, moving pictures, Web links, and other data. This is probably the most useful format for digital artists working in After Effects 7.
Radiance Sequence	This is another high dynamic range image format, which preserves 32-bits-per-channel (floating-point) information.
SGI Sequence	SGI (**S**ilicon **G**raphics **I**ncorporated) computer workstations use this format. It is usually used only by scientific or visual-effects facilities.
TIFF Sequence	IFF is a cross-platform image file format used for lossless compression. Images can include an alpha channel. Use this format to transport images between computers or to store images with fairly good compression.
Targa Sequence	Targa is an image file format used on PCs that have Targa hardware. It has also been widely used for scanners and imaging software.
Video For Windows	This was originally developed as an alternative to QuickTime and is a common video format for Windows computers.
WAV	This file format is the de facto, uncompressed audio format utilized by Windows computers, although it is playable on Mac as well.
Windows Media	Microsoft developed this video codec, which has become a standard of the Windows operating system.

The following chart describes many of the compressor types available in the **Compression Settings** dialog box:

QuickTime Compressors	
Compressor	**Use**
Animation	Use this compressor when you have large areas of solid color, such as cartoons or graphics. The size will be large, and it is best for film or video projects, not the Web or CDs.
Apple Intermediate Codec	This is a special codec developed by Apple to edit video originating on the HDV format.
Apple Pixlet Video	Apple and Pixar designed this to be a high-quality editing format.
BMP	BMP is a Windows image file format with medium-quality compression. Use this compressor to transport images between computers.
Cinepak	Use this option to compress 24-bit movies intended for CDs.
Component Video	You can use this compressor to output through an analog video card, if your computer has one.
DV/DVCPRO - NTSC	Use this codec to transfer digital video to an external digital video recorder. NTSC is the standard used in North America.
DV - PAL	Use this codec to transfer digital video to an external digital video recorder. PAL is the standard used in most of Europe.
Graphics	The **Graphics** compressor creates 8-bit images and is intended primarily for still images.
H.261 & H.263	These codecs were developed for videoconferencing. You can use H.263 for streaming Web video as well.
H.264	This is a highly efficient and scalable video codec, related to MPEG-4, which is currently popular for delivering video on the Web and on high-definition formats.
HDV 1080i50, HDV 1080i60, HDV 720p30	HDV (**H**igh-**D**efinition **V**ideo) formats are a popular consumer and professional format for capturing and delivering HDV. Utilizing a form of MPEG-2 compression, HDV is able to store high-definition images using the same amount of space necessary for the SDV (**S**tandard **D**efinition **V**ideo) format. You can choose between 1080 interlaced and 720 progressive line formats, as well as between NTSC and PAL frame rates.
Motion JPEG A, Motion JPEG B	These compressors are useful for creating video files that work with **Motion JPEG** hardware such as capture and playback cards.

continues on next page

QuickTime Compressors *continued*	
Compressor	**Use**
None	This selection means no compression will be applied. Selecting this results in large, lossless files.
Photo–JPEG	This compression scheme is intended for images containing gradual color changes. It offers a range of quality settings.
Planar RGB	This lossless compression scheme is intended for large areas of solid color. Use as an alternative to the **Animation** compressor.
PNG	PNG is a cross-platform image file format utilizing lossless compression. Images can include an alpha channel. Use this compressor to transport images between computers.
Sorenson Video	This is useful for compressing 24-bit movies to be used as streaming video on the Web. You can also use it to compress movies for CDs. It produces better picture quality and smaller files than Cinepak.
Sorenson Video 3	This is a video codec often used for delivering high-quality video on the Web and CD/DVD. This has improved video quality and performance over the earlier Sorenson Video codec.
TGA	TGA is for use with Targa hardware.
TIFF	TIFF is a cross-platform image file format used for lossless compression. Images can include an alpha channel. Use this compressor to transport images between computers.
Video	This compressor is useful for capturing analog video. It supports both spatial and temporal compression of 16-bit movies with fairly high quality. Use it as an alternative to the **Component Video** compressor.

EXERCISE

4 | Rendering Audio

Just as you can use various image compression schemes, you can also use audio compression to output audio files. In this exercise, you will learn to select audio compression and render audio.

1 If you followed the previous exercise, **Rendering.aep** should still be open in After Effects 7. If it's not, choose **File > Open Project**. Navigate to the **AE7 HOT Projects** folder you copied to your desktop, click **Rendering.aep** to select it, and click **Open**.

2 In the **Project** panel, select (but don't open) the **Orbit Down** composition.

3 Choose **Composition > Add To Render Queue**, or press **Cmd+Shift+/** (Mac) or **Ctrl+Shift+/** (Windows).

Note: The Add To Render Queue command is another way to begin making a movie. You'll probably use it often because you can simultaneously add multiple compositions to the queue this way. In this example, however, we're showing it simply as an alternative method to the Make Movie command you used in previous exercises.

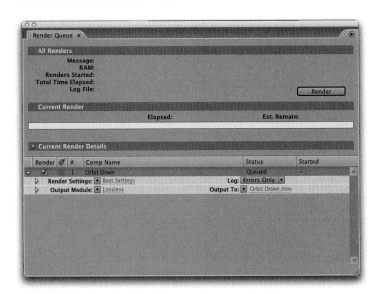

4 In the **Render Queue** panel, click the underlined word **Lossless**.

5 In the **Output Module Settings** dialog box, make sure the **Format** pop-up menu is set to **QuickTime Movie**. Turn on the **Audio Output** check box, and then click the **Format Options** button.

QuickTime is one of the few formats that can include audio.

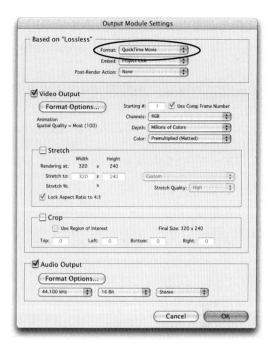

6 In the **Sound Settings** dialog box, click the **Compressor** pop-up menu, choose **MACE 6:1**, and then click **OK**.

See the "QuickTime Compressors" chart previously in this chapter for information about each audio compressor type. You're choosing MACE 6:1 here because it is a good all-purpose audio compression choice.

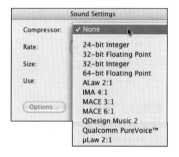
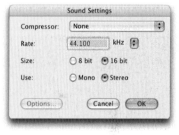

7 Accept the default **Rate**, **Size**, and **Use** options, and click **OK** in the **Output Module Settings** dialog box.

Rate specifies the audio sample rate in kilohertz; the higher the sample rate, the better the quality. You'll generally use high-quality settings if the movie is for broadcast video. You'll use lower-quality audio sample rates when the file size is a concern, such as for Web, multimedia, or DVD output.

You can choose a variety of standard sample rates from the pop-up menu. The Size option refers to the bit depth. Just as images can have 8 bits or 16 bits per channel, audio channels come in 8 bits and 16 bits. A high bit rate sounds better but results in a larger file size. The Use option allows you to specify Mono for one audio channel or Stereo for two audio channels.

8 In the **Render Queue** panel, click the **Render** button.

---

9 When your movie finishes rendering, play the movie in the QuickTime player. You should hear audio when it plays!

---

10 In the **Render Queue** panel, select the **Orbit Down** composition name, and press **Delete** (or choose **Edit > Clear**) to delete the rendered composition in the **Render Queue** panel.

---

11 Choose **File > Save**, or press **Cmd+S** (Mac) or **Ctrl+S** (Windows). Leave **Rendering.aep** open for the next exercise.

---

5 | Saving Alpha Channels or Motion Masks

Sometimes it's useful to output only the alpha channel for a composition. Perhaps you want to import some type you designed in After Effects 7 into another program, such as Apple Final Cut Pro or Premiere Pro. Those programs will honor the alpha channel output by After Effects 7. In addition, many 3D programs use alpha channel information from QuickTime movies to create interesting texture effects. You can even import the finished movie into After Effects 7, and it will honor the alpha channel. In this exercise, you will learn to output only the alpha channel of a composition.

1 If you followed the previous exercise, **Rendering.aep** should still be open in After Effects 7. If it's not, choose **File > Open Project**. Navigate to the **AE7 HOT Projects** folder you copied to your desktop, click **Rendering.aep** to select it, and click **Open**.

2 In the **Project** panel, double-click the **Alpha Mask** composition to open it.

3 Click **RAM Preview** to preview the animation in color. Notice the color circles have feathered edges. When you're done observing, close the **Composition** panel.

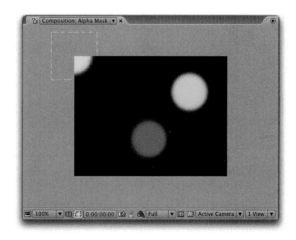

We created all the circles and edges in After Effects 7 as solid layers, and we used mask settings with feathering to create the shapes. Whenever you create masks in this way in After Effects 7, the program creates an alpha channel for the composition.

Tip: Remember, rendering is faster with the Composition panel closed.

4 Choose **Composition > Make Movie**, or press **Cmd+M** (Mac) or **Ctrl+M** (Windows) to open the **Render Queue** panel. In the **Output To** field, click the underlined **Alpha Mask.mov** (Mac) or **Alpha Mask.avi** (Windows) name. Navigate to the **AE7 HOT Projects** folder, and click **Save**.

5 In the **Render Queue** panel, click the underlined word **Lossless** next to **Output Module**.

6 In the **Output Module Settings** dialog box, make sure **QuickTime Movie** is selected for **Format**. Click the **Channels** pop-up menu, and choose **RGB + Alpha**. Accept all the other default settings, and click **OK**.

Choosing RGB + Alpha tells After Effects 7 you want to make a movie with an alpha channel.

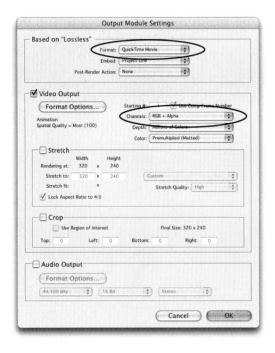

7 In the **Render Queue** panel, click the **Render** button.

8 When After Effects 7 has rendered the movie, open the **AE7 HOT Projects** folder, and then locate and play the movie in the QuickTime player.

This movie looks like a normal movie, identical to what you saw in the Composition panel. The difference occurs when you combine this with another movie by importing it into an After Effects 7 composition or into another program, such as Final Cut Pro or Premiere Pro. When you do that, all the black areas will become transparent, and the three colored circles will float on top of the other content with the feathered edges preserved. You'll get to import this movie file into After Effects 7 soon to see what we mean.

9 Return to After Effects 7. In the **Render Queue** panel, select the **Alpha Mask** composition name, and press **Delete** or choose **Edit > Clear** to delete the rendered composition in the **Render Queue** panel. Close the **Render Queue** panel.

10 Double-click the **Project** panel to open the **Import File** dialog box. Navigate to the **AE7 HOT Projects** folder, and import the **Alpha Mask.mov** movie you just rendered.

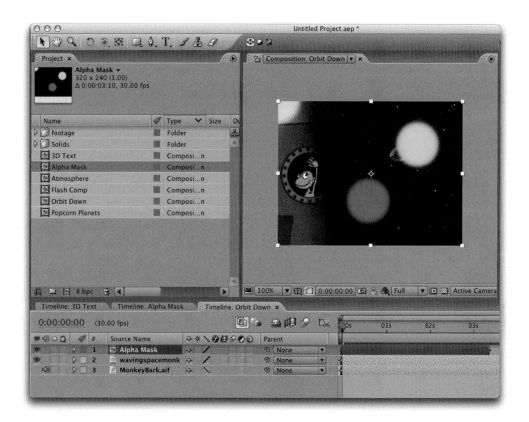

11 In the **Project** panel, double-click the **Orbit Down** composition to open it. Select and drag the **Alpha Mask** movie file to the **Composition** panel. Make sure it is positioned above the other layers—it should appear first, as shown in the illustration here. Press the **RAM Preview** button to preview the composition.

Notice the circles appear to float over the rest of the layers. That's because you rendered the movie with its alpha channel, and the circles are masked as a result. During the course of this book, you've worked with lots of movie files in various compositions created for you. This is how we did that—by rendering the alpha channel.

Sometimes you'll want to render a movie for a layer element instead of for a final output element, as you did in this exercise. Doing so makes sense when you have a lot of layers and your composition is getting bogged down trying to render everything at once.

---

12 Choose **File > Save**, or press **Cmd+S** (Mac) or **Ctrl+S** (Windows). Close the **Orbit Down** composition. Leave **Rendering.aep** open for the next exercise.

Viewing the Alpha Channel of a Composition

When you want to render a movie with an alpha channel, you first have to know whether the composition contains an alpha channel. As described in previous chapters, it's easy to import artwork into After Effects 7 from Photoshop or Adobe Illustrator and preserve the transparency. When you render a composition, however, you are rendering all the layers in your composition. Some layers might have transparency, and some might not. For this reason, it becomes important to know what the alpha channel of the composition looks like before you choose to render a composition with it.

When you open the **Alpha Mask** composition from the **Rendering.aep** project you just worked with, you can't tell right away whether the composition contains an alpha channel. You might be wondering, as you progress to creating your own projects, how you'll know whether a composition contains an alpha channel.

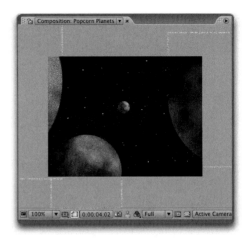

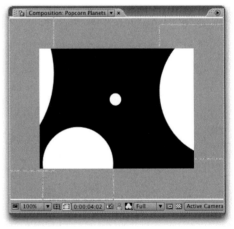

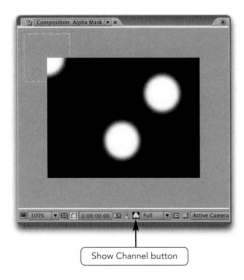

Show Channel button

Every **Composition** panel has a red, green, and blue button called the **Show Channel** button. To see the alpha channel, click the **Show Channel** button, and choose **Alpha**. The other selections allow you to view the R, G, and B channels. You might want to open some of the other compositions in this project and click those buttons to explore their capabilities.

The majority of the compositions in the **Rendering.aep** project you are working with in this chapter show a solid white alpha channel. That's because they use images as backgrounds that take up the entire screen, so the alpha channels for the composition look completely white. Try turning off background layers (which are shown in the illustration above on the top, and you'll see shapes emerge in the alpha channel (as shown in the second illustration above).

For example, open the **Popcorn Planet** composition, click the **Show Channel** button, and choose **Alpha**. The entire composition turns white. If you turn off the last layer in this composition (**space_backdrop.psd**) and click the **Show Channel** button again, you'll see the shapes of the planets appear in white. Before you turned off the last layer, it was showing the alpha channel for the background layer.

If you wanted to put these planets over some live action, you would need to turn the background layer off and render the composition with its alpha channel, as you learned to do in the previous exercise. You could then import the movie into

After Effects 7, where the planets would composite perfectly over the other layers you imported into the composition. Likewise, you could take this movie to Premiere Pro or Final Cut Pro, and the planets would mask over other footage.

In general, you'll use the white areas of the alpha channel to reveal the image in the document and the black areas to mask that image.

Rendering for the Web

Once you get into After Effects 7, you might decide you want to put a portfolio of your work on the Web. Although we haven't included a hands-on exercise to show how to do this, this section covers some of the important issues related to Web delivery.

When creating for the Web, you should work with the QuickTime format because it has more Web-savvy features than the AVI format. In the **Output Module Settings** dialog box, make sure the **Format** pop-menu is **QuickTime Movie**, and click the **Format Options** button.

In the **Compression Settings** dialog box, for the **Compressor** type, choose **Sorenson Video**, which is the best choice for compressing 24-bit movies as streaming video.

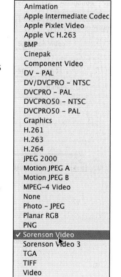

The lower the quality, the smaller the file will be.

Next, experiment with the **Quality** setting. You can also change the frame rate to make smaller Web movies. (Recall that key frames in QuickTime are

different from keyframes in After Effects 7.) Adobe recommends a 3:1 formula to come up with a key frame rate. For example, if you choose a frame rate of 15, multiply it by 3, for a value of 45. To use 45 as the key frame rate, turn on the **Use this frame rate** check box, and type **45** for the value.

The data rate varies depending on the speed of your user's system. Sample data rates are 28 KB modem = 2.5 Kbps, 56 KB modem = 4.0 Kbps, ISDN = 12 Kbps, and T1 = 20 Kbps. These days, most people browsing the Web have some form of high-speed Internet access, so you can use the higher-quality settings.

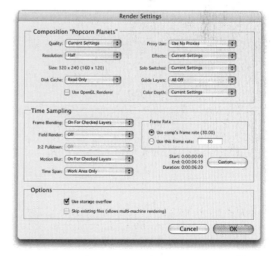

You might also want to set your resolution to **Half**, **Third**, or **Quarter**. Every bit of savings you can eke out of the file will save your users precious downloading time.

Getting the Needed HTML for QuickTime Movies

After Effects 7 doesn't write HTML (**H**yper**T**ext **M**arkup **L**anguage), as some other Adobe products do. Therefore, it's up to you to write this code. The following is the HTML code used to put QuickTime movies on a Web site:

```
<embed src="yourmovienamehere.mov" width="640" height="496" autoplay="true"
loop="true" controller="true" playeveryframe="false" cache="false"
bgcolor="#FFFFFF" kioskmode="false" targetcache="false"
pluginspage="http://www.apple.com/quicktime/" align="middle">
</embed>
```

Feel free to use this code, if you need to do so! If you don't know how to write HTML, see the resources listed in Appendix B, *"After Effects 7 Resources."*

Note: Make sure you replace the source (**src**) footage where we wrote **yourmovienamehere.mov** with your own movie name!

Adding Output Modules

You can add an **Output Module** to any item in the **Render Queue** panel. This allows you to output more than one version from the same item, using the same render settings.

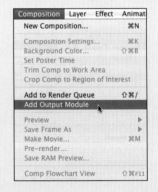

To add an **Output Module**, select the composition name in the **Render Queue** panel. Choose **Composition > Add Output Module**.

This adds another **Output Module** to the item, and you can create different output settings by clicking its settings and changing them. When you click the **Render** button, After Effects 7 actually creates multiple movies with different settings.

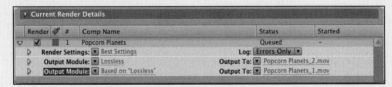

6 | Saving RAM Previews

You can save RAM previews as movie files. This allows you to save a movie file quickly and easily, without visiting the **Render Queue** panel. (Although the **Render Queue** panel opens quickly, you can't change settings there.) Most After Effects 7 artists save RAM previews to be able to view them repeatedly, show them to clients as rough drafts, or import them into a project as source footage for compositions.

---

1 If you followed the previous exercise, **Rendering.aep** should still be open in After Effects 7. If it's not, choose **File > Open Project**. Navigate to the **AE7 HOT Projects** folder you copied to your desktop, click **Rendering.aep** to select it, and click **Open**.

---

2 In the **Project** panel, double-click the **Popcorn Planets** composition to open it.

Note: The composition must be open to save a RAM preview.

---

3 Choose **Composition > Save RAM Preview**.

Once you choose this menu item, After Effects 7 plays the composition for you. While After Effects 7 is playing the composition, it is rendering it; After Effects 7 will prompt you when it is finished.

---

4 When the RAM preview ends, in the **Output Movie To** dialog box, navigate to the **AE7 HOT Projects** folder, and click **Save** to save the movie. Notice the **Render Queue** panel pops up, and your movie renders as if you had selected **Make Movie**.

---

5 After your movie renders, open and view it in your QuickTime or AVI player.

You might be wondering why you would ever use this feature. It's a matter of personal preference; in essence, it performs the same task as Make Movie.

6 In the **Project** panel, notice After Effects 7 automatically imports the rendered RAM movie as footage. You might want to keep it there, or you might want to drag it to the **Trashcan** icon at the bottom of the **Project** panel if you don't need to use it.

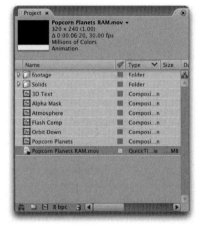

7 Choose **File > Save**, or press **Cmd+S** (Mac) or **Ctrl+S** (Windows). Leave **Rendering.aep** open for the next exercise.

7 | Creating and Using Rendering Templates

As you've seen, rendering settings can get quite complex. Wouldn't it be neat if you could come up with your favorite settings and save them so you could access them when you needed them? You can! **Rendering templates** store predefined settings you can apply easily. Both the **Render Settings** and **Output Module** dialog boxes have a few default templates you can choose from a pop-up menu. These templates have specific settings for rendering and output.

Better yet, you can create your own templates with the settings you need. This means you can store the settings you use often and have them appear via a pop-up menu. When you create a template, you can give it a name meaningful to your work style. In this exercise, you'll learn how to create rendering templates and choose rendering templates when outputting.

1 If you followed the previous exercise, **Rendering.aep** should still be open in After Effects 7. If it's not, choose **File > Open Project**. Navigate to the **AE7 HOT Projects** folder you copied to your desktop, click **Rendering.aep** to select it, and click **Open**.

2 In the **Project** panel, select the **Popcorn Planets** composition.

3 Choose **Composition > Make Movie**, or press **Cmd+M** (Mac) or **Ctrl+M** (Windows) to open the **Render Queue** panel. In the **Output To** field, click the underlined movie name. Navigate to the **AE7 HOT Projects** folder, and save it there.

4 In the **Render Queue** panel, click the **Render Settings** pop-up menu, and choose **Make Template**.

5 In the **Render Settings Templates** dialog box, locate the **Settings Name** box, and type **Quick Study** as the name for the template. Click the **Edit** button.

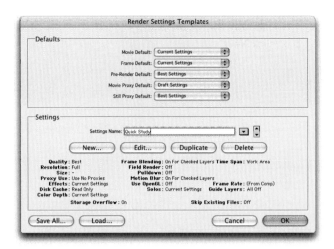

6 In the **Render Settings** dialog box, click the **Quality** pop-up menu, and choose **Draft**.

In the next few steps, you'll create settings for a low-quality, quick-rendering, rough-draft movie.

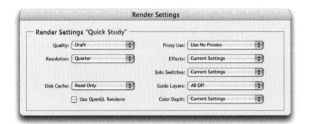

7 In the **Render Settings** dialog box, click the **Resolution** pop-up menu, and choose **Quarter**.

8 Click the **Time Span** pop-up menu, and choose **Length of Comp**.

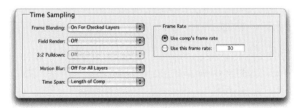

9 Click the **Motion Blur** pop-up menu, and choose **Off For All Layers**. Click **OK** to return to the **Render Settings Templates** dialog box.

In the following steps, you will create a second template for use when rendering high-end movies.

10 In the **Render Settings Templates** dialog box, click **New**.

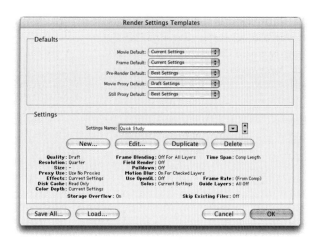

11 Click the **Quality** pop-up menu, and
choose **Best**. Click the **Resolution** pop-up
menu, and choose **Full**.

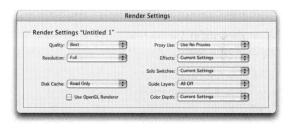

12 Click the **Motion Blur** pop-up menu, and choose **On For Checked
Layers**. Click **OK**.

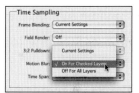

13 In the **Settings Name** box, type
High End for the name of the new template. Click **OK**.

These arrows allow you to
access different templates.

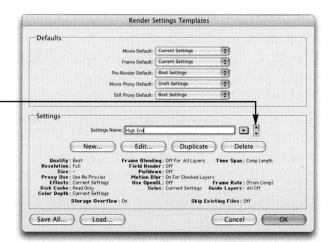

14 In the **Render Queue** panel, click the **Render Settings** pop-up menu, and notice the **High End** and **Quick Study** templates appear in the menu. Choose the **Quick Study** template, and then click the **Render** button.

15 After the program renders the movie, locate the output file, and view it in your movie player. Now try adding another movie to the **Render Queue** panel, but this time use the **High End** template you just created.

Reread the steps if you can't figure this out—but we know you can! Most After Effects 7 artists love rendering templates, because they can use them to easily set up the exact render settings they want for their specific needs.

16 Choose **File > Save**, or press **Cmd+S** (Mac) or **Ctrl+S** (Windows). Leave **Rendering.aep** open for the next exercise.

TIP:

Outputting Module Templates

You create **Output Module** templates using the same process you use to create rendering templates.

You must first add a composition to the **Render Queue** panel by choosing **Composition > Make Movie**. Before rendering a movie, click the **Output Module** pop-up menu, and choose **Make Template**.

In the **Output Module Templates** dialog box, give your new template a name, and click **Edit**. Select the settings you want in the **Output Module Settings** dialog box. Once you've selected the options, click **OK** to close the **Output Module Settings** dialog box, and then click **OK** again to close the **Output Module Templates** dialog box. Your new **Output Module** template now appears in the **Output Module** pop-up menu.

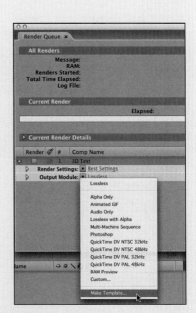

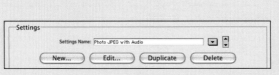

---

8 | Collecting Files

In this exercise, you will learn to use the **Collect Files** command. This is an important automation command available in After Effects 7, and you will undoubtedly use it frequently to help organize your work. The **Collect Files** command allows you to automatically create a copy of all the footage used for a project, along with a copy of the project file, and place the copies in a single folder at the location of your choice. We cannot overstate the usefulness of this command, which makes it easy to collect all the files for a project in the form of a copy you can use to archive, render, or transport the project. You can apply this feature to an entire project or to an individual composition.

---

1 If you followed the previous exercise, **Rendering.aep** should still be open in After Effects 7. If it's not, choose **File > Open Project**. Navigate to the **AE7 HOT Projects** folder you copied to the desktop, click **Rendering.aep** to select it, and click **Open**.

---

2 Choose **File > Save** to save your project.

Note: You must save your project before using the Collect Files command. Otherwise, you'll see a prompt notifying you that you must save your project before collecting files and giving you the option to save the project.

---

3 Choose **File > Collect Files**.

---

4 In the **Collect Files** dialog box, click the **Collect Source Files** pop-up menu, make sure **All** is selected, and then click the **Collect** button.

The **All** option collects the project file and all the footage items used in the project. It also generates a report.

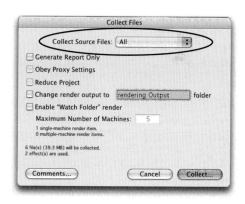

---

5 In the **Collect files into folder** dialog box, navigate to the **AE7 HOT Projects** folder, and click **Save**.

---

6 Once the collection process is complete, locate the folder, and open it to see the project file and footage file copies inside the folder.

7 Close the **Rendering.aep** project.

Writing Macromedia Flash Files

It's pretty easy to output After Effects 7 movies to the Macromedia Flash file format (SWF). The question is, why would you want to use After Effects 7 for this purpose?

Flash supports sound, graphics, motion, and inter-activity. For this reason, the scope of what you can create in Flash is different from the scope of what you can create in After Effects 7. Specifically, you can create an entire Web site in Flash, with working buttons and forms for visitors to complete.

After Effects 7 has different capabilities and strengths. It is a stronger tool for creating bitmap motion graphics, because of its superior blending, blurring, masking, and keyframing features.

The advantage to outputting After Effects 7 movies in the Flash format is that you may not know how to create motion in Flash but you know how to do so easily in After Effects 7. For this reason, After Effects 7 is attractive because you are probably more skilled at producing animation in it than you might be in Flash. As well, After Effects 7 has much more sophisticated motion-control capabilities than Flash via keyframable effects and the independent **Transform** and **Mask** properties in the **Timeline** panel. For this reason, you might want to use After Effects 7 because you can achieve a different kind of animated image than you can in Flash.

In addition, many After Effects 7 production companies use Flash to create their Web sites because the format is so much more visually liberating than

HTML. This is because you can produce full-screen animation and use any font you want in Flash, which is untrue of HTML.

It's important to understand that After Effects 7 outputs pixels, and Macromedia SWF for Flash distinguishes between vectors and pixels. If you use only vectors in your Flash work, your file sizes will be quite small and will download more quickly than if you use pixel-based artwork. Flash treats anything with live action, an effect, or blur in After Effects 7 as pixel-based artwork. This almost ensures the download will be larger if you choose to incorporate After Effects 7 work in your Flash work.

It is possible to output vectors only from After Effects 7. The key is to use vector-based artwork from Illustrator or to use solid layers and non-feathered masks. You should also avoid effects, blurs, and live action. However, After Effects 7 is best suited for pixel-based animation, and most people will want to use live action, effects, masks, and blurs freely in their After Effects 7 work.

After Effects 7 offers you a choice to ignore pixel-based artwork when you output to the Flash format. You can also choose to rasterize frames containing unsupported features and add them to the SWF file as JPEG-compressed bitmaps. If you add bitmaps for each frame, however, the file size of the Flash movie will be larger, making it less efficient and less appropriate for the Web. The following exercise will walk you through some of these issues firsthand.

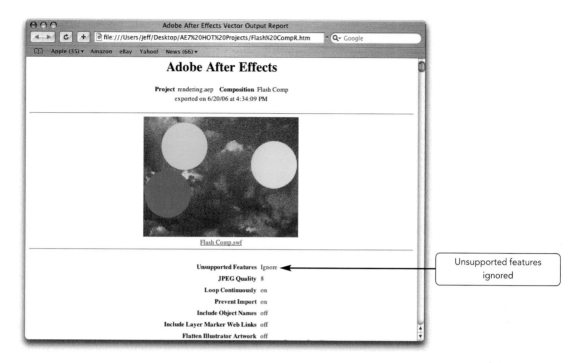

Unsupported features ignored

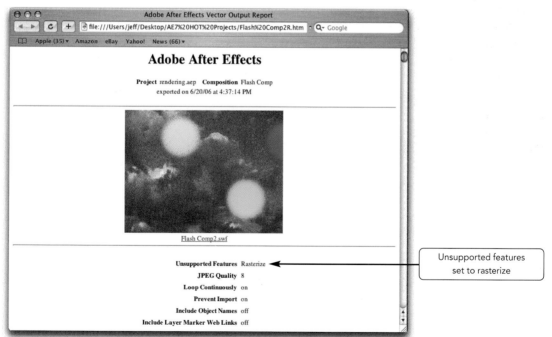

Unsupported features set to rasterize

Once you output to the Flash format, you can import the resulting file into Flash. The program accepts both SWF and QuickTime formats, so you could also elect to output to the QuickTime format from After Effects 7 for Flash work. You might choose to experiment with your specific content to see whether it's better to output your After Effects 7 work to SWF or QuickTime.

9 | Outputting to the Macromedia Flash Format

This exercise walks you through the steps to output to Flash SWF as your final movie format. You'll see it's quite easy; you have a choice of ignoring pixel-based effects in order to write pure vectors for a smaller file size.

---

1 In the **Project** panel, double-click **Flash Comp** to open it, and then press the **spacebar** to preview the movie.

In this exercise, you'll try different settings when outputting to Flash SWF.

---

2 Choose **File > Export > Macromedia Flash (SWF)**.

Unlike the other movies you have made in this chapter, Flash SWF is supported only through the Export menu, not through the Render Queue panel.

---

3 In the **Save File As** dialog box, leave the file name as **Flash Comp.swf**, navigate to the **AE7 HOT Projects** folder, and click **Save**.

---

4 In the **SWF Settings** dialog box, notice the **Images** group of options. For this exercise, leave **JPEG Quality** at the default settings.

This setting affects any pixel-based content, such as a photograph or live-action footage. Choosing a higher quality results in larger files.

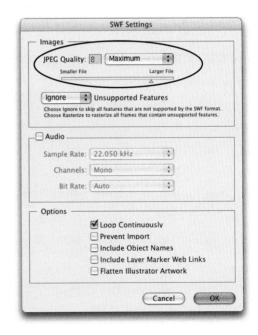

5 Click the **Unsupported Features** pop-up menu, and notice you can choose to ignore unsupported features or to rasterize them. For this exercise, keep the **Ignore** setting.

The Rasterize option converts any unsupported features as JPEG images and increases the file size.

6 Notice the **Audio** section. This exercise doesn't include audio, so leave the check box turned off.

Audio is encoded in Flash files using MP3 compression. If you use audio in your Web project and you want to create the smallest files possible, keep the sample rate low (11.025 kHz or 22.050 kHz) while still maintaining acceptable quality. Mono audio creates less data than stereo. A lower bit rate also reduces file size.

7 Turn on the **Loop Continuously** check box, which causes your movie to play repeatedly. Turn on the **Prevent Import** check box, which prevents the output SWF file from being accessed by someone else who could then modify your content.

8 Take note of the remaining check boxes, and then click **OK**.

The Include Object Names check box includes the names of any layers, masks, and effects in your composition. This increases the file size. The Include Layer Marker Web Links check box allows any layers that have markers with Web links to be included and active in the Flash output file. The Flatten Illustrator Artwork check box merges Illustrator artwork. See the following tip for more information about this option.

TIP:

Exporting Adobe Illustrator Files

Illustrator files are vector files (although Illustrator files can contain bitmaps, too) and are supported as an export item. However, be aware that After Effects 7 supports only stroked paths and filled paths in the CMYK or RGB color spaces.

9 When the export is finished, After Effects 7 creates an SWF file and an HTML file. Open the HTML file in a browser.

If you have the Flash plug-in installed in your browser, you will see the output playing in the HTML page.

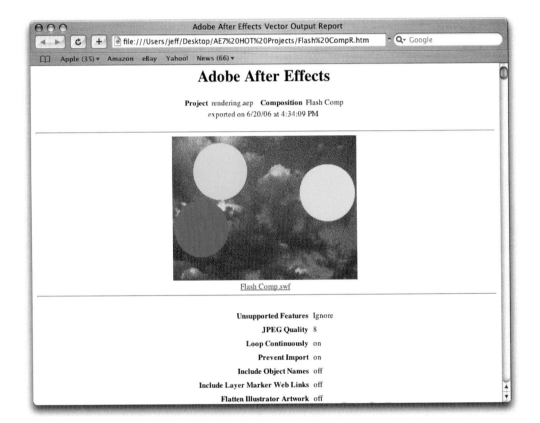

10 Scroll down the page, and notice the report created regarding your Flash output. When you are done viewing the animation, close the browser.

After Effects 7 creates this HTML file to help you preview the final SWF file and its settings only. It is likely you would want to import the SWF file into Flash and would discard the HTML.

11 Choose **File > Save**, or press **Cmd+S** (Mac) or **Ctrl+S** (Windows). Choose **File > Close**. You're finished with this chapter!

This was a big chapter with a lot of technical information. You can always refer to it as you begin outputting your own projects. By completing this chapter, you have learned all the rendering basics, and you are prepared to discover each detail necessary for the types of output your projects require. As usual, the more you use the rendering tools, the more you will learn.

We hope you enjoyed working through this book and that it turned you on to the tremendous possibilities of After Effects 7. All we can say is the more you create, the more confidence you'll build. Be sure to check out Appendix B, *"After Effects 7 Resources,"* for other training and reference resources. Enjoy!

Technical Support and Troubleshooting FAQ

If you run into problems while following the exercises in this book, you might find the answer in the "Troubleshooting Frequently Asked Questions" section in this appendix. If you don't find the information you're looking for, use the contact information provided in the "Technical Support Information" section.

Troubleshooting Frequently Asked Questions

Q Why Do I Get a Gray Frame at the End of a Composition?

A The After Effects 7 **Timeline** often shows a gray frame if you manually move the **CTI** (**C**urrent **T**ime **I**ndicator) to the end. This is because the **Timeline** often extends one frame beyond the true end of the composition. Move to the last frame by pressing the **End** key on the keyboard or by clicking the Last **Frame** button in the **Time Controls** panel.

Q Why Does My RAM Preview Stop Short?

A For RAM preview to work properly, you must have enough RAM (**R**andom **A**ccess **M**emory) in your computer. The amount of RAM you need varies depending on how complex and large your After Effects 7 project is. The good news is that RAM is getting less expensive every day.

Q Apple QuickTime Isn't Working—What Should I Do?

A Go to the Apple Web site, and download the latest QuickTime plug-in. Make sure After Effects 7 is not open while you do this. If you are using Windows XP, make sure you have installed the latest updates. You can accomplish this by choosing **Start > All Programs > Windows Update**. Oftentimes updates can affect QuickTime compatibility, so don't forget to check for the latest version when you run into a problem.

Q What Can I Do When the "Missing Footage" Error Message Appears?

A Missing footage will appear in the **Project** panel (you might have to click the **twirly** icon to find it) as italicized text with a **test pattern** icon. If you double-click the name of the missing footage in your **Project** panel, After Effects 7 will let you navigate to your hard drive to locate the missing footage.

Q Why Is My Movie Playback Jerky?

A When you play a QuickTime movie on your hard drive, it will be jerky if you don't have a fast enough processor, a fast enough hard drive, or enough RAM. If this is a movie you created from After Effects 7, you might want to render it again using a higher compression method (smaller file size). The bigger and less compressed the movie file, the harder it will be for your computer to play it without the proper hardware.

Q Why Do I Get an "Untitled" Warning?

A When you open a project file in After Effects 7 that was created in After Effects 6, you will encounter the following warning:

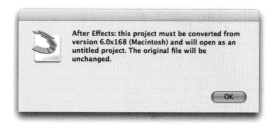

Click **OK**, and the project will open as originally intended, except it will appear as an untitled project until you save it.

Q What If I'm on a Laptop and the Keyboard Shortcuts Don't Work?

A Not all keyboard shortcuts work on a laptop. For example, most laptops don't have a **Home** key or an **End** key, which can make it difficult to jump to the beginning or end of a composition. However, you usually can use equivalent shortcuts. Instead of using the **Home** key, you can press **J** on your keyboard to go to the beginning of a composition, and you can press the **K** key to go to the end.

Technical Support Information

The following sections contain technical support resources you can use if you need help.

lynda.com

If you run into any problems as you work through this book, check the companion Web site for updates:

www.lynda.com/books/HOT/ae7

If you don't find what you're looking for on the companion Web site, send Chad Fahs and Lynda Weinman an e-mail at the following address:

ae7hot@lynda.com

We encourage and welcome your feedback, comments, and error reports.

Peachpit Press

If your book has a defective CD, please contact the customer service department at Peachpit Press:

customer_service@peachpit.com

Adobe Technical Support

If you're having problems with After Effects 7, please visit the Adobe technical support center at the following location:

www.adobe.com/support

B

After Effects 7 Resources

Many great resources are available to After Effects 7 users. You can access a variety of newsgroups, conferences, and third-party Web sites to help you get the most from the new skills you've developed by reading this book. In this appendix, you'll find the best resources for further developing your skills with After Effects 7.

lynda.com Training Resources

lynda.com

lynda.com is a leader in software books and video training for Web and graphics professionals. To help further develop your skills in After Effects 7, check out the following training resources from lynda.com.

lynda.com Books

The **HOT** (**H**ands-**O**n **T**raining) series was originally developed by **Lynda Weinman**, author of the revolutionary book *Designing Web Graphics*, first released in 1996. Lynda believes people learn best from doing and has developed this series to teach users software programs and technologies through a progressive learning process.

Check out the following books from lynda.com:

Designing Web Graphics 4
by Lynda Weinman
New Riders
ISBN: 0735710791

Adobe Premiere Pro 2 HOT
by Jeff Schell
lynda.com/books and Peachpit Press
ISBN: 0321397746

Macromedia Flash Professional 8 HOT
by James Gonzalez
lynda.com/books and Peachpit Press
ISBN: 0321293886

Macromedia Flash Professional 8 Beyond the Basics HOT
by Shane Rebenschied
lynda.com/books and Peachpit Press
ISBN: 0321293878

lynda.com Video-Based Training

lynda.com offers video training as stand-alone **CD-ROM** and **DVD-ROM** products and through a monthly or annual subscription to the **lynda.com Online Training Library**.

For a free, 24-hour trial pass to the lynda.com Online Training Library, register your copy of *After Effects 7 HOT* at the following location:

www.lynda.com/register/HOT/aftereffects7

Note: This offer is available for new subscribers only and does not apply to current or past subscribers of the lynda.com Online Training Library.

To help you build your skills with After Effects 7, check out the following video-based training titles from lynda.com.

After Effects Video-Based Training

After Effects 7 Essential Training
with Jeff Foster and Lynda Weinman

After Effects 7 New Features
with Garrick Chow

After Effects 7 Animation Techniques
with Jeff Foster

After Effects 7 and Photoshop CS2 Integration
with Jeff Foster

After Effects 6 Essential Training
with Lynda Weinman

Motion-Graphics Video-Based Training

Learning Motion
with Lynda Weinman

3D/Animation Video-Based Training

Maya 6.5 Essential Training
with George Maestri

Carrara 5 Essential Training
with Jack Whitney

Animation Principles
with Chris Casady and Lynda Weinman

Flashforward Conference and Film Festival

The **Flashforward Conference and Film Festival** is an international educational conference dedicated to Macromedia Flash. Flashforward was first hosted by Lynda Weinman, founder of lynda.com, and Stewart McBride, founder of United Digital Artists. Flashforward is now owned exclusively by lynda.com and strives to provide the best conference for designers and developers to present their technical and artistic work in an educational setting.

For more information about the Flashforward conference, visit **www.flashforwardconference.com**.

Online Resources

DMN Forums: Adobe After Effects
www.dmnforums.com/cgi-bin/displaywwugindex.fcgi?forum=adobe_after-effects

Web Sites

Creative Cow
www.creativecow.net

Fxguide, a visual effects blog
www.fxguide.com

MGLA (**M**otion **G**raphics **L**os **A**ngeles)
www.mgla.org

media-motion.tv, an After Effects mailing list
www.media-motion.tv

AEP, an After Effects portal
msp.sfsu.edu/Instructors/rey/aepage/aeportal.html

Toolfarm, which has an After Effects forum
www.toolfarm.com/forum.html

Trapcode, where you can find plug-ins for After Effects
www.trapcode.com

Books

Creating Motion Graphics with After Effects,
Vol. 1: The Essentials
by Trish Meyer and Chris Meyer
CMP Books
ISBN: 1578202493

After Effects and Photoshop: Animation and
Production Effects for DV and Film
by Jeff Foster
Sybex
ISBN: 0782143172

Adobe After Effects 7.0 Studio Techniques
by Mark Christianson
Peachpit
ISBN: 0321385527

After Effects 7 for Windows and Macintosh:
Visual QuickPro Guide
by Antony Bolante
Peachpit
ISBN: 0321383540

Index

T

T option, Preserve Underlying Transparency, 363
tab, panel, 14
takes, 27
Targa Sequence, Output Module formats, 469
technical support, 494–496
templates
  project, 4
  rendering, 483–486
temporal interpolation
  icons, 119
  settings, 124
  vs. spatial interpolation, 107
Temporal Phase Wiggly selector property, 231
text boxes, Wiggly selector and, 226–230
text effects
  with Bézier masks, 328–329
  expressions and, 417–420
  with masks, 330–332
text layers, 206–249
  adding/animating, 208–212
  Advanced selector properties, 220–223
  animate text menus, 207
  animation presets, 244–246
  animator properties, 213
  boxes and Wiggly selector, 226–230
  Character Offset, 232–240
  importing from Photoshop file, 247–249
  multiple animators/selectors, 217–219
  Offset introduction, 216
  overview, 206
  putting on a path, 241–243
  Range selector, 214–216
  Range selector properties, 224–225
  Wiggly selector properties, 231
TGA, QuickTime compressor, 471
thirty-two bit graphics. see alpha channels
three-dimensional layers. see 3D layers
three-dimensional switch, 156
Threshold, Specular, Lens Blur effect, 263
TIFF Sequence, Output Module formats, 469

TIFF, QuickTime compressors, 471
time, 106–125
  editing Speed graph, 113–114
  Graph Editor and Keyframe Assistant, 108–112
  Hold interpolation method, 115–118
  keyframe interpolation, 124
  morphing painting over, 307–309
  moving/trimming, layers, 168
  overview, 106
  remapping, 182–185
  roving keyframes, 120–123
  spatial vs. temporal interpolation, 107
  stretching blending layers, 178–181
  Temporal interpolation icons, 119
Time Controls panel
  play modes in, 130–131
  preview settings, 147
  previewing, 127
  RAM previewing, 68–69
  workspace introduction, 16
Time Navigator slider, 61
Time Remap graph, 186
Time Span Render setting, 458, 460
Timecode, 49
Timecode Base setting, 50
Timeline panel
  adding audio, 440–441
  alpha channels, 347
  centering footage, 52
  creating a composition, 42
  creating keyframes. see keyframes
  preview settings, 147
  viewing, 61
  workspace introduction, 14
  Zoom control, 287
Timewarp
  defined, 4
  effect, 187–188
  time stretching vs., 181
tips, showing/hiding, 11
tolerance, color, 368
tools
  After Effects introduction, 8
  Clone Stamp tool, 314–316
  custom camera views, 391
  easing, 108–112
  eraser tool, 310–313
  mask. see masks
  painting, 297. see also painting

Pan Behind tool. see Pan Behind tool
Pick Whip, creating relationships, 411–412
Pick Whip, parenting, 277–279
rendering. see rendering
Type tools, 208–209
Tools panel
  keyboard commands, 345
  organizing panels, 15
  workspace introduction, 17
tools, navigation
  Keyframe Navigator, 71–72
  Timeline panel, 61
track mattes, 346–363
  alpha channels, introduction, 347
  animating, 353–354
  creating, 350–352
  importing alpha channels from Photoshop, 348–349
  luminance-based, 355–356
  masking modes, 360–362
  overview, 346
  Preserve Underlying Transparency option, 363
  soft-edged with masked solid layer, 357–359
track types, motion tracking, 427–428
tracking camera tools, 391
Tracking text animation property, 213
tracking, motion. see motion tracking
trails, motion, previewing, 144
training resources, 499
Transform properties
  3D layers. see 3D layers
  adding/animating camera, 400–401
  keyframe. see properties, keyframe
  parenting layers, 275
  parenting vs. precomposing, 291
  shortcut keys, 81
  text animation, 213
transitions
  applying effects, 258–260
  sequencing layers, 195
transparency channels, 347
trimming layers
  bracket key commands, 175
  with keyboard methods, 172–174
trimming time, 168
troubleshooting, 494–496
turning off expressions, 421–422